The Polar North

The Polar North

Ways of Speaking, Ways of Belonging

Stephen Pax Leonard

Francis
Boutle
Publishers

First published by
Francis Boutle Publishers
272 Alexandra Park Road
London N22 7BG
Tel/Fax: (020) 8889 7744
Email: info@francisboutle.co.uk
www.francisboutle.co.uk

The Polar North © Stephen Pax Leonard, 2014

ISBN 978 1 903427 94 1

Printed in Malta by Melita Press

This book is dedicated to Ane-Sofie Imiina
who helped me through the dark period

Contents

Acknowledgements

I am indebted to a number of institutions and individuals for making my time in the Polar North possible. Firstly, I would like to thank the Master and Fellows of Trinity Hall, Cambridge for allowing me to intermit my Fellowship to undertake this fieldwork, but more importantly for providing a superb place for me to live and work over these last three years. I should also like to thank the British Academy and the World Oral Literature Project who part funded my stay in the Arctic and supported my academic work which has been the subject of other and forthcoming publications.

Living in such small, remote communities, I got to know many, perhaps the majority, of the Inugguit. Throughout my stay in the Polar North, there were a few outstanding individuals who became and have remained friends. David Qujaukitsoq is the exceptional *inuk*, full of ideas and ambition. Understanding the value of his language, he provided much support over the course of the year and beyond. The Qujaukitsoq family have done their best to preserve the Inugguit culture and traditions. I spent much time working with the older members of the community, documenting their stories and hearing about the old way of life. I should like to thank Taatiraaq, Savfaq and in particular Pauline Kristiansen who was always the voice of wisdom and is the link between the past and the present for the Inugguit. Sadly, some of them have passed on over the last two years. Aijakko Miteq will be particularly missed. I also owe my gratitude to Emily Lethbridge and Chris Paton (Krissi) for the entertaining discussions and friendship. I am most grateful to Ibbi Qaavijaq, Tornge Qaavijaq and the Hendriksen family in Hiorapaluk for all the fun times and for the assistance they gave me with documenting their tiny language. At home and before I left for the Polar North, Les at the Salvation Army in Cambridge helped to kit me out and saved me a small fortune. I am extremely grateful for his kind assistance.

Finally, I should like to thank Ane-Sofie Imiina for all her patience, for helping me get to grips with what be must one of the more difficult languages to learn in the world, and for bringing such warmth and fine spirit to my freezing hut day after day. She was always the smiling face when there was no sign of sunlight and not much reason for hope. It is to her that this book is dedicated.

Spelling Conventions

The people I lived with for a year call themselves the Inugguit (pronounced 'inohwee'). They are also known as the Polar Eskimos (note the word Eskimo is not pejorative in this part of Greenland), and both terms were used during my stay there. The famous Danish-Greenlandic ethnographer, Knud Rasmussen, used the term Polar Eskimo, but throughout this book I have used the two terms interchangeably. Sir Wally Herbert, the inspiration for my own journey, referred in his books to this part of the world as the Polar North. A term used infrequently elsewhere, I have adopted it for the title of my own book.

The spelling of the difficult 'gg' sound found in the word 'Inugguit' could be much discussed, but the 'gg' spelling is the form we agreed on. Elsewhere, you may see the sound written as 'gh'. Throughout the book, I have used spellings that reflect how the Inugguit (singular Inugguaq) would pronounce the place-names (and not what is to be found on maps) and attempt to spell their words. Thus, it is Hiorapaluk and (not Siorapaluk), Haviggivik (not Savissivik) and Qeqertarhhuaq (and not Qeqertarssuaq). I have decided on this convention because I think it is what they would prefer. On the odd occasion, I have used the old Greenlandic spelling system to write old personal names which were (and sometimes still are) written that way.

All the references to temperature in the book are in Celsius; DKK is the abbreviation for Danish Kroner.

To ensure anonymity, the names of all the local people that appear in the book have been changed to pseudonyms.

Map of the Arctic, showing north-west Greenland

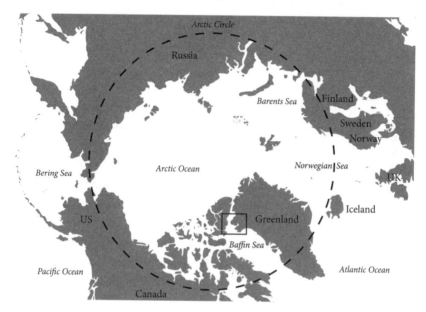

Map of north-west Greenland, showing inhabited and abandoned settlements

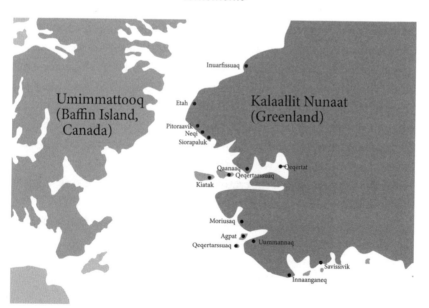

Prologue

It is the end of May in the High Arctic. I am skiing alone out towards the edge of the sea ice in the Murchison Sound, north-west Greenland. A skirl of Kittiwakes overhead breaks the silence. The lure of the uncircumscribed wilderness and grammarless landscape draws me further towards what seems like my ineluctable destiny. My only wish is that the sea ice will continue, taking me deeper into the icy, Arctic nothingness. Out here, the only evidence of human life are the partially hidden tracks of hunters' sledges. The thrill of going beyond the human horizon is powerful and emotional, taking me back to a former age of simplicity and equilibrium when there was an innate correspondence between man and nature. Here, the overwhelming whiteness and loss of distinction promises the bliss of transcendence, mingling the ephemeral worlds of past and future. A moment of *prajna*. To get mentally lost in the wilderness in this way has now surely become an impossibility in twenty-first century Europe. We have lost something special, broken a fundamental relationship which once informed us what it is to be human.

Despite living in the age of up-rootedness and environmental crisis, we all need to belong *somewhere*. From the time I was a teenager, I knew that I did not belong in the crowded, soulless suburbia of south-east England where I grew up. To me, suburbia, wherever one is in the world, is the least attractive option. Here, living in a detached cocoon of inbetweenness, the bond with nature is severed and the suburbanite subscribes instead to the treadmill of a dull, salaried life dependent on machines and first and foremost the motor vehicle. Here, the *open* 'nature' is an alien notion for lives are built on concepts of 'enclosure': ubiquitous, monochromatic vehicles piled up on cramped driveways and clogged streets, walled gardens, sterile 'anywhere-in-the-world' shopping

centres, locked rooms and private property. Here, freedom and wilderness have been traded for the lie of material happiness and imprisoned
reality. Prisoners of monotony and 'ownership', their bilked lives are lived
out behind steering wheels, in grey offices and expressionless commuter
trains. Chidden by their superiors, they pursue 'careers' which make
their mothers proud. Toing and froing from work to home, they speak in
the same platitudes and live the lives of automata.

In suburbia, there is none of the thrill and excitement of the great
cities and none of the serenity of the vanishing green English countryside. It is here where the orchard trees and woodland have been long
chopped down to make way for modern housing estates and the next
generation of indebted youth whose ugly demotic hurts one's ears.
Here, lives are mortgaged in big houses full of shiny possessions that they
never 'need'. Toasting the lowest common denominator and the celebration of idiocracy on television and magazine, talk is of nothing but
soap-operas, football and motor vehicles. Not stopping to ponder the
loss of standards and decency, the absurdity of post-modern Britain is
embraced.

It was during these teenage years that my search for belonging had
subconsciously begun. From this young age, what mattered most to me
was adventure and it is perhaps not surprising that I read endlessly about
those that had sought adventure in some form or another, those that had
escaped the *et cetera* of life. Having been touched by the extraordinary
gentlemanly spirit of Captain Scott and his men, I began to read everything I could about polar exploration. Long before I had even gone there,
the North and Scandinavia in particular held a special appeal. With blue
eyes and hair the colour of snow, I was always asked as a child whether I
had Nordic heritage. Sometimes it felt as if my issue of belonging had
already been addressed for me. Later in life, my Swedish dentist would
insist that I had a Scandinavian jaw. Upon telling him that I grew up in
Kent, he would nod his head knowingly and declare me a Jute. I have no
idea whether it was this or a combination of other things that led me to
the North, but what I know is that from a young age my sights were set on
the North, the Arctic and the polar regions. Sometimes if one is to
deconstruct these little life mysteries, one risks taking something away
from them and tampering with their value, so one shall leave it at that.
All I know is, having read so much about exploration, I came to admire

the likes of Sir Wally Herbert, Fridtjof Nansen, Helge Ingstad and Thor Heyerdahl and wished to identify with them and their achievements.

As a schoolboy, I was taken to one side and told that I had a special gift for learning languages. Language for me was the conduit for exploring another world of 'belonging' and it became more than just an interest. I discovered that through speaking another language, I found a new voice and sense of 'embodiment'. I have always loved words; the most precious ones were always those just beyond my comprehension, those that were just beyond my reach, shielded by enigma. I came to realise that I had a remarkably sensitive acoustic memory, storing voices, intonation patterns, accents and dialects in a rich, mental discography that would play to me when alone in my freezing hut during the Stygian days of the dark period in north-west Greenland. Soon, I appreciated that there is a difference between being able to speak a language fluently and to speak a language like a native. The latter requires first and foremost a mastery of the language's paralinguistic features. To be able to speak a handful of languages as a native, you have to be able to act and act well, reproducing exactly certain collocations of words to the rhythm, gestures, flow and timbre of its speakers. This is always more important than just having a large vocabulary or putting the verb in the right place. Each language of the world requires a different voice and it had become obvious that I had a taste for an intellectual life built on a musical pell-mell of voices and idioms. Having this special gift, I would have an immediate advantage over researchers who try and conduct fieldwork in their own language and who end up with an incomplete understanding of the societies they are working in because they understand so little of what is going on.

I had studied French, German and Spanish at school and after short periods abroad was able to pass off as a native. The French told me that I suffered from *l'exotisme*, the desire to constantly discover new places and things, to belong in *other* places. From a young age, it was obvious that I had a passion for being elsewhere. Later, and whilst working as a merchant banker in London, I had learnt some Danish and Swedish, but ultimately decided on Norwegian as my main Scandinavian language. As a student at Oxford, I wrote a D.Phil on Icelandic and studied in my spare time Faroese and Greek. Having completed my D.Phil early, I spent the remainder of my time in Oxford studying Arabic. Subsequently, I would take up a Fellowship at Trinity Hall, Cambridge, where I would study some Russian. In Cambridge, my plan was to continue with my work on issues of Icelandic anthropology. With the financial crisis in Iceland in 2008, the funding for the proposed collaborative project disappeared. I had a window of opportunity and knew that I had to take it. The lure of the Far North had never left me and was becoming too much.

Out of all the reading that I had done on polar exploration, there was one book that stood out in my memory, 'The Snow People' by Marie Herbert. I had bought this book second-hand in a bookshop in Rochester at the age of about twenty. I knew already about Sir Wally Herbert's journey across the Arctic Ocean in 1968, but had not realised that his wife had written a book about their time in north-west Greenland in the early 1970s. The couple with their baby daughter had taken the ship to north-west Greenland and spent 15 months living with the Polar Eskimos of the Thule region. Marie Herbert's book is not a book about bravery and exploration, but a book of human relationships. It is an emotional account of some of the trials and tribulations of living with a small child in a remote Arctic community. In her book, Marie describes an exceptional community of proud Inuit hunters who had clung onto their old way of life, using traditional hunting techniques and travelling on the sea ice by dog-sledge. The book left a lasting impression on me and I knew that one day I would want to visit these people at the 'top of the world'.

After a period of research, I had discovered that the Polar Eskimos or Inugguit spoke a dialect that was not readily understood elsewhere in Greenland, that there were just 700 or so speakers and that the community was being rocked by climate change. Whilst the language was not in immediate danger, it was obvious that the prospects of the community or at least those living in the outer settlements were not at all clear in the longer term. There appeared to be a sense that for various reasons a unique way of life was coming to an end. Very little work had been done on the language, and the oral traditions (storytelling and drum-dancing) were endangered. I was advised by the only living linguist that knew much about the language, to 'go now'. The research project brought all my interests together. What I could not have known at the beginning was that, language and oral literature documentation work aside, the project would take me to the heart of the question of 'belonging' and the human condition and would thus take me back to my childhood in more way than one.

My stay in the Arctic would also instill in me a form of poetic thinking that would remain with me throughout my fieldwork, but that is totally absent here in England now that I have lost the privilege of being the 'outsider'. The transient Arctic landscape, the existential mimicry and transcendental voices of the hunters blurring the poet's insider/outsider distinction, the intimacy of the enmeshed natural and human environment, the vicissitudes of life in the polar desert, the liberty of thought that the open spaces of the North offers, the awakening of primordial intuitions, the isolation and solitude, the sense of self that one discovers in the remote polar night, the colours and sounds of community and wilderness would lead me to conjugate and juxtapose words and images in new and novel ways. The blurred soundscape would reverberate through my mind and out in the white desert I was exposed to the possibilities of poetry in the begetting and forgetting of cold days.

This poetic thinking defines inevitably the shape and feel of this book which at times must seem more like a tapestry of vignettes than a narrative. But it is this poetic and perhaps unconventional association of words and images that defined my time in the Polar North and is for me the essence of 'being' in the Arctic. At times, the poetic was a natural response to the need to intellectualise difficult moments or encounters. It was perhaps a response to what Jackson (2007: xx) calls 'existential aporia', the puzzles of life. But, the important point is that this was a 'natural' output and not something managed or contrived. Poetry is seldom objective, and the style of this narrative (and not ethnography) is unapologetically subjective. It wishes to challenge the sterile, soulless approach to standardised academic writing. My poetic thinking was a window onto my own consciousness. Often, it became a means of connection with my natural environment and a means of detachment from my human environment. Always, it showed me, however, that there is no substitute for the richness of the direct ethnographic experience.

I received funding for the project at the end of May and had just six weeks to prepare for my departure to Greenland. The plan had been hatched many years ago in my head, but now it had suddenly become a reality and I had just weeks and not months or years to actually prepare to go and live with the Polar Eskimos. The excitement of the looming adventure built day after day and the thought of achieving a rusting ambition and of actually living in the Far North was now tantalisingly close. There is almost no available written material on the language I was to learn, and so instead I crammed as much Standard West Greenlandic as I could in these few weeks. This is the dialect spoken on the west coast of Greenland, the principal language of Government and effectively the second language of the Inugguit. It is a standardised written language with sufficient resources available to learn it. This and my Danicised Norwegian were to become the two initial lingua francas once I reached the community.

I was to live a year with the Polar Eskimos from August 2010 until August 2011 without leaving the region during this time. During my stay, I lived in three different settlements. It was my intention to arrive in the community in the small window of the Arctic summer and to get settled in before the 'dark period' began. The days leading up to my departure were exceedingly hectic, working my way through endless to-do-lists. With so much focus on the human dimension to climate change, the Press had become very interested in my project. Within the 72 hours prior to my departure, I had given radio interviews for the BBC Radio 4 Today programme, BBC World Service, Radio 5 Live, BBC Radio Cambridge, Swedish National Radio, Japan National Radio, CBC Radio in Canada and National Public Radio in the US to name but a few. There had been a full spread on page 9 of the *Guardian*, two interviews for local television and finally a live television address on CNN to 300 million people. Coming down for breakfast at Hotel Opera in Copenhagen, I was greeted by a gaggle of Danish journalists wishing to interview me and take photographs. The response was rather overwhelming, but I took heart in the fact that the media were taking issues of linguistic and cultural endangerment and the human impact of climate change so seriously. But, let us not forget, the true heroes are the Inugguit (and not me) who have survived in such a hostile environment for centuries.

My first sight of Greenland, the largest island on Earth, was the greying and thinning ice sheet: it looked old and tired, grown melancholic with age, mumbling chapters of disregard. Dotted all over the ice lay brilliant, sapphire blue melt-water lakes, some of them a mile or so across. I felt a sense of remorse; the lakes symbolised a collective human failure, a tragic testament of the all too rapidly changing natural environment. My neighbour, a self-confessed businessman, shaman and healer thought the West had not listened to the Inuit people and that we were destroying Mother Earth.

The short onward flight from Kangerlussuaq, a former US military landing strip that now acts as the Air Greenland hub, skirts the ice sheet northwards. Icebergs litter the fjords like lumps of polystyrene; a magnificent iceberg arch provides a window onto the mysteries of the icebound world. On the ground in pretty, picture-postcard Illulisaat, brightly painted, Scandinavian style wooden houses lie scattered amongst the rocks. Despite the relative warmth of the Arctic summer, colonies of icebergs drift slowly past. It is a surreal picture of transition that speaks dislocation and a sense of foreboding. The icebergs go nowhere, sitting and collecting dirt before sinking into oblivion.

Unlike in Sir Wally Herbert's day, it is now possible, but not always likely, to fly from Denmark to north-west Greenland in two days. Leaving Ilulissat early in the morning, the scenery from the vantage point of the red Dash 7 Air Greenland PT6A-50 turboprop was Lord of the Rings-like and it seemed as if I was going to be lucky with the weather. Mountains rose steeply out of the deep blue water, topped with greyish receding glaciers, but not snow. Glaciers spread out their icy digits, weaving their way through deep channels of rock between the mountains. This is raw nature: no evidence of any human inhabitation whatsoever, just the oldest rocks on Earth. Icebergs, some of them the shape of giant doorways, sit in the fjords like Roman Janus figures.

We make a stop in Qaarsut, not far from Ummannaq. The airfield lies in what appears to be the middle of a desert. The solitary, blue terminal building measures the size of an average living room and keeps vigil over an utterly remote, barren wilderness of rock. I have never seen a land so derelict, an empty husk. I revel at having escaped from the endless suburbia of cluttered modern Britain and am excited at the prospect of going back to a more simple life. Nestled a short way behind the airfield lies a settlement fewer than 200 strong in a sunny, sheltered bay. Bright coloured wooden houses sit implausibly in a wild and forgotten landscape beneath the morning Promethean sun.

As we head further north still, few words are exchanged on the Dash 7, Nipki ('the silent one'). Most of the passengers are young Inuit who are returning from vocational training or further schooling programmes in south Greenland, but there are also a small group of geologists and prospectors from Northern Minerals poring over maps. There appear to be one or two tourists, but they disembark at Upernavik. Out of necessity, these small turboprop flights are part freight and part passenger aircraft, and this one is no exception. The back five rows of the aircraft hold cargo and there is in addition an enormous sack of mail lying at the front of the aeroplane. One can sit anywhere one wants and there are few concerns about security or the size of the carry-on-luggage which is fortunate in my case as mine must surely exceed any allowance. Those Greenlanders or hunters who travel with guns are required to give the bullets to the captain. This is one of those special journeys that harks back to the age before burdensome security measures and large scale transit: a reminder of how life used to be before the multiplication of discount airlines offering flights to hundreds of destinations at the price of a pack of peanuts degraded the romantic spirit of adventure and travel to a commoditised, characterless commute. For the final leg of the journey from Upernavik to Qaanaaq, there are seventeen passengers on the aircraft including myself and the Danish captain.

There is finally a break in the vacant wilderness of bare rock stretching up the west coast of Greenland and the infinite journey that separated me from the Polar North errs towards its end. Soon, by dint of being elsewhere and apart, the granulated dream will give rise to new perspectives. Living apart, I would be able to question the tenets of modern existence and speak out about what I had suspected for a long time, the fact that there are more simple, more gratifying ways to live. This was to be a journey of discovery of my own senses, a journey that took me back to a pre-linguistic world.

Clouds linger just above the icebergs, sitting in the Murchison Sound, sculpted by the wind, and then a flash of colour from the brightly painted wooden houses of Qaanaaq – almost the first evidence of human habitation for the best part of one thousand miles. Fifty years ago a tiny hunting settlement, the town with the palindromic name now boasts a population of 650 people, living with their back to the Greenland Ice Sheet. Beneath, live the northern most indigenous people in the world, located in a quite implausible polar desert environment, vanishing between the clouds. Rocks, boulders and scree imprimis, this barren tundra and unfenced, mythological wilderness is to be my home for the forthcoming year. It was Pytheas and Polybius that manufactured the ancient myth of Thule, a name etched in my memory from long ago and for whom many this part of the world remains a reference point. Today and with a touch of tragic irony, this ancient onoma is borne by the nearby US Air Base which I would visit later in my stay.

1: Introduction

This is a book about my year living in a remote Inuit community at the top of the world, and is concerned with what it is to be human and to 'belong' or 'not to belong' in a society whose cultural values are quite different from your own. The issue of 'belonging' became a perennial struggle and was impossible for me to ignore because my day-to-day experience was framed in these terms. This is *not* a 'realist' monograph or an objective ethnography of the Inugguit that attempts to display and explain the life of the indigenous 'other', although inevitably that makes up part of its content. Instead, this book is a narrative that uses this special experience to reflect on my own 'being'. It is thus written in the style of a kind of auto-anthropology or memoir, undertaken in a certain existential state of mind and reflexive awareness triggered by the experience itself. The narrative is concerned very much with the 'lived' experience, and not with the process of language documentation. During the course of the year, there were many times when nothing much happened, but there was always lots to talk about. My time there was characterised by what one might call 'eventful nothingness'. Instead of couching ethnographic moments in terms of existential events, my narrative follows the arc of a year-long-stay in north-west Greenland. The book comprises a sequence of vignettes with intermitting chapters focusing on ways of speaking and ways of belonging.

My account is based on the premise that human existence can only be grasped within ourselves, but also that human sociality is no longer simply the object of our understanding, but the very method whereby we achieve it. It is my belief that our understanding of the world cannot arise from reflection alone, but that it must pass through a medium external to ourselves, such as language. And it must go through others. This kind of inter-experience is richest when these 'others' share different parameters of 'belonging' from your own.

This book is therefore concerned with the experience of living in a society that is alien in many respects and using this experience to say something about the *human condition* and the essence of language. Moreover, it is the story of a person who discovers a new sense of consciousness of his own world by being an 'outsider' in an extraordinary place – a subject that is taken up in the Epilogue. For me, the overall objective of fieldwork is first and foremost to undertake a journey that broadens your horizons and enables you to understand better 'your' world. It is a chance to 'hold infinity in the palm of your hand and eternity in an hour' (Blake, 1977: 506).

Aware of the work of previous anthropologists in the region, I wished, as a linguist, to avoid at all costs what I came to call the 'Minik Syndrome'. From the beginning, it was obvious that the Inugguit did not wish outsiders to treat them or their culture as objects of enquiry. Minik was a Polar Eskimo child who Peary took to New York to show New Yorkers what an *inuk* looked like. He and his father were treated as museum exhibits with his father's skeleton being exhibited at the American Museum of Natural History in New York. Peary had promised to take Minik back to north-west Greenland, but it was 13 years before Minik was able to return. By that time, he had forgotten the Polar Eskimo language. On their arrival in New York, the adult Inuit got tuberculosis and Minik's father died. Minik wanted his father to be given a traditional burial, but Mr Wallace, the museum curator wanted to have the body for 'research' purposes. To placate Minik, the museum carried out a fake burial filling a coffin with stones and a stuffed body. The boy was led to believe that he was witnessing the burial of his father. In the meantime, Minik's father's body was defleshed and subsequently put in a cabinet in the museum without his son's approval.

Most of all, they did not want their cultural practices to be museum pieces. Documenting their oral traditions was a sufficiently difficult issue that I became grateful that the fieldwork was such a self-reflexive process and that I was able to focus more on the philosophical issues that invariably arose from it (as well as of course the linguistic ones). The fieldwork became the lens through which these issues could be tackled. Reflexivity was not, however, an instrument of political correctness, but was a *natural* response to my environment. To my mind, pursuing ontological problems and issues by living in and embracing an alien culture is the rightful task of anthropology in a post-colonial, globalised twenty-first century where the 'other' might deem the scholar to be practicing an intellectual neo-colonialism. The time for the 'description' of the 'other' appears to have passed because it is based on a supposed opposition of 'here' and 'there' which in many respects is no longer tenable. The concept of culture is problematic in a 'mixed-up' world where everything is overlapping and inter-connected. There are still some parts of the world where cultural alterity makes fieldwork a worthwhile pastime, but these are rapidly decreasing in number and mass tourism will render them much less interesting anyway. Tourism may well help the economy, but it will make the job of the anthropologist in a place such as I worked ultimately impossible.

The irony of this way of thinking is that one goes into the field aiming to 'study' an aspect of a foreign culture or language, but one ends up becoming an ethnologist of one's own world and society. An approach to anthropology which is based on a phenomenological description of perceptual consciousness is grounded in the paradox that the life of the individual is also a universal life. But, this approach does not make fieldwork any less problematic in practice as the indigenous people that the researcher is working with will probably still perceive the fieldworker as somehow trying to get at the reality of the 'other'. This perception of the researcher as a 'collector' became, as I was to discover, the perennial problem of fieldwork. Worse still, whenever one describes daily life in the region – the honest truth and not a glossed, theorised account for a sterile, politically correct audience – one is accused of victimising one's informants. But, a story should be told as it was, with the positive *and* negative aspects, without having to avoid all the difficult issues for fear of offending somebody. That way, the reader can be made aware of the real issues and help can be provided as I have tried to do myself by raising awareness of the problems of imposing hunting quotas on the Inugguit.

I had gone to document the language and endangered oral traditions of a tiny Inuit community fewer than a chiliad strong, but ended up benefiting from the privilege of immersion into a different 'lifeworld' (Merleau-Ponty, 2002) by getting 'outside' my own world and language, to the extent that it is possible. I had hoped to study the communicative practices of the Inugguit with the aim of writing an Ethnography of Speaking. The language I discovered was, however, one where there are almost no proverbs, where raised eyebrows frequently replace words and where jokes are practical and not oral. I was left to decipher the perpetual maybes of the indigenous mind and its chiasmus with language. The fundamental premise of the Ethnography of Speaking is a relativistic one, the understanding that speaking, like other systems of cultural behaviour is patterned within each society in culture-specific ways. It soon became apparent to me that actions spoke louder than words in the community where I was working. It is true that knowledge and socio-cultural experience are constructed, transmitted and performed through the filter of storytelling, but a more significant medium of instruction and relaying knowledge today is through actions themselves. Elderly people told me in plain, matter-of-fact fashion: 'there was not much need for language in the olden days'. From that moment on, my interests shifted to pure language documentation which will be the subject of a separate book, and my own narrative which focused on the issue of 'belonging' and 'being'. The two are related: the need to 'be' results in a search for 'belonging'. But this search for 'belonging' was perhaps more of a search for 'belonging in the world' to use Merleau-Ponty's terminology. 'Belonging' is fundamentally defined through a sense of experience, a phenomenology of locality (Lovell, 1998: 1). Memories of belonging can become powerful identity markers in themselves.

It became rapidly apparent that Arctic travel literature is full of false accounts and inaccuracies in its descriptions of the Inuit. The first flawed myth was that the Polar Eskimos kiss with their noses: something which I never once witnessed and which local people denied and laughed at. The accounts I had read were, however, right about the Inuit reception to outsiders. Even if I expected it from having read Arctic ethnographies, I struggled to understand in these first few months why it was that I so frequently felt ignored. In Inuit communities, it is normal to watch and observe the 'outsider' for a while before making contact with him, but there were clearly other issues at work here. Researchers have a low status in the community and as a visiting researcher, one is certainly rather low down the pecking order. There is a lack of trust between researchers and local people. Quite understandably, researchers are not seen to be offering anything to the community and their intentions are not always appreciated. I imagine this must be especially the case if one is an anthropologist.

The 'experience of language' helped me formulate my own views on what one might call the phenomenology of speech. Working in a primarily oral culture, I discovered that the primacy of the 'perceptual' experience of the language and the existential framework of my work were connected by the issue of phenomenology. Merleau-Ponty (1962: viii) in the Preface of his *Phenomenology of Perception* says that 'phenomenology can be practiced and identified as a manner or style of thinking'. It should not therefore be thought of as a fixed system of philosophy. It is more a way of describing as opposed to analysing. It is an approach to philosophy which says that knowledge comes from experience. It is opposed to the mechanism and reductionism of logical positivism or reductionism. Inuit society is experiential and therefore it would be difficult to find a more fitting way of doing philosophy within this kind of fieldwork than phenomenology itself.

Merleau-Ponty (2002: 216-18), the phenomenologist, said that language is gesture and working in a context without a written tradition, I came to recognise the gestural or existential significance of speech and words. Voice quality and facial gesture are an important means of 'embodied' linguistic meaning in this community. Here, it is the living use of language, the un-writeable that gives the spoken utterance its illocutionary force. The voice of the Arctic hunter was something 'transcendental', reverberating in my head long before I could formulate a correct grammatical sentence. In a place where the soundscape intermingles with human voices, music seems to precede grammar. For me, language has always been first and foremost music. Learning a new and completely alien language rekindles a sense of linguistic and intersubjective surprise because words once again become representations of certain meanings. Words regain their agency because the ready-made-meanings are not yet known. Speech is deinstitutionalised. In such an environment, one becomes sympathetic to the idea that words imply verbal experience in which the word carries a meaning that conveys a thought as a style, an emotional value rather than just a conceptual statement. Hearing their language brought a new dimension to the overall linguistic experience: the long silences were a window onto the primordial, inner world with all its unspoken words and thoughts; the link between the 'way of speaking' and the natural, sensory environment. To know the meaning of a word is not just a question of acquiring an appropriate phonetic motivation. It involves a familiarity with an entire universe of meaning where language and society interpenetrate the *lived* value of words.

Phenomenology, where 'phenomena' are the objects of 'perception', is the science of experience or a method of reflective attentiveness that discloses the individual's 'lived experience'. The very notion of 'experience' implies that the experiencing subject is not contemplating the world from some position outside it, but is itself part of that world. The world is not something we merely contemplate, but something we inhabit. This is what Merleau-Ponty means when he asserts, as a central theme of his philosophy, that as experiencing subjects, our being is necessarily 'Being-in-the-world'. Merleau-Ponty (as indeed do the Inugguit) avoids the dualism of objectivism and subjectivism through the conceptualisation of the body-organism as a mode of 'Being-in-the-world' or belonging in the world through its openness to the solicitation of the world.

Phenomenology is concerned with the relationship between Being and 'Being-in-the-world'. Fieldwork gave me phenomenological insights into the whims of human consciousness – drifting between an ontologically secure sense of self and at other times an overwhelming instability. The fieldwork experience provided me with a consciousness of myself and of my world – a consciousness that was often unsettled and fluid, oscillating constantly between speech and silence, solitude and sociality, frustration and calm, aimlessness and purposefulness. It showed me that experience is knowledge and that being human means first that we possess consciousness of ourselves and our world. This phenomenological basis for my fieldwork meant that I was concerned with what Husserl called the *Lebenswelt* and the 'spoken word'. The phenomenologist tries to recover an awareness of what a speaking subject really is, and it is the intersubjectivity that is the path to knowledge and consciousness. Experiencing subjects such as ourselves could not be 'in the world' unless we had a position in space, and to that extent we are ourselves objects like any others. But, 'the world' is more than simply the spatial container of our existence. It is the sphere of our lives as active, purposive beings. What it is to 'experience' the world, therefore, can be explained only in terms of such 'inhabiting', rather than simply in terms of representation. Indeed, we can 'represent' the world only because we are already present in it and involved with it. We must 'be in the world' before we can have a science of the world. In accordance with Merleau-Ponty's philosophy, perception is not an inner representation of an objective world, but a relation of inhabiting a world. The sense in which our being is 'Being-in-the-world' is that we do not simply represent the world as pure object of knowledge from a point outside the world, but actively participate in it.

It should be clear therefore that the general attraction of phenomenology for the framework of my narrative is that it represents a desire for a philosophy rooted in description of the experience of beings who were 'in the world' rather than attempts at general 'theories' or 'systems'. It engages with a sense of reawakening of the world. And with this in mind, the phenomenology of speech 'tries to determine the place of speech with regard to the totality of human experience' (Verhaar, 1963: 13).

Today, many linguists wish to reduce language to a fixed synchronic cognitive code pitted in a universe where man is absent, but a year in an Inuit community reinforced my belief that utterances are artefacts in social space that derive their meaning from their place in diachronic processes of human interactions and cultural production. Working in the context of a language with no strict written tradition, one cannot help but focus on the 'user of language, the speaking subject', moving away from the notion of language as something static and objective to the experience of the spoken word and the power and memory of the voice. Merleau-Ponty makes the distinction between a spoken language and a speaking language. The spoken language is the acquired linguistic meanings that I have at my disposal, whereas the speaking language is the expressive gesture which engenders language. From a linguistic perspective, 'Being-in-the-world' means becoming part of and internalising the sensory-perceptual observations that one makes with reference to the speaking language.

In a corner of the Arctic where the words share the rhythm and lilt of the local soundscape, language seems to lie at the deep structure of the sensory landscape and to be much more than a disembodied, purely formal set of grammatical and syntactic relations. With a host of almost indistinguishable palatal fricatives sounding like the wind blowing across the ice sheet, one cannot help but focus on the inner content of language. Amongst the Inugguit, the performative utterance conveys extraordinary nuance. Our experience of language leads us to objectify the world around us, writing and speaking of every entity as though it were a determinate, quantifiable object without its own sensations and desires – as though in order to describe another being with any precision we first had to strip it of its living otherness, or had to envision it as a set of passive mechanisms with no spontaneity, no subjectivity, no active agency of its own. Through language, we isolate human awareness apart from the sensuous world by making language a container for our thoughts. My 'lived experience' in the Arctic showed me that the Inugguit were to have a quite different notion of language. Insights from my fieldwork showed me that the ontological bearing of language may be clarified if we draw a distinction between *language* as an objective structure studied within the field of linguistics and *speech* which is the value language acquires when it is turned towards expression. It is the latter which tends to be neglected nowadays within linguistics, but that was always of more interest to me during my fieldwork. I became sympathetic to the phenomenological approach to language which would state that ultimately, language is not a system capable of revealing the genesis of its own meaning. The reason for this is that we are the language we are talking about. A phenomenologist would wish to put it in terms that state that we are the material truth of language through our body, which is a natural language. It is through language and the existential significance of gesture that I came to discover my 'new world'.

2: First Encounters

It was the sense of being 'somewhere else', the otherworldliness and overwhelming emptiness of the place that struck me first. It felt like a journey to the primordium of the Arctic. After four and a half hours of flying up the West Greenlandic coast with nothing to see but chiselled basalt and granite, meandering glaciers and icebergs sitting like solitary, glacial offspring in the distant fjords, the dry, desert environment of the Thule region suggested a world of paradoxes. The ancient glaciers, the deciduous icebergs; the Martian polar desert flanking the inky, frigid Arctic waters; the heat of the sunshine, the coolness of the air; the geographic remoteness, the surprising connectedness with the outside world; the meteoritic coastlines just 800 miles from the North Pole that mirror the moon – a place somewhere between poetic imagination and an implausible reality. But, people had lived here in this place, not quite out of reach, for over a thousand years, so far north, so far from anywhere. The mercury in the thermometer read only a few degrees, but it felt considerably warmer in the dry air of the Arctic summer sunshine.

The hut (342B) where I was to be living for the next year, the most dilapidated in a line of bright, pastel coloured wooden houses leading up one of the dusty tracks towards the top of the town, looks run-down with a rusting blue van leaning against its wooden walls and an outside porch door that does not close properly. Inside, we are assaulted by an armada of semi-anaesthetised flies, and on the floor lie the casualties of a dipterous genocide. Window-sills act as funeral parlours for regiments of the fallen. Through the thin pink curtains, the view is magnificent: columns and pinnacles of ice drifting towards Herbert Island. Unusually for an Inugguaq house, a vast polar bear, and a musk-oxen skin decorate the floor. There is an old-fashioned television (with one Danish channel) on which a thin layer of tangled dust spangles in the afternoon Arctic sunlight. The house is an uninsulated, pre-fabricated Scandinavian style wooden house with an extremely sturdy front zinc-plated door – the kind of door that one finds as an entrance to 'cold rooms' – with a polar bear proof handle which you have to push up to open. The house would have come as a flat-pack on the supply ship. It is a 'summer house'. There is oil heating and electricity, but no running water or washing facilities. The bathroom is a bucket, lined with a yellow plastic bag that is collected twice a week. There is no waste drainage. Here, as in other parts of the Arctic, they use the honey-bucket system. There are only two tracks in Qaanaaq which are on the mains water supply – these adjacent roads are where the shop, the fire station, the police station hut, the electricity generator, the municipal building or local council (*kommune*), the laundrette and a few residential houses are located. There are two dirt tracks leading into Qaanaaq – one leads to the airfield and the other to the cemetery: a symmetrical metaphor of entrance and exit. There are no other roads. Qaanaaq is linked with the settlements by the sea ice (when it comes) and helicopter.

The sense of hunter-gatherer society meets modern consumerism is obvious from a brief glance at the place. The town seems tatty, shabby, dysfunctional somehow with rusting prams, outgrown shoes, discarded toys and various bits of broken furniture typically scattered around the perimeter of each house. In amongst the white goods and modern accoutrements, hangs dried narwhal skin (*nikkoq*) on lines, dead Arctic Hares (*ukaliq*) on hooks and skinned Arctic Foxes (*tiriganniaq*) on gibbets. On the ground, there is a small kennel for a bitch and her puppies who play in the chaff and the dirt. The sandy beach serves as a storage place and dumping ground. It is home to a collection of boats sandwiched in amongst blood-stained wooden chests (*neqauhivik*) containing meat and blubber, empty shipping containers, the packed, rotting, wood of unassembled houses and curled up sleeping dogs.

The Inugguit straddle two very different universes with opposing values. Wealth here is not yet properly expressed in terms of ownership of material possessions. The Inugguit all live in more or less the same houses, just painted a different colour. Some own dogs, some do not. Some are better hunters than others. Being an excellent hunter is still the means to gain prestige and recognition. Everything is shared, children (and previously wives) included. It is almost the atmosphere of a kibbutz, the ethic of collective ownership. This manifests itself in the way that they go in and out of each other's homes. They just walk straight in. Private ownership is very alien to them; the few houses privately owned in Qaanaaq belong to one *kadluna*. People swap homes frequently, just for a change. Nothing is quite permanent. If wealth is defined in any way, it may be in terms of the number of children that people have. This is an excellent example of different cultural perceptions of wealth and interpretation of different cultural categories. With consumerism, the encroaching Western cosmology might turn these values on their head. The levels of personal debt indicate that the desire to own the latest consumer goods might be as insatiable here, as elsewhere in the world.

Prior to having a superstructure of a Danish welfare benefit system imposed on them in the 1950s, the Inugguit were living in a sort of acephalous, non-tribal communistic anarchy – a form of voluntary and integral communism. Within this mould, Inuit kinship is bilateral. Relatives on both the father's and mother's side are equally recognised as belonging to one's own kin group, and social solidarities are primarily embedded within family and kinship groups. Many households consist of an extended family with three generations living in one house. There is little, if any, hierarchy in Inugguit society. Generally speaking, each household is related by kinship to a certain number of other households in the same settlement. During these first few weeks, I was busy establishing who the members of these family networks were and how they inter-connected. It is principally within these groups of related families that food is shared, visiting occurs, and various domestic services are rendered. Marriage tends to be still based on a strict division of labour, and space is therefore gendered to some degree. Women would not participate in the hunts during the winter. At this time of the year, there is often much to be done in the home with the preparation of skins, necessary repairs to clothing, making of *kamikker* for their grandchildren, etc. The wives join their husbands in the summer months when they go to camps and the settlements empty out.

Shortly after midnight, the sun disappears towards Hiorapaluk leaving whale-shaped Herbert Island awash in crimson in the late, scumbled sky. An easterly breeze speckles the sapphire sea. It is my very first evening in the settlement. Two tipsy hunters invite me into their wooden, A-framed house and quiz me on who I am and what my purpose is here. Clothes and shoes are piled up in the fetid porch. The pungent whiff of blubber and sea mammals hits you as you enter the house. The kitchen is crammed with dirty plates piled up on one another, a dried up narwhal steak sits in a frying pan. Stepping over the narwhal blubber spread out on newspapers on the kitchen floor, I am channelled into the corner settee in the chaotic living room and introduced to the various ancestors whose photographs line the walls, one of whom, Qâvigarssuaq, travelled with Knud Rasmussen to Alaska. There is a television in one corner of the room and a great number of toys strewn over the floor. I am asked repeatedly if I am a Norwegian from Greenpeace. There is paranoia in the community about Greenpeace and the threat they pose to their hunting culture. The younger of the two, Aningaaq, a 48-year-old hunter, offers me a choice of red or white wine from the carton inner bags that slop over the corners of the stained table. I am furnished with a slice of *mattak* 'narwhal skin with blubber'. The skin is very tough and I spend an inordinate amount of time chewing it in comparison with my hosts who seem to swallow it almost whole.

As is often the case in a place where there are relatively few outsiders, my hosts jump at the opportunity to vent a few of their concerns with the visitor. They explain how Greenpeace is making their lives difficult. The older gentleman tells me that he will hunt them with guns if they dared approach Qaanaaq. The mental image that I conjure up is almost reminiscent of the scene in Erik the Red where the Norsemen encounter the *Skrælingur*.

Some of the tiny wooden shacks close to where these hunters live down by the shore are now in a very bad state of disrepair and are the original homes built in 1953 when the Inugguit were forcefully relocated from Dundas (Ummannaq) to make way for the construction of a secret US Air Base at Thule (Pituffik) at the height of the cold war. At this point, Qaanaaq was just a tiny hunting camp with no permanent residents. The Inugguit were still semi-nomadic when Greenland became a colony of Denmark in 1953. They would move from one settlement to another in pursuit of sea mammals and sea birds. The Inugguit number 770 people living in four settlements, but fifty years ago the population was about half that and they were living in fourteen different camps. The shift from semi-nomadism to a more sedentary life has been sudden (and one might say bungled), but is not quite complete as their movements in the summer months show. However, there has been urbanisation in this part of the world too. Today, 660 people live in Qaanaaq – the smallest town in Greenland, leaving the remaining three open settlements with tiny populations. A number of the older people still feel as if they are people of exile, remembering the move from Dundas. As the population has grown, the infrastructure has grown around it. There is a modern school, an oil-fired electricity plant, a large shop, a sports hall, community hall and a small hospital. In addition, there is a small care home for the elderly and thus many of the older people who were previously living in the settlements have moved to the town to seek care. Two supply ships, operated by Royal Arctic, service the town and settlements. They come from Aalborg in Denmark, one arrives in July and the other in September when the bay is free of sea ice.

From what these two hunters are saying, it is clear that those who are held in the lowest esteem are environmentalist groups and representatives of the Government in Nuuk. The tension between the Self-Rule Government elected in 2009 and the Inugguit was increasing during my stay. The Government is advised by biologists when determining the quotas placed on the animals they can hunt. The trend is for the quota to decrease year-on-year. The Government also withdrew the subsidy that used to exist for the goods that were shipped to the 'outer settlements' and thus the cost of living has increased significantly. The Inugguit feel 'squeezed' by their own Government who does not wish hunting to be the face of a modern Greenland, regarding it as something primitive and backward. The hunters feel strongly that climate change has made the movement of animals less predictable, and therefore it is harder to determine how many animals there are in total. Quotas are set for narwhals, walrus, musk-oxen, caribou and polar bears, but locals would tell me that the scientists have never completed an in-depth study of the number of bears in the Kane Basin, the Arctic waterway lying between Greenland and Ellesmere Island and the place where they retreat to with the disappearing sea ice.

With a system of quotas and higher fuel prices, the hunters are less inclined to travel long distances (for example to Etah), if they can only hunt one walrus. There is a clear sense that the physical and social space of the Inugguit is shrinking. With the disappearing sea ice, travel between the different settlements in this roadless place is becoming more difficult, and thus the nature of social interaction is changing. Climate change is forcing urbanisation upon the Polar Eskimos and is interfering with hunting cycles. From the beginning of the 1990s, the sea ice has started to come much later. By the time the sea ice is thick enough to go out on, it is the middle of the dark period and hunting in the twenty-four hour darkness is a lot more demanding. Hunting prospects used to determine movement, diet, social life and even games. As climate change impacts their daily life, the Polar Eskimos are, however, increasingly subject to very different movement patterns. This transition coincides with a loss of animist beliefs; the bond between animal and *inuk* is weakening and not what it used to be. For instance, silence is no longer held after an animal is killed and *a'diqtoq* or the system of taboo regulation covering many aspects of life died out long ago. Few hunters believe nowadays that animals have souls (*tarneq*).

Three days later, the settlement is suffused in drizzle and the dank tracks resemble those of a remote Faroese village hidden in wisps of low brume. Mist-hewn houses sink into nebulous oblivion. The uneven, dirt tracks become puddled, the landscape beyond the church bespattered with mire. This was one of just three occasions during the course of a year when it rained. With the exception of the shop, everything seems to be closed for the weekend. The silence is timeless and immutable. The drizzle is unrelenting. There is barely a soul to be seen on the vertiginous slopes. August is a quiet month for hunting, and just at the moment at least it would seem that much of the traditional, hunting life has disappeared. It is too warm to wear traditional sealskin boots (*kamikker*) or polar bear trousers (*nannut*). There is barely a kayak to be seen. Instead, Gore-Tex clad Inugguit putter across the glassy expanse of the Inglefield Bay in their small outboard engine boats. At Arctic Food, two rubber-clad young men sidestep small puddles of poppy red blood, cutting up the occasional narwhal.

Clumps of cotton grass raddle two teams of barking, brawny dogs which are about to be fed. The sledge dog teams are kept on the periphery of the town with the town itself tending to be more the domain of the bitches and their puppies. By law, every Greenland Dog over the age of seven months has to be chained up, unless it is a pregnant female. Just behind the cemetery is a flattened area which used to be the helicopter landing strip until the airport was built in 2001. Today, the area is used as a football pitch.

The cemetery is relatively small and probably contains up to about 200 plots. A number of them seem to be recent burials, judging by the artificial flowers that decorate the graves and the clear engravings of the brass plaques on the white, wooden crosses, all of which face the rising sun. This is a cemetery of youth, perched above the sea; a charnel of lost ambitions and misplaced futures. Stillborn babies neighbour victims of unrequited love and suicide: closed minds in a closed, inward-looking society (conceptually, not materially) where emotional decrees stem from community wide taboos. Many died in their teens, twenties or thirties.

One of my initial observations in this first week was that the *raison d'être* of the Inugguaq is to have children. There are about 250 children in Qaanaaq. They are left unchided; enjoying complete freedom and a world devoid of discipline. In the twenty-four hour daylight, children play outside at all hours, without supervision and are very seldom chastised. Track-suited and puffing smoke, Inugguit parents spend their days sauntering around town with empty expressions and toddlers in tow. The laughter and cries of young children aside, in these first days, one had to get used to the more alien, primordial sounds that define Greenland. The shrieking, squealing and howling of the dogs, marking their territory just as the wolves of Ellesmere Island do, is unceasing in the near perpetual light. Some of the puppies, trying to fend for themselves, make the most appalling, high-pitched sounds as if they are being ripped to pieces in some bloody massacre, fighting over scraps of flesh. The eerie sound of anguished cries, tormented pleas and discombobulated heckles is unrelenting. At times, it is distinctly human-like as if one of the small children is screaming for his or her life. Many of the dogs seem quite desperate for food. As soon as they are offered a scrap, the dogs are fighting like mad and practically killing each other. The real Greenland Dog was apparently twice the size of the current one, but it died out in Qaanaaq in 1988 when the dogs got distemper. A new breed was subsequently introduced from West Greenland.

It is Sunday and the distant peal of the church bells can be heard just before ten o'clock. The lay-preacher or catechist (*ajoqi*) sits on a chair by the side of the lectern dressed in jeans and jumper with a white collarette around her neck. Most of the people in the church are elderly and dressed in fleece or Gore-Tex jackets. The service is Lutheran and based very much on the Book. It is stony and solemn. The bronchial stand-in catechist reads from the Bible, stumbling over the West Greenlandic polysyllabic words. Some of the words are so long and difficult, she has to make several attempts at them. It is a decalogue of sin read out formulaically in a muttering staccato. The hymns are sung in a very slow, purposeful dirge-like, monotone. There is no personal message for this troubled community, just a medieval-style fostering of a sense of collective guilt. The unengaged Congregation is barely audible. There are three hymns, interspersed by short readings, all given by the lay-preacher. There is a chorus of coughing, shuffling and snorting in the back pews. Hymn or threnody, the service feels purposeless.

We stand for the last two hymns, but not for the first. I tower over the elderly Inugguit, many of whom are not much more than five feet tall. Afterwards, the candles are snuffed out and the solemn Congregation leaves in a cloud of tubercular disinterest and disengagement, just exchanging a few words before disappearing in silence into the mist which enshrouds the town. The *ajoqi* retires to her office without greeting the church-goers. Outside the church, icebergs explode in the crisp, fresh Arctic air and a sudden splash of consciousness washes over me; a moment of pre-reflective self-consciousness that is hard to pin down and define, but that is responding to the experience of this new world.

Pondering the service, I stray down to the shore. It is clear that the Inugguit were christianised very late. The process did not begin until 1909 when the missionary Gustav Olsen arrived in the area. Up until that point, they had no institutionalised form of religious practice, but there were shamans and animist beliefs were widely held. It is believed that the entire community was Christian in name at least by the time of Knud Rasmussen's death in 1933. Only in 1937 was the Thule region incorporated into the rest of Greenland. Prior to that point and from the time of his arrival, the entire region had been effectively the private property of this Danish-Greenlandic ethnographer. Some of the more animist beliefs have, however, remained. The complete lack of discipline vis-à-vis Inugguit children can be explained by the fact that some of these children (*atsiaq*) have been named after dead ancestors, and are therefore believed to be the embodiment of these ancestors. In a community that has changed so much so quickly, it is curious that this ostensibly non-Christian feature has remained very much a hallmark of their society.

The Christian iconography that one finds in people's homes is largely symbolic. Christianity was embraced not a religious construct, but as part of a trade agreement. Therefore, the Inugguit do not connect with institutionalised religion at any deep level. I overheard once a discussion between a group of Inugguit who were trying to work out which of the priests believed in God the most. Most Inugguit would say that they believe in God, but they are not educated in the Bible. The Inuit see hypocrisy in Christianity. Christianity is seen as the religion of the rich, the white man, and yet one of the key messages of the religion is that the rich man never goes to heaven. The symbolic aspect of religion shines through the Inuit love of confirmations and other ceremonies which are little more than an excuse for a good party. Almost everybody is confirmed in Greenland. It is a necessary rite of passage to adulthood. Children look forward to it because they are given so many presents and often a very significant amount of money which is quickly spent on iPods, video games, mobile phones, etc.

Subsequently, it became clear that it was going to be difficult to even appear to 'belong' to either of the two diametrically opposed social groups upon which Qaanaaq life is increasingly divided: the welfare benefit dependent, heavy-drinkers and the teetotal, abstaining Born Again Christians. There does not seem to be any middle path; evangelical Christianity with its openness is a safety net for certain members of the community. The solemn Lutheranism that speaks in terms of sin and misdeed is of no assistance to a young man considering suicide.

The leaders of the Free Church, Naaja and her husband, organised a 'cultural exchange' with Canadian relatives, and there was feverish gossip in these first few weeks about the pending visit from their Canadian relatives in Grise Fjord (Ellesmere Island). These Canadian Inuit were given a warm welcome, and yet people from the south of Greenland might be treated with disdain. Here, identity is not defined by national borders and the cultural links between the Inugguit and this part of Canada remain strong. The event is meant to be an annual cultural reunion bringing together what is effectively one family that has been divided by climate change. Since the early 1990s it has not been possible to travel by dog-sledge across to Canada because the Smith Sound is now partly open all year round. There are no scheduled flights between Ellesmere/Baffin Islands and north-west Greenland. A fortunate few can afford to charter a Twin Otter. Otherwise, they might need to fly to Denmark, then across the Atlantic and back up again. A journey that costs several thousand pounds and which nobody can afford.

I arrive early at Naaja's house and meet a Samoan gentleman called Sila who lives in Alberta and has travelled from the Canadian Arctic to be here. Naaja and her husband used to be alcoholics up until five years ago, before they embraced Jesus and this Church movement which has changed their lives completely. Then, I meet Roger Ambruster – a white Canadian missionary. Thus far, the whole Canadian Inuit-Polar Eskimo reunion seems a bit of a farce as the visitors are clearly not family members.

The house starts to fill up, some faces familiar, others less so. There are now about twenty-five of us and there is a long wait in a hot room for the Canadian Inuit. Eventually, four Canadian Inuit turn up. They have come from Resolute and Grise Fjord. They are all in their sixties. Not so many years ago, the planes used to land on the sea ice at this time of the year. There was even a time when the sea ice was so thick DC-10s from the Air Base would land on the ice. Today, all aircraft have to land at the airstrip by law where their passports will be checked.

Naaja goes round the packed room, placing loo roll strategically on the tables. Just before the service begins, a small group of people convene in the front room to 'preach'. The noise from the room sounds like something from a mystic cult – people speaking in tongues, making rapid babbling, bah-bah sounds interjected with the ecstatic shout and clap. With his staring eyes and expressionless face, Piita plays the keyboard and we all stand up to sing the gospel on the small printed sheet. People sing with their right hand on their chest whilst waving their left arm in the air, eyes closed and everybody looking very intense. The guitarist is sobbing throughout the song and looks desperate, as does our Canadian visitor, Thomas. The Congregation shakes, trembles and shouts. At the end, Naaja shrieks 'hallelujah' whilst jerking and starts talking in tongues again, as does her husband. I feel as if I am in the house of a voodoo priest in West Africa, not the High Arctic. This seems like mindless emotionalism bordering on the hysteria of a Pentecostal

Church. Several people are reaching for the loo paper and wiping their eyes, having worked themselves up into something of an emotional frenzy. I look blankly at the long words of West Greenlandic on the sheet in search of an explanation. I feel horribly conspicuous at the front, towering over my Inuit neighbours. People are shouting out for Jesus and booming out 'praise the Lord'.

Afterwards, the missionary, Roger, gives a short sermon about how the language of the Polar Eskimos and Canadian Inuit ties them together and gives them one voice in front of God. It is horribly contrived and based on inaccurate information at times. Then, Preben tells a story of how he was forced to move to Resolute – the same time that the Polar Eskimos were relocated to Qaanaaq in 1953. He sobs uncontrollably through the story (in a way that looks very unnatural to me) and by the end it is just Roger and myself who have not shed a tear. This tremendous collective outpouring of emotion seems so sudden, intense, but then just moments later it is all smiles again. The second story is similar to the first and dwells on the tragedy of exile and the struggle for recognition in a world dominated by white men. It is by now a familiar discourse.

We finish up with another song and more pathetic, desperate grimaces from the guitarist and end finally on a note of glossolalia from Naaja. Her intense babbling and jerking brings yet another tear to her neighbour's damp cheeks. I am relieved that it is over and hope that we can soon start on the cake. It is certainly a strange undertaking to come to a small house at the top of the world on a Sunday morning and be surrounded by alcoholics and former alcoholics seeking redemption in such a dramatic, hysterical, over-emotional manner.

A meeting has been organised in the sports hall to welcome the Canadian Inuit. At 7pm, the room is packed. There must be about 150-200 people there, perhaps one quarter of the population. Teenage mothers skulk whilst scores of obstreperous children run amok. It is impossible to hear a word Roger is saying, but nobody thinks to heed their children. The event is hijacked by the Christian fundamentalists. There are readings from the Bible and happy-clappy songs. Interestingly, Preben tells a story to the packed crowd, giving a more extended version of his account of his exile. But, this time there are no tears. So, I conclude that this morning we were treated to a display of false emotion.

The audience seems somewhat apathetic to Naaja's speaking in tongues and a little unsure about the whole evangelical spirit. The highlight of the evening is the Canadian Inuit throat singing. Throat singing was never established in Greenland, but was practiced by the Canadian Inuit women when their husbands were away hunting. It was kind of a breathing game really, and not considered music at all. Roger makes an appeal for people not to forget their spoken traditions. There is clearly an attempt at forging indigenous solidarity with the Samoans being greeted and with links being made between exiled groups of indigenous people.

Roger is trying to whip up emotion. He encourages people to remember their songs and their throat-songs, perhaps not appreciating that throat-singing was never practiced here. When one of the Canadian Inuit asks for forgiveness and tells a story about her father, Roger starts crying like a baby, but then two seconds later he is thumping the air and shouting like a cowboy. The more emotional and upsetting the story is, the more he shouts and bellows at the end of it. One third of the town is here. I am not sure if they are here just because there was nothing else to do, or whether it was some kind of snowball effect. The programme is the same for tomorrow night, but we are told that the 'service will continue past midnight'. Roger holds out his hand in the air and shouts out to the crowd that the service will be 'five hours long'. This charismatic evangelism feels increasingly fundamentalist.

Towards the end of the meeting, Roger's shouting builds up to a crescendo as if a football match is about to end. Sila, the large Samoan gentleman, tells us that he found Jesus after a life of crime. Sila reminds us that it is 'evil to have sex before marriage'. That message is surely lost on this fertile and promiscuous community, and there is little reaction from the Inugguit, all of whom practice sex with multiple partners long before marriage. Once the theatre is over, walrus soup is served in poly-styrene cups. Contented faces smile and utter *mammaktorruaq* ('it is very tasty'). Then, it is time to go home.

Roger and his missionaries were not always welcome. He had asked the Headmaster if he could come and preach to the school children. The Headmaster denied him permission, knowing a good deal about the church that he represented. But, he turned up anyway. Roger has a website and details of his trip to Qaanaaq had been posted there. On his website, Roger describes Qaanaaq as 'sin sick and ripe for transformation'. The missionaries had come here to prey on the weak and vulnerable. They know that the Inugguit are not critically minded, and that they represent therefore easy targets. Certainly, it seems to be the case that some Inugguit are able to embrace fundamentalist Christianity without posing any questions, which is rather alarming. They are sitting ducks, and the Canada Awakening Ministries is fully aware of this. Next stop is Cuba. The Headmaster told me at great length how he believed that this Free Church in Qaanaaq was corrupt with members paying ten per cent of their salary directly to Naaja and Piita. Naaja, a teacher at the school, has repeatedly tried to introduce her Born Again teachings to the school children even with the opposition of the Headmaster. Some would say that by calling themselves a 'Free Church', they have licence to do what they want. According to the Headmaster, if you leave, deciding it is not for you, you are abandoned and castigated. By trying to belong to another group, some of the Inugguit were distancing themselves from the group they have always belonged to.

Visiting the Inugguit, the conversation would often come back to cultural disconnects and the desire for connectedness, the need for an attachment, a connection. This manifested itself overwhelmingly in the comfort of the spider web of extended, interconnected families, but occasionally there was reference to a kinship with the natural world, a form of reciprocity with animals, plants and the elements. Inukitsoq would like to tell me how this is a community whose pace of life has always been dictated by the sun, moon, stars, etc., but now the reference points are increasingly clocks, opening hours, deadlines and day-night distinctions. Hunters used to navigate by the wind, moon, stars and the feeling of the Earth. Then, he laughs and says that knowledge has all but disappeared and that they now they use GPS. Religion aside, it is obvious that the transition to Western life has been difficult for them and that they resent it. The effects of the demands of a Western cash economy on an indigenous group are obvious. People tend to eat when they are hungry and sleep when they are tired, but schools and hospitals cannot operate on this basis. Their old way of life and mindset does not fit the modern timetable. There is a culture clash; this society is in the throes of rapid and fundamental transition.

Hunters cannot survive and feed a family from hunting alone, and thus they need to have one foot in the modern, Western system with a job and its starting and finishing times. So much of the hunting way of life has disappeared: the Inugguit would now starve (primarily because of the imposed hunting quotas) if it were not for the shop. For the first time ever, they are no longer completely self-dependent; the export market for their hunting wares disappeared some time ago. All of these factors have threatened in a sense their phenomenology of locality as 'being' and the 'experiencing' of the Polar North is changing. Belonging is fundamentally defined through a sense of experience and this sense of experience is clearly exposed to dramatic modification as the wholeness of their world risks being conceptually severed.

Reflecting on this cultural disconnect and trussed up in my sleeping bag, I fall asleep to the yolk and splutter of the oil-heater, and awaken to the resplendent pink-yellow sunshine filtering through the curtains on the last of these cornerless days. The blue skies of these endless, halcyon days of August go on day-after-day. These days are pristine, marvelling in their perfect, prismatic clarity. One can see for almost 100 miles. It is a graphic tableau of an unspoiled place, an untranslated gobbet of Arcadia. The light, its gleaming sheen, ricochets around the room.

Now, already, I see natural phenomena in a different perspective. The ark of the sun has never interested me so much before, but now it governs the rhythm of my day. It rises from behind the cliffs on the cemetery side of the town, arcs high in the sky and then dips on the side of the airfield in the late evening. By looking at where the sun is in the sky, I can have a reasonably accurate idea of what the time is. When the sun is above the middle of Herbert Island, I know for instance that it is about seven o'clock in the evening. This kind of simplicity and harmony has a primordial appeal, and is giving me a new sense of consciousness about the world I am living in.

Down by the shore, rhombus-shaped lumps of ice measuring two metres across are parked on the beach. The protean ice has broken off the splintering icebergs in the bay and has drifted towards the shore, across the sun-dappled water in a dazzling panoply of optical delusion. Their chatoyant bellies shimmer glaucously in the morning sunshine. The scene is paradoxical and otherworldly. Further along the beach lies a dead Harp Seal, the fresh blood staining its wishbone shaped markings. Further along still, an up-turned sledge, rusty pram wheels and then a decaying dead dog.

At 10pm, I go to the tiny den of the bar (*taffi*), and am greeted with a scene of devastation. Three middle-aged women are barely able to stand up on the balcony they are so drunk and launch themselves at me as I try to squeeze past. The door to the ladies' loo is open and a woman in her fifties, perhaps, lies barely conscious on the floor. A 'security' man (in his teens) walks over and tries to get her onto her feet. I have a peek in the bar, wondering if things can get any worse and witness drunkenness which I have not seen anywhere else in the world. Raven-haired women lie flopped over tables like sacks of flour, soused in alcohol. Old men with glazed almond eyes and lonely tooths hanging from faces of misery and self-destruction spar like narwhals with one another. Some stagger around shouting out my nickname 'Stiffi'. The only white man feels uncomfortably conspicuous, waiting to be abashed by sneering. The Danes do not come here. The only sane person in the place is the young barman, Umik Petersen, who is looking as serious and composed as he was last week. Terribly inebriated hunters stare at me as if I am their quarry. Here, there are no piquant glances, just schizophrenic Friday nights. Belching, wanton old women yank at my jacket, arm-lock me and drag me onto the dance-floor.

The atmosphere is tense and neurotic: the clenched jaws and fixed, expressionless stares speak suspicion and jealousy, fuelled by the alcohol running insidiously through their veins. Gone are the daytime toothless grins; now ladies' faces are marred with tears. Here, it is perhaps believed that the road to excess does indeed lead to the palace of wisdom. I buy a 330 ml can of Tuborg beer for 45 DKK (£6) and escape to the balcony, hoping to meet some relatively sober people. Outside is a circus of laughing black irises. A forklift truck driver wears a Thule Air Base baseball cap and speaks in broken English with an accent that is the result of watching one too many violent American films. He constantly recycles his tiny repertoire of one-liners: 'Fuck you, man; I love Tony Blair; your mother is a bitch'. All rather lamentable and not exactly what I came to document.

I am more fortunate in meeting Tikkili who intriguingly goes by the nickname 'Jarmel' for the apparent reason that his skin is slightly darker than his peers. He is the great-great grandson of Matthew Henson. He shows me a tattoo on his shoulder with the name 'Jarmel' emblazoned across it which seems like an odd undertaking given that he does not approve of the sobriquet. He is just 19, one of eleven children and speaks very good English which he says he learnt from television. He speaks of curdled friendships and jealousy amongst the Inugguit. He thinks he should leave Qaanaaq because at every turn, he meets an ex-girlfriend or a male opponent.

The contrast between his articulate, sober state and the slurred drunkenness inside could not be greater. With a gaggle of comatose women trying to escort me into the bar, we abscond to his girlfriend's parents' house. The house is modern with central heating (oil), is relatively neat and tidy and is right down by the waterfront enjoying the most magnificent views. It is located just behind Uumaaq Jensen's prominently placed blue house which is the closest to the waterfront. With all the mod cons in the house (compared to mine), it feels almost as if I am in Europe again. There is no whiff of sea mammals and there are even wardrobes. A peek in the freezer reminds me where we are as a caribou's head (with the frozen eyes still in place) stares back at me. I am then introduced to the various body parts of the beast which sit in a variety of neatly organised polythene bags.

We go through the normal ritual of looking at and commenting on photographs of the extended family and I am introduced to countless cousins. I am shown a picture which is perhaps twenty or thirty years old with twelve family members. The girl tells me that eight of them are now gone. They all committed suicide. I am speechless, offer rather pathetically my condolences and am told that she does not know what motivated the deaths. I have only been here a few weeks but realise already that this community is blighted by suicide and that everybody knows somebody who has taken their own life. It is said that young boys do it for reasons of unrequited love. Many of the suicides occur under the influence of alcohol, and normally in the summer months. For the vast majority of people, there is no way in or out of Qaanaaq. It is prohibitively expensive to fly. If a young boy were to fall in love and that girl became his entire focus and yet the love was not reciprocated, he is stuck in a condemning, loveless trap understood by all, but for which there is no escape other than down the barrel of a rifle.

I look at the magnificent moon in the east and the still, serene bay full of shimmering monoliths of ice. Panning the bay, my glance moves to the sun inching around the corner. The sky is a seesaw tipping west, sinking the sun and rising the moon, breaking the momentary equilibrium. Away from the chaos of the bar, tilted-eyed Greenland Dogs bay the waning gibbous in an eerie concert of evening solitude. The contrast between the sublime and the lowly; the magnificent vista across Murchison Sound and the problems of this troubled community is almost too great for words. On the way home, I walk past any number of locals slumped outside their homes and staggering down the coiling, dirt tracks following in the spoors of previous party-animals. This particular drinking spree was triggered by a tax-rebate that the local people had received. The Danish doctors had arrived to test for radiation from the nuclear accident from the US Air Base in 1968, but they were unable to do any work for the first week because the level of alcohol in their blood was too high.

Very regrettably, the issue of alcoholism was impossible to ignore during my stay in the Polar North. I would find on countless occasions that the Inugguit would always wish me to join them when they had been drinking, just to find that on the next encounter I would be more or less ignored. Worse, in the case of two particular hunters, I would be subject to unpleasant verbal abuse. Some of the people in Qaanaaq are, what is called in Danish *alkoholisert* (FAS: Fetal Alcohol Syndrome), recognisable through various facial stigmata such as a smooth philtrum and a thin upper lip. That is to say that they were born with mental deficiencies because their parents drank through the pregnancy. In Polar Eskimo society, it would seem that alcohol and violence are even more closely coupled than in other societies that I know. It is clear that those who drink most and who are most prone to violent acts are already on the 'emotional scrapheap' (Riches, 1986: 17). In some of the recent years, there has been an average of one murder a year in Qaanaaq, which for a community of 700 people equates to one of the highest murder rates in the world. Sadly, every family has a tragic story to tell; there is an appeal to tragedy everywhere you go in the Polar North. It was not long before I started to unearth the dark underworld of Qaanaaq life.

I have not been home for more than a few minutes when I hear the familiar heavy, stumbling footsteps of a drunk coming up the steps to the house. I move towards the front door and try and lock it, but the tall character who Marie Nielsen warned me about, forces his way past me. He has never been here before and I can tell by the cut of his jib that he is not the sort of gentleman I want to deal with. He stares at me with fixed eyes: an unwanted glance that is becoming too familiar. A single tooth hangs down from a desperate, weathered looking face. Standing just centimetres away, he looks like he wants to kill me. It is past 11pm on a Friday evening and apparently he wishes to speak to me about the Polar Eskimo language in response to the advertisement that I placed at the shop. Firmly, I suggest that he can perhaps come back another time. He pushes me out of the way and stumbles into the room. Such an aggressive guest is really most unwelcome at this time of night. After a drawn out foray of miscommunicated slurs, I tell him that he has to leave because I am tired. He refuses to get up and I consider calling Hans, the policeman. It is a last resort, but increasingly this does not feel like an average encounter with a drunk. I have been out all afternoon and left the heater on low and the temperature has fallen to nine degrees. He complains that it is freezing in the room and starts to kick the spluttering oil heater, shouting and groaning like a deranged man. On this occasion, the oil heater is for once my saving grace. Complaining of the cold in the hut, he finally leaves, but not before asking for 200DKK.

I discovered subsequently that this was Taiko Peary: a man who the policeman considered the only 'dangerous' individual in the town. He attempted to kill a woman by hitting her over the head with a hammer. He had been kept in the tiny cell at the police station in Qaanaaq, but was now awaiting charges. Some believed that the attempted murderer was angry with me because I had mentioned the Peary name in the context of polar exploration in a radio interview. There are those Inugguit who are proud of this heritage and will boast their links publicly whereas others wish to have nothing to do with the polar explorers and their achievements. Either way, the Inugguit cannot understand the fuss about the polar explorers when they have been surviving 'up there' for centuries. Early on in my stay a Norwegian billionaire arrived in the town and unveiled a plaque of Eivind Astrup, a relative of his and an explorer who had travelled with Peary in the region. The indifference that the local people showed towards the unveiling of the plaque was palpable. Objectively speaking, it is of course true that some aspects of the discourse of 'discovery' are absurd. Allen Counter, a Harvard Professor, wrote a book about the ancestors of Robert Peary and Matthew Henson living in the region of north-west Greenland. Anybody who knew anything about the Polar Eskimos knew that there were descendants of Henson and Peary in the community, but that did not stop this Harvard professor claiming to have 'discovered' Henson's ancestors in a mission that was somehow 'personal' because the author himself was black. Such books are an embarrassment to every *kadluna* who has travelled in the region.

My closing remarks were supposed to motivate the local people, to get them to do more to preserve their language. It had been an appeal to their heroism, their ability to survive and a reminder of the importance of their language to their culture. This member of the Peary family had decided that he did not like the message. Subsequently, he disappeared for a while and I wondered what had happened to him. I discovered that a group had turned on him and that he had been beaten up.

Throughout my year in the Polar North, the Inugguit were very seldom violent towards me. In my experience, the alcohol-related violence was typically between couples (often initiated by feelings of jealousy), or between single men. It is very unusual for Inuit to be violent towards Europeans. Whilst there may be tensions, the Inugguit have a certain respect of the white man simply because he is in a sense symbolic of power. This must hark back to the very first sightings of the Europeans when Sir John Ross appeared in a ship with guns, smart uniforms and any number of goods and machines that the Polar Eskimos could not previously even conceptualise. Elderly people would tell me about when they saw an aeroplane for the first time in the 1950s. Even though they had heard talk of them, they could not believe that such things existed. When they first saw an aeroplane fly over, they shouted *quvdhardardoq* ('it can fly in the air').

The Inugguit were only properly introduced to alcohol one hundred years ago when Knud Rasmussen established his trading station. Unlike Europeans who have been drinking for centuries, the Inugguit have not had time to build up a tolerance to alcohol, and thus lack certain enzymes. Alcohol is often described as the 'cancer of Greenland', and the alcohol-related problems seem to be worst in the outer settlements, i.e. north-west Greenland and East Greenland. The local authorities have tried to tackle it in different ways, but have never found a solution. Some would say that they have never tried very hard, and that the income from the alcohol sales is too good for the community to turn down. Following the revelations of a Danish sociologist about alcohol-induced child abuse in Qaanaaq, a complete ban was introduced in 2007. However, this was not workable in the longer term. In the view of the policeman, the welfare benefit system upon which about fifty per cent of the population is dependent is too generous and the cause of the problem.

This is a hunting community where one will find a gun in most households, and the combination of guns and alcohol has never been a good one. Anybody can buy a gun in the shop. There are no regulations, and no licence is required. One can keep the gun anywhere one likes. Some are kept in unlocked wooden chests on the beach. Shortly after I arrived in the community, a woman living in Hiorapaluk received a letter from the hospital in Qaanaaq telling her to go for a routine cervical cancer smear. The woman had been drinking and misread the letter as saying that she had been diagnosed with cancer. In front of her husband and children, she picked up a rifle and shot herself. The bullet went through her shoulder and she survived. The man picked up the rifle and threw it out the window. And, life went on.

Adapting to modern life has been difficult in many ways for the Inugguit as my first encounters with them showed. This is and always has been a static society, but the Inugguit are now increasingly surrounded by the accoutrements of a modern economy. Despite that, life is here in fact still characterised by a *carpe diem* mentality (but food is stored over the winter). In times when there was a shortage of food, the Arctic hunters would surely have taken more risks and therefore the philosophy with money was simple: spend it whilst you can as you might be dead tomorrow. The Inugguit are paid on every other Friday. Money in hand, they go to the shop and spend it as soon as possible. In a way, the advent of credit cards has made this habit even more pronounced. Seeing as one is not actually handing over hard cash, one or two wished to convince me that it was not money at all.

According to Gilberg (1948: 83), it is said that when the Inugguit first started using money at the beginning of the twentieth century, they could not understand the point of it. They would go to pay for something in the store and at the counter would just hand over all the money they had. It was not understood why when they sometimes paid for something with one coin, they would get several coins back. It seemed illogical and was not like handing over a narwhal tusk in exchange for tobacco. Some did not appreciate that exchange rates are arbitrary and assumed that I was eight times richer than them because an English pound was worth eight Danish kroner. A Norwegian couple who were in Hiorapaluk wanted to charge their computer, and thus use somebody's electricity for half an hour. The man asked them to pay DKK 8,000 for the pleasure.

The *carpe diem* mentality can surely also be explained in part by the fact that life was very short until recently. Accidents and drownings were more common than today, and the Inugguit were afflicted by tuberculosis, tubercular meningitis and pneumonia. The very high rate of tuberculosis, still today twenty per cent of Greenlandic children show symptoms, is explained by the cramped, crowded living conditions. At one point during my stay in Qaanaaq, there were eighteen people living in one of the houses, two down from me.

Unlike so many of the explorers who died of scurvy, the Inugguit have never suffered, however, from vitamin deficiencies. Medical reports show that they are better supplied with vitamins than the average Dane. *Mattak* and the liver and kidneys of walrus and seal are very high in Vitamin C, A and D, and thus they managed to stay healthy in the 'dark period'. Up until the 1950s, there had not been a single case of cancer amongst the Inugguit and heart disease was very rare. Now, cancer is almost as common as it is in Europe and heart disease is on the increase. As an amateur, the only explanation I can see for this is the shift to the Western diet and the prevalence of smoking. The number of sea mammals that are caught is limited and once the hunters have fed their families and dogs (the semi-wild dogs need to eat meat and not the processed dog-food available at the shop), there is little to go round. Else, a woman in her fifties, thinks that the restrictions imposed on the Inugguit have forced them to gradually give up their traditional diet.

Adapting to a more Western lifestyle, the problem has been primarily that the change has been so very rapid. It is a familiar story with indigenous people all over the world. Elderly people would tell me that they were living in 'culture shock'. In one hundred years, the Inugguit had gone from living in the Stone Age, in houses made of stone and turf, heated and lit by blubber lamps and hunting with bows and arrows to modern Scandinavian housing, automatic fire-arms, mobile phones, DVDs and iPods.

However, this is still a community-based culture where the collective comes before the individual. People do not tend to be singled out and told what to do or how to do things. And, most importantly of all, people are not criticised in the workplace or elsewhere: if one criticises somebody at work, it is unlikely that they will turn up for work the next day. The reason for this extreme sensitivity to criticism must stem from the communal basis of their society, but also the size of the community. In other small, bounded societies such as the Faroe Islands, one finds a similar reluctance for residents to be critical of each other. There is a concern that by speaking out about the actions of a person, that individual might retaliate by making public a secret concerning the informant. In such a small, bounded place, if relations break down, life can rapidly become intolerable. The sense of communality is so strong that being singled out as an individual, particularly one that has made a faux pas, is most undesirable and results in the loss of face. There is little room for individualism and the ancient system of customary law was based on the exposure and public ridiculing of individuals. It may be due to this very clear sense of a communal and distinct identity that the Inugguit are very self-conscious of cultural differences, and like to highlight them whenever the opportunity arises. According to the traditional Eskimo penal code, murder is only a personal crime. Something is only a crime if it weakens the social body itself for the Inugguit live as one non-hierarchical social body, and not as a collection of individuals. Had a 'crime' been committed, the accused would be pilloried mercilessly, excoriated for their mistakes and made to listen to a string of insults in front of an appreciative crowd. Their sense of humour and the metering of justice was based on ridicule and mockery with the recital of extremely insulting verses.

It was in these first few weeks that my fascination with the community began. There was of course the excitement of living in a new, alien place where I had to fend for myself in a simple hut. However, it was perhaps the degree of inter-relatedness that was the source of the original fascination with regards to how the society functioned. One of the very first observations one makes is the overwhelming sense of kinship as a principle of social organization. The divide between insider and outsider seemed more like a chasm in this initial period. Everywhere I went, there was a constant appeal to an all-pervasive concept of kinship. I would ask

Eva, the great-granddaughter of Robert Peary, whether she had any relatives in Haviggivik and she would respond immediately by saying that her deceased husband's older brother's daughter's son lives there. Everybody knows exactly how they are related to each member of the community. This is knowledge of 'Being-in-the-world' for the Inugguit. When it comes to kinship, their knowledge is encyclopaedic and unfaulting.

People were introduced to me by the kinship term, more often than by name. Rather than building a mental registry of names, I was invited instead to formulate complex networks of relations in my mind. Communal and familial identity preceded any sense of individual identity. Those who were not originally from Thule were highlighted in discussions. There was also a distinction between those who could claim a Canadian (Baffin Island) heritage, and those who could not. A significant minority could trace their ancestry back to the nineteenth century wave of immigration from the Baffin Island region. Many have still family there, and some would proudly display a small Nunavut flag featuring the *inuksuk* ('an Inuit land marker') and a blue star representing the *niqirtsuituq* ('the North Star') on top of their televisions.

It is easy to speak of the Inugguit in terms of semi-nomadic Arctic hunter stereotypes, but of course the truth no longer quite reflects that. There are those who fit this description, but there are many more who do not interact with their natural environment in the way that their ancestors did. In the context of very rapid climate change in the Arctic, identity paradigms are beginning to shift and will transmute further as indigenous ecophilosophies (Drengson & Inoue, 1995: 56) have to battle with other perspectives on the world and our environment. Hunters' spatio-temporal relationship to this local cosmos will be reconfigured as dramatic change occurs in the local ecosystem because the amount of visible human changes to the Arctic environment is relatively small. Travelling and idioms of orientation are not taught, but part of the broader task of 'dwelling' (Heidegger, 1990: 80), which implies a comprehensive and continuous engagement with the environment and emphasizes the bond to 'place'. This is accomplished through an emotional attachment redolent with memories of significant places. Stories and dreams are spatially situated through wind bearings. Place-names in these stories are becoming less meaningful because of climate change, undermining the Heideggerian sense of 'dwelling' and immersion in one's environment. One name for a local glacier translates as 'the small glacier that stretches out to the sea', but the glacier no longer exists.

Despite this, there is certainly no evidence of an identity crisis amongst the Inugguit as there may be in other parts of the Arctic. They have a very clear sense of what an *inuk* is. Allusions to *inuk* and *kadluna* are in fact unnecessarily frequent. This may be because they feel threatened or because of an inferiority complex when it comes to the white man, but the distinction is embedded in ideology. There is an appeal to racial categories and a sense of uniqueness. There is a very clear sense that the *inuk* is 'better'. They see themselves as the prototypical Inuit at a time when Inuit groups in other parts of the Arctic are losing their language and culture.

The biggest and most conspicuous of puzzles for the outsider is to fathom how in such a tiny, inter-related community one manages to find a partner. Analysing the comprehensive genetic and medical evidence collected by Aage Gilberg who was a General Practitioner living with his wife in the Polar North in the late 1930s, it would seem that the Polar Eskimos go to some lengths to ensure that they marry the person whom they are least related to. Gilberg had travelled to Greenland as a visiting Danish doctor in 1938. Whilst he was there, war broke out and he ended up staying in north-west Greenland for more than a year: an experience by which all accounts changed his life. He had no desire to return to Denmark, but was forced to because he had promised his father-in-law that he would not keep his daughter away for more than a year. She had fallen pregnant and there was widespread tuberculosis in the community at the time. He returned to the district on a number of occasions, and he and his son, Rolf Gilberg, continued to collect great swathes of data on the Inugguit. From a genetic perspective, the information and data that we have on this community is extraordinary, and one might say, unique. The Gilbergs passed the data onto Prof. Edwards of the University of Cambridge who has produced a number-based genealogy of the community from 1881-1951. The computer print-out of this genealogy measures about 12 feet long by three feet wide and was shown to me on the floor of his garage.

Analysing the data, it is clear that up until the 1950s, there were relatively few first cousin marriages amongst the Inugguit, and not that many more after that. The genetic analysis shows that the inbreeding coefficients are surprisingly low. This might seem surprising given that the population up until the 1950s was no more than 300 and at some points as low as 150. There were, however, a great number of second and third cousin marriages. It would appear that this is the fashion in which Polar Eskimo society has managed to continue throughout the centuries without resorting to incest. And this is surely one of the reasons why everybody possesses such complete and remarkable genealogical knowledge, knowing exactly how they are related to each other. This body of knowledge is passed on at a young age to the child. In such a small society with such a high degree of genealogical awareness, the choice of potential partners is small, and also to some extent pre-determined. The incest taboo runs deep. I had heard rumours of father-daughter incest in Qaanaaq, but these always came from outsiders and could not be verified with locals. A friend of mine was married to his first cousin and had just had a child with her sister with whom he was co-habiting (alongside the wife at one point). That kind of behaviour might have raised the occasional eyebrow.

The footprint that some of the early twentieth-century explorers have left on the community is really significant in terms of identity politics, not least because one of them, Matthew Henson, was black. In a semi-joking manner, the members of the Henson family would always be 'singled' out for being 'black'. Standing in the queue at the shop behind a Henson, a fellow Inugguaq would tap me on the shoulder and point to the man in front, whispering that he was 'one quarter black', and then roar with laughter. In a community as homogeneous as this, having a different racial heritage is to invite comment and the Inugguit love to highlight these differences. This sense of ridicule was often self-imposed: on every occasion that I met Qaaqqu Henson, he would introduce himself as the 'black man' and then chortle.

Acute focus on physical differences is perhaps not surprising given that the Inugguit lived in extreme isolation for centuries. It is often said that they thought that the Inuit were the only inhabitants on the planet until they were 'discovered' by Sir John Ross in 1818, who like so many explorers was looking for the North-West Passage. Thalbitzer, a Danish philologist, who travelled widely in Greenland, but not in Thule, said this about the Polar Eskimos:

> 'With respect to the inhabitants of Cape York (76-78 degrees),
> they have not time out of mind had any communication with
> the other Greenlanders. The inhabitants of Upernavik, their
> nearest neighbours to the south, have never met people from
> up there, but have only occasionally seen their sledge tracks
> without knowing where they came from. The people of Cape
> York have not, so far as is known, any tradition about their
> southern countrymen. But there have repeatedly come immi-
> grants to them from some unknown tribe in, or south of,
> Ellesemere Island, whose language they say is somewhat
> different from their own' (Thalbitzer, 1904: 184).

People have been saying the Inugguit are 'disappearing' for over a
century. In the preface to his 'People of the Polar North' (1908), Knud
writes: 'When others (researchers) come, if they do come, they will be
too late'. This was written at a time when the group looked to be perpetu-
ally at risk from epidemics and tuberculosis. *National Geographic* articles
from the 1970s talk of the 'disappearing' Polar Eskimos, but there are
now more of them than ever before. Now, they face a new threat: climate
change. If Qaanaaq does close, then it will probably take longer than
most people think. Commercial oil and opportunities opening up in
mining may be a catalyst. That is likely to damage the sea life still further,
and the oil industry will bring with it jobs but not to the Qaanaaq region,
or at least not for the Inugguit.

The twentieth century was of course quite different, and from the
1930s onwards, some form of contact with Danish administrators would
have been quite the norm. Centuries of isolation, and on the whole a
rather 'difficult' history of cultural contact with Europeans, has meant
that the Inugguit are still sometimes wary of 'outsiders'. In these first few
weeks, I was the subject of many rumours. People would keep an eye on
me, but not always talk to me. The business of doing fieldwork in such a
densely networked, inter-connected place is very taxing, initially at least.
The bonds which tie the society together are the same links which act to
exclude you. One rumour could completely undermine your position
and credibility in society.

Like societies all around the world, the Inugguit like to categorise.
There are different categories of residents in north-west Greenland
which might be roughly grouped as: (1) Danes (not integrated, socially
invisible, with a few exceptions they are here for very short spells); (2) the
employed Inugguit, i.e. those that are not full-time hunters, but are

employed typically as labourers or in some blue collar capacity and hunt occasionally; (3) the full-time hunters; (4) the non-working people which can be broken down into three sub-groups, the unemployed and benefits-dependent; the elderly – this group for the most part live up at the residential home, and there are half a dozen other elderly people living on their own and finally young parents with small children. And, then there is me and the issue for some people here was that I do not fit any of these categories and was therefore an anomaly.

It was in these first few weeks (and perhaps months) that I felt particularly conscious of not fitting any of these groups, of not 'belonging' in any way. At large social gatherings in particular, I felt completely invisible. Often, not a single question was asked of me and not a single glance was made at me. The major exception to this was of course the children whose parents' preconceptions had not yet been instilled in them. It was this and the apparent lack of intellectual curiosity that struck me most. The mentality is still that of survival, even if in daily life 'survival' is no longer an issue. There is a tendency not to rationalise and come up with reasons for their actions. Things are just done. On many occasions, I was given no time whatsoever to prepare for a journey across the frozen sea. A hunter would just walk into my house and say that 'we had to go now'. Then, when I discovered out on the sea ice that I had forgotten something, he would roll around laughing and tell stories about how useless *kadluna* were.

In order to be accepted in an Inuit community *ab initio*, one needs good, reliable local contacts, somebody who will effectively act as one's patron. This is probably always the case in small, remote places. Once one has the right contacts, one needs to be hard-nosed and be patient. Appointments are missed, schedules are not kept to, teachers leave their positions just as term starts at a time when it is not possible to find a replacement and a friend might sleep with his best friend's partner. On a number of occasions, people would come to my hut on the pretext of having a Polar Eskimo-English conversation exchange, and then drink all my beer at break-neck speed, defecate in my yellow bag and then be on their way. Often, I could feel a sense of 'silent revenge' for the way previous white men had apparently treated them. There was never an apology and the size, intimacy and complete lack of privacy in these settlements means that everything is out in the open.

The lack of a private sphere in this treeless place might explain the lack of interest in covering one's tracks: when everybody can see what one is doing, there is no place to hide. There is no privacy in the world of communal hunting. It is often not possible to withdraw to oneself which explains why perhaps thoughts are concealed. The hunters are the product of the natural environment where they have been seeking to survive for centuries: there is no shame in tricking the quarry. This form of hunting relies on cunning. Creeping up on seals when they appear from their breathing holes. The same procedures are used with fellow men. One never knows when they will come and visit. Often, I felt like I was being crept up upon. As a joke, the men like to creep up behind you and then grab you by the leg. Then, they howl with laughter. The size and homogeneity of the community seems to ensure that a small repertoire of practical jokes are shared and practiced in exactly the same way by its members, its male members at least.

The absence of privacy impinges inevitably on relationships. Couples do not tend to, and indeed are not able to keep secrets from one another. The dynamics of the community size mean that it is not possible to have an affair in a remote settlement without somebody finding out more or less immediately. The limitations of place create their own problems.

There might not be secrets, but gossip is rife and the fuel of remote Inuit settlements. Gossip is typically vibrant, personal and 'sexual' in nature as is the non-stop male-to-male banter. Sex is a major preoccupation which is openly discussed. One is reminded that sex is 'normal' and it is therefore 'normal' to discuss it. Given the level of promiscuity, it is surprising that the genetic data suggests, as noted, that there is a careful screening process when it comes to finding a wife or a husband. It is difficult to reconcile the facts with the perception, but it is clear once again that the collective concern outweighs the individual concern. Husbands occasionally offered me to have sex with their wives, knowing that this would grant them a credit to sleep with another woman. On other occasions, women would follow me home to my hut, knowing perhaps that they had a credit in hand. The family is based upon economic factors rather than reciprocal sexual monopoly.

Throughout my stay, I always felt a sense of excitement upon entering a hunter's home. A whole new sensorium awaited. One felt as if one were entering another world. There was an element of surprise, of not

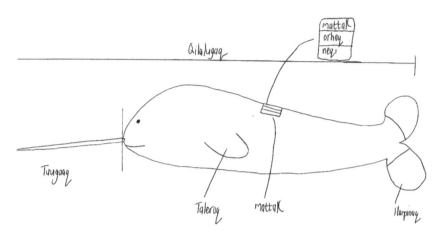

Author's drawing of a narwhal with Polar Eskimo terms for different parts of the body

knowing what to expect. One could not be sure how one would be received, what one would find on the floor (a dead animal, a faulty sledge), whether the house would smell of blubber, fermented Little Auks or boiling seal, whether a dead seal would be suspended from the ceiling and whether the residents would be present, sleeping or eating. The dysfunctionality, the pedestrian pace of life, the openness and hospitality, the overwhelming sense that *hila* (meaning consciousness, mind and weather) determines everything were the ingredients that defined these visits. At times, hunters sit in their kitchens and wait for days for the weather to change. The constant grin, the bemused long silences; the sounds of the dogs when the wind eventually died down all characterised the places where I lived. Time did not matter much here. The immediate juxtaposition of tradition and modernity is everywhere. One goes into the most modern homes in Qaanaaq and one might find the man of the house squatting on his knees, hands the colour of claret, quartering a dead animal on the kitchen floor. Living spaces become makeshift, temporary mortuaries. It might be a seal, musk-oxen or narwhal. This is no place for the squeamish. Young children, completely used to the sight of dead animals, are not remotely curious or concerned by it.

3: The Dogs: Saints and Sinners

Leaving the town, I walk along the beach, heading east towards Qeqertat. I am pleased to see that the dead dog which I spoke to the *kommune* about appears to have been taken away and hopefully given something of a burial. The animal will no doubt be sitting on a rubbish heap at the dump. I get to the point on the beach where a team of particularly large and aggressive looking sledge dogs skulk on the grassy verges, on the other side of the church, standing sentry for another summer. One of the particularly tatty, peevish wolf-like dogs watches me approach what he clearly regards as his territory. He sits there proudly like Cerberus guarding the entrance to Hades. For a moment, I am not sure if I should continue as I cannot see if this louche looking Fenrir-like creature is chained. This burly, brindled dog stares at me, watching me every step, but thankfully stays put.

Around the corner of the bay awaits a rather splendid, sandy beach without all the paraphernalia of an Inuit settlement: the jumbled up discarded furniture, the uncloven driftwood, rusty boats, scuffed, peeling hulls and tired freight containers wallowing in the waftage of the sea. With the exception of the odd fragment of a whale carcass, the beach is empty. Out to sea, a vast, tabular iceberg (*natsinnarraaq*), the size of a small English village, sits in the fjord. The beach becomes pebbly, and then the pebbles become boulders. Haunting rock formations resembling statues called *inuihet* ('the stones that look like people') rise vertically to my left, grimacing and scolding. I come across another dead dog much further up the beach. It is beginning to feel like a deserted battlefield, scattered with the corpses of the losers. I reach a stream of glacial melt-water, pouring off the Greenland Ice Sheet and decide to turn back. Walking along this forgotten beach towards Qaanaaq, a small motorboat comes chugging around the corner, headed in my direction. There is a young family on board and I wonder for a moment if they are going to give me a lift. They must be surprised at seeing somebody out here along the beach, walking so far from the town. But, apparently not. A quiet and unobtrusive family disembarks in silence without acknowledging me, and ambles up the beach, settling down on a small rug to a picnic.

It is the first week of September and at 4pm in the afternoon, the Royal Arctic Line supply-ship arrives. Although she was expected three days ago, her arrival appears to have surprised the sore-headed, sleepy residents. They stumble out of their dolls houses, clutching their heads, weaving their way through dirt tracks to the shore. Others stay at home, watching the proceedings through binoculars and telescopes – the standard furnishings of every living room. With the reef and breakwater a few hundred metres from the shore, red freight containers are ferried on floating platforms at high tide. It will take several days to unload all the cargo.

Up above the town, I scramble over never-ending piles of indiscriminate rubble and stone, bypassing the occasional cairn (*hakamattaq*) – navigation markers and a reminder this is not terra incognita. Once I make it over the top of the slope, it is not long until I see the Greenland Ice Sheet before me. At first, I am not sure if the layer of white on the cake of igneous rock – spliced and incongruous – stretching right across the horizon is cloud or ice. It seems remarkably close, but in the Arctic distance and scale are almost impossible to judge. The rays of the sun bend and twist – a polar Fata Morgana, distorting and confusing. A place without fixed definition. I feel tiny on this vast expanse of lunar infinitude. The consciousness of space fills my being. I have travelled all over the world and many extraordinary places have made an impression on me, but the emptiness of the Arctic was conducive to a different way of thinking. It was a poetic journey and that was the Arctic difference. I stop for a breather on the eternal rubble. There is absolutely nothing but silence. I enjoy one of those seldom moments in life where there is no other sound but the thump of your own heart and the steady ticking of your wristwatch. This is an easy, but extraordinary escape from the problem-ridden town below. The baying of dogs and the bellowing of the residents are silenced. Here, you cannot hear the sea or the wind, just nothingness. It is almost as if I have lost one of my senses, but that it is not to the detriment of anyone or anything.

I continue to cleave a path through the rocky wilderness, climbing over small mountains of scree, dumped there by something greater than man. I labour over rock, lichen-covered boulders with painted faces and stone for over two hours, but have still not reached the elusive ice. The Arctic desert landscape and clean air have conspired to fool me again. What seems so tantalizingly close is in fact many kilometres away. Eventually, I get what I think is very close to the Ice Sheet but decide to turn back as to climb onto the ice itself involves a steep climb down and then up a gorge. I decide to tackle it when I have more time and am better equipped. The dry desert rock lying immediately adjacent to the largest ice sheet in the world is a surreal juxtaposition that belongs to another world altogether. I feel as if I am walking in the spoils of a meteorite in a never-ending and negating landscape. The air becomes brittle in this inexpressible nothingness. I return to the hut.

The night of the 8th of September proves to be a memorable one as I experience the first equinoctial storm. The hut trembles in the northern stiff wind; the table jitters, edging across the floor as the wind whips underneath the house. When the weather turns colder at the beginning of September, strong winds blow from the North. The wind's pelt battered thoughts and syllables around the icy room. The ill-fitted porch door flung open and the caribou antlers, aluminium ladders and random cuts of plywood sitting on the unfinished balcony were rearranged by the wind buffering the house. I may as well have been sleeping in the bleachers.

I wake up to propitious blue skies, high pressure and a cool breeze. The surrounding houses appear to be intact, and the weather looks so promising that the terror of last night seems almost like a distant memory. In the bay sits a P570 Danish frigate and in my first-thing-in-the-morning incoherence my mind seems to think that the arrival of the Danish Navy is somehow connected to the adverse weather conditions. The chuckling, Danish speaking Tullu Eipe at the *kommune* jokes that they always come when the weather is bad, but concedes that it is just a routine visit and that the Danish Navy patrol the Greenlandic coast, mooring in Qaanaaq once or twice a year.

With stiffened air, the streams are iced over. Walking on the thin, brittle ice is akin to treading on glass, cracking as one skates across it like a spoon skirting the circumference of the hard caramel of a crème brûlée.

The other memorable thing about the night of the 8th of September is that this is the first night since I have been here where it gets properly dark. I have become so used to the light that the darkness seems almost like an odd sensation, and I stand staring out of the window at the broad shoulders of street lights, whose noses point down inquisitively on the partially hidden landscape trying to imagine how it will be when it is like this all day and all night.

The afternoon sunshine is unbounded, a divine metaphor for enlightened individual consciousness. It feels like one of those last days of summer that just has to be enjoyed *en plein air*. Lazily, I stroll back up the sandy, sun-blazed inclines towards the hut and on the way am delighted to be summoned into Masautsiaq's house for a coffee or something stronger. He lives alone in a rather long, canary yellow bungalow with a splendid view. Always cracking jokes, Masautsiaq is extremely cheerful and it takes just a few words of mispronounced Inuktun to light up his face. Masautsiaq is very much amused that I have been greeting him with the words, *hainang hunai*: a slightly old fashioned salutation used perhaps when spotting somebody from a distance who one has not seen for quite sometime. He finds this very amusing and insists on repeating it several times when he sees me. The result is reciprocal room-filling laughter.

His house is very sparsely furnished and there is nothing about it that would suggest one is in a settlement whose basis is hunting. There is no pungent whiff of sea-mammals, but there are of course the obligatory family photographs adorning the walls above the settee. The corner-sofa is, compared to other Inugguit homes, uncluttered. I am poured a cold coffee and in a mixture of West Greenlandic, Inuktun, English and Danish, Masautsiaq tells me that he is an ex-seaman who served in Qaanaaq as the policeman for one year. He flexes his muscles as if to prove that was qualified to do so. There seems to be some confusion when this was – at first I am told 1987, then 2000 and then he reverts back to the original date. A collection of certificates and documents proving his ex-status are stuffed into my hand for my perusal. Once again, I note how the homes of the Inugguit are devoid of books but full of certificates and written attestations confirming their status. In a context of colonial encounters, these documents were perhaps perceived as evidence of legitimacy. The conversation then continues on its familiar path with the normal limited repertoire of questions about my age, family and marital status. The basic facts always matter, but that is all. Masautsiaq is 52 and I understand from the Danish that he suffered a blood clot in 2003, has not been well since and is no longer able to work. This is an extremely familiar story in Qaanaaq. Not working means invariably a diet of alcohol, depression and a basket of social problems. Masautsiaq is one of six brothers and a younger brother (*nagu*) joins us subsequently. He has come with an unopened carton of red wine, lots of roll-up tobacco and I think I know what is in store for the rest of the day. Still, their company is enjoyable and the afternoon is peppered with some extraordinary tragic-comic moments all dished up with a cocktail of Monty Pythonesque sign language and the shreds of various spoken languages that we attempt to package together.

There is no doubt that the Inugguit employ sign language in contexts which would be completely inappropriate in my own culture. The starter on this menu of tragic-comedy was when Masautsiaq repeatedly told me that he was unable to father children (perhaps the worse possible dish that could be served up to any member of Inugguit society). The information that Masautsiaq was 'not able' to have children would have been quite enough, but to ensure that Masautsiaq had made his point with the requisite accuracy he jabs his index figure towards his groin, grimaces in a childlike fashion and says *ajorpoq, ajorpoq* – 'bad, bad'. Just in case there was any doubt what Masautsiaq was trying to relay to me, he then folds his erect little finger to make a right angle immediately before me so as to indicate erectile dysfunction. This marvellous piece of theatre is reproduced several times during which I am clearly invited to look as solemn and sympathetic as can be reasonably expected. Predictably, I am then asked whether I have children and one can surmise the nature of the pantomine that ensues. Bearing a great grin, Masautsiaq points at my groin and enquires as to whether I have the same problem. Perched on the edge of the settee, I can see that he is almost excited at the prospect of enjoying at last some much needed solidarity with a fellow sufferer in this ostensibly fertile community. I am quick to answer in the negative, but then immediately recognise my mistake. Confusingly, questions are invariably couched in the negative and by responding in the negative, one is in Greenlandic actually answering in the affirmative. His eyes light up and he practically shouts for joy, clinking his sullied plastic beaker with my coffee cup. This farcical scene almost turns into an act unto itself with repeated renditions of him pointing towards our respective groins, shouting *ajorpoq* and then wishing to collectively toast our alleged infertility.

Having confirmed to his delight that I did not in fact have children, the conversation then moves on in its all too predictable path and I am then asked whether I have a wife. Here, Masautsiaq is also quick to detect common ground and then the main course in this tragic-comedy is served up. He tells me in Inuktun that his wife is dead, and then to ensure there is no doubt at all about his marital status, he says slowly in a matter-of-fact fashion and in English 'dead, dead, dead' pulling the sides of his mouth down in a childlike manner to produce a semi-circle of sadness. There is no need for niceties or euphemisms here. One is simply alive or the emphatically pronounced 'dead'. Once again, this would have been more than enough information. But, then in a Faulty Towersesque sort of way, he makes the shape of a revolver with his thumb at right angles to his extended index and middle figure and points at his head. He then grunts the sound of a small explosion and says one last time 'dead'. I do not know whether to laugh or cry. Another suicide, another widower. Masautsiaq bows his head for a moment, totally oblivious of the comic effect of his rendition of this tragic event. After a few moments of silence with a tinge of gloom in his meditations, he is once again pointing towards our respective groins and rolling around in paroxysms of giggling, practically watering the sofa with red wine.

The dessert is more of a petit-four really, but amusing nonetheless. Masautsiaq, for all of his alleged mental problems, is the first Inugguaq I have met who knows anything at all about England (English football players do not count for my purposes). He knows that England has a Queen and seems to want to have my views on her figure. For a moment, I think this a misunderstanding, but apparently not. He is quick to tell me that Her Majesty is 'no good' for the apparent reason that she is too diminutive, which is a bit much coming from a gentleman who stands no more than 5 feet 4 inches in his stockings. I am led to believe by the thrusting of his hips and the gyrations of his groin that Her Majesty The Queen of Denmark would, however, make an excellent bed-fellow. With his undulating hands he paints a picture of the ageing Danish Sovereign's curves. I know that the Danish Royal Family is very popular in Greenland, and indeed Frederik, Crown Prince of Denmark, has spent quite sometime in Qaanaaq, but really, this seems most misguided and almost unchartered territory in terms of fantasies.

A lambent light creeps across the shadowed polar bear skin. The sunshine pouring in to the hut clasps the September morning. It is getting colder by about one degree every day. Over the centuries, the Inugguit have adapted to the cold and their natural environment, and do not shy away from vaunting this ability. It is freezing and many just walk around with a few layers on, bearing the sinews of this group.

I spend the afternoon with Iihaaq who has a kind, gentle face. His pleated wrinkles smile at me, forming a network of narrow channels and tributaries meandering between low banks of skin across his forehead. A relief map modelled in clay. His etched, furrowed face tells a thousand stories of an unimmured life lived in the Arctic tundra. The occasional scar, the symbol of a vetoed urban existence. He smiles with his dark, dusky eyes and lights a pipe, apologising for the smoke. A hunter, a man of nature, an unregenerate capitalist.

The *kaffimik* to celebrate his 85th birthday is in full flow. Cakes, buttered currant buns and small bite-size portions of reindeer meat sit in small bowls dotted around a collection of tables in the living room. Black coffee served in plastic cups is available from a Thermos. In a stream of imperatives, I am invited in, told to eat and go outside where there is more food. The custom is to come in, remove your shoes, greet the other guests and then go over to the host, wishing the person celebrating their birthday 'happy birthday' *pi'dluarit* ('congratulations') and then offer a small gift, normally a few coins in the case of children. I come with a box of chocolates. I go outside to explore the other savoury options. As per usual, there is a folding trellis table propped up against the wall and on the table the local manna, a selection of various catch and scummed broths to choose between. Sitting by the table is my cheerful friend, Masautsiaq, tucking into a bowl of *puihi qajoq* ('seal soup'). It is traditional to start with *qajoq*, normally seal or reindeer, at a *kaffimik*. I laugh at the thought of how small this society is and how familiar many of the faces already are. On the table is a lump of fresh *mattak*. The guests cut off small rectangles of meat, and then using the *ulu* ('the semi-circular woman's knife') divide it width-ways into very small, mouth-sized manageable strips which can be bitten off. Also, on the table is the black, twisted dried narwhal skin. It looks like burnt wood, can be seen hanging around the town on drying racks and tastes like the sea, full of iodine and vitamins. Next to the *mattak*, there is a shoulder of frozen musk-oxen meat. Small slithers are cut off from the thawing meat. The frozen meat is very red and melts in your mouth. Also, on the table are reindeer ribs and musk oxen liver.

The close of the evening, sprawled out in front of me, is continuous, perpetual. At low tide, the glossy icebergs straggling the mottled water feel closer than ever before. The sun is still dipping, turning the sky shades of soft citron and cantaloupe. The percussive chitter of the Snow Buntings falls silent. It is mid-September and the Snow Buntings are gathering and are preparing for their journey south. The only birds that over-winter in this part of the Arctic are the Raven and the Ptarmigan. I remember Ole Danielsson's first words in the *taffi*, 'welcome to paradise'. I peer through the cracked window-pane at the hypnotic landscape, the blue-tinted icebergs through the shards of evening light and think to myself that in one respect at least his description is apt. His words replay in my head: 'all the time you are in Qaanaaq, the door to my house is open anytime. You are always welcome'.

I fall asleep to the diminuendo of dogs whining wistfully in the distance. I wake up to another cool, blissfully crisp day. I feel a fillip of energy with the morning sunshine. I hop out of my warm sleeping bag and race around the cold room, donning my clothes as quickly as possible. Every day would begin with steaming porridge amidst trains of breath chugging across the icy room. In the town, all the talk is about the settlement, Moriussaq, which closed last week. The last resident, Qaaqqu Henson (one of the grandsons of Matthew Henson – the Afro-American polar explorer who accompanied Robert Peary to the North Pole), has moved into a small house in Qaanaaq behind me. According to Else, he did not want to leave and was forced out. People from the *kommune* had visited him on a number of occasions to try and persuade him to leave. The policeman tells me that the Government has spent millions keeping one person in Moriussaq, providing an expensive helicopter service and shipping goods there. He thinks these costs are completely unjustifiable. Until recently, the population of the settlement had been three. As well as Qaaqqu, there were two brothers. One of them was a manic-depressive. There was a drinking bout and it became violent with one brother shooting at the other. The man who had been shot at called the police and was advised to shoot the brother in his leg. The man shot the brother, but killed him. The man who shot his brother suffered badly with a variety of mental problems after the event. He went to Sisimiut for treatment, but could not afford to keep going there and eventually moved back to the settlement.

It is mid-September in the High Arctic, the outside temperature is -3C and there is little hope of the sea ice forming any time soon. Local hunters tell me they know it is warmer than it used to be because the frozen moisture of the dogs' breath used to be more dense in the cold. Else who has spent nearly all her life in Qaanaaq stands in my green prefabricated wooden hut, on the polar bear and musk-oxen skins that cover the floor. Dried, pungent blubber sits on the racks outside. Looking out across Inglefield Bay and the whale-shaped Herbert Island, towards the exploding Leviathan icebergs that sit like vast lumps of polystyrene in the Murchison Sound, there is a sadness in her eyes: 'Twenty years ago, my children used to go skating on the ice at this time of the year. Just 15 years ago, the sea ice in the bay was up to three metres thick. If the sea ice goes completely, there will be no need for the dogs and our culture will disappear'.

Else sketches for me how life is changing so drastically. At Christmas time last year, there was no snow at all. If there is no snow, this makes the dark period especially difficult. Fifty years ago, it was as cold as -50 degrees in the winter. Nowadays, the temperature seldom goes much below -30 degrees. Then, the discussion switches to the education in the school. She thinks that the standard is lamentable. In her opinion and others, many teenagers cannot read and write and the teachers are teaching them nothing. 'A poor education never used to be a problem because the children would become hunters. Going to school was a distraction. But, now young people are trapped in a community where there is no future as a hunter and where they cannot leave and do something else as they have such low levels of education and training'. Eight per cent of pupils go on to the equivalent of A levels.

Like Else, Josef cannot comprehend why anybody would object to hunting, providing endangered species are not being killed. 'We were all hunters originally, so what is the problem?', Josef complains. Josef thinks vegetarianism is ridiculous. He says that a vegetarian came here once, but that she was gone in no time. Once again, Josef repeats Ole's words 'my home is your home' and that I am welcome there at any time. He tells me not to knock, but just to come in and help myself to anything I want. The Inugguit do not like people to knock at doors, standing awkwardly outside people's homes.

Tonight, after another serene day of lavender northern skies, the sun dips below the horizon at 9pm. The evenings are drawing in very fast now. The disappearing light at both ends is being squeezed in a pincer movement. The sun sits much lower in the sky than when I first got here. It still arcs right across the bay, but at a lower point on the horizon. Majestic Snow Geese pass through the bay, in flocks of 4-20. With their black-tipped wings, these birds that cannot be hunted, fly effortlessly, but at great speeds, across the horizon. Soon, it will be October, and there is no evidence of the incipient, oily skim of frazil ice that one would expect to find at this time of the year. The scene across the Murchison Sound is in constant flux, a canvass of permanently shifting, tumbling white objects. The titanic iceberg has broken up and the tide has brought a trail of its fragmenting glacial brood to the shore. The shoreline is now littered with dirigible and diamond-shaped cakes of ice the size of a small motorcar. They are like gargantuan, ship-wrecked chess pieces beached in a strange place.

Fighting, hectoring Ravens produce remarkable somersaults over-head. Fulmars, the Albatrosses of the North, fly just above the surface of the sea, gliding and banking on stiff wings and shallow wing-beats. High-pitched shouts and cries can be heard in the distance. Towards town, young boys play baseball using lumps of driftwood as bats and pebbles as balls. As the squarking Ravens fly past, the little boys point their makeshift clubs at the birds, holding them as if they were rifles, and make the noise of a pot-gun.

Out by the airfield on the steep, lichen-covered scree banks by the beach, small charms of cheery Snow Buntings (*qupanuk*) flitter and chatter. Several dog teams are kept chained up in between patches of purple Saxifrage whose semi-sweet petals provide clusters of brilliant colour. Frenzied dogs shout and cheer in the distance and all around – it is feeding time and the pandemonium is just beginning. There is a tremendous barking and howling. It is infectious, and the cries and songs escalate into an infernal crescendo circling around the town. Listening to the capriccio, a laughing Raven wheels overhead, confident of picking up a scrap or two. The dogs are hysterical, launching themselves at their feeder and practically strangling themselves in doing so. Lumps of seal meat are tossed to the ravenous dogs, one-by-one. The meat is wolfed down, barely touching the backs of their throats. Their main concern is being absolutely ready for the next chunk. The other dogs on the adjacent teams whine and squeal in desperation, trying to inch closer to the black buckets containing the dark chocolate-coloured seal meat. I walk all the way down the steep, rocky slope to the shore and get my first real sight of the hunters' catch. There is a hive of activity around an impressive cache of narwhal meat. The meat has already been chopped up and put into large see-through bags. A long wooden chest is overflowing with fresh, black narwhal meat and deep, pomegranate, coagulating red blood. The huddle of hunters quickly transforms into a makeshift market with the hunters donning aprons and weighing chunks of meat before handing them to eager customers. None of the hunters engage with me and it is at these hunter-gatherings in particular that I feel especially invisible, an unanatomised bagatelle to this hermetic community. The stranger, not a member of the kin group, is ignored. Am I an invisible flaxen halo amongst black hairs? The peregrine Blond is ubiquitous but invisible, except to the gabble of cheery children, who are spies for those who do not speak. Small, smiling faces wave to me from the window, without preconceptions or judgement.

Mist lingers over the sea; Herbert Island is nearly lost in the cloud; the town is enshrouded in *pujoq*. The sea looks grey, no longer blue. The view could not be more different than just ten days ago. With a flick of a switch, the world has turned from colour to the faded black and white of an old postcard. The break in the very stable weather has finally come. With the exception of a small group that gather at the shore to pore over the most recent catch, the Inugguit sit in their overheated homes, glued to Danish cartoons and the universal Mr Bean on their television sets. Baying dogs wait anxiously on the hillside, sensing that feeding time is approaching. Soon, they will be unshackled and will be ferrying the Inugguit in their blood-stained chariots across frozen seas, unfolding a new world whose emptiness is the pneuma of the place.

The oppressive weather brings lethargy, but not quite silence: Hip-hop music blares from a blue cabin behind the water tanks and teenagers wave as I saunter past. A man stripped to his waist smiles from a cracked kitchen window. An ageing hunter pushes a wheelbarrow full of fresh blubber up a steep, sandy slope, leaving a meandering trace of ruby-coloured seal blood behind him. A cold wind whips around the place, forcing the Inugguit to zip up their thin coats and to bury their chins in their tracksuits. A man walks past with a gun slung over his shoulder. He is wearing a blue uniform with the name of the Qaanaaq council emblazoned on the back. On the way down to the shore, a sledge-dog sleeps, sprawled out over stones and dirt as if it has collapsed from exhaustion.

Further down the track, outside Fritz & Søn, a sort of haberdashery, a large, adult male Greenland Dog lies dead on the track. It looks like it has broken its leash. The blood from his mouth has frozen on the stony surface and its expression is one of absolute terror. His broad, wedge-shaped head lies at an oblique angle, pulled back towards its withers. The dog must have died very recently. I am not quite sure whom to call about this grisly matter. The *kommune* were rather indifferent about my protestations of a dead dog on the beach last time, and I cannot imagine they would brook my interference today. After much hesitation, I decide that I should call Hans, the policeman. He asks me if the dog has been shot. I could not see a bullet wound, but it seems that this dog has indeed been shot by the man who I saw patrolling with a rifle earlier in the morning. I ask why a man is walking around the town, shooting dogs and I am told that it is policy. A subsequent encounter with John-Peter allows me to fill in the details of this new chapter of Qaanaaq life. An unchained dog can and might kill a child. I am told this is a particularly dangerous time at the moment. The dogs are hungry, the darkness is soon upon us and the ice is everywhere. If a child slips on the ice and falls to the ground in the dark, then an unleashed dog might take his chance to attack the child, seeing it as nothing more than a piece of meat. These dogs behave as if anything at their own eye level is fair game. There is a long history of children (and indeed adults) being killed in this way, ripped to pieces by these semi-wild dogs. Parents have come running out of their homes to find nothing but the bones of their child and the dogs licking their lips. Some years ago, a man fell over and was eaten alive by dogs. These are dogs that are so brave as to taunt a polar bear – an animal which can kill a Greenland Dog with just one swipe of its paw.

Life is tough here. Death is discussed in a matter-of-fact fashion. Blood and guts are everywhere. The shortest of sojourns will furnish the visitor with skinned Arctic Hare hanging from hooks outside homes, drying narwhal skin and pungent blubber on food racks down by the shore, stretched seal skins and dead animals adorning kitchen floors. On the way home, I see Marie Nielsen. I tell her that there is a dead dog outside her house. She shrugs her shoulders and hurries off to work, not having the time for vacuous chit-chat about such macabre things. The wind begins to howl in the afternoon. The town is once again lost in cloud and we are cloaked in the grey, snowy air of winter. If the bad weather continues, the airfield may close. The plan to go to Haviggivik shortly appears to be already scotched. Space is closing in around us, almost tangibly so. On the way back, the dog that I had thought was asleep is rigor mortis, a white sheet of snow covering its stiff, frozen body lying in a street-side morgue. Just a few metres away, young children play without a care in the world.

It is now snowing sufficiently hard that visibility is almost zero (*nittanngitsoq*). Qaanaaq seems to almost sway in the wind. The sky lours. There is a tossed silence; a gaunt landscape on a bleak afternoon. The settled weather and August sunshine have gone, and there is an air of vulnerability about the place: wooden dolls houses cling to the steep permafrost hillsides and worried wives, armed with binoculars, wait behind four-panelled rectangular wooden windows scanning the blurred horizon for misplaced husbands. Approaching one of the six wooden bridges that span the frozen stream, an unfettered adult female dog scampers past me, beetling off in pursuit of a scent. The broken leash is short and difficult to get hold of without getting too close to her. By slapping my thigh and gesturing enthusiastically to the dog, I try to entice her to follow me, knowing that I can offer her some musk-oxen meat in the fridge. Rather than persuading her to follow me up the hill and across the frozen puddles, she runs off in the opposite direction, apparently distracted by something else. Clumsily, I scout around for her in my heavy Baffin boots, but she has disappeared into the cloud and greyness of this snowy afternoon. I cannot find her anywhere. I decide not to mention it to the locals. I am confident that they would not see the animal as anything other than a threat to their clans of toddlers, and thus her chances would be diminished.

It is dark at about 8pm and the evening light is so very different from previously. It is achromatic, the sky has lost her hue – gone are the shiny vivid, pure colours of the endless Arctic summer days. Here, in the bosom of the Arctic, winter has arrived. The landscape is now frozen and the view is a wintry one. The cliffs to the east with their concertinaed folds forming the shape of a granite accordion have thus far been radiating red and purple in the late evening summer sun, but are now uncompromisingly white. Low cloud sits on the horizon and the North is now a spectrum of various shades of grey and white. There is that certain silence and stillness to the place that one only finds immediately after a snowfall.

This was not to be the first day that such issues with the dogs would arise. I have always been a dog-lover. Over the year, I was to form a special bond with the dogs in each settlement where I lived, becoming acquainted with their rich theatre of expressions. Cautious of the males, I would make a special fuss of the more friendly bitches. The unleashed pregnant females would sense that dogs are special to me and would follow me around the settlements, sometimes sleeping on my balcony hoping to get the odd scrap or two. Throughout my stay, I made every effort to live just as the Inugguit did, eating their food, learning their language, hunting with the hunters, but my relationship with the dogs reminded me that I could never be like them. They related to their dogs in a way that would never be acceptable for me. More than anything else, it was this that set us apart.

To an extent, my time in the Polar North was defined by the dogs that I was surrounded by. These intelligent animals that can smell a seal breathing-hole from a great distance and that have homing instincts driving lost hunters' home would make a great impression on me. For the Inugguit, they were principally 'tools'. If they are not well trained, they are more of an hindrance than an aid. For me, they were objects of great admiration and the foundations of the Polar Eskimo culture. The Inugguit would not be who they are if it were not for the dogs. My plan had been to go the Polar North and have my own dog-team. There was always the difficult issue of what I would do with the dogs once I left. It was made clear to me that no *inuk* would wish to have the dogs that a *kadluna* had previously owned because they know that the white man treats them like pets, and therefore they become soft and uncontrollable. Out on the sea ice, one has to be absolutely certain that a dog will do as you say. Otherwise, you might be putting your life at risk. If a dog will not jump over a lead or if a dog will not do as it is told on thin ice, then it might become a life-death situation. I often discussed the dilemma with Josef. He could not understand the problem. He told me I should simply let the dogs off the lead when I left. Unleashed adult dogs have to be shot, and Dennis would therefore come round and shoot them all. Problem solved. I could never have done that. A part of my polar experience was therefore always missing, but I could at least live with a clear conscience.

I would soon become accustomed to the sounds of the dogs in the different settlements and come to understand what their different shrieks, howls and barks would come to signify. The hysterical barking of early evening would tell me that the dogs were about to be fed; the dogs' silence would indicate the worst weather or the calm after feeding time; the baying of the dogs resembled a form of evening communion to which I would fall asleep. The dogs were like an eclectic Fellowship of saints and sinners whose personalities shaped every event.

The howls of the dogs echo around the town on this frozen morning. The colourful wooden houses stand like beacons of light in an otherwise confused, indistinct landscape. Tilting and bobbing lumps of ice freckle the dove-grey sea which merges with the snowy, blurred, off-white slopes of the town. It is Friday morning, pay-day and there is the normal activity at the shop with people buying up all the beer they can afford. The pensioners are first in the queue. Some of them have lost a finger or two to the cold. Collapsing and falling asleep outside in winter drinking sprees leaves one with severe frostbite and the digits are the first to go.

Outside in the bitter cold, Ole is cutting up seal, tossing lumps of meat and blubber onto a wheelbarrow to feed all of his 18 dogs. In the severe cold, dogs may be fed two or three times a day. Ole cuts up the seals whilst his wife keeps daring puppies at bay. They are desperate for any scraps they can get. Wearing a traditional Eskimo anorak and arched over the dead animal, he struggles to hold the knife in the cold with his bare hands. The northern wind is absolutely biting. The seal lies on its back and Ole draws the knife from bottom to top. Then four cuts are made, two on each side, one set at the shoulder and the other two at the bottom of the animal. The skin and blubber are then drawn back. Beneath is the chocolate brown meat. Small rivers of blood run from the carcass; vermillion, forked tributaries on the frozen ground. The dogs are going berserk, knowing that soon they will be fed. Ole tells me how the trade in furs and skins has all but disappeared. Now that there is an EU export ban on all sealskin products which are not the result of indigenous subsistence hunting, the market has dried up and Great Greenland A/S has a surplus of skins they cannot sell.

A small flurry overnight has now turned into heavier snowfall. Suddenly, and with little warning, we are in the depths of winter – or at least, winter in my terms. The outside temperature has dropped to -10 degrees Celsius and is forecast to fall as low as -25 degrees next week. Still, this does not stop Josef coming to visit in the evening wearing a grey, US Air Base T-shirt and a thin blue jacket. He wanders around as if it is still late summer. He pats his impressive, Falstaffian bulk and tells me how he has been feasting on seal meat. Children are brought up to eat meat in large quantities to keep heat and generate it in their bodies. Poring over maps, Josef shows me where he has been hunting in the Bowdoin fjord (named after Donald Baxter Macmillan's schooner). He shot a *kivihoqtoq* ('seal with little blubber at the beginning of summer, and thus one that sinks easily'), but it sunk. Josef tells me how my detailed map of the Thule region is now out of date. Many of the glaciers have receded so rapidly. Josephine Peary island (Qeqertaarrhhuharhuaq) is no longer connected to the Tracy Gletscher (Qeqertaarrhhuharhup hermia), but is an island to itself. This change has happened over the last ten years. Josephine, the wife of Robert Peary, had come to north-west Greenland in 1891 and they overwintered in McCormick fjord (Iterdlagssuaq). The calving of icebergs in that area has become a problem, affecting narwhal hunting in the summer. Many of the glaciers in the region have receded so rapidly that they are no longer productive: the once icy fingers that reached the fjord, are now greying stubs. Hunters used to travel to Pituffik and Haviggivik over the Greenland Ice Sheet by going up the Politikken Glacier. But the glacier no longer reaches the sea and the dogs will not pull sledges over rocks on sharp inclines. Some hunters believe that glacial fronts in the Qaanaaq region have receded by at least 500 metres over the last 10 years. There is far less snow than there used to be and the stronger winds in October/November blow the snow off the slopes in Qaanaaq, making the dark period appear darker than it did previously. All of these factors conspire to make climate change a real threat, even if the Inugguit are practical people, adapting to problems rather than discussing them.

There is a break between the clouds and one can see the sun struggling to make it above the skyline at 9.15am. It is not until 10.30am that the sun finally sits on the horizon. The Arctic light is pale. It was a very cold night. The darkness and cold are galloping in now. The view has changed again. The driving wind overnight has blown the snow off the higher slopes, exposing the sand around the house. The wind has dropped, the temperature has risen and the snow falls in small, graceful flakes. Young children are sledging down the snowy slopes of the tracks. *Nilas*, the thin, elastic crust of gray-coloured ice, are forming on the calm sea. Down by the shore, the bellies of the bubble-free lumps of ice on the beach are a distinct blue colour making the shoreline look more otherworldly and luminous than ever before. Whilst admiring the different shades of ice, I hear a horrible high-pitched screaming sound come from behind me. I turn round to see an adult male dog about twenty feet away savaging a puppy. The dog has the small puppy in his mouth, and is shaking him violently. The puppy is screaming for his life. This is not the normal rough play, but the puppy is in fact being mauled. The adult tosses the puppy to the snowy ground and runs off. It is all over in seconds and I feel like a hopeless observer. The puppy has broken both of his hind legs. He is in terrible pain, tries with all of his might to walk, but at best can just drag his two disabled legs along behind him before collapsing in the snow. It is a heart-breaking spectacle. He is yelping and whimpering with the pain, defecating with fear. Within a few seconds, he has gone from being a healthy puppy to an invalid. He keeps trying to stand up, but just falls pathetically to the ground. There is fear and confusion in his eyes.

I summon a man walking past. He shrugs his shoulders and is not interested in helping. Then, an angry hunter behind me, sorting out blubber on racks, tells me to kill it and points to a boulder, suggesting I should club it over the head. He tells me that people kill each other in Pakistan, and that that never happens here (not quite true). His point seems to be that we Inuit put humans before animals unlike you white men. He is clearly upset that I am so concerned about the plight of a disabled puppy. He is missing the point and I do not want to entertain a discussion with him. I have been warned many times that the treatment of dogs is the ingredient of a major culture clash. A dog with two broken legs has no chance here. He is suffering terribly and I decide that the kindest thing is to arrange for somebody to shoot the poor thing as soon as possible. He is crying out with pain. I speak to Frederik in the green house just behind the shoreline. He walks over to the dog with me, and whilst this is nothing unusual for him, I can see that he appreciates the wretchedness of what has happened. He tells me to go and knock on Dennis Qujaukitsoq's house which fortunately is the next house up the track. Dennis is the dog killer and it seems horribly ironic that I am now asking him to help, after having cursed his previous actions. Frederik picks up the dog and puts him down by the boat with his siblings and the mother. The mother seems to understand what has happened and looks concerned as she watches her offspring try and drag himself towards her across the snow using his two front legs.

Dennis comes down straight away. We make a beeline for the upturned boat, but I cannot see him anywhere. He is not able to walk and it is not possible that he could have gone more than a few feet. And then, Dennis points to the sheltered area by the heel of the upturned boat. The mother sits upright, looking away, aloof and enigmatic, but acting as a guard over the grisly proceedings beside her. The siblings to the puppy are eating him alive, ripping off lumps of his flesh. We thought we had left him in the security of his mother and siblings, but they could only see it as an offering of food. It is too late to do anything. The meal is almost over. I stand there, completely helpless and apparently stuck to the ground, trying to come to terms with the abject horror of it. It never occurred to me that these dogs would be cannibals. Dennis shrugs his shoulders, says in Danish that they must have been hungry and makes off back up the slope, slightly frustrated that this has been a wasted journey. But the grim reality is, his siblings sensed that he was fair game, and the mother could not deprive them of a meal. If he had been shot, I suspect the dead body would have been tossed to the dogs to eat anyway. Here, meat is meat, for both dog and human alike, or so it would seem.

This macabre episode highlights very clearly how different their mindset and ontology is from my own. In my view, there is a tendency to rather romanticise the relationship between the Inuit and the animal. Josef and other hunters tell me that traditions such as holding silence after the hunt are now long gone. What is clear to me is in fact that there is here a great gap in the hierarchy between human and animal (dog).

The Inuit cannot understand our notion of pets, and I suspect that they think it is perverse to put a dog on the same level as a human (but there are one or two cats here, which I think probably are pets). Conversely, they are incensed at the way we treat humans. In the absence of alcohol, it is probably the case that there would be (almost) no homicide in Greenland. The fact that some people still smack children would, I suspect, make them as angry as the way some animals are treated here may be disagreeable to a Westerner. Here, the child is the king, often ruling the household. They are after all the embodiment of their ancestors.

As the light is fading, the feelings of suspicion towards me seem to be growing rather than dissipating. There is no avoiding the fact that there is a massive cultural discrepancy between us. Often I feel as if all my movements are being watched, but people remain reluctant to come and talk to me. Behind the eyes that are always eluding mine are people who are enigmatic, unpredictable, resourceful, but also cheerful, utterly carefree and always survivors. After all, they are the inhabitants of a desert of ice and there is a harshness to their way of life. Here, ridicule can be cruel and pitiless. Everyone will join in, even the wife of the husband being scoffed. Deformities are quick to be spotted and are made public, often making them the subject of ridicule and nicknames. Family members will not hesitate in highlighting very publicly the mental illness or physical disability that a sibling suffers from. But, there is no better object for ridicule than the *kadluna*. Everywhere one goes, one hears *kadluna ajorpoq*, 'the white man is bad'. The origins of this phrase lie in the belief that the white man can contribute nothing to a hunter-gatherer society because he does not know how to hunt. They could not contribute food and therefore their value was perceived to be nothing. They were seen as a liability, and not an asset. In that respect, he is quite genuinely 'useless'.

If the outsider is seen to be providing a service, teaching their children, working as an engineer at the electricity plant or working as a carpenter, then he can be accepted (but probably not integrated). If he is not seen to be providing a service or a tangible good, it is assumed that he is there to take something away. The discourse of exploitation is widely shared. If one looks at the home page of the Greenland Trade Union website, SIK, it talks of how Greenlanders have been exploited and underpaid over the years. Ironically, it was the *kadluna* that felt constantly exploited. Even to do a small task such as washing my laundry at the laundrette, I would have to pay six times what a local would pay. For the first three months, I was ignored completely by the people that worked there. On a number of occasions, locals wanted to charge me 100 DKK for one drum-song which lasts a minute long and my rent was multiples of what a local would pay. The people that wanted to charge me these absurd amounts (over ten pounds for a minute's work) were men and women that I had worked with a lot previously. One felt shattered, being treated like this after having put in so much time and effort to establish a bond of trust.

Attitudes to the 'other' aside, they continue to benefit from a very generous Danish welfare benefit system. Previously, the Inugguit only had one objective in life – to hunt and survive. Now, with Danish supply ships bringing Western goods, survival is guaranteed. They are left in an existential vacuum, and a small number of hunters have lost their motivation to hunt. Some consider the community to be 'paralysed' because 'hunting has been taken away from them' through a system of quotas, and it is easy to sympathise with this view. In my experience, many hunters would sit at home and try and find an excuse not to hunt. I heard any number of unfeasible excuses during my stay. Sixty years ago, that mindset would have been unthinkable as it would have resulted in death for the community. Some fishermen were brought from Illulissat to show the hunters how to fish. They complained that it was too cold to go fishing in Qaanaaq and so the *kommune* had special huts designed and made for them. These small huts were built on sledges and can be pulled by dogs. Initially, they were hardly used, however. Hunters sat there and played cards, not seeing any other use for them.

Two of these mobile huts can be found down at the shore where with the lack of wind, the turgid, inarticulate sound of thickening sea ice can be heard. The wind is a crucial agent in sea ice formation and preservation. Without the wind, the snow sits on the ice and acts as insulation. It holds the heat in and the result is thinner ice. The dots of small, scattered icebergs are joining up with a grey film of thin, slushy ice. There is now a wide strip of ice covering the sea a few hundred metres from the shore. The laid-back Inugguit have not brought in their boats and the ice is forming around them. The view from the shoreline is now one of ice rubble and grey, thin ice. Icebergs are no longer free to float through the channel, but are instead being locked in place. For the first time, I can now see how it will look when the sea is frozen over. However, it is in fact the splintered ice from a massive exploding iceberg that has frozen into the sea. Initially, this seems unlikely but an iceberg might be fifty metres high, and thus there is five hundred metres of ice beneath it. This ice from the collapsed iceberg will probably be blown away and subsequently in a few weeks time, the sea ice will begin to (properly) form.

At this one point in the year, the Inugguit might feel in a sense 'trapped'. They are no longer able to hunt seal from their boats and the sea ice has not yet formed, providing the freedom of hunting on the frozen sea. There is little to be done at this time, except for repairing sledges, nets, tools, making handicrafts to sell to the US soldiers at the Air Base, etc. For some members of the community, this restriction on their freedom brings gloom, saturnine expressions and depression. The light is fading and space is closing in around them. For the hunters of the Polar North, this is the hardest time of the year. Up until the late 1980s, this period might have lasted for a maximum of few weeks in September and October, but now this nothing in-between stage can last for months in the warmer climate. It becomes a battle between the wind and the temperature. It might be cold enough for the sea ice to form, but then an early winter storm might blow it away. And then the process starts again.

In the following days, the weather changes again and the strong winds and the blizzard like conditions reduce visibility to about two hundred metres. With the inchoate rage of the winter storms blowing down the chimney, the oil heater will not light. The oil does not seem to last two minutes. I put twenty litres of oil in the tank in the kitchen, but it has disappeared within a day and I have not had the heater on all the time. As was so often the case this time of the year, I go for a walk to get warm. Cohorts of crepuscular perambulators, young fathers and mothers push small children in little, wooden sledges (*qamutik*) before the sun sets at about 6.30pm, which is much later than I would have thought.

4: The Dark Period

I wake up to cold integrity: it is another freezing start to the day, and getting the house warm is becoming a troublesome and time-consuming task. The lethargic sun struggles to make it above the horizon at 11am, breaking the faint Arctic blue twilight. As the temperature started to fall at the beginning of October, more and more time was spent wrestling with the faulty oil heater whose soft warble would send me to sleep. Waking up in a silent room, I would curse that the heater had gone out in the night; my expletives would be lost in a train of smoky breath lingering in my hut and I could feel the temperature of the cold air plummeting around my snug sleeping bag. Having lost my computer and some data to one very cold night when the heater went out and the temperature dropped to -10 degrees in the hut, I started to become fixated with the thermometer LCD screen as the digits would tick down before my eyes. Throughout the course of the winter, I became extremely accurate at guessing the temperature in the room. It got to the point where I knew exactly what 12 degrees felt like. I knew that if I were sitting around with any number of layers on, 12 degrees was bearable, but anything much below that soon became uncomfortable. It was often the case that the heater would either just splutter, giving out a minimal amount of heat or it would roar like a furnace and the room would rapidly become unbearably hot. The room could seldom be kept at a normal room temperature for any amount of time. Magnus, an unemployed bachelor with a constant grin, was a very frequent visitor to the house and would come and 'fix' the oil heater and be typically paid 200DKK for doing so. There were two 'regulators' (one being a spare) and typically he would come and just take one 'regulator' off and swap with the other. Over a period of a few months, he must have done this half a dozen times and became very proud of his reputation as the 'master oil heater repairer'. We both found the procedure rather comical especially as he thought he had convinced me that he was somehow providing a long-term solution. On one occasion, he stoked up the fire with a steel rod which he had found on the balcony. The rod caught fire and he ran around the house like a madman, trying to put the flame out.

During this period, Josef would like to come and visit in the evenings and the conversation would often turn to their beliefs. It is obvious that the concern in this community is tangible reality: any views expressed on the intangible, if they are articulated at all, are normally contradictory and misleading. The conversation turns to the history of shamanism in the area. Josef laughs and says that it has all long gone. There was a famous hunter, Qaviunnguak Qisuk, who passed away in Qaanaaq not so many years ago. It is thought that he had some of the skills of a shaman. For instance, he was able to forecast the weather accurately many months in advance. He would go hunting on his own on very long trips, often going north of Etah.

Throughout my stay, a pot-pourri of subjects was avoided, but there was always much discussion about shamans, but it was a false discourse primarily used as a means to joke with the outsider, knowing that he would be interested in such matters. This is what Clifford (1997: 22) calls 'stranger talk'. It acted as a means of mocking the Westerner who was seeking to uncover a secret, mysterious indigenous system of beliefs which has surely disappeared. Not only is shamanism no longer observed, but also the complex system of spirits and taboos has partly gone from public life (it is still taboo to mention the name of a dead ancestor before it has been 'recycled'), and been largely lost from collective memory too. Their belief system has undergone massive transformation in the course of less than one hundred years. Previous ethnographers such as Knud Rasmussen have documented many of the taboos that the Inughuit and other Inuit groups observed: taboos concerning how animals should be killed, what should be done following the slaughter of a caribou, how to deal with the dead, which kind of food should and should not be eaten (during, say, pregnancy), the role of evil spirits, etc. All these beliefs were bound up in the mythical stories, most of which have now been forgotten.

Even if shamanism has not been practiced for a long period of time, there are still many who are very sympathetic to supernatural phenomena. Inukitsoq waves me into his house and tells me that there are killer whales (*aa'rdluk*) in the bay, and that they are scaring off the narwhal making the hunting difficult. He has also seen a *qivittoq* down on the beach, half-man, half-beast according to his account. There is solemn nodding all round, and no laughter. The man is clearly serious. These are outcasts who cannot integrate into a community. It is believed that they have special powers. They go out onto the *hermeq* (the 'Greenland Ice Sheet') and often die. Sometimes they come back to the community and haunt people.

The supernatural often crops up in conversations and ghost stories are common. The Inugguit are hypersensitive, armed with an almost chthonic sense. Once they have seen it, it becomes the object of a story which can be passed on. If there are no patients at the hospital in Qaanaaq, local people will refuse to work there overnight in an empty building because they are worried about ghosts and the spirits of the dead that haunt the place. The ghost stories circulate and stay with them forever. Arqioq Jensen told me that he was once walking along the shore in Qaanaaq when he heard a dog-team come past, but there was no hunter. Arqioq saw a man float almost across the top of the ice in old, traditional clothing. He could not see the face of the man, but saw instead a figure floating above the sledge. Arqioq could never quite explain this supernatural experience, but it left him believing in *tuurngaq* ('the helping spirits that guide shamans'). Arqioq thinks that there are people with shamanic abilities in Qaanaaq, but that they would not admit to their powers. They are frightened of gossip and what people would say about them, but also the risk that they might lose this knowledge if it were to be out in the open. Arqioq Jensen often told me that he 'needs more than one conventional God'.

Subsequently, Arqioq told me about the radio interview with Angaangaq Angakkorsuaq. This was the healer, shaman and businessman that coincidentally I sat next to in the aeroplane to Greenland. Arqioq was very convinced of his ability as a shaman. The radio interview was done on the telephone. Arqioq called him from a withheld number. The line was very bad and kept cutting out. Without having any way of knowing the number, Angaangaq called Arqioq back at one point. If anything is remembered from this rich indigenous system of belief, suspicion and taboo, it is perhaps the role of *hila*. *Hila* was an omnipresent power that played a role in man's fate. It was a power that shamans who acted as a sort of intermediary could invoke. By observing all these taboos, a balanced relationship was maintained with the power of *hila*, and there would be harmony.

Sitting with Arqioq and listening to his ghost stories, he would often drink several litres of coffee as if it were water. As with many indigenous groups, and most obviously the Aborigines of Australia, the Inugguit are sadly very prone to addiction. The most obvious addictions are tobacco, alcohol, caffeine, carbonated drinks, sweets, chocolate and Bingo. For a group of people that do not like numbers or arithmetic, their addiction to Bingo is baffling. They have become slaves to commodities for which they previously had no need. Unknowingly, they have exchanged a healthy, free life for the trivial luxuries of the West. Now, ten per cent of the population suffer with Diabetes Type 2, obesity is on the rise, nobody exercises, over sixty per cent of the community smoke, some people drink over two litres of coffee a day and others play Bingo three times a week. It seems that for the average person, few of these things are done in moderation. The sudden switch to a high sugar diet surely explains the appalling dental health that blights the community. Many young people have lost a tooth and elderly people might just have a single tooth dangling down. Not having any teeth causes in turn intestinal and digestion problems.

In the afternoon, Susanne, the girl who introduced herself to me in Danish when walking up from the shore last week, comes to visit. She is a very sweet, well-behaved girl who enjoys helping me learn her language. We have fun listening to my various recordings and playing around with my audio equipment. Despite the many phonological differences, she has no problem understanding the speech of the older people. The speech of this age group which I came to call Polar Eskimo Variety B is characterised by palatalisation, in particular of intervocalic /h/, e.g.: *kamahuk-toq* 'he hurries because he has spotted a polar bear in the distance'; the /ai/ diphthong, e.g.: *tittaihuitsoq* 'he never writes' (cf. *tittahuitsoq*); the /iu/ diphthong, e.g.: *iu'di'ddu* 'you are welcome' (cf. *i'di'ddu*); apocope and very indistinct articulation. In this variety, affixes are often accentuated, and the final phonemes 'swallowed'. In rapid speech, a /q/ can change to an /r/. Plosives in particular, (/t/k/g/) often cannot be determined with any certainty, and are even pronounced as nasals (/n/ng/). Susanne and I spend many hours together, trying to agree on the spelling of Polar Eskimo words. She reminds me, as so many others have, that her language is much harder than West Greenlandic.

Josef also comes to visit with the news that some hunters have spotted Belugas (*qilalugaq qaqortaq*). The hunting quotas set by the biologists are in his opinion far too restrictive. Nobody is allowed to kill more than one Beluga on a hunting trip. Interestingly, the number of killed sea mammals is not officially monitored, but the dynamics of the community are such that if somebody exceeds the quota, people will notice and find out almost immediately and that hunter's reputation would be destroyed. In a place like this, reputation and rumour is everything and thus the system can operate on trust. With such inter-connectedness, so few families and rivalries between them, the mechanism for monitoring the quotas is built in to the community. The way sea mammals are hunted has not changed, but the magnitude of the hunts has changed dramatically and to the detriment of their traditional way of life.

A week or two later, the sea ice in the bay is about 3 inches thick. The hunters have formed a narrow, curving channel with their boats, running between the thin sheets of sea ice, allowing them to still get out to the open water for the foreseeable future. There is a grey, thin layer of ice sitting on the top of the water. It begins to thicken, but then it is blown away and broken up by the wind. For the more permanent ice to form, the temperature needs to be consistently very low with little wind.

There is a pale, wan light at 9.30am, and the sun finally makes it above the snow-capped mountains in the east at 11.15am. The low Arctic sunshine pours into the kitchen, highlighting small patches of crumbs and dirt on the worn and tatty kitchen surface. Light, wispy cirrus cloud cover hangs sublimely over the eastern tip of Herbert Island. Its intriguing triangular rock formations are first pink, then orange before turning a light butter-yellow colour. *Isblomster* decorate the corners of the hut windows and sparkle in the late morning light.

Down at Eva's house, we talk at length about the inter-connectedness of the place, about the dynamics and tensions between the different families. They all have their own individual characteristics. The biggest and leading family at the moment are the Qujaukitsoqs. They have become well known because of Ole who was a member of the ICC and has been involved in pan-Inuit politics. This is a very big family whose reputation is that they are very proud, open and friendly, which I have certainly found to be true. The Dunneqs are reputed to be aggressive, confrontational and rather brutal. The Daoranas are philosophical and introspective whereas the Qaerngaqs are prone to depression and suicide. Irrespective of which family they come from, the Inugguit treat everybody as the same. When the Crown Prince of Denmark stayed in Qaanaaq, he was treated exactly as everybody else. Nobody made any fuss whatsoever. Here, everybody is equal and attempts to trade on a name or on a way of life are very much frowned upon.

Almost no household in Qaanaaq is living purely off hunting now. The woman has gone out to work in order to be able to put food on the table, but it is also the woman that is expected to bring up the children. She tells me how there are many problems with young children who come from difficult families. These children are not being looked after. There is no social welfare to speak of, and little interest in birth control. This is a laissez-faire, frontier society which is content to just expand its population. Before I go, she tells me about Qeqertat, the settlement at the end of the fjord where there live twenty-two people. There is no electricity (with the exception of the occasional portable generator), and one landline telephone that is shared between all the people. There is no mobile phone coverage. One wonders what it must have been like there during the last great storm in February 2006 when people in Qaanaaq could not leave their homes for two days because the wind was so strong.

We get three or four inches of snow overnight. A thin layer of snow over the incipient sea ice gives the impression of a flat, white landscape stretching out endlessly towards Herbert Island. In reality, the sea is a viscous, greyish soup of slushy spongy lumps of shuga. The latest arrival of snow leaves people sledging to the shop. Grown men racing down the steep slopes like young children is an amusing sight. The wooden sledges are parked outside the shop, their tall upright stanchions visible from a distance.

It is not yet light. Lens-shaped, puffy lenticular clouds the shape of UFOs created by gravity waves take my thoughts away to a universe of numinous experiences. Ten minutes later, the first light of the day shines on these stationary sooty puffs, and they are burnt different shades of pink, red and orange. The sun reflecting on the water makes the incipient sea ice look red; the flame in the sky flickers. It feels like a glorious sunset, but it is 9.30am. It is dramatic and beautiful: a masterpiece of an oil painting. I stroll back down the lazy slope towards home. We are now blessed with the most marvellous midday sunless sunsets. The sky exudes soft, amber light which fades into light blue and then dark blue sky. The cliffs in the distance sit like black slag heaps against a milky, pale orange horizon.

The sun draws a low, sluggish arc across the horizon, and disappears just after 6pm. Teenage boys play football in the dark, with the aid of the light from their mobile phone screen displays. Small candles sit in the windows of simple wooden huts without lampshades or pelmets, oriels, gilded edges, gauds, lace trim or nets. There are no books on the shelf, no libretto, no Delft. Inside, homes are almost bare, except for the clutter of toys. Home is the Ministry of Children, a fairground of fun and freedom, and not a dwelling of domestic discipline. Outside, the snowy tracks are lit up by the yellow light beaming down from the broad shoulders of the street lights. The circadian rhythms of the Arctic animals will be soon lost to the diuturnity of dark days and nights that lies ahead. I cling onto the ephemera of the light-dark cycle, but daylight and timekeeping will be of little relevance as we move inexorably towards the dark period.

Inugguit straggle from one house to another in thin tracksuits. There is silence except for the crunching of snow underfoot and the distant obstreperous banter of Ravens overhead. The dogs are asleep, curled up into tight balls. Large Greenlandic flags flutter in the breeze: two semi-circles of red and white on a white and red background. Forgotten laundry sits on lines above discarded furniture gathering snow. The landscape and the sky form a patina of subtle blends of grey and white, a mackerel coloured façade, mirroring rather precisely the shade of the solitary Kittiwake flying over the thin sea ice with such a sense of purpose. After 11am, the sun peeks above the mountains in the distance. Its slothful rise reflects my own increasing tiredness. On the beach lies a frozen adult Harp Seal (*aataaq*) like an unexploded bomb, patches of blood trace its journey up the snow-covered beach. Hans Miunge walks past, carrying a bag of walrus meat. Josef and Hans killed a walrus up at Etah yesterday. The Inugguit have a unique way of carrying heavy goods. They sling the plastic bag onto their backs, holding the bag over their heads, with their hands firmly clasped on their foreheads. It looks quite uncomfortable, but seems to work well.

In the evening, I am summoned to Josef's house to dine on the walrus that he hunted yesterday. Josef's wife, Bodil, has been boiling it for two hours. In the adjacent pot is a *qajaq*, a soup with rice, carrots and small chunks of reindeer. The walrus meat is very dark, almost black, and very tasty. There are no forks. The meat is held in your left hand, and slithers are sliced off using a knife in the right hand. Both hands are used to get the remaining meat off the bone. The blubber is also eaten, and this I do not much care for. It tastes like any other fat and is almost impossible to swallow and digest. When Josef is not looking, I put the small chunks of fat that I cannot digest into the dog's bowl. Josef always likes to emphasize how important meat is to the local diet and how they need the meat to stay warm in the winter. There is no pudding, but we have coffee and some biscuits and cheese. It seems odd to switch to a quintessential Western dessert after dining on hunters' food.

After supper, Josef shows me several hundred photographs on his Canon point-and-shoot camera. The pictures are all from this summer and include one confirmation and two funerals as well as photographs of narwhal hunting at summer camps near Qeqertat. One of the funerals was for his closest friend who hung himself in August. Josef tells me he does not know why he did it, but that he was suffering from depression. Death is gestured and described in the usual manner: a noose being pulled round somebody's head and then labelled 'dead'. Josef shows me a photograph of the gentleman shortly after he died. I am rather shocked to see a photograph of the dead man in his bed. In his capacity as ambulance driver for the hospital, Josef says that he has counselled six adolescent boys, all of whom were close to committing suicide. He thinks that in every case they were considering suicide for reasons of unrequited love. Josef is the first person with whom I feel close enough to explore this delicate topic of suicide. It is so pervasive and tragically defines the community to an extent.

Josef's photographs include pictures of the coffin, of the coffin lowered into the ground, of the mourners, etc. It reminds me of a conversation I had with a visiting Dane who told me that if you die here and do not wish to buried here, the body has to be transported in an extremely expensive zinc coffin in case the body fluids leek. It is more complicated if you die in one of the settlements as there is not room for a coffin in the helicopter. This Danish nurse told me once how she was standing at Nuuk airport with the bereaving family of the deceased and how shocked they were when they saw the helicopter arrive with the coffin suspended underneath.

Josef has pictures of funerals just as he has photos of confirmations. He tells me that we all must die and that it is just one of those things. We are born, we struggle and then we die. *Memento mori.* I am intrigued to see in the confirmation photos a balancing game being played. This is a traditional game and amounts to one sitting on a small seat of wood which in turn sits on three balls. The objective is to balance the bit of wood without your feet touching the ground, and it is clearly a game to test or indeed improve one's kayaking skills. The house where they now live is owned by Josef's wife's father who recently celebrated his 75th birthday and is called Ole-Peter Kristiansen. He is the grandson of the well-known Polar Eskimo who travelled with Knud Rasmussen to Alaska. Josef has a fantastic photograph of this man standing in Ummannaq (Dundas) with his wife, wearing *nannut* and *kamikker.*

At midday, I hear an announcement on KNR about Gustav Poulsen's funeral. I race down to the church. Else Qaerngaq, the tintinnabulist, is standing at the door and says that the service will begin at 12.45pm. A crowd begins to gather outside the church, many of them holding small wreaths of plastic flowers. With the exception of the Parka-clad pall-bearers, people are dressed in normal, everyday clothing. The crowd gets bigger and half of the town descends on the place. At 12.45pm, we are invited in and I am seated between Susanne Qujaukistoq and Helge who appears to be growing a handlebar-moustache. It is bitterly cold and my toes are freezing. The church is packed, and a queue forms outside.

Gustav Poulsen had been the head of the *kommune* and thus effectively the mayor of Qaanaaq: an intelligent man that I had got to know quite well. He was a Dane who had lived in Greenland for 25 years and had a sound understanding of local issues. We live today in a globalised world, inter-connected via an online platform that reaches even the more remote corners of our planet. Gustav Poulsen had a mail order bride from the Philippines which is not that uncommon for Danish men in their late 50s or 60s living in Greenland. She had come to the top of the world from Manila, a noisy and vibrant city of nearly twenty million people. She had expected to find skyscrapers, shopping centres and a 'green land', but instead found that her future home was the Arctic tundra. She did not speak a word of Danish or Greenlandic and came with two teenage children. They had been living up there for two years when I arrived, and it is fair to say that they had not been accepted. The schooling of the children had been a disaster and his wife was desperate to leave. Gustav Poulsen had a small stroke one Thursday evening. He was in good health, but was a heavy smoker. He was taken to the hospital where he was given Aspirin. There was nothing they could do for him and four days later he was dead. Had he been in Copenhagen, he would have survived without doubt. Imelda, his wife, pleaded with the only doctor to send him to Copenhagen for treatment, but he was not able to fly after a stroke.

There is one emergency plane for the whole of Greenland which can get you from Qaanaaq to Illulisaat in about 2 hours. They will only send for it if it is critical and if there is a reasonable chance that the patient will survive the flight. In the event of bad weather, there is no guarantee that the plane can be sent. With a staff of five on board, the cost of running the plane is very high. There is only one doctor in Qaanaaq. The visiting doctor to Qaanaaq is invariably a retired Dane who comes on an inflated salary. He might stay for a few weeks and will often treat the trip as a holiday, stating when he will not work on arrival. Depending on the doctor that they get, they may have no surgical experience at all.

In his will, Gustav Poulsen had left everything to his daughter from his first marriage. Imelda had been widowed for the second time before the age of 50, but now had nothing. Angry, Imelda admitted that she had only married him to get Danish citizenship. But, she had not done her homework. The Danes very sensibly changed the law to try and put an end to these scam marriages, and thus one cannot be guaranteed citizenship through marriage in accordance with Danish law. Her subsequent plan was to leave for America, not being able for some reason to return to the Philippines. She seemed to think that she could just move to America, but was held up at the embassy in Denmark.

The service is relatively short. We start off with a well-known hymn. There is a prayer and then the catechist reads out from a sheet an account of some of the events of his life, what he did and where he worked. As far as I can work out, it is all rather factual, a bit like reading somebody's

Wikipedia page. There is a reference to his wife, killing speculation that they were not in fact married. There are also references to a son and daughter who are in Illulissat and who could not be here because the Qaanaaq flight was cancelled because of bad weather. Helge tells me that he is not confident that either of them have been properly consulted. I certainly hope that his children knew that he was going to be buried today. Subsequently, Puto Dunneq tells me that the *Selvstyre* ('Self-Rule Government') insisted that the funeral had to go ahead. There is perhps a regulation about how long one can wait before a body is buried.

There are no readings from his family, but another hymn, prayer and then unconventionally we finish on a carol, *Silent Night*. The pall-bearers raise the casket to their shoulders and solemnly tote it out of the church past the mourners where it is placed into the back of the Mitsibushi L20 pick-up truck. The simple, white wooden cross which marks graves in Greenland is carried by a woman leading the pall-bearers out of the church. Here, there are no funeral directors, undertakers, priests, hearse or grave-diggers, but a strong community of family and friends. Then, the pick-up truck driven by Jan ascends very slowly the snow-covered dirt tracks and a cortège of fifty silent mourners skitter across frozen puddles, following the vehicle along the meandering track, out to the cemetery.

The burial site is very close to the arched entrance to the cemetery. In the darkness of the December afternoon, the coffin is lowered into the shallow grave which is just two feet deep because of the permafrost. In Upernavik, the graves are raised because the permafrost is so high. Torchlights beam on grief-stricken faces. The catechist reads a short prayer and faint voices sing a hymn. Then, more prayers and a hymn which is sung from a song-sheet with a little more vigour marking another premature coda, lived out in an ill-equipped hospital. Devoid of emotion or expression of any kind, the catechist reads the committal in West Greenlandic: an all too familiar meaning cloaked in alien sounds. A handful of men pick up shovels and fill the grave in there and then in front of the mourners, quickly, mechanically and with no fuss. The discordant, grating sound of the spades on the frozen ground, the rasp of the metal passing the tiny stones in the soil's gravel, breaks the mourners' silence. Stones and brightly-coloured wreaths of artificial flowers are put on top of the grave. Not a word is spoken, but the ceremony is complete.

Once the plot is filled in, everybody lines up to offer their condolences to the family who stand by the grave, trembling with grief. It is rather formal and very much like a line-up at a wedding, but without the happiness and joy. I am told to go to the house for the wake where there will be coffee and cakes.

Under a dark sky, bespattered with distant smidges of very faint *arharniq* ('Northern Lights'), I walk heavy-footed back into town, feeling the sadness of the occasion. One of the pick-up trucks stops and I am offered to join a group of teenagers sitting on the rim of the open-top rear cargo area. It is exceptionally cold: the wind whips my face, turning my head numb. Everybody is joking and the atmosphere has switched completely. The teenagers make quips about opening a strip-club up in Qaanaaq. The tragedy is already the past.

The following day, I turn up at the *peerarsarfik*, hoping that I can join the Greenlandic class. I have a peek at the work set for the mathematics class. Much of it comprises the simplest arithmetic possible with sums like 7+9+2-1. Jens Ole's replacement is a sensible and pleasant man of perhaps 23 or 24 years. The new teacher, Frederik Kristensen, tells me that he is not trained as a teacher, but is just trying to help out. There are about 15 of us in the class. The people here are aged between 17 and about 24. These people have struggled at school and are here to catch up a bit and hope to gain some qualifications. We are set a task which is to introduce yourself to the group in Standard West Greenlandic, telling people who you are, when you were born, who your family is and what your hopes and aspirations are. With the various breaks, they spend about two hours on what is clearly a taxing task. After lunch, the group is invited to present themselves. One after the other introduces himself only to break down in tears after the first few lines. They are talking about siblings who have died. It is a case of either infant mortality or more typically suicide. Infant mortality is relatively high here and there are no medical facilities to deal with pre-natal complications. At one point, there is barely a dry eye in the class. Two of the girls who are sobbing when asked to present their family are taken outside. This sudden outpouring of grief is extremely reminiscent of the events at the poetry reading at the *taffi* on Saturday night. They are not providing any detail on these deaths, merely mentioning that they have lost a sibling, but this is enough to trigger a collective emotional outpouring. One is reminded once again that this community is essentially one family, and the feeling of inter-connectedness is perhaps never stronger than at the time of the loss of a loved one. As is always the case, the drama and melancholy does not last long, and just minutes later it is all smiles, laughs and practical jokes.

It has got to the point where there is much speculation amongst the locals as to when I might leave. When it came to them setting up a betting syndicate and taking bets on the departure date, it was very noticeable that they did not share my sense of time. On a Tuesday, I would be frequently asked if I was leaving tomorrow. I would tell them that I was leaving in August, but I could see that this did not mean anything to them. They knew that August referred to a month in the year, but the fact that it was nine months away was conceptually a vacuous thing to say. Times, days, months – the bits that we use to break up time – seem to be rather meaningless reference points. Instead, it is better to say that one will spend the winter here or that you will return to England when the narwhal return or something of that sort. Time is not measured by hands on a clock, but by the movements of nature and importantly events. The Inugguit are interested in the event itself as a reference in space and time, not in the telic relationship between acts, the chronological sequence of events or the period between. The focus is on the event minutiae, but not the grand scheme or context. They would describe in detail visits from the Inuit of Canadian Baffin Islanders by dog-sledge, but they could not tell me when they occurred and could not always see the relevance of the question. The few relevant dates are birth dates and Christmas which take on a peculiar significance. Young people and non-hunters have all embraced this concept of time.

The last sunrise is on the 24th of October. We will not see the sun above the horizon again until the 17th of February. We had a small ceremony up on the hill this morning above the satellite dish to mark the occasion (it is 'illegal' for the school to be open on a Sunday and so we had to celebrate it today). The children had painted some pictures of the sun and a small verse was read out in West Greenlandic and Danish, along with a speech from one of the teachers about the merits of what the darkness can bring. It had not occurred to me that there could be any. We had assembled at 11.30am, but I knew of course that was too early as I have been watching the sunrise and sunset like a hawk. It was bitterly cold and the teachers decided not to wait for the penultimate sunrise. Instead, the children performed a variety of skits at the school, and subsequently currant buns and hot chocolate were served. The sun appeared finally above the mountain at 1.30pm.

The sun dips below the horizon again two hours later at 3.30pm, and produces subsequently the most extraordinary sunset I have seen since being here. The sky is a rich, carmine colour. My thoughts go the blood-red sky of Edvard Munch's Scream, and whether this sangria-coloured sky is too a symbol of forthcoming anxiety vis-à-vis the pending darkness. Dogs howl at the dark sky which is lit up with shooting stars falling to Earth like troubled aeroplanes in a dramatic, meteoritic light show. I do not feel overcome with melancholy. On the contrary, the dark nights are splendid as on a clear night the sky comes to light with a maze of constellations, planets and shooting stars; a spangled firmament providing celestial bliss. As the air is so clean here, all these natural phenomena seem extremely close and immediate in a way that I have never seen before. These simple things are difficult to appreciate in a polluted, overpopulated urban landscape. The light from the refulgent moon was white this morning; so bright that I could not even capture it properly with a camera. Despite the lack of light, the hunters are getting ready for the sea ice. The sense of anxiety is palpable. Down at the shore, a hunter is training his new dog team, walking alongside the sledge, shouting commands and expertly cracking the whip just inches above their heads. Dogs can start pulling when they are six or seven months old and each male dog can pull up to about eighty kilos.

The darkness is really upon us, and the remaining light is rapidly disappearing now. At 11.30am the next day, it is still not properly light. The mountains in the East are as black as coal against a pale, orange sky. During the brief midday twilight the horizon burns pink and orange, and the wind blows the snow in sweeping arc-forming patterns across the scree slopes. There is a sunless sunset at 1.30pm, providing theatrical colour to translucent clouds. The days are growing very short and the shadows lengthen forebodingly in the moody light.

Wistful looking dogs, the tenants of the scree slopes, watch my gait with quizzical expressions, heads rotating hypnotically, as I wander past in the fading light of mid-afternoon. The orange wan stain on the horizon loses its early afternoon freshness, and the soft, diffused light of late October is vague and uncertain; a crepuscular incoherence. Wooden sledges jounce noisily over bumps in snowy tracks and candles flicker nervously behind frosted windows. The slush and shuga has spawned a sea of pancake ice: a grid of colliding, frozen giant lily leaves with elevated rims. These plates of ice, roughly circular in shape and perhaps two or three feet in diameter creak and groan as they wrestle with one another. The boundary between sea and land is smudged by the shore ice. Icebergs of different shapes and sizes are now locked into place and sit like protruding teeth from off-white gums. A tall iceberg sits in the corner of the bay like a frozen, crumbling castle – its passage halted for many months now.

In the evening, Inunguaq Imiina, my neighbour, comes to visit. She says it is too cold to stay in my house and thus we decamp to her place for a cup of cha. The wind is absolutely biting, and going into a warm house my whole face tingles at the shock of a sudden thirty degree change in temperature. Inunguaq is a kind woman in her forties who has two sons in Sisimiut. With a population of 2,000, a 'big city', she tells me how she could never live in such a built-up place. She is recently divorced and is a former alcoholic. Today, she is teetotal, a Born again Christian and a member of the Free Church. She went to Nuuk in 2008 for treatment for her addiction and has not touched a drop since. She was also addicted to Bingo and has stopped that too. This is a society of addicts and former addicts. In her house, there is Christian iconography everywhere: vast tapestries of Christ adorn the walls, along with small crucifixes and paintings of the Messiah. And yet these ornaments are apparently nothing more than vacuous symbols as she admits that only now is she learning about her religion. An unthumbed Greenlandic Bible lies open on the bare dining room table; it is not long before she makes a pass at me over a cup of steaming tea.

At the beginning of November, literature started appearing in the shop about meetings that were being held across Greenland to discuss the future of the remote settlements. Not one of the meetings took place in north-west Greenland. People became increasingly concerned about the Self-Rule Government's intentions, writing messages on the posters saying: 'it looks like we have been forgotten again'. We have been here before. There was a plan in the 1950s and 1960s to close Qaanaaq and Upernavik and move the entire population of these settlements to Nuuk.

This was part of the infamous G60 policy whose objective was to foster a few villages and towns in Greenland, so that service provision could be centralised. Many politicians in Greenland believe today that a modern economy cannot be run effectively with a tiny population of 55,000 people living in such scattered, remote places. This previous policy was a disaster – hunters were moved from remote fishing settlements and housed in huge Soviet style apartment blocks. One of them, Blok P, was so enormous that one per cent of the Greenlandic population lived there. People could not adapt to urban life and this created a plethora of social problems. By the end of the 1980s, Greenland had the highest suicide rate in the world. According to the Self-Rule Government, one in five Greenlanders have tried to kill themselves at some point in their lives.

It is still pitch black at 11am and at midday we are trapped between the light and the darkness: a dim cloak of different shades of grey and white that envelops the place. The sky is hoary and timeless. Drifting, swirling snow reveals terracotta coloured scree. The blurred grey and white of the liminal land- and seascape merge into one like a tatty, faded postcard. The twilight and the persistent wind lends a hazy, indistinct feel to the town: an out-of-focus, developing sepia photograph wobbling in the water of the bathtub. The Inugguit stand shivering on wooden, cluttered balconies taking a quick drag on the late afternoon cigarette before hurrying inside to attend to demanding toddlers in overheated homes. It is dark again by 3.30pm and the muted light is now rapidly losing the battle to complete darkness. The town is now a cluster of greenish-yellow lights on an otherwise uniform landscape. Lugubrious November offers time to the pensive one in a forgotten corner of the Arctic. Sequestered at home, in the hut, the poet lost in sub-fusc, cloaked in the beetle-black gown of the now silent Raven, has misplaced his mettle but there is no hiatus in the brumal palinode. In the hut and following the neighbour's advice, the single-glazed windows are now taped up with black bin liners to prevent the cold draught getting in through the cracks. The battle with the cold is beginning.

Josef continues to visit in the evenings and fleshes out his plans for the *nuna inugguit*, the land of the Inugguit which he thinks should be an autonomous region. This region is called Avannaarsua and is the area which runs just north of Kuvdlorssuaq on the west coast diagonally across the ice sheet to the Danish weather station in the north-east of

Greenland called Nordvejrstation where eleven Danes work (some scientists are based there in the summer). These Danes are members of the
Danish Defence Command and live there for periods of twenty-six
months. It is a base for the Sirius Patrol. The station was built as a
weather and telecommunications station for the Americans in the fifties.
There is no ship to Nord, as it is called, and ice conditions are such that a
ship can get there every five or ten years. This is a vast area and is,
according to Josef, the land of the Inugguit.

Josef is concerned that one day the Prime Minister, Kuupik Kleist, will
announce that he is closing Qaanaaq and that the Inugguit will have to
move south. If that happens, he will announce his plan which is pure
fantasy, but immense fun. Although it is fiction, he has put a lot of
thought into it. Jokingly, he says that he will be President of this
autonomous area and that I will be Minister for Languages or perhaps
the Education Minister.

The language of the region will of course be Inuktun and that will be
the language taught in the schools. A written standard will have to be
established. Josef thinks that this region is rich in resources. Firstly, they
have the pure, excellent water. At the moment, the Thule region imports
drinking water from Denmark which is ludicrous when we are surrounded by glaciers. Josef thinks that there is gas beneath Qaanaaq, oil by
Herbert Island (where incidentally he thinks tourists could go skiing as
the top of the island is very flat), minerals (iron) at Etah and Haviggivik.
There are thousands of birds in Hiorapaluk, fish in Qeqertat where he
would have a factory and a landing strip built with direct flights to other
countries so that they can export their fish to China and the US.
Interestingly, the plan is all based on socialist principles. There will be no
private ownership and all food will be heavily subsidised, so that it will be
cheap and so that the money can be reinvested into infrastructure. Half
of the profit will go to the state treasury of the *nuna inugguit*. Josef would
install solar panels and wind turbines in Qaanaaq as there is sunshine
here from February to October and so that they can profit from the
strong winds in the winter.

Although this is all a bit of fun, and tongue-in-cheek, it is tremendous
to discover somebody who has the motivation to do something and to
recognise the potential of this area. Josef does not believe in anthro-
pogenic global warming. He says that there have always been periods in

history where the earth has been hot and that this is one of them. Josef thinks that the world is in a warming stage because we have moved closer to the sun. He says that it is nothing to worry about and that we will return to one of the cold periods in a matter of decades. In 1979, the sea ice did not melt at all in Haviggivik. The supply ship arrived in the summer and it could not reach the settlement. They had to use the dogs to get the supplies off. 1979 was a year without a summer. They used the dogs all the year round. The older hunters think that the Earth will cool down again because that is what has always happened. Nature and climate are cyclical according to him and many others. The Polar Eskimos are more concerned about the quota systems than climate change. The biologists go looking for the animals and birds and find that they are not there, but that is because they have moved. Walrus hunting has got much harder because the walruses are on the other side of Herbert and Northumberland Island, but they cannot get to them because the ice is too thin there. With the melting sea ice of the Arctic Ocean, the ice shelf where many of the sea mammals like to feed is moving further and further away from them. Contrary to the view of the rest of the world, the Inugguit are, however, firmly of the view that hunting quotas imposed by the Self-Rule Government will make the hunting way of life impossible before global warming does.

The Inugguit hunt seal in nets when the new sea ice forms. It is dark at this time of the year, and thus it is difficult to shoot the seal. Seal is the main source of food for the dogs. With global warming, the new ice is often thin and that makes it difficult to hunt the seal using nets because the new ice keeps moving. The Inugguit are of the opinion that Greenpeace have put so much pressure on the Greenlandic Government that they are practically dictating Government policy without being aware of all these facts. The Government is focused on the towns in south-west Greenland, and not the outer settlements.

It is almost light outside; the full moon sets the scene for the most splendid of nocturnal chiaroscuros. The Inugguit believe that the polar bears come closer to the settlement when there is a full moon and one has been spotted near the dump, less than a kilometre from my house. It is extraordinary what a difference the moonshine makes, casting a dim light on the whole area and turning the sky a deep, dark blue. It is

complete, permeating my mind with all its consciousness. It is sufficiently light to be able to see stretches of open water far away in the
distance towards the fast moving and rapidly retreating Politiken glacier.
It is approaching the end of November and the sea ice still does not cover
the whole of the Inglefield bay. According to the DMI data, the average
temperature for Qaanaaq for November (thus far) has been -10 degrees.
The average for the same period in 1961-1990 was -17 degrees. We
cannot be sure how accurate this data is as meteorological data is only
modelled for Qaanaaq, but that is at any rate a significant difference.

The Inugguit have lived the life of a hunter for thousands of years, but
the generation of people born in the 1960s decided that they wanted
something else and many left Qaanaaq. It is sometimes said that they lost
a generation of hunters. Many of those that stayed did not have the skills
of being a hunter and got jobs in the *kommune* and the shop.
Greenlanders were told in the 1960s that if they wanted any future they
had to learn Danish and many went to Denmark to do so. More than
once I hear that when they did so, they started to think differently:
learning Danish made them think like Danes. There is a clear concern
that the schooling does not prepare young people for a traditional life of
hunting in any way, and yet the subjects they study at school are no use if
they wish to stay in Qaanaaq. In Josef's fanciful autonomous region for
the Inugguit, the education system would give people the skills to stay in
their homeland. The fact that the education system was ill-preparing the
young people was one of the points that was made most forcefully during
my stay. Some thought that the region that the Inugguit occupy should be
part of Nunavut and not Greenland. It is clear that culturally and linguis-
tically at least, that would make a lot of sense, but is of course in every
other respect problematic.

With the move away from the traditional hunting life that defined the
community for centuries came a different set of values tied to the cash
economy that the Inugguit were increasingly dependent upon. Speaking
to David Nielsen, a hunter originally from further down the coast and
one of the most respected hunters in north-west Greenland, I was told
that this was the biggest change in Inugguit society over the last twenty
years. David is something of a celebrity hunter. He took part in the Sirius
patrol in 2005 with Hans Miunge, Uumaaq Jensen and a hunter from
Illulissat. They travelled for three months in the winter up the east coast

of Greenland with the Danish military elite, right up to the station at Nord. They were not allowed to hunt and ate instead a 'Western diet' of soup and pemmican. David says that north-west Greenland used to be a communal society where everybody would help each other, and never think about money. In his view, now it is seldom that people will help you without asking for money. That is something that struck me repeatedly.

In the morning, I turn on the radio and Christmas carols are playing. I draw the curtains and the stars lit in neighbours' windows tell me that it is the first day of Advent. Everybody lights a star in their window on the first day of Advent and the lights on the Christmas tree outside the church are turned on. The town has turned into a lethal ice-rink. It is almost too slippery and unpleasant to go out. Slipping and sliding everywhere, I make it to the Church just in time. There is a big crowd there, perhaps a two hundred people, many of whom are children of course. The Christmas tree came on the supply ship, I am told, but I am not sure how it is still alive. I suspect it might have come on the plane. Either way, the tree has come from Denmark and we are grateful to have it. The Norwegian Spruce is only about five feet tall but looks significantly taller as it is sitting on a pile of crates. Greenlandic and Danish speeches like solemn prothalamions thank the people of Denmark for the tree. Carols are sung in the pitch black (there is no moonshine today) and then the children hand-in-hand dance and chaunt around the Christmas tree. The spirit of Christmas has arrived and it is a joy to be in a place where there are no shopping centres beaming out vulgar 'Happy Holidays' signs in bright lights. This feels authentic and how it should be.

The christening party is hosted in the evening. It is not what I expect at all. It is held at the school and there are forty guests. Everybody is very smart. Frederik from the *peerarsarfik* is wearing a suit and most of the other men look like snooker players with dress shirts and waistcoats. Many of the women sport very fancy dresses. I turn up in my oversized gorilla Icelandic woollen sweater and cumbersome Baffin boots with self-made studs (hanging off the bottom) made from bits of wire coat hangers. One is feeling rather uncouth. Seated at the table, I am opposite Storm Sadorana. The dinner is a buffet and is a spread of musk-oxen, reindeer and pork served with mashed potatoes and berries. There are soft drinks only and a variety of party games on offer. Everybody is given a one kroner coin to hang round their necks. The idea is to get the coin off somebody by getting them to say 'no' to a question. I soon lose my coin and Storm manages to build up quite a big collection. One annoying gentleman along the end of the table insists on shouting *iih* ('yes') all evening. It is funny for the first minute or so, but after that becomes rapidly tiresome.

Then, there is a singing competition. I join my elderly neighbour and somehow we win. The highlight of the evening is the game where a man and a woman have to pair up and exchange clothes under a bed sheet. I team up with Ingeborg Jeremiassen who must be about 4 feet 10 inches. I wear her tiny top and skirt and she is wearing my trousers and boots. It looks very funny and we win that game too. My present this time is a candle which is sure to be of use.

We also play the party game 'yet'. Everybody stands around in a circle. A selection of gifts and presents are put in the centre and everybody rolls the dice. If you get a '5', then you are entitled to take a gift. Once the gifts have been distributed, you can then take a gift off somebody else. This continues for 10 minutes when the time is up and those with a gift at the end can keep it. I win a pack of biscuits. At the end of the evening, all the coins that have been hanging around people's necks are thrown on the floor. Children and adults throw themselves at the money as if it were the Holy Grail. I pretend to participate in this game, but in fact hold myself back and should be embarrassed to do otherwise. The whole evening is a lot of fun but I leave early as I have a thumping headache and am feeling terribly jaded. The effects of the constant darkness now are making themselves felt.

A few days later, it was the Old People's Home Christmas Party. There were forty people in attendance, twenty employees (everybody that works there) plus a guest. The party is held at the *forsammlingshus*. Instead of nametags, numbers are put at each seating place. There is plastic cutlery and the same very cheap plastic table cover laid out on Formica tables. The layout is identical to that of the Christening I went to on Sunday. We draw numbers to see where we seat. I am seated next to Aima who is a young girl I have seen at the *peerarsarfik*. She was the one that cried through the course of her presentation when she spoke about suicide in her family. I tell her that I have forgotten her name, she repeats it and looks away, putting in her iPod. She has no interest in talking to me. I ask my neighbour who he is and he ignores me. Not a good start and we for the most part eat in silence. The food is a selection of lamb, boiled potatoes, gravy and boiled tin peas and sweet corn. It is not very exciting, but the meat is good.

Once the dinner is over, the evening pans out exactly as it did on Sunday. There are a series of games and we all end up getting presents. Embarrassingly, I get the biggest present again. We sing the same songs we sung on Sunday and there is the same game of exchanging clothes with somebody of the opposite sex under a bed sheet. Although I have seen it only once before, I am bored of it already and cannot wait to leave. We play the 'yet' game, this time it is a number six that you need. As per usual, it ends with a rugby scrum of Inugguit trying to hoover up the last Kroner. The highlight of the evening is the 'Suck and Blow' game, where a playing card is passed from your lips to your neighbours by inhaling and then blowing onto the lips of your neighbour. The playing card lands on the floor much of the time and I think it is very unhygienic, but I cannot back out now. As players drop out for not managing to pass the card in the correct manner, the circle gets smaller and the rhythm of sucking and blowing gets quicker. The participants find this game most amusing, marvelling in the sexual innuendo of it all. They roll around laughing as I have to crouch down to pass the moist playing card onto my diminutive, toothless neighbour. As the evening progresses, the jokes become progressively more bawdy.

Games have always been an important part of life in the Polar North. As with every other part of the world, many of the traditional games that were played just fifty years ago are no longer played, but when it comes to parties a long repertoire of traditional and less traditional games are still staged. During my stay in the Polar North, I went to any number of parties to celebrate Christmas, special birthdays, Easter, etc. Generally speaking, these tended to be very joyous, but also emotional occasions, often gyrating very suddenly between sadness and tears of laughter. There was a tendency to get very excited about such emotionally charged social gatherings and exhibit very few adult inhibitions. Unexpectedly, these were times when suppressed thoughts about the dead would also surface. I went to 50th birthday parties and Christmas parties which would begin with a minute silence for the dead, with thoughts reserved in particular for the recently departed. The giving of presents was always especially central to these parties, and there would be great fuss and applause even for the smallest of gifts such as a bar of soap. At some parties, there would be unexpected ritualistic re-enactments of wedding ceremonies. The married guests would leave the room and then re-enter, arm-in-arm and with beaming smiles to great applause and act as if they are walking down the aisle of a church.

The day after one of these parties, Kunuk Mathiassen from Hiorapaluk comes round in the morning to collect the walrus tusk from the loft. He will carve figurines out of the walrus ivory, selling them to American soldiers at the US Air Base. He opens the heavy door and cold air billows into the hallway as if one is entering a cold room. Only the contours of his face are initially visible through the clouds of freezing air filling the icy entrance. In order to get up in the loft, I go outside to collect the ladders on the makeshift balcony and my skin sticks immediately to the icy, thermally conductive aluminium. Cursing not wearing gloves, I rip my hands away from the sticky metal and for a moment have no feeling at the tips of my fingers.

I spend the afternoon at Iggiannguaq's house. A dead Ringed Seal hangs from the ceiling in the kitchen with a pool of blood in a bowl beneath it. A young, inexpressive girl stands over the kitchen sink, bored and silent, working her way through endless piles of washing-up. I almost feel sorry for her. The scene has become a very familiar one: once in the house, the men relax whilst the women do all the work. Arqioq Jensen, Iggiannguaq's nephew, sits on the sofa with three of his five children climbing all over him. On the news on the television, we are told that there will be no weather forecast today as KNR has not received the data from DMI. These small things make Greenland special. The men talk of hunting. The hunters are catching Greenlandic Shark (*iqalugguaq*) at the moment. Holes are made in the ice and they are simply hooked. These sharks are twenty feet long and it is believed that they can live for over 200 years. The flesh of the Greenlandic Shark is poisonous, but it can be eaten if boiled in several changes of water or eaten fermented, as the Icelanders do. Iggiannguaq mentions that he will go out tomorrow and I ask him if I can join him which is replied with an emphatic *iih*.

I am looking forward to going out on the ice to look for the *iqalugguaq*. It is the first week of December, and I have waited so long for the sea ice to form that I have almost become nervous about it. I turn up slightly early and find Iggiannguaq's house full of people as a *kaffimik* is taking place. The house smells of dried blood and dead animals. A small mountain of boots and jackets discarded by all the visitors makes it almost impossible to enter. On the floor of the living room, on bits of cardboard, lie dead musk-oxen and reindeer. Halibut and Arctic Char sit in small pots. A group of people are knelt down with a knife in one hand, eating chunks of raw meat from the knife. Visitors parade in, eat something savoury followed by cake and coffee and then leave. Iggiannguaq's three daughters are busy doing chores. Abelonie, his wife, has been collecting fresh-water ice (*nilak*) for water; a viridian ice cube is parked outside her home. She is dressed in *kamikker* and a seal skin coat that she made herself. Iggiannguaq sits in the corner in typical Polar Eskimo fashion, back straight, his legs make an arc of forty-five degrees like a pair of scissors. He wraps seal gut around two bits of wood. This is a sort of bungee cord that will be attached to a sledge. It is remarkable how the Inugguit have adapted and used nature for their own ends. The atmosphere is jovial in the house. The family realises that this is the first time I have been on the ice and there are therefore lots of jokes at my expense. Iggiannguaq wishes me to believe that I will be driving the dogs, and I am spurred on by the daughters who find the prospect of the *kadluna* running a dog-team utterly implausible.

In preparation for the dog sled ride, I have donned seven base layers and a pair of orange *salopettes*. I am wearing two pairs of Meindl socks and my Baffin boots. Iggiannguaq gives me the reindeer rug or sledge skin (*inguriq*) to sit on. Clad in a sealskin parka called a *naitsiq*, he unleashes two dogs which are tethered on the slope just down from his house. He is carrying a whip (*iparautaq*) which he cracks with great expertise, the long whip unfurling just a few centimetres above the dogs' heads. The use of the boot is less impressive. I try not pay too much attention and am busy avoiding his whip which looks lethal. The first thing I notice is the reaction of the dogs to him is entirely different from their reaction to me. When they see me, they wag their tail and push their big, heavy heads right into me. They want to play and stand on their hind legs with their front paws practically on my shoulders. When they see the hunter, they cower and are scared stiff. It is not surprising, but it seems to me that the dogs only do exactly as they are told because they are so frightened of the consequences if they do not do so. This goes against what I know about dogs. I did not think you got the most out of an animal by being so harsh with it, but here maybe it is different with these Greenlandic Dogs. Travelling by dog-sledge is still the most effective means of travel on the sea ice and a large dog team of fifteen strong, well-fed dogs is a reflection of a skilled, successful hunter. In the days of mechanised transport, the prized possession for a Polar Eskimo remains his dog-team. These dogs are so strong, not only can they pull a fully loaded sledge, but two or three dog teams tied together can pull a motorboat in addition to two sledges across the frozen sea to the edge of the sea ice as I was to witness many times whilst out hunting in the spring and summer months. On one occasion in May the dogs pulled a motorboat without having been fed for three days.

On the ice, we collect four more dogs. In total, the team is six: five males and one female. They are good-looking dogs and all of them seem well fed with very thick fur. Iggiannguaq has the unenviable task of sorting out the tangled leads of six hysterical dogs. The leads are attached to their harnesses which are connected to a single rope that is attached to the 12 foot sledge. Instead of using a metal hook, the lines are attached to a toggle carved out of walrus tusk. The sea ice is flat and stretches out for miles before us. The shore ice is still quite thin and Iggiannguaq walks ahead of the dogs with the whip by his side, ordering the dogs left and right, *harru, harru, atsuk, atsuk*, expertly guiding them around the thin patches of sea ice. Once we are on thicker ice, the dogs fan out and begin to run. Iggiannguaq has a split second to launch himself onto the rapidly accelerating sledge, and takes his seat on the skins in front of me. The hunters sit with their legs over the side of the sledge, with feet dangling just above the ground. For the most part, they do not whip the dogs but thrash the whip just to the side of them to direct them left and right. On thin ice, it is imperative they do as they are told as the hunter's life depends on it. There is no room for error. The control they have over their dogs is extremely impressive, and they respond exactly to his commands. To travel by dog-sledge on the sea ice is to experience something extraordinary and unique.

The first thing that I notice once the dogs start pulling is the offensive stench of excrement. The dogs are so excited that they more or less lose control of their bowels instantaneously. Months of fettered anguish are at last set free and they are now finally free to pull. It is obvious that they are happiest when working. This is as big a moment for them as it is for me, but fortunately I do not feel the need to pass stools. Their response to the excitement is to defecate which they try do as they run along. The dogs attempt a semi-squat, but of course the sledge does not stop for poopers. It all looks extremely uncomfortable and is surely more or less akin to trying to expel faeces whilst jogging. The dogs soon get thirsty and very deftly drop their tongue to one side of their jaws and eat the snow as they run along the ice. Everything is done on the move. The sledge runs along smoothly and at quite a speed. I ask how we will navigate in the 24 hour darkness and Iggiannguaq produces a state-of-the-art infra-red night vision telescope. The ice rapidly forms around the holes and thus we are just looking for a pole to which the pre-placed net is attached, sticking up out of the ice (in the dark). To me, the task seems more or less impossible.

Headlamp on, Iggiannguaq surveys the contours, lines and bumps of the frozen sea, looking for thin ice, cracks, leads, etc. We are hunting Greenlandic Shark and Iggiannguaq has placed narwhal bait on large hooks at about a dozen places dotted across a vast expanse of sea ice. The principal reason Iggiannguaq hunts Greenlandic sharks is to sell their jaws to the *kommune* who will pay 200 DKK for them. The shark is killed and then dried and fermented for six months before it is eaten.

We travel by dog sled for about five kilometres away from Qaanaaq, navigating our way through icebergs frozen into the sea ice, listening to the soporific sound of the sledge runners bumping rhythmically across the frozen sea. My head begins to dip, but I remind myself of the dangers of falling asleep in these temperatures. It is high pressure, -28 degrees and the sky is a mass of constellations, stars, galaxies, planets and the hazy, winter moon with her whitish areolas. Venus sits low in the sky and looks magnificent above Politiken glacier, shining brighter than any star. This celestial splendour feels like a gateway to another world: a break from the intoxicating obscurity of the scoreless Kaaba-coloured sky. Qaanaaq becomes a cluster of yellow lights huddled together, an army of receding fireflies dwindling in the distance over the brow of a hill, irrelevant compared to this natural light display. Enveloped in nature's ambiguous force, we hie through a city of twisted buildings made of ice: for weeks and months, distant objects through the lens of my binoculars, now up close, magnified and real. The ice surrounding the icebergs is thin and light blue. We do not find any Greenlandic Sharks. The bait is still on the hooks. We return empty-handed, but I have been shown another world of ice and mystery which will be my playground in the coming weeks and months. On our next trip, we will be hunting seal. On the way back to the hut, I climb the slippery slope up to the church. The light is on at the chapel, the tiny shed next to the church, telling the community that a body is lying there. None of the Inugguit have mentioned this death to me.

The most effective way to hunt seal during the dark period (*kapirdaq*) is to lay nets at their breathing holes. That is our task a week later. Sat on the spider-man rug on the floor, Iggiannguaq is repairing a hole in his *nannut*. After a brief conversation comprising a series of raised eyebrows and soft, drawn-out *iih*, we go straight down to the ice where we harness up nine dogs, all males except for one female. Putting a harness on a snarling, excitable male Greenlandic Dog is no straightforward business. One has to hold the dog's head firmly between one's legs with his back between your legs and then try and work out in which hole the dog's head and legs go. The hunters tell me that they have never seen somebody get it right first time, and I was no exception.

Tantalising glimpses of the full moon flicker through the cloud cover. The December shore ice is quite thin and very slippery. Once we are a few hundred metres or so from the town, the ice improves. Suddenly, the dogs are pulling and I have a split second to jump onto the sledge. It is tremendous to be out on the ice again: the familiar soft, scraping sound of the sled runners on the *hiku*, the vastness of the frozen sea and the insignificance of a solitary head-torch bumping along in a dark, refrigerated wilderness. The unmechanised bliss and simplicity of this kind of travel provide a nostalgic warmth to my soul. The dogs are pulling well. We travel twenty miles or so from Qaanaaq, passing haunting icebergs: ancient sculptures with artistic excrescences towering in the darkness. Radiating from the icebergs like a vein of a leaf, leads (*ainniq*) stretch out into the white expanse. Iggiannguaq jumps off and guides his dogs around the thin ice. We stop and lay three seal nets (*qassutit*). To break the ice we use a steel rod with a pointed end. It is very hard work and we take it in turns: the ice is 50 centimetres thick in this part of the bay. That is considerably deeper than three weeks ago. Once we have made a hole through the ice, we shovel out all of the slush as quickly as possible before it starts to refreeze. We follow this procedure three times before lowering the net down the middle hole.

The net is attached to two poles either side of the peripheral holes. The idea is that the seal swims into the net and gets tangled up. The seal dies because it has to come up for air every fifteen minutes. Even when the sea ice is thick, Ringed Seals are still able to keep small breathing holes open by using their heads which must rapidly become a perpetual battle. Once the seal has drowned, it is pulled up by dragging the net through the middle hole. The net is not really a trap, but is more of an underwater fence pulled across under the ice.

We are out on the ice for four hours and get within seven or eight miles from Herbert Island. The open sea is apparently very close, but it seems implausible. The ice is thin and we are surrounded by massive icebergs whose jagged outlines can just about be made out in the polar darkness. We cannot go any further. We return in silence. Iggiannguaq is a man of few words, but his kind face speaks volumes. By the time we make it back to Qaanaaq, the time is 5pm. The fantastic glow from the full moon lights up the whole bay. The light is soft and mysterious with its soothing bluish tones. The dogs are fed again on the ice and seem to be starving. Their eyes glow in the dark; their eyeshine is haunting and surreal. Tomorrow is the shortest day and then after that the light will begin to return which is quite a relief. The winter solstice is reason to celebrate. I have climbed a mountain of darkness and now lying on the anvil of beginnings I can begin very slowly the descent. From now on, it will get a bit lighter each day. The faculae of the occasional magnificent half-moon and Venus casting her light in the western sky might provide relief on the odd day. If you have not experienced it before, it is inevitable, however, that three and half months of darkness will tamper with your mind and leave you feeling drugged and drowsy. Swaddled in Erebus, my view has been at times monochromatic blackness. Deprived of light, my head was sore. The days and weeks would trudge by, but still no sun. Drowsiness and the exigencies of solitude weighed upon me. Hankering after light, I was offered light treatment for Seasonal Affective Disorder at the hospital in Qaanaaq, but to have allowed myself this would have felt like cheating to me. By January and towards the end of my stay in the town, I felt as if I had interiorised the Cimmerian darkness whose toil in this wintry adagio was becoming never-ending and which left my mind addled and somewhere else. I began to count the days left until the return of the sun. No dawn, no dusk, you begin to wonder how long is a day in the dark? It was only when an elusive sun returned on the 18th of February that my pallid face awoke from this lethargic dream and eternal slumber.

There is an annual celebration on the shortest day of the year. The hall is absolutely packed with people: a giant game of *yatzy* with about one hundred children standing round in a circle is being played. Upstairs, children hack away with axes at raw musk-oxen, deer and narwhal carcasses all laid out on the floor. Sitting on plastic sheets, frozen Arctic Char is on offer alongside a variety of frozen meats. There are also hot dog sausages with mustard and dried onions: a nod to the Danes in what is otherwise an extraordinary authentic, indigenous feast.

In the days leading up to Christmas, the shop was heaving with people buying '*kadluna* food'. I must have heard hunters tell me *neqi kadlunap ajorpoq* ('white man's food is bad') a hundred times, but here they were queuing to buy as much of it as they could. If there was ever any doubt as to whether this was still a pseudo-subsistence economy, now there can be none. On a much smaller scale, this reminded me so much of the absurd consumerism in the UK which has destroyed the spirit of Christmas. Many were stocking up, buying goodies to give to people who come round to the homes dressed up in disguise for Twelfth Night (*mitaaqtuq*). Visits to the shop were often a circus of practical jokes with male shopkeepers pinching my bottom and then hiding and people putting things in my shopping (such as tampons) when I am not looking. Snared by their blitheness, it is clearly appreciated that the *kadluna* does not mind always being the object of mockery.

It is at this time of the year that people are particularly needy, emotionally and otherwise. At my lowest point in terms of frustration, I felt as if I was practically running an orphanage, spending so much time with the children who wished to constantly come and visit me. The complete lack of privacy – a strange word in these parts – became rather overwhelming even if I very much enjoyed being with the children, playing, laughing, joking and trying to pronounce their language which was always a source of much amusement to them. The adults consider directness socially crass and most communication is circumlocutory, using conditional phrases, studied silences, pregnant pauses and indirect speech in order to avoid giving the impression that any one person is determining the course of events for others. Unsurprisingly, the major exception to that are of course the children who would ask any number of direct questions.

It is unbearable for the Inugguit to be separated from kith and kin. For somebody like myself to have done so voluntarily was unfeasible for them, and this sense of strangeness was particularly acute at Christmas time. Isolation for the Inugguit is social death. 'Isolating' myself from friends and family as I effectively did for a year would be intolerable for them. For the Inugguit, 'Being-in-the-world' is defined in terms of being with others, being with family. Christmas is celebrated with a dinner on Christmas Eve after two services in the church, one for children and one for everybody else. It is now Christmas Eve and after a supper of divine Caribou, the gospel of St John is read over the Advent Crown in my cosy, Advent-red, candle-lit, window-frosted room.

Christmas Day is devoted to visiting friends and family, going from hut to hut. Much of my time was spent with Susanne, baking, making Christmas decorations, playing a variety of games and of course writing down words. She wanted to spend all her time with me and I was very pleased for her company. Entering people's homes, coffee and a variety of cakes will be neatly laid out and the Inugguit will be dressed in their finery. This is the only time of the year where saucers are used and where the tubs filled with thawing meat and blubber are suddenly absent. Everything will be very tidy and seem more Danish than Greenlandic.

Christmas having come and gone, I awake to the crumpled blackness of the night sky and to the sound of fireworks (*hirhaqtuq*). It is 11am and New Year's Eve. The temperature in the hut drops further overnight, and it is 6.2 degrees. In the morning, it is only about -8 degrees outside. There were a number of fireworks at 9pm to celebrate the Danish New Year, but the fireworks at midnight were quite extraordinary, competing with any capital city in the world and yet this is a town of 650 people. I wonder if the town's budget for 2011 was blown in ten minutes flat. The fireworks are lit outside people's homes, just a few metres away from people and not the requisite thirty metres. No health and safety regulations here. There are fireworks all around us, the finest immediately behind my house. The display lasts for a full twenty minutes and is quite splendid.

Shortly after midnight, the neighbours (the Karlsens) walk over and offer their hand, wishing Susanne and I *Ukioqtarmik pi'dluarit* ('Happy New Year'). Taking the hand, the tradition is to say this to everybody whom you meet on this day and for the next few days. Throughout the course of the evening, I must end up saying this phrase to a couple of hundred people as everybody I meet offers their hand. I can see that the Inugguit revel in this tradition and do not tire of it. These kind of customs have a distinct appeal in a time when their own indigenous traditions have become hazy in the mist of the past, ebbing away, writhing like a Halibut on the ice. At the bar, the atmosphere is rather oppressive. I am surrounded by pervading slurs and blenched by fixed stares as the Inugguit emerge from bosky Bingo. A moving song is sung about the Inugguit, the place where they live and the fact that they have only ever known peace.

Outside, it could be a scene from *Dr Zhivago* with the easterly *nigeq* rapidly whipping into a full-force gale, assaulting sore heads and fuddled minds. Throughout the afternoon, the house is buffered again by a storm as the New Year is blown in with new paradigms from the East. The whole house shakes and the wind makes a tremendous screeching noise, blowing down the chimney. The hinged, wooden flap at the top of the steps whose purpose is to prevent the dogs coming up onto the balcony, makes a loud clacking noise increasing in tempo, faster and faster, until it is blown off its hinges and fed to the swirling scherzo. I go outside to try and get some video footage and meet a small, cheeky boy whom I have seen before. Burying our heads into our scarves to quickly gasp some air, the whipping wind bars an abortive attempt at conversation, but we share a grin in the squall and a smile of solidarity in the face of the elements. We stand with our backs to the wind, barely being able to stand up. He loses his hat and I jib after it, but it is too late and is soon skirting rooftops and chimneys. The dogs have fallen silent amidst the chaos. Further down the track, a few souls under siege, huddle and cower with coats pulled up over their heads. Like an ill-formed testudo, they shield themselves, shuffling to a nearby shelter.

The storm continues unabated throughout the day. Magnus has navigated himself through the windy reverie and perches himself by the oil heater, with his perpetual grin and his hand over the heater, saying *ajor* and then laughing aloud. A garrulous wind chats down the chimney. All of his front teeth are missing, the result of a drunken encounter that ended up not in his favour. He is most content, playing with my toy wind-up penguins (*iharukitsoq* – 'that which does not have wings'). Time and time again, he winds up the two diminutive, black-and-white toys, placing one upon the other, simulating the missionary sexual intercourse position and then chuckles to himself. His constant visits comprise long, grinning silences interspersed with talk about women and sex. He would walk into the house, point to the bed and say *id'di quassi?* ('you, how many?') and then guffaw. Despite our very different backgrounds, we bonded over these first few months in the most unique of ways and spent a great deal of time together.

Later in the afternoon, Susanne comes to visit. As always, she is happy just to do drawings and spend the best part of an hour scraping off dried candle wax from candlestick holders. Boredom is a modern problem: previously, they were just busy trying to stay alive. Over a supper of musk-oxen steaks, Susanne tells me how she is so bored in Qaanaaq and that 'Greenland is a stupid country'. She insists that she wants to go to Denmark and that all her friends have left Qaanaaq except for me. It seems that she always makes friends with people who are from other places or who have connections with other places. Her best friend from Qaanaaq is currently living in Norway, but she does not know where. The story is heartbreaking. She feels trapped here and I fully sympathise with her. She is so different from other members of the community her own age, actually rather exceptional. In her Christmas card to me, she wrote that her dream was that I could be her father. As has so often happened in the past after having spent a pleasant evening here, she asks if she can stay with me and move in. The Greenlanders fear sleeping alone. Many of them are worried about spirits, ghosts, etc.

On the 6th of January in the late morning the lower stratum of sky is a pomegranate red. Slowly, but surely a cosmic fire creeps above the horizon like an atomic empyrean. It is baffling and utterly mesmerising. My neighbour, Avatannguaq, tells me that such a sky is inexplicable so early in the year. Increasingly, celestial phenomena are occurring which the local people cannot account for. People stare upwards at a red sky. Nobody can provide an explanation for the fact that the sky is red as we have not seen the sun for over two months. People joke that there must be another atomic explosion at Pituffik, but this is surely another nameless Arctic celestial phenomenon. Helge tells me that he is not surprised and that he has seen blue sunsets and green flashes of the sun here in Qaanaaq before.

I discuss the phenomenon with Josef who enjoys telling me that he is an *heqaijuk* ('a lazy, apathetic person'). He complains that it is too dark to go hunting, that there are too many polar bears, etc. Extraordinary excuses: I wonder what his ancestors would have made of that. They lived at a time when survival meant that such choices were not available. Well, the polar bears will not stop me. I have borrowed from Rosa Jensen a Marlin883SS .22 (caliber) Magnum bolt-action rifle with low recoil and a Nikko Sterling scope. It is true that the polar bears have now come down from the Kane Basin and the bear-hunting season has begun with two bears being hunted in Qeqertat and Haviggivik respectively; a Snowy Owl has been spotted near the airstrip.

It is Twelfth Night (*mitaartut*). Children are dressed in epiphanic disguise as mummers, wearing black capes and grotesque masks. It looks exactly like Halloween. To dress up in disguise for Twelfth Night is called *mitaartut* and it is a celebration to mark the end of Christmas. Christmas decorations are still hung up in people's homes, but soon they will come down. The idea of the *mitaartut* is that children go from house to house in disguise and if you cannot guess who it is, then you have to give them a gift. Twelfth Night is cause for another New Year's Eve style celebration: Orsino, Viola and Cesario frolic on the sea ice where fireworks gong Christmas to an end. People light two candles in the windows of their houses; others light candles outside their homes. Else has turned lumps of fresh water ice (*nilak*) used for drinking water into two very ornate miniature igloos with lights inside.

With the slightest glimmer of light, I started making preparations to go out onto the sea ice on my own. I was feeling claustrophobic living in a town, enveloped in darkness, prompting gossip every time I walked out to the cemetery or the airfield. By the beginning of January, I was itching to get out of the town and explore the frozen planet. The old name for January is *qaamaaliaq* meaning the 'month where the sun begins to come back'. Parts of West Greenland were at this time getting the sun back and inevitably the return of the sun started to become my sole focus even if it were still a few weeks away. The sun rose two days earlier than usual over Illulissat. This has never happened before and the best explanation is that the melting of the ice cap has meant that the horizon is lower. If so, this would be shocking proof of global warming.

A few months into the fieldwork, the issue of payment for data remains a very fraught issue. I was beginning to feel quite exploited and regrettably could not dismiss the notion that some of the locals were out for revenge when it came to the *kadluna*. Now that I was reasonably well known in the community, Susanne and I went round every house in Qaanaaq with a letter carefully drafted by the Language Committee which I had formed explaining the language documentation work and how I intended on going about it. The meetings would typically be inquorate: no excuses, no apologies, just empty chairs. Empty workplaces, but no comment or cavil from one's peers; silence in a stony place is the apotheosis of expression.

On these visits to people's homes, I would explain in Polar Eskimo what the letter was about and why it was important we tried to document the knowledge bound up in the language whilst we could. Susanne would stand behind me, grinning, correcting my faulty Polar Eskimo as I went along. It took three days in total going from one house to another in temperatures of -25 degrees with a strong, biting wind in your face that felt like the *piteraq* – the very strong, cold, katabatic wind on the Greenlandic Ice Sheet which originates on the East Coast of Greenland. Jibbed at the threshold by lost faces, I was greeted for the most part during these visits with blank expressions and eyes that saw straight through me. The occasional person would take an inordinate amount of time to read the letter before nodding silently in agreement.

Working with Ingeborg on the language intensively for a month was fascinating, enabling me to get a clearer picture of how language reflects culture, but also the immediate natural environment. For instance, there are relatively few colour terms in Polar Eskimo. There is no word for 'orange' or 'pink' even though these words would be most useful to describe the Arctic sunsets. Instead, one speaks of 'dark yellow' or 'light red'. About 30 or 40 per cent of the lexicon I compiled from my older informants is not understood by Variety A speakers, i.e. those under the age of 50. In particular, the very rich Polar Eskimo lexical domains regarding hunting, traditional way of life, climate and weather conditions are not being passed on to Variety A speakers.

As well as language, we discuss of course culture and the way of life 'up here'. She tells me how difficult life used to be. Up until the 1950s, life expectancy was just over thirty years. Today, it is twice that. This is a sobering thought for those who believe that the Inugguit would have been best left alone. Even if there have been many costs and problems, the investment by the Danes in the 1950s resulted in a significant improvement in the standard of living for the inhabitants of north-west Greenland.

Like many here, Ingeborg loves to gossip, but now for the first time I am treated more like an 'insider' on the gossip. She explains the dynamics between the different families and how some are more at the centre of Qaanaaq life than others. She cannot understand why the Imiina family apparently keep themselves to themselves (but that was not my impression). Ingeborg tells me how I need to be careful with some of the people that are coming to the house. In her view, Avataq Dunneq, the schizophrenic who visits the house occasionally is 'dangerous'. Taiko Peary has previously broken into her house and she thinks that the situation that is developing with Susanne who calls up sometimes several times a day now to ask if she can visit to be also 'dangerous', but for quite different reasons. For some time, I have been concerned about the latter and the manner in which she has attached herself to me. We have now got to the point where she wants to spend all her time with me. I know very well how sensitive and fragile these communities are and wonder how she will cope when I leave. I discuss the situation at length with Ingeborg and others who I have come to know and whose opinion I value. Ingeborg spotted a drawing that Susanne left on the table. It is a picture of her and me standing at the airport in Qaanaaq with our names in bubbles, hand-in-hand, off on our travels together. She is such a caring, loving girl and I know that this drawing depicts her ultimate ambition: to leave the town and discover another world with me as her guardian. For her not to get hurt, I have to now 'manage' the relationship by putting a bit of distance between us and not letting her visit every day. One hates to do that as she is so kind and loving, but in the long run it might be in her interest.

My other best friend is a pregnant bitch who follows me everywhere I go and sits on my balcony, howling late into the night. I don't know her name, but she is referred to as *hingaiggoq* ('pregnant dog'). The females become very clingy when they are pregnant and she is trying to seek out the best place to give birth. By the time she does so, it will be rapidly approaching the coldest time of the year. It is now -21 degrees and the temperature is falling fast. The boarding has come away around the sides of the hut and the dog is scouting around down there under the house, looking for a place to give birth.

Even for the Inugguit, the level of gossip can sometimes become too much and utterly stifling leaving them wanting to leave the town. With the establishment of the Free Church, much of the gossip is now channelled into the subject of religion and the activities of Naaja and Qillaq Qaerngaq who have been ostracised by some for being 'too' religious. In such a small society, there is a pressure to conform to the local norms. Ingeborg would get upset if I told her that I had speaking to other people about language issues. She thinks it is best if I just speak to her.

In the third week of January, I awake to a raddled sky with an orange tinge on the horizon and a small patch of blue. A tantalising wafer of light, a transient smidge of unaudited hope peeks through the infinite ether. Then, celestial curtains close the brief skylight and Orion is wheeled on at two in the afternoon. And then, oneiric nights and at dawn more talk of dreams. On these mornings, the view was exactly as it was in the last week of October and the first week of November. The hummocky sea ice and icebergs, hidden in the darkness for months, are slowly coming back into view. Teams of dun, anxious dogs with cambered backs skulking on the ice can be just about identified. The sense of familiar circularity is very welcoming. The small amount of light makes all the difference to my mood: I am over the worst of the dark period now and can begin to really enjoy life here again. Three months of no sun have left me with an ashen white face, dirty blond hair, patches of psoriasis on my hands and scalp and the burden of pessimism, but a fire is now raging beneath the horizon. Treating the psoriasis, every morning I would take an ice pick and break up the ice which would freeze overnight in the water tank in the bathroom, warm up the water, strip down and wash my hair in the sink of the frozen kitchen: a hapless chore. But, there is no chance of doing a Blighty now. I miss the rain, I miss the grass, I miss the soft chime of the Oxbridge College Chapel bell. I have been lost in the indeterminate shadowlands where there is neither sunrise nor sunset. Not being able to cast a shadow, I have felt at times less than alive, sleeping 12 hours a day. Approaching the end of the dark period, constant tiredness is, however, now turning into insomnia.

Outside, it is -28 degrees and the temperature is expected to drop further. With the colder weather, I have started to eat much more, burning off more fat, trying to stay warm. When it is this cold, water forms on the eyelashes and freezes, gluing my eyelashes together within minutes. Adapted perfectly to the cold, the Inugguit with the tiniest of eyelashes do not have this problem. Ittukusuk Kristiansen finds much amusement in seeing me thaw my eyelashes over hot coffee in his over-heated living room. It is another opportunity for them to show their superiority over the European. Not only their mindset, but their phys-iognomy is the result of living for centuries in a hostile climate. Some, like Ingeborg, have connected earlobes.

Perched on the sofa, Ittukusuk is repairing rows of fishing hooks. As I enter the room, he lurches towards me, trying to attach one of the hooks to the groin part of my trousers and then laughs boorishly. Today, he is in very high spirits. Big and jolly with a tremendously dirty, sordid, sort of Benny-Hill sense of humour, he quips constantly, asking me how many women I have had in Qaanaaq and how many girls I have in England. The conversation is one long sexual innuendo. Back at the hut, I throw the dirty dishwater off the balcony in the evening, a drop of about eight or nine feet and it cracks when it hits the ground. Within a fraction of a second, the water has frozen to a solid.

Ingeborg and others with whom I have worked were always keen to address the prejudices that the outside world have of the Inuit. They feel misunderstood and in many respects they are. Visitors and researchers insist on getting even fundamental things wrong. Despite the claims of many, the Inugguit have never lived in igloos. Snow igloos were/are used on hunting trips, but never as any permanent form of accommodation; there are not a hundred words for snow, etc. Journalists and writers such as Gretel Ehrlich always talk in sensationalist terms about travelling in temperatures of 50 degrees below, but it very seldom gets colder than -35 degrees. Ingeborg was always telling me how much colder it used to be. Unlike in North America, there are no 'Elders' in this indigenous community. Ingeborg loves to talk about the past and remembers the sense of amazement at being able to turn a switch and a see a light come on in Qaanaaq. She did not believe such things were possible. The only thing that Ingeborg misses about the old days is her parents.

At the beginning of February, it was -30 degrees outside and I was getting through over 80 litres of oil a week, trying to heat the hut.

Everything is now frozen in the kitchen and bathroom: the water tank, the water in the sink, the water in the hand-washing bowl, all liquids in bottles, washing-up-liquid, toothpaste, etc. All solid. The curtains are frozen to the wall and ice is appearing on the inside of the window frame. The pillow feels like a frozen, hard rock. Even if it feels like I am living in the ice palace out of *Dr Zhivago*, I am in good spirits. Visitors to the hut would complain of the terrible cold and shout *id'di Eskimo* ('you Eskimo') and then roar with laughter. Everybody is now talking about Stiffi living in the freezing hut.

In the early afternoon, the light is such that one can see clearly the slopes behind the town for the first time since the beginning of November. The jet-black Ravens hidden in the darkness for so long are once again visible as their velvety, ebony wings come into view. Bit-by-bit, a new, but familiar frozen world is opening up for me. Curled-up dogs lie in large circles on the hummocky shore ice, their rusty chains leading from a spike frozen into the ice like spokes on an old, buckled wheel. Jaundiced patches of urine and dog faeces decorate the ice, tampering with its aesthetic of purity. Almost all the dogs are on the ice now. There is a hive of activity. Hunters dressed in skins are coming and going like commuters criss-crossing the concourse at King's Cross Station in London. Muffled figures in an early February liminal light shuffle in the penumbra whose in-betweenness is neither one thing nor the other: a twilight of imprecision and vagueness. Tinctured skies are hidden behind a blurred white nothingness.

As I arrive, Iggiannguaq turns up with some fish to feed his dogs. With this team of seventeen dogs, he caught his first polar bear on 30th of January not far from the town. A pin-balled conversation reveals that the ice is at least 50cm thick and goes beyond Herbert Island. Behind us dog teams pull heavy sledges in silence, weaving their way through the stained shore ice rubble. The sound of sledge runners on the ice is like the steady rhythmic chug-chug-chug of a sleepy night train disappearing into the distance. Frozen dining cars snake their way along well-defined tracks and icy sleepers, rekindling a dying romance.

Keen to discover the stillness and ethereal beauty of the new frigid blanket of ice that lies before me, I do a recce on skis, rifle slung over my shoulder. The first few hundred metres is very heavy going, clambering over collided sheets of ice jutting up in the air. Bleached battleships of ice rise out of the sea. The scene is reminiscent of Caspar David Friedrich's The Sea of Ice or a twisted, fractured road following a major earthquake in the months of winter. Beyond the first 500 metres of shore ice pressure ridges, the sea ice is absolutely flat. There is very little snow on the ice; the surface is hard and unforgiving. With the exception of the occasional patch of inelastic, young grey ice, the view is miles of unrelentness whiteness. It feels like a heavenly view created by my poetic imagination. There is nowhere to hide. There are few signs of life. Aside from the parallel sledge runner tracks, the dog and the Boeing 787-shaped Raven footprints, there is absolutely nothing. I feel free at last.

The sky is that haunting and delicate, deep Arctic twilight gauzy blue. Pushing with my poles diagonally opposite to my Rossignol Classic NIS skis, I find the steady rhythm of classic cross-country skiing. With a slight tailwind, I head in the direction of Herbert Island, the frozen Mecca, getting about half way. Losing my nerve a bit, being out on here on my own for the very first time, the incoming cloud cover prompts me not to push my luck any further. On the way back, the weather deteriorates slightly and visibility is restricted. Double stride, double poling, I up the tempo and focus on the icebergs ahead which I use as beacons, weaving my way through them, avoiding the thinner ice around the edges. I have waited for months to step out on the ice with my skis and experience a freedom as boundless as my memory in a place where it is only the sounds of nature, the wind and the creaking ice that speak to me and tell me stories. I have entered a new fantastic, sublime world. For a moment, it is as if the world is empty of people. It is difficult to believe that there are billions of people living and sleeping below me in cramped poverty, just adding more to the daily misery. To rise above this chaos feels like the greatest privilege. The sea ice has been here since December, but now we have the light and there is nothing more to stop me. Already in my head I am hatching a plan to ski to Herbert Island and stay in Wally's old house there.

I see a sledge pass by in the distance. A team of dogs pulls a silent hunter across the sea ice. Its primeval simplicity, but also its timelessness takes one far away from noisy engines and mechanical toys which disturb the sense of equilibrium. There is something majestic about the sight of a solitary Polar Eskimo driving a dog team across the frozen sea ice, navigating his way around icebergs, sitting contentedly, listening to the crunch of the runners on the snow and reading the wind from the *aijupinak* ('striae') on the ice. He reads the ice with refined ken, not from books. It is a short trip, but I enjoy it immensely. The combination of the appeal of a risk, the unknown, and the silent, white wilderness makes for a cocktail so enticing that one almost trembles at the knees with anticipation.

There are some adjustments to be made with the strap of the gun which has really cut into my shoulder, but the combination of base layers and outer layers was about right. On my way back to the hut, I stop off at Eva's house where I am offered part of the boiled arm of the polar bear which Ole caught. She serves it with rice and a yellow, saffron sauce. It tastes very much like mutton – a bit stringy, dense in texture and a little coarse and heavy. There is no pungent smell or after taste. I did well to turn when I did. In the evening, the town is battered by the *nigeq* again, the easterly wind that brings snow. The wind brings warmer temperatures too and within two hours the temperature has risen a full twenty degrees and the frozen hut has turned once again into a sauna. The West Greenlandic news on the television in the evening lasts eleven minutes and there are two news stories. The first news story is seven minutes long and is about the problem of dog poop in Nuuk.

Down at the shore the next day, Iggiannguaq is busy getting the dogs ready. They are excited and the normal chaos prevails as we assemble the team, picketed two-by-two at each stake. They are fed and socialised in pairs, often one dominant and one submissive. Newcomers are seldom accepted in a pack. Leashing all the dogs to the fan-hitch is always the hardest point as the social structure of the dog team is put to the test with respective dogs questioning positions in the relevant hierarchy of the fan. I tell Susanne to ask Iggiannguaq whether she can come along and he says *na'aa*. That is rather harsh and I am puzzled as to why he would say 'no'. I wonder if he thinks hunting is the domain of men and that girls should stay at home, or perhaps he wants to bond with me. She looks terribly disappointed and it is rather embarrassing. As we unleash the dogs, jealousy boils over and the dogs begin to fight. Scolding and chiding the dogs for their disputes, rivalry and love interests, Iggiannguaq loses his temper with the scrum of snarling fur. Bellowing orders to sit (*aulaitsit*) and with a long whip swishing and cracking just an inch or so above their heads, the dogs cower and finally the social hierarchy is reinstated. We need to move fast now before the fighting begins again. A few seconds before we launch ourselves onto the accelerating sledge, Iggiannguaq tells Susanne that she can join us. *Ikigit* he shouts, and she jumps onto the sledge.

We head into the fjord, eastwards. The ice is hummocky at first, crumpled, warped and challenging, but then it is perfectly flat like a smooth, oblate stone. With a fresh layer of snow on top of the ice from the *nigeq*, the conditions are excellent for dog sledging because the new snow provides a soft blanket over the *puqaq* ('the granulated sharp snow crystals which hurt dogs' paws'). With twelve dogs and a light sledge we are moving fast. Following the frantic kerfuffle on the shore ice, two of the twelve dogs came unharnessed and run along side the sledge. They will not go in front of the lead dog (*ittuqut*), but run just behind him, careful not to undermine his leadership. Even if they are not harnessed, their instinct is to run and stay with the pack.

Far in the distance sits an *i'duaq* ('a hut built on a sledge where you can escape the cold on fishing trips'): a small speck on a landscape of white nothingness. We travel for about fifteen minutes before we come to the two tiny mobile huts, several hundred metres apart. Outside the huts, deep sea heavy duty fishing reels are attached to stakes locked into the ice. In this part of the bay, the sea ice is about a metre thick and making a hole in the ice with a shovel is hard work. At these temperatures, it is a battle to make a hole before it starts refreezing. The lines are lowered to about two hundred metres. Iggiannguaq attaches twenty-five short subsidiary lines and uses a stone as a weight. Small bits of Halibut are used for bait. It is all very straight forward. Once the lines are lowered, Susanne and I sit in the hut where there are two large Primus heaters placed in front of a tiny sleeping platform covered in skins. The huts are made of ply-board and have two tiny windows. It is cramped, measuring just seven feet square, but remarkably cosy. Iggiannguaq sits outside on his sledge, drinking tea from his Thermos. I have no tea and am not offered any. Few words are exchanged.

Iggiannguaq thinks he might have spotted a polar bear. He is not joking. I cannot see anything. He does not wear glasses and has extraordinary eyesight. After a few moments, I do, however, spot a black snout way in the distance. Occasionally, dogs break loose from their harnesses and run off. Normally they can follow a scent and make it back to

Qaanaaq, but tens of miles from the nearest settlement they are likely to die on the sea ice. The Inugguit senses are very refined; they can connect the 'seen' with the 'unseen'. Gilberg's tests show that the eyesight of some hunters is roughly twice as good as the average *kadluna* who does not wear glasses. They also have a refined sense of smell. If I wore eau-de-Cologne, the women would screw up their faces and make a tremendous fuss. They found it unnatural and disgusting. Pouring the twenty litre jerry can of oil into the tank for the heater, I would often spill some, missing the funnel or slightly over-filling the tank. The Inugguit who came to visit would act in the same way, screwing up their faces and complaining about the smell even if I were barely aware of it.

Iggiannguaq has gone to the other hut, apparently not wanting our company. After several games of cards, Susanne and I decide to join him. Approaching the hut, I hear the creaky voice of a man and offer the traditional greeting of *inugguarunai* on entering (this is a word used by older people to mean 'hello', but means literally 'look, there are some people' – an indication perhaps of how language reflects culture). Going inside this diminutive raised room perched on a sledge is a surreal experience and one of those defining moments of a fieldwork trip. Here, miles from anywhere on the frozen sea in a forgotten place, lies Piitannguaq Kristensen asleep on a skin on the sleeping platform. Three men, clad in bearskin trousers and reindeer skin anoraks, sit huddled together listening to a storyteller regale his company with an account of a polar bear hunt. It is rude to interrupt a story and thus my greeting is not reciprocated with the conventional *ahukiaq*. There is nowhere to sit and even though my head rests awkwardly on the ceiling of the hut and my bulky down coat fills the little remaining space, I feel paradoxically rather invisible. Disengaged faces puzzle the Western mind. When stories are offered for payment, it is tempting to think of this oral literature as commoditised and effectively dead. But, here on hunting trips, these traditions do just about continue in an unforgettably unique atmosphere of breathy voices lingering over steaming cups of cha. The story over and it is time to check our lines, leaving the fugitive hospitality behind. We have caught seventeen Greenland Halibut and one Northern Wolffish: a splendid return for two hours tea-drinking. Despite the ease of fishing, most Inugguit are reluctant to give up hunting to focus on this. Hunters might spend weeks looking for the elusive walrus and come back empty handed, but a real hunter does not fish (unless he has to).

Reharnessing the dogs proves to be quite a challenging chore. This time two male dogs are fighting, neither wishing to be subordinate. Iggiannguaq smacks the culprit with a steel rod. The dog screams. He has had enough and starts whipping them. They cower and huddle together in a small group, absolutely petrified. Eventually, we are off. He tells me to hop on but I misunderstand him. The sledge spins round so fast and I am left running with all my might after the rapidly disappearing stanchions, much to the mirth of Susanne who finds the whole business very entertaining. We arrive back in Qaanaaq under a pink sky. Iggiannguaq tells me it is a sign the sun will soon return. The porch of his house smells of blood and pungent sea mammals. Leaving the grey-coloured doll's house, I have a sudden pang of consciousness. The smell triggered something and I suddenly ask myself what it means to be in Greenland.

Strolling down to the shore, I try and articulate my thoughts on this subject. It is the smells of blood and blubber, but perhaps first and foremost the sounds of the dogs barking and howling, dotting the snow-covered landscape. The sky is cloudy and the view over the fjord is one of whiteness, snow, ice, icebergs, hummocks and rubble, peeking through strips of grey-white cloud in the distance. It is utterly wild. There is a sense of 'living on the edge'. It is the precariousness of life, but also the immediacy of nature. That feeling is very strong here, both physically and psychologically. This is a tiny place on the edge of an ice sheet. The sea ice emphasizes that sense of wilderness in the way that the open sea does not. The open sea shows a way out to another world, whereas the never-ending white of the sea ice is an unknown whose foundations maybe shaky. It is the sense of dysfunctionality found in the clutter outside people's homes and the shabby, worn appearance of the housing which in a way has its own appeal. Or at least, if everything were shiny and functional, I would feel as if I were somewhere else. But, it is also, the sense of communality. There are no street or house names. Identity and location of one's homestead is merely expressed in terms of the colour of one's house and the approximate direction in which one lives. The imprecision is significant. Nobody tells you exactly where they live. It will just be *hamani* or *pikani*, demonstratives which exaggerate the distance. The implication is that Qaanaaq has grown big and can no longer be negotiated using more precise orientation terms.

Greenland would not be the same without the dogs, but the numbers of dogs are depleting each year. Down on the west coast, Ummannaq has finally got the sea ice but the decision has been taken to shoot two hundred dogs. If it comes at all, the sea ice is only there for weeks or a couple of months a year, and people cannot afford to keep their dogs for such a short hunting period. The ancient culture of keeping the Greenland dogs will of course die out relatively soon unless climate change can be reversed.

Freuchen (1961: 243) said 'there is no place in the Arctic for weaklings or non-producers'. I was certainly never seen as a weakling, but I was most definitely regarded as a non-producer. And, not unreasonably so. I was not a hunter and was not providing a service of any kind, be it teaching their children, servicing the power station or delivering water. There is little respect for research as it does not meet any immediate needs. However, I was one of many non-producers. Indeed, most of the people living around me were non-producers. But of course I was quite different as it was not my community. I was a visitor and it is expected that visitors are producers of some kind. Otherwise, their presence and contribution is very questionable. By this stage, it was clear to me that the Inugguit are interested mostly in the necessities of life; not the add-ons.

5: Ways of Speaking

With an eye firmly on the horizon, Inukitsoq Dunneq smokes a pipe on the balcony of Aipilanguaq and Equilana Qaavijaq's house. Inukitsoq lives in Hiorapaluk, and is here to visit his sister, Equilana. He does not like life in Qaanaaq and prefers to spend his time in the settlements which are quiet and peaceful. As I pass, he waves at me and says abruptly *kaffi*. Inside, a young hunter sits on the floor of the kitchen, cutting up narwhal into tiny slithers and eating it raw. The remains hang, suspended from the ceiling using a pulley-system. Equilana is rolling cigarettes and her bored granddaughter, Inge, is trying to entertain herself with anything she can. She skips around the living room, breaking wind audibly. Everybody laughs and the windows are opened ajar for ventilation. Somewhat amusingly, she addresses me as *aataq* ('grandfather'). It is not unusual for people of my age to be grandparents in this community. The flickering screen of the silent Danish television programme lights up the room. Glued to pictures, images, and not words, the Danish is not understood and the volume is down. The smiling and cheerful Aipilanguaq Qaavijaq is a joy to be with, helping me patiently with my Inuktun, breaking down the difficult to pronounce words. Syllable upon syllable upon syllable and then breathe. When he speaks, he whispers like the wind through the vents. How can our tongues be so different, we both wonder.

After a while, I am offered *kaffi*. It seems the protocol here is just to help oneself from the pre-prepared Thermos, and not wait to be asked. I want to try the *mattak* ('narwhal skin and blubber') and my request is met with an imperative. Increasingly, I approve of eating raw meat. Every time I offer a Greenlandic phrase, they say *na'aa* ('no') and tell me that is the language of the south. They then offer what they deem to be the correct version – the language of the Thule region. However, they are often reluctant to write these phrases down in Inuktun and not being a standardised, written language they are unsure as to how these words should be spelt. Typically, I am told the word in Inuktun and then the word is written down in Standard West Greenlandic. There is a constant appeal to an Inugguit linguistic identity and the fact that their language is not the one taught in the schools is for some a bone of contention.

The conversation turns to education and the spelling of Standard West Greenlandic. The new orthography which was introduced in the 1970s has made the language quite inaccessible. The previous spelling system was much easier and logical. To indicate vowel length, one would put a circumflex over the relevant letter. Now, the words are so long, Greenlanders themselves stumble over them. The result is that any educated Greenlander would prefer to read a book in Danish than Greenlandic. The Inugguit have little respect for alphabetised understanding – the premise on which their schooling is based. The great majority are literate and have a written norm, but it is a different dialect, the standardised language of West Greenland. When I would ask how a word should be written (*qanuq titaqtutin auna?*), they would either shrug their shoulders and say *nalorrhorruiga* ('I don't know'), or write it in West Greenlandic, reproducing it in West Greenlandic phonology. I was often told that their language *could not* be written. When I would try and write down their words, the Inugguit would shake their heads. They wished me to prioritise the ear and learn their language without resorting to trying to write words down which is a nigh impossible task for somebody steeped in academic learning and a written tradition. For some, there was a distrust of writing as it was symbolic of the Western way of thinking. The feeling was that it was the spoken word that represents the sharedness of basic perceptual experience; the written word objectifies language. Literacy disembodies language, removing it from the body of speaker.

One of the greatest frustrations during my stay was the often lack of engagement from the local community. This issue really came to surface during the dark period. The omnipresence of the word *nalorrhorruiga* ('I don't know') began to blight my stay. This was the standard response to almost every question, making it more or less pointless to ask anything directly. This response can in fact mean a number of different things such as: (1) I could explain it to you, but you would not understand (for reasons of language or culture difference); (2) I do not want to tell you as it is too sensitive; (3) mind your own business (4) that he or she genuinely has not considered the issue and cannot therefore respond to the question because they do not have a view or (5) I cannot comment on it because I have not experienced it, or not been there. The response *nalorrhorruiga* was used for any question which might be perceived to be slightly abstract, or for which the Inugguit had no personal first hand experience. Any questions regarding life after death would for instance be met with this standard response. It was futile to ask such questions. I got the distinct impression that for the Inugguit there was much that would always lie beyond the ability of human comprehension, and therefore there was little point speculating on it. There were days when it was almost impossible to get beyond this wall of *nalorrhorruiga*. The small number of West Greenlanders who were living in Qaanaaq and whom I got to know were also struck by this complete lack of engagement, and the sheer frequency of the use of the word *nalorrhorruiga* became a source of in-jokes between us. This discourse of obfuscation characterised by extreme caution and an inexpressive way of speaking was impossible to circumvent. This was a function of talking to the 'other' and was not determined by subject matter which might have been considered to be 'sensitive'. For instance, informants wished invariably to talk about sex and personal issues. A person with good verbal skills was seen as somebody who could bring a sense of banter and amusement to the conversation (something which I was apparently good at and that was much appreciated by the local community, by the men at least whose appetite for such repartee is boundless). Laughter is at the centre of any male-male conversation where mockery, teasing and sexual innuendo might be used to enforce social solidarity. Humour strategies amongst the Inugguit are quite different from the West. It is personal in orientation, often explicitly so, especially so if one is a bachelor, and many of the conventions for normal conversation in the Western world do not apply. As a white, male European one is expected to fulfill certain roles in conversation. The issue of learning from observing, watching and listening (and not asking explicit questions) was one of the hardest lessons. Liberman (1985) in his book on interaction in an aboriginal community in central Australia talks about 'congenial fellowship' as a social imperative and the need for a consensus orientated discourse. On occasions, one felt as if the Inugguit were anxious not to break the confines of this socially orientated discourse by going out on a limb and expressing a personal view. But also, there was so much emphasis on non-verbal communication. I came to realise that sometimes my questions had probably already been answered non-verbally and yet a verbal response might have been the only one that seemed definitive to me and thus I had continued to seek it.

Dell Hymes (1974: 445) talked of 'ways of speaking' because he understood that speech is culturally patterned. The Inugguit can be understood to an extent through their 'ways of speaking' and 'ways of knowing'. Using an ethnolinguistic framework, one can do this by employing an *holistic*, phenomenological approach to language and embark on a journey that takes one back to an embodied, experiential conception of language. Merleau-Ponty's approach to such a subject would have been to focus on the immediacy of speech and voice and the primacy of perception as a manifestation of 'Being-in-the-world'. If Merleau-Ponty had been looking for a 'deep structure' in language, it would have been a primordial and not a cognitive one. But before discussing 'ways of speaking', let us first see what we can say about the ethnolinguistic identity of the Inugguit which was a reoccurring subject at such visits. The Inugguit is a self-imposed demonym and means the 'big people'. The language has various names, but is known internationally as Polar Eskimo and is a member of the Eskimo-Aleut family of languages, which to an extent form a dialect continuum around the circumpolar region, reflecting the previous nomadism of some of the Inuit groups. Polar Eskimo is typologically speaking a dialect of Canadian Inuktitut (North Baffin Island dialect) spoken in Greenland. A significant proportion of the population had travelled in various waves of migration, the last of which was in the nineteenth century, across the Smith Sound from Baffin and Ellesmere Islands in Canada to Greenland (probably for hunting reasons). Reflecting the aberrant phonology of the dialect of North Baffin Island, the language is not typically understood elsewhere in Greenland, and this is one of the reasons which makes it rather anomalous. UNESCO considers the language to be 'vulnerable'. The transmission process is intact, but Polar Eskimo has a small number of speakers, and the community *per se* is to some degree threatened by political factors and climate change. Polar Eskimo is spoken in a bilingual, diglossic context:

the language of education, media and the Church is Standard West Greenlandic, a related written language which all the Inugguit speak.

As with many Eskimo-Aleut languages, Polar Eskimo makes use of a small phonemic inventory providing the language learner with the difficulty of a plethora of near-homonyms to distinguish between. The Inugguit are well aware of this and like to invite the learner to mix up words for comedy value. In finding one's way around these, the learner of the Polar Eskimo language is constantly minded of Saussure's structuralist view that the defining feature of phonemes is how they distinguish themselves from other phonemes (Saussure, 1916). To explain the pronunciation of a difficult phoneme, a Polar Eskimo speaker will choose minimal pairs in two or three near-homonyms, so that the very subtle phonemic difference can be heard as in *anaq* ('excrement'); *arnaq* ('woman'); *aniq* ('woman's older brother'); *anuq* ('dog harness'); *angak* ('maternal uncle'); *anngaq* ('woman's brother's child'); *aanaq* ('grandmother'); *amiq* ('skin, hide'); *amauq* ('great grandparent'), etc. This is often done with a rather ribald sense of humour, the speaker choosing near-homonyms, one of which typically refers to genitalia.

In an ethnolinguistic context, a phenomenological analysis would be concerned with the meaning functions of language in its primary character as speech or communication. The chief task of a phenomenology of speech is to regain an awareness of the speaking subject. A phenomenology of speech lends itself to analysing ethnolinguistic identity in this Arctic society for the following reasons: (a) the phenomenological approach to language is based on the paradigm that rejects the subject-object division and the Inugguit are sympathetic to this non-Cartesian way of thinking; (b) gesture and silence which are central to Merleau-Pontian views on language are important features of this linguistic culture; (c) language and nature are enmeshed in the psyche of the Inugguit through an appeal to primordiality, a concept which lies at the heart of Merleau-Pontian phenomenology. In accordance with the view, this enmeshment would be evidenced in the coalescence of the noises of nature, the Arctic landscape, and the sounds of the language, taking us back to the origins of language and poetry in the Heideggerian sense.

There are undoubtedly many complex features that make up any ethnolinguistic identity. By ethnolinguistic identity, I mean 'people's intuitions of social belonging emerging from certain cultural assumptions about language'.[1] Ethnolinguistic identity is not a mechanical institutional fact; it is a fact of a psychosocial sort that has emerged where people ascribe a certain primordiality to language and a certain consequentiality to language difference. The first feature of the Inugguit ethnolinguistic identity is the perception that their language is moulded by nature. Language and nature are for them intertwined. Language is seen as inseparable from the *inuk* and the *inuk* is embedded in the *nuna* ('the local cosmos'). Whilst the *kadluna* draws boundaries between the Self and the world, the Inugguit define their relationship with the cosmos in terms of connections. There is a pervading discourse of harmony and an ideology of unity which links the *inuk* with his natural environment. If the natural environment is an extension of the human mind, then speech is the primary focus of meaning. It would be going too far to say that the Inugguit view their language as emanating iconically from the sounds of nature, but the resemblance of the hissing, palatal fricative sounds with the sounds of the wind are in their view not coincidental either. The Inugguit construe their language as constituting a fundamental basis for their distinction, and this distinction can be mapped onto racial differences. In their view, the *kadluna* language is not equipped for the Arctic environment with its generic terms and lack of semantic specificity. Previously, it was believed that one could not survive in this society without being able to speak the Inuit language as there is so much knowledge bound up in the language. Inversely, one might argue that it is the language that is world creating, just as Heidegger claimed, and their world is different from ours. As Jenkins (2005: 64) tells us, the Copper Eskimos had no generic word for fish, but there were distinct words for 'Arctic Char', depending on whether the speaker meant Arctic Char that were swimming upstream, Arctic Char that were moving down to the sea, or Arctic Char that remained all year in the lake. There are many other examples of this such as all the words for ice formations, but no generic word for snow. The Inugguit differentiate between *aput* ('snow on the ground') and *qaniit* ('falling snow').

1   C.f. Silverstein (2003: 531-57).

Similarly, there are a large number of words for different types of seal, but no one generic word for 'seal'. So, for example, an *uuttoq* is a 'seal that has crept up on the ice to bask in the sun'; *qakiqitoq* 'seal that has crawled up onto the ice'; *puigaqtoq* 'seal that has come up to breathe'; *ippigaqtoq* 'seal that dips its head down while the rest of its body remains on the surface', etc. The Inugguit do not tend to verbalise categories or concepts, but prefer words with internal semantic distinctions enabling them to refer to very specific things. In a pseudo hunter-gatherer society such as this one, there is a premium on specific knowledge and less need for abstract concepts. Much emphasis is placed on movement, direction and location with very frequent use of action verbs, demonstratives and tenses such as the ablative, allative and locative which frame this constant spatial referencing. Describing one's actions and activities, one is always going towards something or moving away from something. This spatial thinking is heavily influenced by the Inugguit hunting culture.

The second feature of Inugguit ethnolinguistic identity is the morphological structure of the language itself which facilitates this great precision. Whilst the Inugguit would not consider themselves poets, the plasticity of their language borne from its morphological structure lends a degree of linguistic innovation and creativity which is poetic in nature. If we take the phrase:

Stiffi, muminguahoq, hinikkadlarhanngaaqihoq 'Stiffi, the one who sleeps all day, he just slept (when he could have been doing something else)'.

This was a phrase that I heard during the dark period when there is no sun for three and half a months and when on average I was sleeping for 12 hours a day. *Stiffi* was my 'nickname' (most people have six different names in addition to nicknames), *-nguaqhoq* is an affix which means 'in a state or position of doing something' and *mumi-* is a stem meaning something that is 'reversed' or 'upside down', the implication being here that a person is fast asleep on his front. The postbase *-ga'dlarhanngaaqi-hoq* means 'is just -ing' (when he could be doing something else) and *hini-* is the stem referring to sleep.

If we are to subscribe to the Inugguit and Merleau-Pontian view of language, then there are reasons why we should think of the Polar Eskimo language as more of a 'being' than a 'thing' or a 'means' (Merleau-Ponty, 1964: 43). To perceive language as a 'being' implies a lack of control which historically has been a hallmark of this society. With a high degree of morpho-semantic plasticity, the language is alive with an ontological dimension and open to new shades of meaning through the addition of potentially a very large number of affixes. This means that language has the ability to surprise, perhaps through the unusual compounding of affixes. Not exactly neologisms as new words are not being 'coined' in any way, these lexical innovations which are based on stems and affixes already used in the language are able to conjure up elaborate images through concise morphological packaging. With a suffixing morphological structure where there tends to be a one-to-one ratio between form and meaning, semantic meaning does not tend to be lost.

In a context of affixation where a basic stem is qualified semantically and grammatically in very complex ways, the value and meaning of lexemes or words in a dictionary sense is very limited. Breaking language up into stems and affixes and conveniently parcelling everything into neat, semantic boxes is for them a meaningless abstraction. Structurally, the language is not static, allowing one to create new words that have never been uttered before, moulding words to precise thoughts through the use of highly productive morphological patterns. For example, one could take the affix -*lugginnaqtoq* 'in vain, not seriously' and add it to a stem where you might not expect it such as *neri-* 'to eat'. It may seem like an unconventional thing to say 'to eat in vain, not seriously', but the fact that *nerilugginnaqtoq* is a 'potential' word in Polar Eskimo is important. In such a language, one can define the stems and affixes but not all the lexemes as one can in English. The morpho-semantic plasticity of the language lends it an unique expressive power by which to articulate social and cultural representations encoded in the Inuit way of knowing.

A polysynthetic language such as Polar Eskimo where words are composed of many morphemes with highly productive morphological patterns presents new grammatical algorithms all the time. Being an agglutinative language, words are formed by gluing lots of segmentable affixes together to create what would be sentences in English. The affixes can be single or compound morphemes and have independent semantic and/or grammatical meaning. There are over four hundred affixes to learn and every verb can conjugate potentially up to seven hundred different ways with thousands of potential compound affixes. With a system of agglutinative affixes, it is possible for words to be at least fifty letters long as in the example below (Fortescue, 1991: 178):

Aivvaqatauqattarhamamhukkalaanga ilaanni, qanuq agkurniggaa taunna aavirhuup amir'dahiunguqpagguaqatauqattarramanngitsurru-ugama nalorrhorruiga

'Although I have taken part in walrus hunts I don't really know about how walruses are divided up since I haven't taken part in hunts involving many people.'

The penultimate word of the sentence is 49 letters long and can be parsed as follows:

amir'dahiu-ngu-qpaggua-qata-u-qattar-rama-nngitsur-ruu-gama

'because I have not taken part in (hunts) many involving so many people'

Many (verbal quantifier stem)-be (infix 'to be' after double vowel)-greatly (quantifier infix)-participant-be-repeatedly (iterative aspect affix)-have (perfective)-not (negation infix)-intensifier-1sg. causative

It should be clear that the Inugguit are conscious of the complexity of such sesquipedalians, but that the complexity only becomes an issue once an attempt is made at writing them down and the words assume a visible independent existence. Few attempts are made at writing the language and in fluent speech, there is no real space between words anyway. The key point here is that in Polar Eskimo, one does not just take down words unthinkingly from the mental shelf and reproduce them. Sometimes, one does that as in non-compositional nouns such as *nanoq* 'polar bear'. But often, one thinks about 'the realities we talk about' to quote Austin (1962: 182) and then shapes the word exactly to the thought. If we take the example of *ihumaninahorjamahunga*. The word *ihumaninahorjamahunga* comprises the stem, *ihumani*, meaning 'thought' followed by three derivational affixes and one inflectional affix, *-na-* means 'in order to', *-hor-* 'open to', *-jama-* means 'want' and *-hunga*, the 1 ps. sg. indicative. There is no dictionary for Polar Eskimo and because it is a whole sentence expressed in one 'phonological word', the meaning had to be explained morpheme-by-morpheme. We, as speakers of heavily codified languages, are used to working with the notion that if we cannot find the word in a dictionary, then we assume that it does not exist and is therefore an incorrect form. If your language has never been codified, it is unlikely you will think in these terms and instead you will shape the word in your head by gluing affixes to a stem.

Here is another example:

haaviniarru'dluuarhinnaqtorleqihoqqahortuuhaaqihor'dluhoq

'and so he had probably begun to be completely deprived of anyone to turn to'

haag-vvik-niar-erut-'dluarhinnaqtoq-leqihoq-qqahoq-tuuhaaqihoq-lu-hoq

This sixty letter word was used by an informant when describing how he felt when he came across a *qivittoq*, an outsider who has been rejected from society and taken on a supernatural guise. It is possible to tailor words so that they can provide the most exact of descriptions, where we would need a whole sentence in English. Absolute referential accuracy can be produced through just one word. And, this is what makes the language so rich, and presumably lends itself to linguistic innovation and creativity. The old Inuktun word for 'bachelor' is *qaangiunniq* which also means 'food that has been kept too long'. This one example shows very clearly how language is a reflection of culture. For the Polar Eskimos, there could be few things worse than to live on your own, without a wife and children. Indeed, the only people that would do so would be folk who were deemed to be past their sell-by date. The old word for chocolate was *qirhauhoq* which probably referred to 'dried blood', the Inugguit perhaps thinking on first glance that that is what chocolate resembled.

As words are constructed on such a morpho-semantic transparent basis, one gets the impression that language and meaning in a Polar Eskimo speaking environment sit almost on top of each other giving the sense that language is perhaps less of a detached object. With gesture acting as an important form of communication in this community too, there is for the Inugguit more the notion of 'generating the world' to quote Lanigan (1972: 84) from the verbal and non-verbal language you use. Speaking Polar Eskimo, words regain their agency because the ready-made meanings are not yet known and thus speech is to a degree deinstitutionalised.

A third feature of their ethnolinguistic identity is the fact that native speakers are very much aware of the non-arbitrariness of their words. The word would be given followed by its literal meaning. I do not wish to suggest that the stem and affixes are independently 'motivated', but when affixes have a compound meaning that is equal to the sum of the parts, as is often the case in polysynthetic languages, collectively and sententially this morphological semantic transparency seems to challenge the conventionally arbitrary nature of the signifier/signified relationship.

If one takes the example *nerrivik*, it is not just a 'table', but is literally a 'place where you eat' coming from the stem *neri-* 'to eat' and *-vik* the nominalizing suffix meaning 'the place' (i.e. 'the place where the food is eaten'). We might take the Saussurean example which he uses to make his point about the arbitrariness of the form-meaning relationship, the word for 'chair', *igguavik*. This comprises the stem *iggua-* 'to sit down' followed by the suffix *-vik*, 'the place where one sits down'. Similarly, the word for 'bed' is *hinigvik* which is made up of the stem *hini-* 'to sleep' and the same suffix *-vik*, meaning therefore 'the place where you sleep'. The word for 'refrigerator' is *ni'dlataaqtitsivik* meaning the 'place where it is rather cold' with the same affix added to *ni'dlataaqtoq* 'is rather cold'.

These words are not arbitrary, but are motivated at the level of the 'word' (and not morpheme). The phonemes chosen to represent the word for 'chair' may well be arbitrary, but the composition of morphemes selected to articulate this are not arbitrary. Unsurprisingly when it comes to loan words, one witnesses arbitrariness in Polar Eskimo. Bloomfield (1995: 145) used the example of 'horse' when talking about arbitrariness of the sign. The Polar Eskimos have never had horses but would use the West Greenlandic word *hesti* which is a Greenlandicised version of the Danish loan-word *hest*. Based on my knowledge of Polar Eskimo alone, it would seem that a language shows relatively less arbitrariness of the sign in the absence of language contact. In the case of Polar Eskimo, there are words that are non-arbitrary, but this does not necessarily make them phono-semantic. Native speakers are very much aware of the non-arbitrariness of their words and break them down morpheme-by-morpheme when explaining the meaning of such words. It is this point which seems significant.

Reading back through a year's worth of fieldnotes, I found time and time again scribbles about the Inugguit having apparently no concept of the 'abstract'. Despite my best efforts, I found it impossible to engage my informants with abstract thoughts. Abstraction is expressed in dreams and other media, but not verbal expression. The Inugguit dream all the time and spend much time talking about their dreams. The dreams are perhaps a condensation of these 'signifiers' which are not expressed verbally. In terms of speech at least, what matters to the Inugguit is first-hand information of the world based on personal experience. They believe that you cannot know something unless you have experienced it. If asked about something they have not experienced, they would typically answer with *nalorrhorruiga* 'I don't know', answer tangentially or give you contradictory information. And, yet, I discovered towards the end of my stay that there is a word for 'abstract'. The word *erqarhautainaq* means literally 'just a thought' and comprises the stem *eqqar-* 'to think about' followed by two derivational affixes. The people told me the word followed by its literal meaning. Once again, it is clear a high degree of semantic transparency is still very present in their conceptualisation of language.

The lack of historical linguistic contact with speakers of other language families means that the language has a pure, primordial feel to it, and surely explains in part the pervading morpho-semantic transparency. If the language of north-west Greenland had been heavily influenced by the colonial language, Danish, which is not the case, it could not have the same sense of lack of arbitrariness as lexical composition in Danish does not have the same transparency. It is possible to create this semantic transparency, but in an artificial context. In doing so, the languages that are subject to these policies (Icelandic, Hebrew and Finnish for example) have a different 'feel' because the purism is contrived and sometimes the result of lexical or morphemic recycling. The Icelanders have a puristic language policy which replaces incoming English words with Icelandic neologisms based on recycled Norse roots.

These words tend to be semantically totally transparent. The word for 'telephone' is *sími* which comes from the Norse word for 'thread', and the word for mobile telephone became *farsími* or literally 'travelling bit of thread', the *far* morpheme coming from the verb 'to travel'. The logical appeal of these neologisms explains in part their success. To some extent, Polar Eskimo and the other dialects of Greenlandic work like this too, but this is more for reasons of lack of contact and takes us back to the primordial conception of language. In the dialects of Greenlandic, the transparency is grammatical as well as semantic. The cultural assumption with regards to the relationship between form and meaning is probably motivated by the fact that the morphemes in the Inuit language are already in use in the language and can be used to define anything in the universe; it is just a question of packaging and compounding them in innovative ways. All the meanings are in place; they just need to be interwoven into a new form.

Working with a language such as Polar Eskimo, one is minded of the issue of form-meaning arbitrariness which Merleau-Ponty engages with in his discussion of Saussure. Merleau-Ponty does not find the linguistic sign arbitrary in the same way that Saussure does because he sees the movement of the body in making the sounds of language as a form of 'motivated' embodiment. This is part of his gestural theory of language where speech sounds are integrated into bodily behaviour. The Saussurean opposition between the 'sign' and the 'signified' is less relevant to Merleau-Ponty because language (gesture) and its meaning are not two opposing realities. As with the Heideggerian ontology, he sees the perceptual act and linguistic expression emerging from silence and his philosophy of language focuses on *parole*, the 'signified', or meaning which is enacted in a verbal and non-verbal sense but which is inseparable from it, and not *langue* which refers to the total structure of 'signs'. Unlike Saussure, Merleau-Ponty does not subordinate speech to language and does not reduce language to something contingent on thought.

In the Saussurean sense of the word, one finds 'arbitrariness' in all natural languages, but it would seem that in such a rich polysynthetic, agglutinative language, there is relatively less arbitrariness. Arbitrariness is normally discussed at the level of the word, but there is the question of what arbitrariness means vis-à-vis words, when the words we are talking about represent what are sometimes known as 'phonological words' or long concatenations of morphemes.

At a different level, the issue of 'ways of speaking' came up in the language programmes that I organised on Kap York Radio. One evening, we got quite a number of callers and the feedback was positive. Calls came in from Else Dunneq, Bertheline Kivitoq, Ole Danielsson, Minik Qujaukitsoq, Niels Udoraq Johansen and Gedion Amalortoq and there were several callers whom we did not have time to respond to. The first caller makes the point that a 'way of speaking' amongst the Inugguit has disappeared. According to Bertheline, in the old days people used to sing when they spoke. He says that the intonation pattern of the language has changed and that people speak in monotones nowadays. It is also the case that singing used to be perhaps a larger chunk of their culture than it is today. Gedion also believes that the youngsters speak quite differently from the older people in Qaanaaq. Young people might say *ingahaqtuq* 'exaggerates', but older people would have said *hugaluktuq* 'to go too far'. He thought that children are speaking differently because of the influence of the West Greenlandic in the schools. There is a general sense that parents should take the responsibility of teaching them the old language at home, but the problem is that the young parents in the community (in their twenties) do not know this older form of the language.

Some of the best work completed in the Ethnography of Communication paradigm has been on what might be called 'ways of speaking' and there is no doubt the Inugguit way of speaking helps define them as a group. Even if shamanic and ritual language has long disappeared, this is still a community of storytellers. Stories are related with eyes lowered and told using a distinctive 'way of speaking', an earthy, creaky voice that speaks in a slow, steady rhythm in an authoritative, un-interruptible tone. It is a way of speaking and a primordial voice that takes you back to the rootedness of human language, to the interiority of words as if the *nuna* is speaking through them. The speech of the storyteller is guided by his environment. When the Inugguit speak, they are listening at the same time to the sounds of nature. Speech is therefore used in a careful, measured way. Speech is not just verbal noise, but words are listened to. Sitting in hunters' homes, storytellers might say they could hear the breathing of the walrus. If the storyteller starts crying, it is common for those listening to all start shedding a tear. Storytelling requires a refined use of the language's paralinguistic features – in the case of Polar Eskimo, a rich and never random repertoire of sighs and groans and a specific mix of intonation patterns and gestures accompanying particular words and phrases. Certain bundles of these features are used when one listens to a story being told: the particle *ijaii* has no specific lexical meaning, but is a cue to the storyteller that the listener is engrossed in the story and that he should continue; a very soft, breathy and drawn out *hunaa* is a mild expression of surprise and a certain two-pitched low-high groan means 'oh, I see. Is that the case?'

Storytellers are 'memory systems', but in storytelling it is the act of speaking in a 'storied' way that is as important as the content. Storytelling is a social, humanising occasion and it is the familiar heavy, nasal voice and way of speaking that brings people together after the hunt. The storyteller's voice conjures up the Arctic environment outside from which the hunters are seeking refuge, sitting together and enjoying the warmth and the coziness of the hut.

The mechanics of social interaction in an Inuit community were quite different from anything I had known elsewhere in the world. Here, it is not acceptable to ask direct questions. A direct question might elicit shrugged shoulders or a meandering story about an unrelated topic interspersed with spontaneous weeping, but hardly ever a clear answer. As in other Asiatic cultures, one has to pose a question periphrastically. It is assumed that you know the unspoken rules, such as not asking how much should be paid for something. In turn, those who did not know me would channel their questions through somebody who had previously had contact with me. On a number of occasions, I would be sitting in somebody's house surrounded by a family whom I was getting to know, when a woman immediately next to me would ask somebody in the room who I was. This was not an issue of trying to circumvent what might be for them a potentially embarrassing situation where there is a problem communicating. This occurred even well into my stay when I had gained some fluency in the language. It seemed to be more of a case of a Polar Eskimo woman not being able to look a male *kadluna* in the eye, perhaps for reasons of not wishing to make her boyfriend or husband jealous.

Direct questions are typically ignored, furnished with tangential responses or answered with *ammaqa* meaning 'maybe'. The Inugguit live in a world of probabilities (not certainties): there is no guarantee that the seal will appear at the breathing hole and the weather is becoming increasingly unpredictable. The Inugguit inhabit a cycle of *ammaqa* and their monistic thought patterns are characterised by an unrelenting indeterminacy. *Ammaqa* reflects the constant uncertainty of the world they live in, but also the cultural importance of a collectivist community and the fact that an individual wishes to avoid making a false statement.

The Inugguit have clear views about what is 'their language' and what is not. Certain phonemes have particular salience in language, acting as identifying agents. If one cannot get certain basic sounds right, it cannot be considered that one is speaking the language irrespective of how good one's vocabulary is. One such sound is the uvular plosive, the popping sound made at the bottom of the throat. Learning about 'ways of speaking', one also learns about different 'ways of knowing'. In this part of the Arctic, lived practical experience represents in fact a better way of knowing than that which is spoken. To understand this world requires a negotiation of the spoken and the unspoken, the expressed and the unexpressed. Knowledge is encoded in non-linguistic modes of 'Being-in-the-world'. Engagement with things produces knowledge, not language alone. Polar Eskimo is a metaphorically weak language with almost no proverbs, and is a community where ways of learning and knowledge are experiential. A father will construct a sledge in silence with his son watching, but will not tell him how to do it. Children are hardly ever instructed to do anything, and coercion of any kind appears not to exist. In fact, there is opposition to spoken instruction, and it might be that the Inugguit subscribe to the belief that linguistic constructs place boundaries on thinking. In terms of speech at least, what matters to the Inugguit is first-hand information of the world based on personal experience – yet another premise shared with phenomenology.

Silence is valued in Inuit culture, but does not appear to be structured or 'regulated' as it is in Athabascan communities. In this post-shamanic society, both speech and silence have lost their inherent power. Writing in 1908, Knud Rasmussen tells us that words used to be magical and could actually be traded. Today, the long silences are a window onto the primordial, inner world with all its unspoken words and thoughts – a sort of inner speech; gaps in tangential conversations become meaningful and represent the link between the 'way of speaking' and the natural, sensory environment. The Inugguit spend much time talking about their dreams; an activity that is sometimes known as 'dream-sharing'. The dreams are perhaps a condensation of these 'signifiers' which are not expressed verbally or of the spirits that used to inhabit the land; they seem to have a strong collective, social dimension and might be significant to their daily lives. Amongst the Inugguit, there is also a curious ability to read each other's thoughts. Silence might mean that the hunters were trying to read somebody's thoughts or were listening to the 'language' of the animals; the mind of the animals and humans are inextricably linked in these communities and previously it was believed that they shared the same language. In the world of the Inugguit, animals are on the whole treated with respect, as equals. Unlike in the West, the assumption does not always prevail that human language is primary. Silence is not seen as 'negation' or 'non-talk', but instead it is non-verbal communication just as gesture is. Hunters would wander into my hut, sit down silently and say nothing for what seemed like (initially at least) an unfeasibly long period of time. Learning to understand the dynamic of this 'non-talk' became important and reminded me that getting to know a language is always much more than just learning a list of words.

Two hunters meeting on the sea ice might say next to nothing to each other, brew a cup of tea and only then begin to exchange the news. Integrated into their landscape, listening and silence have traditionally been essential to the Inuit. Out hunting on the sea ice, standing at seal breathing holes or sitting in kayaks waiting for pods of narwhals, hunters would remain completely motionless and silent for thirty minutes or longer, often in very low temperatures. Traditional games such as *aaqhiiq* were based upon silence – the first person to make a noise was the loser.

During the first months when I was visiting, listening, watching, talking, waiting and waiting, I adopted as much as possible the norms of community life. I soon discovered that one cannot conduct interviews in a place like this. One can have well-defined research questions, but it is unlikely you will get answers to specific questions. Anthropological research with the Inugguit that makes extensive use of the interview will be flawed. It takes months and years to gain the trust of the *inuk* and the result is that in these early stages it is often the community that will dictate the focus of one's research.

At the beginning, I had to decipher the cultural value of gesture and 'embodied interaction'. Facial expressions and gestures are used to relay language. I was non-plussed by the sometimes total expressionlessness of the Inugguit. But, if the 'linguistic' culture is one of embodied gesture and you do not wish to express anything, it is perhaps the case that one has to be totally expressionless. Facial gestures are entirely homogeneous among the Inugguit and act therefore as a collective identity marker. Everybody makes the same gestures, young children included. The facial 'yes' and 'no' gestures are the same in the Canadian Arctic as they are in north-west Greenland (Kulchyski, 2006: 155-67). This shows how much the Inuit sub-groups have in common. This most basic of linguistic elements, the affirmation/denial binary is facially inscribed. The Inugguit raise their eyebrows for 'yes', pinch the top of their nose for 'no' and shrug their shoulders for 'maybe'. Sometimes these gestures accompany the words for 'yes', 'no' or 'maybe' which when used in certain contexts do not mean what they 'should' mean. In response to a yes/no question, the word *ammaqa* 'maybe' typically means 'no'

Reading these gestures and analysing these 'ways of speaking', I began to gain a sense of their culture: not locking doors is a gesture of openness, trust, solidarity and community, but also an indicator of notions of ownership. Nobody would lock their door in the settlements unless they were going away for a week or so. Trust has an operational meaning in this society. There is some evidence that this is breaking down in the town, Qaanaaq. As well as incidents of oil theft during the night, during my stay, one of the men who worked on the 'honey-wagon' stole from a household. The doors need to be left open so that the men can take away the yellow loo bags, rubbish and fill up the water tank. The word got round instantly that something had been stolen, and the person was caught. A society this small cannot operate without trust. Just as open doors represented trust, the sharing of food and drink was a reliable indicator of hospitality. If it were not offered, then one knew one were not welcome.

Polar Eskimo is a language of glottal stops and outsiders have described it as not sounding like a language at all, but as a series of sighs, heavy breathing and broken, jerky sounds. Impressionistically, Polar Eskimo is a language that comes from the stomach or the middle of the body. Outsiders wishing to learn the language are told that as a first step they have to learn to make the sounds of a polar bear. There can be no doubt that historically hunting in a subsistence society must have influenced Inugguit 'ways of speaking'. Language was used directionally, 'I am going out hunting', 'I am doing this or that', but there was little debate or discussion about anything. This is only beginning to change now with the discussions that they have on the local radio and in the hunters' association. The radio plays an important part in the lives of the Inugguit, bringing together effectively one family living in the different settlements. Loss of sea ice positions the Inugguit in a static environment rooted to the town and cut off from their relatives in Canada. In addition, there is increased contact with the outside world as the Inugguit become more connected with the market economy. My preliminary findings indicate that these developments are leading local people to speak in terms which place far less emphasis on the interconnectedness of humans and nature. Consequently, the significance of traditional knowledge is now diminishing and this is reflected in language, for example in the loss of terminology for names of the wind, geographical features and place-names which embody ecological knowledge, relate implicit connections between personhood and geography and inform hunters of land and sea use. Hunters' spatio-temporal relationship to this local cosmos will be reconfigured as dramatic change occurs in the local ecosystem because the amount of visible human changes to the Arctic environment is relatively small. But there is also the question of what will happen to this ethnolinguistic identity once increased contact with the West leads to the introduction of new cosmologies and perhaps a more globalised consciousness. In this society, the interface between the spoken and written word is complex. The Inugguit live in two worlds: one of primary orality framing their spoken language, Polar Eskimo, where the spoken word still has an impact on the senses even if its magical quality has been lost, and one of secondary orality (Ong, 1982: 136) expressed through television and radio but based on the use of writing and print in both Standard West Greenlandic and Danish. With the imposition of a written norm and the shift in experiential frameworks, a new discourse or linguistic ideology will surely emerge.

Previously, and certainly for some still today, there is an isomorphism between language and landscape in a place where language might have been seen as 'shaped breath' (the words for 'breath', 'wind' and 'spirit' all come from the same stem, *aniri-*) and where the air is full of the noises of nature, animals and humans. Now, with just the remnants of animist beliefs left and with the codification of language (of Standard West Greenlandic at least), the Inugguit see language increasingly as an explicit human construct. The cultural assumptions that the Inugguit hold about language are defined by the language's linguistic structure, the lack of codification and the experiential nature of society. Their conceptualisation of their spoken language is such that they are less inclined to recognise it as a separate ontological category because it is not objectified to the same degree as it is in Western societies. The formal linguistic conception of language as an abstract code disconnected from the material world and from the body of the speaker is inadequate for the Inugguit. The high degree of semantic specificity results in the sense that the language is interwoven into the details of the landscape and natural environment, and therefore does not stand apart. This sense is enforced by the fact that the absence of a standardised written norm for the language they speak means that the language cannot be pinned down and boxed up in a reified form, but instead floats above other phenomena. In a society where many children are considered the embodiment of their ancestors and thus assume the deceased's name and kinship term, one might even speculate as to whether the language they use is their own or not. It might be that the reborn ancestors have the requisite knowledge at birth, hence there being no need for instruction and language even being perceived as an epistemological interference.

Historically, when animist traditions, taboo beliefs and shamanic language were more prevalent, and when the bond to nature was even closer, the role of language would have been more evocative than it is today. More evocative still would have been the mnemonic landscape, the contours of the land, the smells of the winds and the sounds of the creaking ice. Living so close to nature, the Inugguit's extraordinary memory, olfactory sensitivity and proximity of sensory pathways might seem almost synesthetic to us.

In Inugguit society, sounds relate to the world because they are a primordial reflection of the natural environment that embraces them. The Inugguit have always lived in a framework of thinking where man and nature are largely co-extensive, where language is not an object but part of this man-nature enmeshment. By examining these indigenous cultural assumptions about language, it is possible to see how the Inugguit articulate a sense of belonging to their extraordinary, but rapidly changing environment, but also to see an ethnolinguistic identity which is now disappearing. The ethnolinguistic identity in one settlement, Haviggivik, proved to be particularly complex and with the onset of the 'cold period' that was to be my destination.

6: The Cold Period

On the 19th of February, the sky is orange with horizontal wafers of iridescent pastel coloured nacreous cloud. After months of waiting, the sun climbs very slowly over the Politiken Glacier. At 2pm, the top part of the sun, a brilliant yellow disk, is just visible above the opalescent smidges of cloud. An elusive, uncauterised aubade is finally mine bringing light, hope and thoughts of future days. Basking in the coldest days of the year, it is farewell to unredeemable darkness and solitude. Light is now warmer than heat. The night is now broken and the hazy, wobbly forms of the last few weeks have become the lucid borders and edges of the landscape. New tumid horizons have opened up before me.

Completely oblivious of this ever so important event, hunters walk past the hut with shambling gait, the reality of *ennui* weighing heavy on their shoulders, and not as much as a backward glance. It is business as normal and they have seen it all before. Standing on the balcony, I make a video recording of this yellow mass just peaking above the horizon. One can see no more than the top part of the sun for about forty-five minutes before it begins to dip again below the horizon, but I am already feeling more positive about my stay here even if I am shocked at how depressed I sound when I listen to the recording.

A day later, like a behemothic dahlia, the full sun can be seen above the mountain for the first time this year. Three days ago, we all gathered up on the hill for the first sunrise and songs were sung in the bitter cold. But, the dense cloud cover soon led the children with their cardboard cutouts of the sun skipping back to the school in the extreme cold. Today, it is high pressure and -33 degrees. The density of the smoke chugging out of people's chimneys is a reminder of how bitterly cold it is. I have seven layers on and with the faulty heater am struggling on some days to heat the hut with candles alone. At night, the freezing air quivers, making me shiver as I try to fall asleep on my hard, frozen pillow. There were weeks where I was more or less dependent on candles alone for heat. I would typically get through about thirty candles a day at the cost of about seven pounds. I am not sure I know anybody else who would have put up with that kind of cold for weeks on end. I enjoyed the challenge immensely and by this stage had warmed very much to the simplicity of life there.

With their backs to the yellowish-ochre sky, polar bear-skin clad hunters are getting their dog teams ready. I manage to take a few photographs, but then my camera freezes up and will not work in the very low temperatures. The sun rises vertically and then drops again after just ten minutes, like mercury rising and then falling in the thermometer. The light is a boon. Sitting just below the horizon for such a long time, it stays light until 6pm in the evening. When the sun comes back, people used to say *kiangnaii* which is a reference to the heat that the sun brings, but paradoxically this is the coldest time of the year. The Arctic is full of paradoxes, but the greatest paradox is surely the fact that the 'cold period' starts when the sun returns. The sea ice is bright and reflects eight per cent of the sun's radiation back into space, reducing the temperature further. Once it begins, the sun returns unimaginably fast with twenty minutes more daylight each day. Hours flit away in never-ending blue skies and spectacular sunsets mark the shank of the evening. I marvel at the clarity of the Arctic light and maintain it is one of the most fantastic things about being here. But, such a thought is perhaps not surprising having gone through a period of prolonged darkness. Looking out the window later on, marvelling at the flaming, molten sky, I see a car drive past Qaanaaq on the sea ice. It looks absolutely tiny and represents the most surreal spectacle: a pair of headlights moving across a, frozen white sheet. The car comes from the East and drives right past Qaanaaq towards Hiorapaluk.

The afternoon is spent again with Eva, recording songs and stories. She offers me currant buns and we have a fun time, talking and laughing about the old days. Eva tells various stories about the daily life at home when she was growing up, how they cooked, prepared skins, etc. She shows me her worn down teeth from all the years of chewing the skins to keep them soft. She also speaks about her life with the dogs. She was so busy as a child that she did not have time to make friends. It was a tough life, but also a good life in her opinion as people drew together. It was one community where everything was shared.

I need her to sign the consent form, but she does not know what it means 'to sign something'. So, on the consent form she just writes her name again where she should sign it. When she was young, people only had Christian names. There was no concept of surnames, and she was simply Eva. It was only much later when they were colonised in the 1950s that they were forced to have surnames. She took her mother's name as many others did. Just as she tells me how she has not passed the stories onto her teenage grandchildren, one of them appears with his girlfriend and child. Perched on the sofa, glued to the television, the endless flicker of this visual age bringing lethargy, passive minds and dampening tongues, the sulking teenagers ignore Eva and myself. No attention is paid to the child who just sits there and stares at me. One thing I have learnt is that all roads lead to Eva Kristensen. She has five sons (Piitannguaq Kristensen, the friendly gentleman who works at the shop and is currently sporting two black eyes is her eldest), fifteen grandchildren and is in one way or another related to just about everybody here.

It was at this time of the year, the cold period, just as the sun comes back that the 'explorers' arrive. The first to come are two Poles who seem to think they can ski to Ellesmere Island, blissfully unaware of the fact that it has not been possible for years. There would have been a time when I would have wished to speak and get to know these people, but having slogged it out on my own through the dark period, I now have little time for these outsiders who appear the moment the sun comes back. They have no interest in the people or community where they are based. I remember thinking how superficial their experience was compared to mine. Had they shown any interest at all in the people around them, they would have soon found out that their costly proposed expedition is not possible, and that months of planning was all for nothing. Slowly, I was coming to understand the locals' take on these kinds of *kadluna* and see what they meant when they spoke of their ignorance, misplaced ambition and narrow vision. My thinking was drifting in the direction of the indigenous mind.

It is the end of February and the tiny room at the airport is empty except for a young woman with her small child. They are taking the

10.50am helicopter to Hiorapaluk and as they are the only passengers, the flight leaves half an hour early. At the check-in desk, the policeman tells the girl in West Greenlandic that the pilot should keep an eye on me because I am an offender and I am leaving the country. The girl seems to believe him. It is very amusing. Hans has a tremendous sense of humour. The pilot for my helicopter is a Norwegian from Oslo called Bent. His co-pilot sitting on the left is Steffan Rahmberg, a Swede who retired as a helicopter pilot from the Swedish Army aged 55. He has run over 2,000 rescue missions and in his retirement now works up here. Bent works part-time as a helicopter pilot for the Oslo police, chasing criminals around the capital.

At 10.50am, the three West Greenlanders who work in the kitchens at Pituffik turn up. Including myself, there are four passengers in the Bell 212. I am the first to get in and am sure to grab the window seat on the right-hand side. My seat belt will not fasten, but I do not worry. I put on the ear-defenders, but there is no safety advice whatsoever. The sea ice stretches as far as the eye can see: an unblemished, perfect expanse without end. There is no sign of the open sea. This naked landscape leaves my head aswarm with floating ideas and ambitions. Sitting in the helicopter, leaving the memories of my battles in the frozen hut behind and with the deafness of the lonely ear defenders, a moment of existential aporia unfolds. Fighting the bitter cold, I would struggle through the museums of my mind, the empty cabinets of forgotten knowledge, the abstract exhibits of lost languages where words wander down grammar-less avenues and affixes are parked at the end of an uncertain street. During the coldest moments, my thoughts were of a jumble of memories and foreign words on scraps of paper lost in a windy place, trading dreams on unwrapped mornings. I would reflect on how we are all but experiential patches of films, books, photographs, friends and family sewn together. A quilt of stitched and tailored composite identities whose whole is the sum of the parts and a little bit more. The deceiving sunshine of late February stirs me from my introspective thoughts.

Most of the ice must have formed since mid-December. Once the temperature is consistently below -20 degrees, the sea ice rapidly thickens. It was not until I got up in the helicopter and saw the landscape beneath me that I realised what an extraordinary place it is where I live. Being dwarfed by the sheer magnitude of nature holds such appeal in a world where we are constantly trying to overcome the natural elements. Cooped up in an icy house for months on end, steeled to understand a strange idiom, suddenly it all felt worthwhile.

Herbert Island looks quite different from the air. I am still not able to see the abandoned settlement. We cross Inglefield Bay and fly very close to the mountains opposite Qaanaaq bordering Olrik Fjord. Climbing over the mountain, the view is nothing but glaciers and mountain plateaus – an extraordinary open wilderness where there is absolutely no evidence of life ever having been there, man or otherwise. This part of north-west Greenland is described as 'unexplored' on the map. It is deeply beautiful and utterly enticing, but extremely hostile.

Flying into Pituffik and over the Wolstenholme Fjord whose waters are fed by four large glaciers and is therefore sometimes known as the 'world's largest ice machine', Dundas is on my left and Saunders Island is on my right. My first view of Pituffik through the low cloud is rows of silver-coloured barracks housing and several large aircraft hangars. The helicopter lands on a trailer which is subsequently wheeled into the hangar to protect it in the event of bad weather. I am given a very warm welcome by the Danish policeman (John) and the deputy Danish Liaison Officer (DLO). They know who I am and nobody asks to see my passport or transit visa. This is not what I expected. After a brief chat, I am back in the helicopter again. I am the only passenger to Haviggivik, making the journey feel even more special.

Bent starts the twin-engine helicopter, but then Jens Ole Nielsen, a Dane working for Air Greenland on the Base, saunters over to the helicopter indicating that there is a problem. The weather is too bad in Haviggivik and it is not safe to fly. It is difficult to imagine as the weather is so good here. Before they depart, the pilots are sent a fax of a weather report from the man that runs the shop in Haviggivik. Slightly disappointed, I disembark and the pilots take me to the Air Base canteen. Before me is a massive buffet with a bewildering choice of dishes. This is a world away from what I am used to and is quite a cultural shock. All the food is flown in from Baltimore every week. American soldiers sit around in military uniforms which look more suited to Iraq than North Greenland. There are men and women here, and as the Inugguit informed me, there are black people too.

Steffan cuts a dashing figure: a tall man with a fur hooded, padded pilot leather jacket and an IWC pilot watch on his wrist. He speaks very slowly and with a distinctive Swedish accent. Inevitably, the conversation turns to polar bears. Steffan has been flying helicopters in Greenland since 1998 and has only ever seen two. He tells me that fifty-eight people live in Haviggivik today, but I suspect the true number is smaller than that. According to Steffan, at one stage in the early 1990s 80 per cent of the population had syphilis.

Back at the hangar, Hans – Lars Iversen's boss – calls to say that he and his wife (Lisbett) would like to meet me and show me around Pituffik and Dundas. This is very kind. He will pick me up from the hotel where I am staying (North Star Inn, Room 209) at 5pm Pituffik time. The instructions are conveyed in a manner suggestive of a military operation. Pituffik is on its own time zone or rather on Canadian Halifax time, and not Qaanaaq or New York time. The Americans do not think of Pituffik and the 570 square mile Defence Area as part of Greenland, but as part of the US. The currency is US dollars and the jurisdiction is that of the US.

I am dropped off at the hotel where walking round with a static charge, I get an electric shock from everything I touch. The hotel could be anywhere in the world except for the fact that the girls' rooms are to the right and the boys' to the left. Breakfast is from 5-8am. I can see that we are in a military compound and I am left wondering whether I will be able to manage 8am. Dinner is from 5-7pm. Jens Ole tells me that there is nothing particularly secret about Thule anymore and that I am free to take photographs. The only place where I cannot go is out to where the radar is which is half an hour or so in the car from Pituffik. There are only one hundred and fifty soldiers based here now whereas at one point there were eighteen thousand.

The afternoon is spent exploring Pituffik in the relative warmth of -25 degrees. My first impression is that this is a surreal, utterly Orwellian dystopia. A tannoy system broadcasts the weather status at the various stations scattered around the Defence Area. These tannoys which are permanently on, are to be found in every living area too. In other respects, it is like a Siberian ghost town without the sense of decay, but clearly one organised by a military or regiment obsessed with order, surveillance and sense of imminent threat. There are occasional silver, steel-plated hangar like buildings which house the hotel, the hospital, the post office, the multi-purpose gym, the bowling alley and the supermarket.

Every attempt has been made to turn the place into a microcosm of modern America with added sterility. It feels like a station on a distant 22nd century planet where everything functions perfectly, but where any personality or individuality has been sucked out of the people. Free taxis can be ordered by punching in a code representing the departure and terminus. They are driven by people who sit and talk like robots. The roads are deserted, but the occasional car stops dutifully on the empty streets at large, red 'stop' signs. All the cars are red pick-ups – brand new and basically identical. Black cables lead from the ultimate weather-proof, barracks housing, feeding pan heaters. All the housing is a grey, steel plated-silver colour with red trim. The roads are marked with red poles every ten metres with red reflecting discs on one side of the street and orange on the other. Anyone would think the personnel working here are blind. There is a strange overcaution about the place.

Civilians are all dressed the same, in big Canada Goose jackets. People's surnames are emblazoned on their jackets to tell them apart. They wave as they drive past slowly in their identikit vehicles. Just outside the hotel, tame Arctic foxes are scavenging. They are very small animals, much shorter and smaller than a fox in England. Their fur, the warmest of any animal, is inexplicably still the dark brown, chocolate colour of their summer coat. Their heavily pigmented orange eyes protect them from the extreme glare of light off the Arctic ice. A Canada Goose clad civilian steps out of one of the identikit red pick-up trucks and addresses me with 'howdy' which I believe to be a North American greeting. We may as well be in Alaska. He tells me that some Canadian military personnel are staying at the hotel. They use it as a stop-off when flying to Alert, Ellesmere Island.

Hans Hartmann (which seems like an appropriate surname) is a balding man with a very serious demeanour and a mean handshake. He has been in the Danish Navy for thirty years which must put him in his fifties. He picks me up at the hotel at exactly 17:00. We cannot go out for a drive because the weather is too bad, but it seems fine to me. More overcaution. They are extremely safety conscious here and the American military seem to take this to absurd extremes. The weather warning system has to be adhered to at all costs. The system is based on Alpha, Bravo and Charlie. In the event of a Charlie weather warning, one is not allowed to go outside unless one is a member of the emergency services.

No questions asked. If that is not depressing enough, there is also a curfew in Pituffik at 1am. Nobody is allowed out. One can call the free, automated taxi service but they might report you. Three people were caught outside in a Charlie storm on the 1st of January and were sent home. That explains perhaps why they went out.

The base is run by a Danish company called GC or Greenland Contractors, not the American military. The Danish contractors come up from Copenhagen once a month on the Airbus. They are well paid and that is their principal motivation for coming here. One exception to that is a Danish woman who has been living on the Base for thirty-seven years. She is a dendrophobic and has finally found peace in this treeless environment. It sounds like a bad joke, but it is not. There are more Danish, Greenlandic and American citizens here than military personnel. The main task of Pituffik is nowadays BMEWS – Ballistic Missile Early Warning System. The other is monitoring thousands of satellites and space aircraft. With the equipment they have they can see a distance of five thousand miles. If North Korea were to launch a missile, they would be able to spot the launch here in north-west Greenland.

If the weather is fine tomorrow, he suggests giving me a tour of the Base and putting the flight back to 11am. I am the only passenger, so providing the weather is good I can more or less determine when I want to fly. Hans is keen to take me to Dundas at 8am in the morning. It is 1am by the time we leave the DLO's house and that is not enough sleep for me. I try to put back the time of our meeting, but I can see that he is not impressed. This is an Air Base after all.

I am up at 9am and call Jens Ole Nielsen. They are still waiting for the weather report from Haviggivik, but it is Alpha here and the skies are clear. It is the 1st of March and cold with a -40 degrees wind chill. I speak to the DLO. He thinks I should have lunch and then meet him immediately after to go to Dundas, thus delaying the flight. Before going to Dundas, I visit Heritage Hill which serves as the Pituffik Museum and discover that there was a missile system at Thule which was dismantled in 1965. There is no attempt to conceal the history of the base. Dotted around the museum are various photographs of Camp TUTO and Camp Century. The intention to build a network of tunnels and a town with a hospital and theatre under the Ice Sheet with mobile nuclear missile launch sites sounds like the ambition of a Bond film villain. But it was the

Cold War, and this was the reality. The plan was to build four thousand kilometres of tunnels housing six hundred nuclear missiles. Electricity was supplied by the world's first mobile nuclear reactor. There is a photograph of the entrance tunnel taken in 2005. On the entrance hangs a sign, 'To Little Siberia, Greenland'.

Hans and his wife pick me up at exactly 11.30am and we drive to Dundas. Today, there is very little to be seen at Dundas, the ancestral home of the Inugguit. There are two cemeteries: one for adults and one for children. Wooden crucifixes struggle to peak above the thick white snow. The church was dismantled and moved to south Greenland. Peter Freuchen's red wooden house is boarded up, but is in good condition compared to the two very scruffy adjacent houses where hunters stay when they come here occasionally to hunt polar bears. One of the huts is in an appalling state with filth and rubbish strewn across the soiled floor. Three hunters from Qaanaaq have stayed here recently.

The first European to arrive in the area was William Baffin who arrived in 1616 and named several places in the area, such as Wolstenholme Fjord, Saunders Island and Smith Sound. There is no reference to him having made contact with the Inugguit. In 1909 the first buildings were built at Dundas when Knud Rasmussen established a trading station in this area that he called 'Thule'. The settlement was vacated in 1953 when about one hundred and thirty people were moved from Ummannaq (Dundas) to Qaanaaq to make room for the construction of the US Air Base.

In the distance, the stony remains of the original housing can be seen: evidence of a different, but not distant age. In front of us, there is a memorial to Knud Rasmussen lost in deep snow, decorated with indistinct polar bear footprints. Hans takes some pleasure in carrying a rifle over his shoulder and is always keen to remind me of the seriousness of everything. Anybody leaving the Base has to inform the radio controller and stay in radio contact all the time. His wife tells me that her husband is 'very important' which is undoubtedly the case, but absurd sounding nonetheless. There is little scope for banter or self-irony. Hans tells me that a polar bear and a cub were spotted not far from Pituffik. The whole Base 'went on Delta' which meant that absolutely everybody had to stay indoors. That seems rather ridiculous to me. Forty years ago and not far from here, the Americans were building a clandestine town in the Ice

Sheet stocked with enough nuclear weapons to destroy the planet, but the sniff of a bear and they are all cowering behind locked doors. Survival shelters line the roads around the Base. If one is caught in a storm, one should aim for one of these where one will find a survival blanket, emergency rations, etc. Alternatively, one would have thought one could seek shelter in the eight-lane bowling alley or the high-tech fitness and sports centre instead. It is all rather over-the-top, and one cannot but help think that they might benefit from taking a few lessons from the Inugguit.

Armed Forces Day is on the 24th of April and this has been used as an opportunity to try and rebuild some rapport with the displaced Inugguit. An annual sledge dog race is held for them at Pituffik, and I know from gossip in Qaanaaq amongst the hunters that this has become an important event in their calendar. Lavish prizes have been dished out in recent years, the top prize being normally a rifle. Hans tells me that the Inugguit are not grateful and that they want more and more each year. There has been alcohol available and this has unsurprisingly caused many problems too, leaving a number of people on the Base wishing to put an end to the event. Dundas is a sacred place for the Inugguit. However, nowadays every year during the summer, the American military organise the Annual Dundas Open which is a nine-hole golf tournament on top of Mount Dundas. Given the history of the place, I find this rather obtuse.

The flight lasts forty-five minutes before we descend towards an implausibly small collection of colourful houses huddled together in the frozen North – Haviggivik, a few half-deserted crumbs on a vast perfect white table cloth of snow and ice. The scenery is quite different from Qaanaaq. A steep mountain rises immediately behind the tiny settlement which is almost lost in deep snow. It is this time of the year that Haviggivik is battered by the *nigeq* ('a strong wind from the East'), bleaching the sky white. Land, sea ice and sky become the same and grey, tatty A-framed houses with sealed up windows and ladders on their roofs act as beacons to carry hunters home during the worst of the storms.

The thudding red machine lands with much ado on a flat bit of rock right in the middle of the settlement. The entire population has turned out. The post is eagerly unloaded onto a sledge and the blue bags are dragged through the thick snow. The gathering disperses. The houses are just metres away from the sea ice creating the sense of a small, tight-knit community living in a place where *hila* determines the rhythm of life and that is all, offering a spyhole onto a pantheistic vision of man living in unity with nature.

For me, the appeal of the remote settlement was immediate and unforgettable. Smiley children were magnetised to the stranger and the adults invited the visitor in for a supper of polar bear or fermented Little Auks, followed by endless refills of black coffee. It is a place where men smoke pipes, sitting with lost expressions and uncritical minds in chaotic kitchens at sixes and sevens, a place where raised eyebrows replace words and signal welcome, a place where unconcealed flatulence breaks the silence in otherwise mute houses.

There is no doubt in my mind that I had come to one of those few places in life which one can label 'special'. I had discovered the cold heaven that I came looking for. Here, for a community of forty hunter-gatherers clinging on in an exceedingly remote place, life was stripped to its basics: subsistence, family and lots of goodwill. A life measured out by spoons of sugar and yellow bags. Empty huts (*inuerunnikud igdlut*) had been smashed to pieces by unforgiving storms, their entrances lost behind walls of snow ten feet high. Vulnerable lives sit in shaking houses waiting for the *anuri* ('wind') to unhinge the door to an uncertain future. Every Sunday the wind threatens to blow the tiny place off the map. The unrelentless wind draws contorted pictures in the ice, broken circles and sculpts miniature mountain ranges. Castles on the sea ice and grave-stones lost under a carpet of deep snow are a playground for toddlers.

There are no women left for the many unspliced for whom hunting comes first. Single male hunters whose wives had left them long ago would live in the simplest of conditions: an oil heater in one corner, a bucket in the other, a bed, television, crucifix, a few family snaps on the wall and no more. There would be no hunting trophies on the wall, but dead seals with bags over their heads would be lined up on the kitchen floor amidst skins, bloody pots and pans. The door to their homes was always open; no need to knock. Privacy, discretion and subtlety are strangers' notions.

The eldest hunter in the settlement and a storyteller with whom I worked, Nukappiannguaq Danielsson, gave Haviggivik ten years.

Climate change has meant that the settlement is almost impossible to get to by dog-sledge and there are few who wish to live in complete isolation in the twenty-first century with no medical facilities. Frank Suersaq can remember how in 1994 he and his father travelled for four days on sledges south of Haviggivik and still they did not see the sea. That is unlikely to happen now. I had planned on just staying a week or two, but from the moment I got out of the thudding, red Bell 212 helicopter, I knew I would be staying longer. The telephone line had been down for six weeks, but once reconnected I spoke to Air Greenland. I was the only passenger and they were happy to send a helicopter down to me whenever I wanted to leave.

Standing by the helicopter (in a black down jacket) and bearing a rather stern expression stands Titken. He introduces me to Qaordloqtoq Johansen and Jens Ole Uumaq who has the key to the house where I will be staying. Constantly grinning, cheery Jens Ole takes me up to the house straight away. He has warmed the house up for me; it is a relief to live finally in a house warmer than the one in Qaanaaq. The house is a fairly respectable red A-framed house just in front of the school. Jens Ole calculates that I will have to buy ten litres of oil every day which will cost 44DKK. There are two jerry cans which I can use to collect the oil from the shop. The Inugguit drag their oil and water jerry cans across the snow with a string. Nobody carries things here unless absolutely necessary. Why put yourself out? At a brief encounter of jerry cans on packed snow, sighs, grins and a few words are traded. Heavy lidded eyes spot a hunter from afar. It is Ingaapaluk, *iih, iih* and then a *taima* gongs the conversation to an end.

There is no oven or fridge, but the warmth and cosiness of the house is instantly appealing. There are two very large velvet red settees opposite each other and it reminds me very much of the Exeter College, Oxford Middle Common Room. In a very narrow alcove is the bathroom: a bucket lined with the all too familiar yellow bag and nothing more. The alcove is sufficiently narrow to not permit me to urinate standing up. There is an old dilapidated piano in the spare room. It is immensely exciting being here. I drop off my expedition kit-bags and go to the shop with Jens Ole to buy some rations. The shop has a tiny annexe which acts as a post office and a largeish store at the back. The shop area itself is not much larger than the living room/bedroom in my house. Rows of black ten litre jerry oil cans with green screw tops and strings attached line up outside the shop in the morning for Vittus to fill. Once they are filled, Vittus leaves them outside the oil depot and people collect them later. It is a system based on complete trust. Everything is terribly expensive, even more so than Qaanaaq. The milk has a January expiry date on it. One by one people come into the shop and shake my hand, sharing some joke or another. I buy some oil and Vittus writes *tuluk* ('Englishman') on the receipt. Knowing their love for word-play, I joke with him that it should be *ittuluk* ('the old man') and there are tears of laughter.

Their warmth is quite overwhelming and very different from the reception I got at Qaanaaq. It might take twenty minutes to get the water from the tank 200 metres away simply because you would inevitably meet somebody on the way who would want to speak with you. At the moment, the talk is about nothing other than who and who not has killed a polar bear. In terms of status and social pride, there is much at stake here. With so few people tied to such a remote, bounded community, any outsider is immediately conspicuous and the subject of gossip. One gets the impression that they believe such a community can only function with complete cultural homogeneity. Outsiders are welcome, but they should not stay too long as they may be a threat to this social fabric.

People here want the quiet life away from Qaanaaq where the Lords of jealousy reign over spoiled futures. Many of the people here are quite poor. Families of four live in the smallest of cabins. Bodil Peterson cooks over the oil heater. Very few people have an Internet connection, the phone network might be down for several weeks at a time and power cuts are common. Nobody has running water and everybody has ten litre oil heaters. The settlement got electricity in 1989, provided by a small generator at the other end of the settlement. The person who manages it, Kuulut, is currently away. Haviggivik got oil heating in the 1960s. Before that, they had coal, before that blubber.

Nature feels closer here than anywhere else I know in the world; that proximity to the wild and its implied vulnerability is at a personal level enormously appealing to me. At the closest place of human civilisation, the US Air Base, Star Wars Technology monitors movement of satellites in the sky and the soldiers living there are ready for twenty-first century warfare. Here in Haviggivik, people live the slowest, most simple, uncomplicated life imaginable with the absolute bare essentials. There is no pollution, no industry and when the dogs are quiet, no noise. There is just one quad bike which drags a wooden *anaqtauharvik*: a wooden box on a wooden sledge carrying the black poop bags. Two entirely different worlds with people living in different centuries are juxtaposed in a remote corner of the Arctic. One world lives by the clock and military precision is a must; in the other, clocks have almost no function at all. Days merge in to one another, but quite happily so.

The sun is now quite high in the sky. Thronged in nothingness, whiteness everywhere, one may as well be on another planet. Unfurled Greenlandic flags flap in the wind; massive polar bear skins hang outside people's homes to dry. Out hunting every day, the active hunter (*assak*) is leaving with his dogs. Nukappiannguaq is busy preparing sealskins at the *kommune*. They are washed, hung up to dry and then put in the freezer. Everybody told me in Qaanaaq there is no market for these skins, but that is not stopping the people of Haviggivik preparing them every morning. The contrast with Qaanaaq is considerable: the dogs are well fed and bushy tailed. Every single one is in good shape and I soon make some new friends.

Small hillocks of fatty, pink seal blubber lie dotted around the settlement. The dogs do not go hungry here. Things look good at the moment, but the hunters tell me that the ice is no more than 50cm thick. Global warming could wipe out this community. Unlike Qaanaaq, it is very difficult to see how this community could survive without the sea ice. A way of living would have to come to an end. On the ice, I play a game of tag (*atoush*) with a group of giggling children who wish to accompany me everywhere. Back at home after lunch, I hear somebody come in the house. A 50-year-old man staggers in. Two rotten teeth dangle from a smiley face. He has a sort of Hitlarian moustache and seems to have been drinking. This is Ingaapaluk, Jens Ole's younger brother. He appears to be to Haviggivik what Magnus is to Qaanaaq – a loner, a bachelor, which is not a good thing in this society, but ultimately a very kind man. He does not work and has trouble writing. I ask him if he works and he shows me his left hand which has just three fingers and a thumb. He has not lost a finger, but was just born with a defect. Questions of overbreeding immediately come to mind. I have never seen that before, but try not to be shocked when he shows me. Scarred faces are exhibits for the visitor here. Unlike Magnus, he likes to tell stories.

I make him a cup of coffee and he starts telling me how Haviggivik was when he was growing up. The population in the 1960s was 150-200; today it is 38. He has the same body language as Qulutanguaq in Qaanaaq when he tells a story. I ask him whether he minds whether I record it. He disappears for a cigarette and then comes back and we begin recording. He has no problem with the microphone and talks for 1 hour 30 minutes, and is well paid for doing so. At the end of the story, he asks me when I was born and jumps for joy when he discovers that was born the same year as Qisuk Oodaq. He insists that we go and visit him and tell him the news immediately.

Qisuk and his girlfriend, Naja Pedersen, live in the A-framed house towards the eastern end of the settlement. They do not give Ingaapaluk much of a welcome and it is obvious that they do not want to entertain somebody who has been drinking. Like most hunters, Qisuk is a man of very few words. He is a proud man and highly respected as a hunter. They own a cat which is most unusual. She never goes out because it is too cold and because she is terrified of the dogs. Naja tells me how she is looking forward to the arrival of the *akpaliarhuk* ('Little Auk'). The mountain behind us is home to thousands of these little birds which come at the end of April. By the beginning of May, the mountain will be covered in them and the Inugguit will be out with their nets. They ferment them in a sealskin with blubber for four months and then eat them. There is also much talk about the planned annual dog-sledge race in Haviggivik this Sunday. The course will be 20 kilometres and Qisuk Oodaq has won the last two years.

Lying at the southern end of the Polar Eskimo speaking region, this must be one of the smallest bi-dialectal speech communities in the world. Here, the Qaanaamitun dialect is spoken alongside the West Greenlandic dialect from the Kullorsuaq region. Those who speak Polar Eskimo can understand the more southern dialect without any problem. There are Polar Eskimo speaking households and West Greenlandic speaking households where you encounter a curiosity alien to the Inugguit. Then, talking of Kullorsuaq, it is off to see Ole. Three polar bear skins dry on a washing line outside the yellow house, flapping in the wind. It is a symbol of status and prestige in this society. Bent Uvdloriaq is currently the top hunter in Haviggivik and perhaps in the whole region, having won the top prize at the Armed Forces Day event at

Pituffik. Ole's wife, Karline, is a nurse and therefore this building is known as the 'hospital' even though there are no medical facilities here. It also doubles up as the nursery. A polar bear's head sits in the hallway – not a trophy, just the remains of a recent slaughter – and inside people sit on the floor, feasting on fermented Little Auk (*kiviat*).

Three young children run around the house – a two year old boy called Poul which Nukappiannguaq dotes over, a four year old girl called Naduk and a slightly older boy called Lars who shoots plastic darts into the two dead Harp Seals lying like bombs in the kitchen. Poul is an *atsiaq* ('named after a dead person') and is getting special attention. As one might expect, it is noticeable how Nukappiannguaq calls his grandson *aataq* ('grandfather'); the recycled name indicating that he is the embodiment of his ancestor. We talk about the skins being left to dry outside. It is a polar desert and Nukappiannguaq thinks that is good enough reason to shower just once a year, on Christmas Day. During my visit and my umpteenth cup of coffee of the day, there is another power cut. We are then joined by one of the many bachelors; a very quiet gentleman called Jens who sports a peculiar haircut. He joins a small circle of people sitting on the floor who have moved on from the fermented birds and are now playing the card game, 'Olsen'.

In such a tiny, remote settlement that is so disconnected, the personalities of the inhabitants loom large and disproportionately characterise the place. Potentially, this could make life in a tiny settlement intolerable as there is no escape from 'bad' (*ajorpoq*) individuals. One will meet them every day, and probably several times in the course of the same day. For a couple of such individuals in Haviggivik, their reputation went beyond the settlement. The previous shopkeeper, Mads Ole, had apparently 'been moved' to Qaanaaq. People referred to him as the little dictator. Everybody contributes to the social fabric of such a tiny community. Every personality must fit. His did not and therefore something had to be done. Otherwise, the situation might have become 'dangerous'. It is important that social control is maintained where possible as the Haviggivingmiut themselves are responsible for policing their own settlement. Strictly speaking, they come under the remit of the Danish policeman based at the US Air Base, but in practice they have to on the whole deal with difficulties themselves.

I had heard all about Titken from gossip in Qaanaaq. He was one of those that had moved up the coast and married an Inugguaq. I had been told that he was aggressive and greedy, and that he was not allowed to keep dogs because of previous gross mistreatment. A whole dog team of his had starved to death. In such tiny societies, such characters are impossible to avoid. Fortunately, there was no alcohol in the settlement at the time of my arrival: the annual shipment had been drunk in six weeks with the residents drinking day and night. The *carpe diem* mentality looms large again. With the exception of the odd bottle brought in from Qaanaaq, the settlement was effectively dry. He proved to be a man who loved to boast to the outsider and who saw himself responsible for managing relations with the occasional incomer, but who was horribly ignorant and bigoted. He liked to bully the locals, but was protective of the outsider. He flaunted some extreme political views and whilst not perhaps representative of the Inugguit reminded me that the Inuit see the Western world through the lens of a camera or rather through a television screen. The result being that they are convinced that Western societies are more violent than they actually are.

Aputsiaq could not be more different from Titken. He looks like no other Innugguaq I have met. His face is long and chiselled, accentuated by his long, grey goatee which reaches down to his chest. His thick hair is floppy and grey; his bushy eyebrows are black. He has a spiritual air to him; his face tells a thousand narratives. With his looks, his nickname in Qaanaaq is the 'arab'. Casualty of the cold, he is missing three fingers. Like most Inugguit, Aputsiaq seems to have a phobia of insects and responds in a very strange manner to seeing a fly in my house. He becomes very anxious, quite alarmed and pulls a childish face of disgust. One storyteller was not able to finish her story because she had spotted a fly behind the nets. He visits at 3pm and the half an hour trying to make conversation with him strikes me as one of the most unusual half an hours I have ever spent. He is exceedingly shy and does not like the look of the microphone. After an interminable silence waiting for him to start his story, he tells me that he will not tell a story today, contradicting what he had said that morning. Peter Freuchen says that we will never under-stand the Inuit and his words seem particularly fitting for an occasion like this. Another splayed silence over fuming cha. And then, after half an hour, he gets up to leave and asks me if he can come tomorrow. He wants company, co-presence, but does not want to perform. No problem. Subsequently and only when I was back in Qaanaaq, I discovered that Aputsiaq's grandson had recently committed suicide. Understandably, he had taken the news very badly and had become extremely quiet and withdrawn.

Jens Ole Qaerngaq, Appalersuarsuk's son, invites me to eat polar bear meat with him in the afternoon. Both he and his brother, Adolf, live in Haviggivik. Their father, a friend of mine in Qaanaaq, left the settlement and moved to the town in 2003. I enter into a chaotic hunter's kitchen; Jens Ole cuts up polar bear meat in large pots on the floor. The smell of sea mammals and blubber is rather overwhelming. He hands me a polar bear paw to inspect. It is remarkable how heavy it is. At the beginning of February a polar bear and two cubs walked right past the settlement – an unusual spectacle even for the Inugguit. They were not shot because she had young.

In this traditional, hunting society, space seems to be even more gendered than in the town. At Jens Ole's house, the wife and child sit away from the two men, not wishing to disturb their discussion. She is sewing a pair of braces into a new pair of *nannut* for her husband. Jens Ole points out that it is best to use the hair of old polar bears as it is thicker and warmer than the new, thin and brittle hairs of the young polar bears. The meat is eaten on its own and has to be boiled for 24 hours to avoid trichinosis. Walrus and bearded seals can be affected by this as well. The worm might come alive in a warm stomach, then multiply and spread throughout the blood. As is so often the case, the conversation turns to Greenlandic food. Few people eat Arctic Fox, I am told. Those that eat it are normally those that got used to the taste when they were young and like to eat it a few times a year. It is said to taste fine, with a bit of salt. Young dog, say six months old, apparently tastes better. Judging by how many dead dogs there are down at the dump (there are about a dozen – it looks like a whole team has been killed recently), dog is not often on the menu. Most people have eaten dog at some point. The one thing that some Inugguit find unappetising is caribou intestines (*tugto nerukka*). We have barely finished lunch when his mobile telephone rings. It is his brother, Adolf. He has just caught some seal and needs some help. Jens Ole gets ready with tremendous urgency and I am left struggling to put my layers back on and get out the door.

I am awoken at 7am by the storm that is blowing in, pressing against the glass and rattling the front door. The wind growls, groans and whistles as it whips the house, growing in intensity by the minute. It is the *pavanngainnaq*, the strong wind that comes from the North. There will be no dog-sledge race today. Having spent some time chipping the frost off the loo seat, I make my way towards the church which is quite an experience in itself, even if it is only one hundred metres away. It is Sunday and the wind is raging, buffeting the settlement and making it almost impossible to walk past the forlorn glances of the huddled dogs. There is a -35 degree wind chill and the cold is absolutely stinging on the small patches of skin exposed on my face. I sway and stagger, just managing to open the door to the church. I wait and wait in the peaceful shelter of the tiny church, feeling assaulted by the elements, but nobody turns up. I had been told that there are normally two regulars: Bodil Peterson and Regina Oomak. Well, neither them nor the catechist have ventured out today. The settlement is deserted, almost lost in a white, insidious swirl. There is no sign of life at all. Feeling the need to share this moment of drama, I decide to go and see Preben Suersaq who lives at the top of the settlement. The storm is howling, demonic and unrelentless. I can just about make out his blurred A-frame house at the top of the slope in a whirlwind of whiteness. The wind is thumping into me, pushing me back down the slope. It is rapidly becoming a complete whiteout. I lose my footing and trip over a mound of snow, near his house and just in front of his dog-team. I am on the ground and the dogs pounce at me, snarling. Now that I am on the ground, I am fair game and they take their chance. I am lucky. I am about two feet out of their reach. Otherwise, I would have been fighting off the dogs, and nobody would have seen or heard a thing.

Bare-chested (no body hair) and with a perpetual grin, Preben straddles a new, full-length wooden sledge parked in his living room. He has made the *qamutik* especially for the big race that was meant to take place today. Many of the best hunters in the region live in Haviggivik and they relish the competition. It is a question of pride and status. Preben is a very kind, friendly man with laughing eyes. I take to him very much. He got divorced in 2006 and has four children – three daughters and one son. I would guess that he is early 40s. It must be exceptionally difficult for him to hunt and provide for his family without a wife. Preben likes living in Haviggivik, but it is difficult if you are divorced and there are no women. Many think that this is a place to be a young child or be buried, but anything in between is understandably difficult.

Still, three of the children are no longer in Haviggivik. He is one of the many *angatsuduk* ('bachelors') in the settlement. The women have left, leaving empty houses full of memories from distant childhoods. Haviggivik is a place of abandoned men, and not just abandoned houses. When it comes to Haviggivik, the men put hunting before women and sex. And yet I am constantly told that I need a wife to live here and then the problems of heating the home, the endless piles of washing up and the cooking would soon be solved. There are no buyers for the empty houses. The price for the empty house next to Preben is £5,000, but there is no interest. Having watched the storm develop over several slices of frozen Arctic Char and endless cups of black coffee from the luxury of Preben's kitchen window, and once the conversation matter is exhausted, I take my leave. On the way out, Preben tells me that this weather can last days and weeks, and that he and his daughter will visit me this evening. This is a good sign and very typical of Inugguit behaviour: even if there will be nothing more to talk about, they will, if they like you, just want to spend time with you recreating the morning visit with its hidden protocol in another context. This grace period will come to an end, however, as the Inugguit do not like to be 'crowded out' in these small settlements. The addition of just one person could change dramatically the chemistry of the place. On the way back to my house I am followed once again by the three cream young dogs. They walk up behind me and then run off, tails wagging, when I turn around – just like the children playing the tag game.

Two days later and once the storm has abated, a meeting is held in the *kommune* with all the men present. Anxious to take charge, Titken is addressing lots of serious looking faces. They are going to try and hold the dog-sledge race at 1pm today. There will be eight competitors and the distance is 40 kilometres. The course is mapped out around icebergs with a loop around the large tabular iceberg way in the distance towards Cape York. The competitors make the final preparations and lead their eager dog teams down to the sea ice. A small crowd gathers at the start, but it is almost too cold to watch the race. Day after day, the temperature is now about -35 degrees. We huddle into Nukappiannguaq's house, drink some tea and watch the proceedings with his binoculars before reappearing as they approach the settlement. As expected, the winner is Bent Uvdloriaq. He completes the course in one hour exactly. Qisuk Oodaq, the previous winner, is not far behind and third is Nukappiannguaq Danielsson. Nukappiannguaq keeps a staggering thirty-four dogs which means that he needs to catch about two seals a day in order to feed them. Here, there is no dog food in the shop and so hunting really is a necessity.

At 6pm there is the prize giving ceremony at the *kommune*. There are tea and cakes followed by games. It is great fun and everybody is very friendly to me. Unlike in Qaanaaq, here I am always made to feel I belong. I am sat next to Naja Pedersen and she tries to translate the bits that I do not understand. Unprompted, Nukappiannguaq Danielsson tells a long story about the race. Before the party games begin, there is almost a storytelling contest with people getting up and telling stories. Most of the games are all familiar. They are mainly children's games. There is also the game where you have to line up and pass the balloon down the line between your legs. I am standing behind Nukappi-annguaq's wife who is a fun, elderly woman. I have to grind my hips into her in order to get the balloon between her legs. I tower over her; the Inugguit roll around laughing, loving the sexual innuendo of it all. There is also the card game where you have to pass it round in a circle between your lips without touching the card. According to Titken, the atmosphere is so different here because Haviggivik does not have 'the jealousy problem'. There are no 'available' women here, just happily married couples and a horde of bachelors for whom there is nobody to compete over.

It is Sunday and the *nigeq*, the strong wind from the East, is slamming again into the settlement. At the church, Aputsiaq sits on the front row wearing a white anorak. On the back row sits Regina Oomak. Jens Ole Oomak is getting ready to ring the bell which has a nice, soft welcoming peal but there will be nobody else coming. At just gone 10am, Aputsiaq stands up and saunters expressionlessly over to the font where he reads a prayer rather too fast. Then, we sing the first hymn. As per usual in Greenland, we are seated for the hymn. Only Regina, Aputsiaq and I sing. Jens Ole sits behind me in silence. After the first hymn, there is a short reading by Aputsiaq in front of the altar followed by the second hymn. Then, there is another prayer, a longer reading from the pulpit delivered at great haste and then a final hymn. The Lutheran service is very much based on the book, is formulaic and designed so that absolutely anybody could deliver it.

I am meant to be going on a polar bear hunt today with Frank, but it is impossible to leave the settlement in these conditions. If hunters are caught in the *nigeq*, they have to head back to Haviggivik. At his large blue house in the middle of the settlement, the porch is cluttered with skins, *kamikker* and various pots and pans containing blood and meat of a seal. I peel off a few layers and almost fall into the kitchen over the rows of soiled hunting clothes and polar bear fur mittens.

Sitting at the kitchen table are Regina and Jens Ole: two smiley faces through a haze of cigarette smoke, whispering implausible palindromes, enjoying the interstices of everyday life. It is a small world. Frank is Regina's nephew, but he is an *atsiaq* and she refers to him as 'father' as he has her father's recycled name. The kitchen is chaotic with pots and pans strewed all over the place. Seal blood and intestines sit on newspaper on the floor alongside a saucepan containing frothy seal soup. There are small mountains of dirty dishes and used coffee cups everywhere. On the settee in the living room with a long *qamutik* as a footstool sits a bored girl playing a violent computer game. The game is called Resident Evil and is the most ghastly game imaginable. One is in a German concentration camp and one has to shoot as many people as possible. This is how some of the Inugguit youth entertain themselves these days, playing games where the child is required to enact gross violence. Mission accomplished – all dead. Peace and violence are juxtaposed in two realities in the same room.

Birth certificates hang on the wall in the living room. Birth and death are especially significant events in a tiny community where such high levels of inter-relatedness play out on two levels: relations with the living and the web of relatedness through ancestors' recycled names. In Nukappiannguaq's house, there hangs a certificate that the visitor is immediately channelled towards. It is from the Danish Royal Family and labels him a *storfanger*. It is not clear how one achieves this status, but I have seen it before at various households such as at Ole Danielsson's. The Danes understand the symbolic significance of these certificates for Greenlanders.

Jens Ole, a kind and thoughtful man, sits there, grinning, looking over the conversation. His almost perfectly round face is made for laughing. There is a pipe on the kitchen table which Jens Ole wants me to smoke. I do an impression of Knud Rasmussen and everyone falls around laughing. We talk about the dogs and who has been hunting where. Everybody's movements, actions and catch are closely monitored. Anything out of the ordinary is always highlighted in conversations: Enok's name is mentioned and I am told immediately that he tried to commit suicide. Miilu Hanson's bad scar on his chin and his faulty speech can be explained by an attempted suicide. He put the gun to his chin, hoping to blow his brains away but did not manage to kill himself. The scars of the people at Haviggivik each tell a tragic story. Personal information is paraded in front of the stranger. We are soon joined by Aerut Suersaq. He is Aputsiaq's son, suffers with schizophrenia and has a horribly scarred face. He has barely got his coat off before I am told publicly that he was savaged by dogs when he was four years old and is lucky to be alive. I am invited to take a closer look at the scar. Physical and mental deformities are everywhere in Haviggivik: victims of an unforgiving environment.

Frank tells me that his own daughter was attacked by dogs when she was four years old. I am reminded that you have to be firm with the dogs if you want them to respect you. He has names for all of his dogs and speaks of how taxing it is when he cannot find food for them. He lost three last year when they fell into open water. Like humans, they cannot survive long in such cold water. Travelling on thin ice, Frank has seen a polar bear try to attack from underneath the ice. Then, there is silence. Once the *nigeq* has passed, Jens Ole thinks I should go out hunting with his brother, Ingaapaluk. There is nodding, a faint chorus of *iih*, then more silence. I take a very long silence as a cue for me to leave. I get up to go and then everybody wants to know why I am leaving. It is a familiar pattern and I have still not mastered how to read the signals. The Inugguit are very easily insulted and wish you to be comfortable in their company all the time. Social mores here are more or less the inverse to England.

In such a tiny settlement where there are fewer than twenty houses occupied, the cycle of visits can become absolutely suffocating during periods of bad weather. On occasions when hosts have become tired of a train of visitors during the same day, I have witnessed visitors (including myself) being totally ignored with the host just continuing to watch television without as much as acknowledging the visitor. Each house has more or less its own function and characteristics: Frank Suersaq's house was the place where cigarettes were smoked and alcohol consumed.

Ingaapaluk's cabin is the red one immediately in front of the school, very close to mine and almost completely hidden by an *apuhinnak* ('snow that has drifted up to the house'). Young dogs frolic and wrestle with one another, tossing a frozen baby seal outside his house. Ingaapaluk lives in one tiny room, the toilet bucket is in the corner and there are two beds: one which he sleeps on, and one for visitors to perch on. It is by now a familiar arrangement. There are crucifixes and faded pictures of Christ on the wall. The television is on and he is dozing. I feel embarrassed to have disturbed him, but he groans *uniit...uniit* and waves me in. He apologies for his small sledge, but says that we should go out tomorrow morning providing the weather has cleared up.

The following morning, the wind has died down and I prepare to go out dog-sledging with Ingaapaluk. We need to check the seal nets. Titken is standing outside the school where he works as a janitor. He has had a rather brutal haircut and is looking more aggressive than usual. Ingaapaluk appears from the shop. Titken shouts out to him and orders him to come and speak to me. I am abashed by his behaviour as it plays into this troubled, historic notion that the 'rich' European can order the Inugguit around. There was a helicopter in yesterday and that means there was alcohol in the settlement. Titken says accusingly that Ingaapaluk has been drinking. There is a small, but quite nasty tiff between Ingaapaluk and Titken. Ingaapaluk tells him that he does not belong in Haviggivik and should leave. Gossip had been rife about Titken, and I was not surprised to hear this. In every respect, he seemed like an outsider to me. To not be accepted in a tiny, bounded community is intolerable. Even for a hard-nosed character like Titken, this was tough justice and within eighteen months he had moved to Qaanaaq. Titken tells me that Ingaapaluk is a lazy good-for-nothing and that Haviggivik is full of them. He asks me if I have considered why there are so many single men in Haviggivik. There are no available women for these men, and those that have wives have on occasion been frightened to leave them alone. It is perhaps not surprising that the best hunters in

Haviggivik all have wives: Bent, Qisuk and Nukappiannguaq. These three also got the top three prizes in the Annual Dog-sledge Race. Being a good hunter here really does mean status and therefore the hunter gets a wife. Alternatively, you might say the reason they are good hunters is because they have wives to look after the household whilst they are away. Hunting requires a strict division of labour for it to pay. I am not aware of any exceptions to that rule.

Back in the hut, Ingaapaluk walks in, smiling and tells me that we should leave in a few minutes. Titken tries to persuade me not to go, knowing that I will have an experience which through his own negligence he has now been deprived. Titken likes to control the movement and actions of everybody. Titken is disappointed that I have not asked him to tell a story when I have been asking others (who have Polar Eskimo as a mother tongue).

The seven dogs, five males and two females, start pulling a small sledge. Ingaapaluk jogs alongside them, whipping to the side of them and shouting orders, *harru, harru, atsuk, atsuk*. There is the normal chaos and mayhem; high-pitched feverish excitement, growling, jostling for position and wagging of tails. I grab onto the stanchions of the sledge, leaning back as far as I can to ensure the dogs do not shoot down the hummocky shore ice. When they start pulling, it is almost impossible to run with the sledge and the spectacle of a passenger trying to cling onto the sledge with all his might is truly tickling. We get to the bottom of the slope without too much drama and within seconds we are on our way. It is always the same: hours, days of skulking, waiting and then suddenly and in a flash, you are on your way.

Hak-hak, hak-hak, Ingaapaluk navigates using the icebergs, remembering where he left his nets in relation to icebergs whose distinctive shapes make for good markers. Icebergs close to the settlements are particularly welcome because they provide fresh water, they keep the fast ice in place and they enable hunters to set seal nets without having to travel far. The nets are put close to the edge of the iceberg as this is where the seal comes up for air and where the ice is thinnest. As with the rest of the region, the hunters of Haviggivik have noticed that the current is getting stronger. Stones are used to hold the nets in a vertical position, but hunters have found empty nets that are lying flat. The stronger current at Cape York makes it now dangerous to travel by dog-sledge around the peninsular, effectively cutting them off from the other settlements.

We are making our way towards a *maniilaq* ('a large, high iceberg with columns') that sits prominently in front of the settlement. The wind has been blowing from the East for some days and we travel alongside a *qimiaggoq* ('long ridge of snow formed by the wind blowing the snow in one direction'). Ingaapaluk has left three nets in total, dotted around the sea ice, all about five kilometres or so from the settlement. The ice here is a bit thinner than in Qaanaaq and is only about 40cm thick. Just before the melt season begins, the Arctic sea ice is at its thickest at this point. Travelling between the nets, Ingaapaluk spots a seal breathing hole. The Inugguit are able to spot the slightest hole in the sea ice or the tiniest irregular ice formation from a great distance. It is remarkable. All the nets are empty, but Ingaapaluk is his normal cheery self, joking and laughing.

Returning to the settlement, there is a truly vicious head wind from the North (*pavanngainnaq*). With the wind chill, it is -42 degrees. I have never experienced cold like this before. The wind is a treacherous, guileful creature, chilling me to the bone. It does not matter how many layers one has on, one will get cold in these temperatures if sitting still on a sledge. I keep trying to wiggle my toes and clench my fists, but I am rapidly losing all the feeling in my extremities. My buff has frozen to my beard and the tiny patches of skin exposed on my face are freezing over. Sitting behind Ingaapaluk, I bury my head under my arms adopting the brace position in a futile attempt to get the blood running. My head feels like a frozen block of ice sitting on stiff shoulders. The *pavanngainnaq* is blowing right through my forehead. It is unbearable, but soon we will be back in the settlement. Ingaapaluk is wearing a thinnish anorak and driving the dogs is facing the brunt of the wind. He turns to me, grinning and says *ikkeernaqtorruaq* ('it is very cold'). I wonder how the dogs can cope with it, running straight into the wind like that. Squeezed in on a small sledge, I get cramp in my left leg and feel thoroughly disabled by the time we get back to the settlement. We hop off as we approach the shore ice. The dogs race up the hummocky ice, the sledge speeding off towards his cabin. Ingaapaluk jumps back on, waving and laughing all the way. The dogs always race back home, thinking perhaps that they are going to be fed. Even for a very experienced hunter, they are extremely hard to control at this point.

Back in the settlement, the news is that Bent and Qisuk have killed a polar bear out towards Cape York and are on their way back. I think of them travelling all that way in these very low temperatures. The proud hunters are greeted by the entire settlement. When a polar bear is killed, there is a tradition of going round and knocking on every door to tell people the news. They have not just killed a polar bear, but have caught circa one hundred Greenland Halibut. Everybody helps out putting the fish on a sledge and pushing it up to the Arctic Foods premises. These men are heroes for a day and are enjoying their celebrity. The sledges are pulled up to Qisuk's house and the polar bear which has already been cut up and frozen on the way back is put up on the racks out of the reach of the dogs. This bear is special because it had a radio transmitter around its neck. Surely, the hunters and biologists must be at odds at what is going on. I am sure they did not put a transmitter on it, just to see it killed.

There is a beautiful pale, light in the evening. The moon is reflected in the windows of the abandoned yellow cabin behind Thomas' house whose derelict condition has a curious charm. The cabin has been smashed to pieces by Arctic storms; its shabby state is inexplicably photogenic. There is utter silence. Then, the crunch of the hard snow as I stroll past half-dozing dogs who have one eye on me. Their snouts are slightly raised, identifying me by smell. Broken furniture and discarded white goods peek up through the thick snow: the accoutrements of modern day living scattered across the frozen tundra. There is a sense of timelessness here and I have difficulty remembering how long I have been in the settlement and am not sure which day it is. The huddle of small wooden houses disturbs only slightly the omnipresence of whiteness which magnifies the overwhelming sense of a tiny, isolated place almost lost in a vast wilderness. On the way up the slope, Adolf Qaerngaq greets me. The conversation goes along the normal lines: a few comments about the weather, the hunting today, a question asking me when I am leaving and then a series of sighs and grins followed by a quick *taima* signalling that the conversation is finished.

Then, I bump into Titken. He thinks that the women have left the men because they are all drunks. In his view, the drinking is much worse here than in Qaanaaq. Titken is keen to tell me about the darker side of life in Haviggivik: Preben's wife left him for Jens Ole because he was beating her up when drunk. Adultery in a place this tiny and remote could surely have lethal consequences because there is no escape from social dislocation. They are no longer on speaking terms, but it is imperative in this culture never to show your anger. If you get angry and do not apologise, the Inugguit will have nothing to do with you. Later on in the day, I meet Preben and he wishes to know what Titken was telling me. Conversations and gossip are monitored here and recycled into more gossip. Preben thinks Titken is a difficult individual and a failed hunter which is certainly the case. It is clear that Titken wants to be in charge of the community, but he has no power. He called a meeting on Sunday at the *kommune* to discuss the 'problems of Haviggivik', but nobody turned up and he is angry.

I retire at just gone midnight, but am awoken at 2.50am by Qaordloqtoq. He is standing at the entrance to the living room, shining a torchlight in my face, and it is obvious that he is excited about something. He tells me that I have to come immediately as there is a polar bear in front of my house. I wonder for a moment if this is a sort of Inugguit April Fools' Day sort of stunt, to wake up the Englishman in the middle of the night on the pretence that there is a polar bear sniffing round and get him to stand outside in sub -30 degrees in his jim-jams. I curse at how slow I am at getting ready compared to the Inugguit who jump into their skins so quickly when need be.

We run outside into the pitch black. I have my pocket video camera, but no torch, and stumble with sleepiness in the deep snow. I am still half-asleep and in my confusion I forget for a moment that I am in a hunting settlement and have in my mind this image of people watching a polar bear walking rather majestically between the houses and very close to us. Sadly, I am mistaken and the truth is remorsefully other. A dead male polar bear lies directly outside my house. It was shot two minutes ago. He had smelt the seal blubber lying around the settlement and had taken his chance. The hysterical barking of the dogs woke up my neighbour and the animal was killed quickly with two bullets. Ever since I arrived in the settlement I have been going on and on about wishing to see a polar bear, and thus Nukappiannguaq's first words were to wake up the *tuluk* (the 'Englishman'). Despite being three in the morning, there ensued a number of quick phone calls to all the households in Haviggivik and soon a small crowd had gathered around the bear.

The adult male bear (*ittorruk*) is huge, measuring nearly three metres long. One swipe of its massive paws could kill a human being. Ropes are tied around the bear's legs and it takes five men to drag the bear up the slope two metres or so where an electric lamp has been strung to a pole. The bear's jaws are opened. A number of its teeth are missing on one side and its jaw is broken. This is mating time and it looks like he has been fighting with another male. I am shocked to see this vast, majestic animal, this eco-icon of the Arctic, the first one I have ever seen, dead in front of me. The bear is cut up before me but I have no problem with the blood and the guts. I have seen so much of that in the last months that one becomes immune to it. The shock is seeing the bear dead and not alive as I had hoped. It lies there like a huge lump on the snow. I am rather speechless. Nukappiannguaq is excited like a boy and very proud of his kill. The bear is turned on its back and a small cut is made just below its chin, then the knife goes right down its stomach. A bear is cut up in the same way a seal is.

It takes three men about twenty minutes to skin the animal. On the inside of its cheek, a six digit number has been stamped on the bear. The biologists have obviously tracked this bear. The number is jotted down. The bear is very thin with very little blubber. He must have been starving. Such a starving, male bear is very dangerous and would attack a human. All the older hunters agree that the polar bears used to be much fatter in the 1980s and 1970s. The Melville Bay region is one of the best areas to find polar bears in the January-March period in north-west Greenland. The best areas are Innaanganeq (Cape York Area), Puihidluuharhuaq and in particular the region where the glacier breaks off into the fjord and produces icebergs. The ice just south of Sad'leq and around Nad'lortuup nuaa where there are stranded icebergs is also a good bear-spotting place.

This is quite an event as it is the first time a bear has been seen in the settlement itself since 2006. Theses bears are referred to as *tikeraat* ('a bear that comes into the settlement'). Many of the hunters believe there are more polar bears now than there used to be. It is true that more are seen now, but this is almost certainly because they are starving and thus coming closer and closer to human settlements. It is not known how many polar bears there are in the Kane Basin region.

The men are freezing, trying to cut up the bear wearing just thin rubber gloves. Once the bear has been skinned, tea and coffee are served inside Nukappiannguaq's house. It is 3.30am but people are still drinking coffee. The atmosphere is very jovial. I jest that the bear's penis was surprisingly small and Nukappiannguaq is curious to know if Englishmen are rather better endowed. After the tea, I retire back to bed and let the men carry on cutting up the bear. I am surprised how silent the dogs were as the bear was cut up. The dogs are so well fed here. There are no hunting trophies and there is absolutely no waste. I am curious to see whether the meat is shared between all the inhabitants as it should be, and whether the fur is used to make *nannut*. Nukappiannguaq has a reputation as an *hinnaktoq* ('a greedy man'). Elsewhere, I have heard people refer to him as a gangster and a bully. Some told me that many young people left the settlement because of him. I was told that one night Nukappiannguaq got drunk and went around shooting. Nobody was hurt, but a crime had been committed. He called a meeting for everybody and asked them not to tell the police.

It is imperative to differentiate between what we mean by hunting in the West to hunting here. The Inugguit have no concept of hunting for sport. This is subsistence hunting only. They hunt to feed their families, dogs and that is all. Many people cannot afford the prices of the goods in the shop. When you go into their homes, you will generally speaking never find any hunting trophies. You will not see a musk-oxen or caribou's head on the wall nor will you generally see polar bear skins on the floor. My house which was let out to 'outsiders' was the only house where I ever saw that. Every part of the animal they kill is used, but the animal is used for clothing essential for survival in extremely low temperatures. Polar bear, seal, Arctic Fox and Arctic Hare fur are all used for mittens. Polar bear fur is used for trousers, Caribou for coats, sealskin for boots, etc.

In the morning, I am invited into the school by Naja Pedersen because her nephew Aqqa Suersaq from Qaanaaq is celebrating today his sixth birthday party. Greenlandic flags are flying around town. Almost the whole settlement turns up. There are five pupils at the school: three boys and two girls. Aqqa will soon start at the school becoming their sixth pupil and this is major cause for celebration. Interestingly, the boy and girls are taught separately in two different rooms. Polar bear, seal and Greenland Halibut are on the menu followed by an impressive display of cakes and biscuits. Everybody does the normal rounds of congratulating the various members of the Suersaq family, shaking their hands in a sort of mock formal manner and saying *pi'dluarit* before tucking into the food with vim. As always, meat is held and eaten with your left hand whilst your right hand slices off slithers with the knife, pushing the knife towards you. It takes a while to master especially when the meat is so hot.

In honour of the new addition to the school, an impromptu and cele-bratory 'mini' sledge race is organised where only small one-passenger racing sledges are used. The course is short, just one loop around the large iceberg stationed in front of the settlement (approximately two kilometres). The sledges are pulled by a full dog team. The result is probably akin to putting a Ferrari V12 engine in a mini. The sledges move very fast and are harder to control. Bent wins again, Jesper is second and Ingapaluk is third. It is great fun. The ten year old Lars Kristiansen has terrible problems controlling his dogs, being swung around in circles and eventually led back to the settlement amidst a festival of laughter and mockery. Starting school, like confirmations and birthdays are very important rites of passage for the Greenlanders. These events have great symbolic value and the celebration should be public (and never private). It is frowned upon not to attend them. The initial and concluding events are always more important than the process in-between: the confirmation celebration is more important than being religious or pious in any way; starting and leaving school are major cele-brations even if the value of education is not always recognised. Life is a series of milestones, rites of passage and it is these that matter.

In the evening, the moon is orange and the sky is full of constellations creating an almost impossible image, dismantling and reformulating perceptions and conceptions of reality. *Forty Licks* plays in my cabin. The moon is full and it is a lunar eclipse. I have never seen such a serene sky. It is bitterly cold but I am happy to freeze and enjoy the splendour of the syzygy. Far from the Hardyesque continents of moil and misery, this profile is indeed as placid as a brow divine. A storm begins to rage later the night, but I wake up to sunshine and blue skies. A ptarmigan (*aqiggiq*) stands facing the wind, pecking at the ground apparently oblivious to both me and the extremely low temperatures. The wind blows the snow off the slopes, throwing up small puffs of white clouds. The view over the sea ice resembles the Sahara el Beyda, the white desert of Farafra: the icebergs protuding like white desert mushrooms created by the dry wind and the sand; a magical, frozen kingdom whose ice is wrinkled like parchment.

Trying to photograph the bird, my fingers freeze, go numb and rapidly start to sting and burn. The wind today is the coldest yet. I am unable to put the lens cap on and decide to dive into Adolf's hut to avoid imminent frostbite. He is busy making a sledge. He puts his chisel down and welcomes me in. I make a beeline for the heater and slowly thaw my frozen fingers over the flame. He quickly puts some coffee on. The routine is by now extremely familiar. Adolf tells me that they eat ptarmigan here and that it tastes very good. Just like chicken. Like his father, he is a warm, kind man living the simplest life possible with almost no material possessions. Ripped bin liners cover up the windows to prevent the severe cold seeping in through the cracks in the woodwork. As is invariably the case, the poorest are always the most hospitable and the first to give up what they have. I mention that I might go to Qaanaaq tomorrow and he immediately does what all the other men do and asks me if I will be seeing girls. The body language is always the same: they hold out their arms as if they are holding and kissing a woman, and then there are peals of laughter. For the hunters in Haviggivik, a trip to town can only mean one thing.

Adolf sits in the armchair, grinning, with his long Qaerngaq face. He has spent his whole life out in nature and has at times been victim to the hostile, cruel climate. He made the costly error of falling asleep on the sledge. He woke up a long way from Haviggivik. His dog-team had stopped and were lying down. His leg had frozen. I think I have some sense of the terrible fear and agony that he must have gone through. Today, he has a wooden leg and life goes on as usual for him, out hunting whenever he can. That is the Haviggivik spirit.

The sky is very overcast in the morning and I am sure that there will be no helicopter today. However, the beacon outside the shop is flashing which means that Hans Karlsson has sent a weather report saying that the conditions are good and that the helicopter has left the Air Base. Hans Berthelson and Naja Pedersen are busy clearing snow from the landing spot. I collect my things quickly and make my way to the shop which acts as a sort of check-in. No tickets, passports or anything else is needed here. I head down to the shop, dragging my bag along the snow when Hans appears, wandering over and smoking a cigarette. He grins and tells me that the helicopter has turned back because the weather is too bad. They will try again in three days time.

Today feels like the first day of spring. In the afternoon sun, it is a good ten degrees warmer and it is possible for the first time in months to have a conversation with somebody outside for more than a few minutes. Naja and Qisuk are building an igloo for one of their dogs to give birth in. The snow is compacted and very thick and it is simply a question of cutting out large blocks with a saw and building a house in a conventional way, as if they were bricks. They are both my age, but still live the traditional life and have not lost any of the knowledge at all. There is no doubt that here in the settlements the old traditions live on to a greater extent than in Qaanaaq.

Over the last few days, my lower jaw molar has given me some discomfort. The tooth broke last week whilst eating a cashew nut. Knowing that there is no dentist here, I set about repairing the tooth myself with my emergency dental repair kit. Using a tiny handheld mirror, I 're-cemented' the tooth but I am not sure that it will hold. Hopefully, there will be a visiting dentist in Qaanaaq who can improve on my shoddy dental work. In the meantime, it is Ibuprofen all the way as I think I am able to resist the locals' keen wish to remove the tooth for me.

It is bright blue skies at 7.30am and I put my head around the corner at 8am to see if the light is blinking on top of the shop, to suggest that a helicopter is coming. There is nothing and so I decide to go and get some water instead. I bump into Naja Pedersen and change my mind, making for the shop to see if Hans is there or not. He is there indeed and is on the phone to the Danish pilot telling him that the conditions are fine. I am the only passenger, but a lot of freight is loaded onto the helicopter: seal skins and Greenland Halibut, all destined for Maniitsoq and Qaqortoq. Approximately fifty boxes are squeezed into the helicopter. There is just about room for me in the side seat facing the right hand side. Almost all the settlement comes out to help put the freight on the helicopter, and perhaps to see me off. We share a few jokes. They are all lined up as if it is some sort of military parade. I shake all their hands and thank them for their hospitality. This has been an extraordinary few weeks and this special place will never leave my memory: its isolation, remoteness, the smiling faces and *ammaqa* spirit. They have been all very kind and I am sad to leave. I say goodbye to my favourite dog with whom I feel I have forged a special bond, leave the key to the padlock for the house with Hans and I am on my way. It is now slightly overcast, but the weather is good enough.

From the air, the settlement looks entirely implausible. So tiny, so far from anywhere and then lost amidst a sea of white. I still cannot believe that this place exists and the words I have chosen to describe it seem painfully inadequate and do not do justice to the images in my mind. Leaving Haviggivik behind, I am reminded of how such an experience, a thought or even a possibility can shatter and transform us. My thoughts turn to those living in choked cities that we call 'civilised', to the stain of industry that might yet stipple and dapple this white heaven. Living without industry is surely an ideal, swerving 'progress' and 'development' and thus living without fumes. Thinking that this 'gobbet of Arcadia' might one day be transformed leaves me feeling emotional and pessimistic about the future of humanity.

Approaching Pituffik, there is bare rock where the wind has blown the snow away. The whole US defence area with radar screens and listening stations can be seen on top of a hill. Waiting to refuel, I have an interesting conversation with John (the Danish policeman based at the Air Base and nominally responsible for policing Haviggivik). Just as I did not think there could be a dark side to Qaanaaq when I first arrived, I most certainly thought the same of Haviggivik. It turns out that once again I am mistaken. There was a murder in Haviggivik two years ago. I cannot believe it. A man trained to become a catechist and he became a fanatic and started drinking heavily and being violent to his wife. One Thursday afternoon, the wife could not take it any longer. She picked up a kitchen knife and stabbed her husband in the heart in the living room in front of their teenage daughter. The man died. At some point, John was contacted. It was March and the weather was too bad to get a helicopter down there and so John had to try and police the situation from the telephone.

He told the locals to take the woman and lock her in one of the rooms in the school and ordered the community to take shifts through the day and night, keeping an eye on her. Nobody was to touch the body. The weather eventually cleared and John got down there on the Monday. He took a doctor with him and a post-mortem was carried out on his body in the living room where he was killed. Locals were spoken to, the victim was put in a body bag and then the wife and the body were flown to Pituffik and then Qaanaaq. The woman was kept in the police station and was sentenced. The daughter still apparently lives in Haviggivik.

The killer received six years in a detention centre in Illulissat, but will probably only serve four. The only criminals sent to prisons in Denmark are cases where the offender is mentally ill or where it is felt it is too dangerous to keep them in the open correctional system. When the criminal code was drawn up in the 1950s, great emphasis was put on the fact that there should be no prisons in Greenland. At the detention centre, the criminal is given a job in the community where he or she works eight hours a day. At 4.30pm in the afternoon the criminal then has to return to the detention centre where he or she sleeps.

John emphasises the fact that most of the murderers are not really a threat to the community because the murder is always motivated by a very personal, difficult relationship between two close people. The event is normally triggered by jealousy and the offender may not have much of a criminal record. John thinks the biggest problem at the moment is sexual abuse against children which always stems from problems with alcohol. John says that there have been at least six cases of sexual abuse in Haviggivik in the last three years. It is difficult to believe it, having spent so much time with the children the last few weeks. The children and the parents there all seem exemplary, and the children seem really happy. It is quite perplexing.

Whilst talking to John, his phone rings. He has received a satellite call from the two German-Polish 'explorers' who set off just before I left for Haviggivik. They are on the inland ice, north of Hiorapaluk in Inglefield Land and have got into trouble. Their Primus is not working and they have no means of melting ice or cooking. They only took one Primus with them and now they want to be rescued. There is much discussion between the pilots as to what should be done. John says that they can only rescue people in life critical situations where somebody's life is threatened or if somebody has broken a leg for instance. A rescue mission of this sort costs 7,000 Euros. The helicopter can only stay airborne for two hours and it will take an hour to get to them which does not leave much time to look for them. They have a reading from the GPS but there are apparently one hundred different GPS systems and unless they use the 84 system, their reading may not match up with the pilots.

The weather report from Inglefield Land is not good and they have to make a decision soon as to whether to go or not. They decide to fly to Qaanaaq first, refuel and then take it from there. John tells me that these expeditions are a disaster and are creating real problems. They had to rescue three Norwegians last year who were sailing kites on the Ice sheet. The Polish expedition was a failure too as there is open water on the Smith Sound. The current running between the Kane Basin and Baffin Bay runs so strongly that even in the coldest of winters, the water does not freeze over. At Cape Alexander, Cape Parry and Cape Atholl, open water rarely lies far from the shore, and in fact it has never been possible to sledge around Cape Alexander.

There is no sign of the open water on the way to Qaanaaq. The town appears huge in comparison and walking up and down the familiar tracks I am almost shocked to see so many people again and hear new noises. Arpud Qaerngaq collects fresh water ice from the icebergs in the massive Komatsu Hm 300-1 articulated dump truck that beeps and flashes at every turn: thirteen tons of metal moves at speeds of 30mph over seventy centimetres of ice. It is a rather strange sensation being back. I have some idea how the children must feel when they move from the settlements to the town to continue their education. I wish I were still in Haviggivik, but am looking forward to getting my tooth seen to. It is very mild in Qaanaaq. It must be about -15 degrees which feels significantly warmer than what I have been putting up with.

The same cannot be said for my house. The temperature inside is -13.5 degrees which is a new record low, but it could have been colder. I get the oil heater going, but it does not last. On a second attempt, I put too much oil in and the fire blows up in my face, burning my hair, eyebrows and eyelashes. The smell of the sulphurous odour from burnt hair lingers for many days and is commented on by all my visitors. With singed eyebrows, the whiff of burnt hair swings like a pendulum in front of my nose. I decide not to waste any more time and go and speak to Jakob who did such a good job before. He makes three trips in total before it finally starts working. I think Qaanaaq is trying to tell me something. This place is not for me. Qaanaaq feels soulless and within no time I am missing life in the settlements.

7: Herbert Island

It is late March and the occasional day is surprisingly mild. In the afternoon, the sun spills into the house pushing the temperature up to a torrid 25.6 degrees. It reminds me of how it was when I first came here. The weather is changing fast. At 6pm in the evening, the sun is still high in the sky; it will be light until 10pm tonight. For the first time in months, I went out without a hat today. With my lighter RAB coat on and without the Baffin boots, I felt like a new man. I am used to covering obsessively every square inch of exposed skin. The change feels sudden, almost too sudden, jarring perhaps. I love the light. Still, the sun and the light are deceiving. It is still -15 degrees out there and I feel it stinging on my ears. A young man saunters past, stripped down to his T-shirt.

I go to the bar at midnight and find that it is almost completely empty. Canned dance music plays for nobody. I ask Umik where everybody is. They are at home, listening to the radio as people are calling in and telling stories. The radio is on briefly in the bar and I hear Magnus tell a story. I cannot believe this. After all the time I have spent with him and the number of times I have asked him whether he knows any stories, here he is telling a story on the radio. I rush home and turn the radio on. All kinds of people are calling in and telling stories. The programme goes on until 3am in the morning in a fuzz of gravelly voices, clashing cadences and drawn out laughter, all spliced together skilfully by Arqioq Jensen.

Magnus visits in the morning, gushing with enthusiasm about the ice-fishing. There are about forty people in total, standing about a mile out on the sea ice in towards the bay. It is clear that this is a social activity as much as anything else with jokes and biscuits being passed around. Cowered over steaming cups of black coffee, men and women of all ages wiggle small lines in the freezing cold hoping to entice a Polar Cod (*eqalugaq*) swimming by. Holes are made using a hand auger; the ice is nearly a metre thick here in this part of the bay. Once the hole is made, the slush is cleared out using an *ilait*, the line is lowered and then given a distinctive flick of the wrist. Shovels are at the ready once the hole starts to freeze over. Keeping the holes free of ice is a constant battle in these temperatures. No bait is used. The brilliant Arctic sunshine spews over the town's clear skies. Out on the sea ice, it is significantly colder than in the sheltered sun-trap of the town. Whilst we are fishing, Josef points in the distance to the slopes behind Qaanaaq. He has identified a wind that is on its way. I have fished for an hour and am overwhelmed by the boredom of it all. I have caught one Polar Cod and am delighted with that. It is a small fish, measuring about twenty centimetres long. I eat the little thing for my supper.

An hour later, walking home, the *avangnaq* kicks up very suddenly. The wind picks up the powdery snow, blowing it off the slopes to a background of dazzling sunshine. Inukitsoq points to a strange phenomenon in the sky. There are two very large arcs around the sun. The arcs are vast and colourful, a bit like rainbows but without the panoply of colours. They are sun halos and occur when thin clouds containing millions of ice crystals cover the sky. Behind us in the distance, Minik drives a Mazda Bongo (Third Generation) at very high speeds across the ice, oblivious of the extraordinary sky overhead.

Shortly before eleven in the morning, Arqioq walks into the house and announces that 'we are going out for a spin and that he will pick me up at 1pm'. He turns up half an hour early. First of all we stop at the fire station to put some more air in the tyres of his white Mercedes M-Class (definitely the poshest of the seventeen motor vehicles in Qaanaaq and rather fitting for the man I call the *kunngi*, 'the King'). Then, we drive over to his yellow house towards the top of the town and before I know it I am loading the trailer up with satellite phones, VHF radios, sleeping bags, Primus stoves and various comestibles.

This looks like more than a spin on the ice to me and I am delighted to see that we seem to be embarking on some kind of adventure. Then, I understand we are off to the *kommune* to pick up two Government officials who wish to see what the potential is for fishing at Qeqertat. There has been talk about building a factory there and moving the electricity plant from the now abandoned settlement of Moriussaq to Qeqertat. Two cars will be going out on the ice. For longer trips, two cars are always required, in case somebody gets into trouble.

I have the front seat and two serious looking West Greenlanders who barely say a word all day long sit in the back. The ice is initially very hummocky and we are bouncing about all over the place, but soon smoothes out to a vast white, flat expanse stretching right across the bay. Once we are off the shore ice, there are a few largeish icebergs to negotiate near Qaanaaq towards Herbert Island, and then we turn sharp left into Inglefield Bay. It is -18 degrees and we are immersed in the most brilliant blue skies and Arctic sunshine. Despite the temperature, one can get sunburnt in this weather. Arqioq is on the VHF radio to the car in front which is driven by his uncle Tullu Eipe. In the back of that vehicle sits Qaanaaq's oldest resident and one of my key informants and story-tellers, Iisaaq Jeremiassen. Sharing the back seat with him is Iggiannguaq's younger sister.

Driving on the sea ice down the Inglefield Bay to the most remote and tiniest of settlements in Greenland is an unforgettable experience. The population is twenty-two and I am frequently told it is the only settle-ment without electricity. There is no longer a helicopter that flies there. Oil and provisions are delivered once a year by the supply ship, and that is it. Mail must be collected on occasional trips to Qaanaaq. They might pay their bills annually, or more probably they just do not have any bills. There is about a ten week window in the spring when one can drive on the ice out there. Otherwise, it is motorboat in the summer and dog-sledge in the winter. Qeqertat is about 70 miles from Qaanaaq, right at the end of the Inglefield Bay. It is the best place to hunt narwhal in the area, and might become an important Greenland Halibut fishing ground.

The drive on the ice is absolutely exhilarating. The ice is covered in a generous covering of snow and is for the most part absolutely flat. We are travelling at speeds of up to 80mph on what is effectively a motorway on top of the sea. A motorway where there are no lanes, no obnoxious speed limit signs or patronising advice about seat belts, but just two solitary cars moving like two ants across a vast, spotless white bed sheet. About half way we stop for a coffee break. Here we are, a small group of people enjoying our elevenses on the frozen sea in the middle of the frigid bay. There is nothing, but silence. No birds, no dogs, not a breath of wind. There is just ice and alluring emptiness: one big natural freezer. The cliffs here are quite high and jagged with glaciers running down through deep, narrow gorges. On the right, far in the distance, Arqioq points to a memorial which I am unable to see. Three scientists were killed there three years ago. They got caught in a storm and were literally blown off the mountain. One of the bodies was never found. Not far from here, the highest wind speeds on earth were recorded just a few years ago, 208mph – that is a double hurricane.

After two hours of driving down the middle of the bay, an iceberg the size of a mythical Schloss can be seen in the distance, parked just in front of the settlement, dwarfing the tiny houses and shining like a precious stone. A team of dogs circle expectingly and then lie lazily on the ice, basking in the afternoon sunshine. A handful of elderly gentlemen amble down to the sea ice, puffing on pipes and bearing large grins. These people do not get many visitors. I have no doubt the whole settlement has been watching us from a distance through the pairs of binoculars that sit on every Inugguit window ledge. There is no phone network here, fixed line or mobile. No Internet. The community has a VHF radio and one satellite phone which they can use in an emergency. Otherwise, they are cut off from the outside world. These hardy people do not worry about emergencies. They have lived in complete isolation long enough to know that if something goes wrong, they are on their own. When the sea ice has not properly formed or has not quite melted, it could potentially be months before it would be possible to reach the settlement. By any standards, these people are living an extraordinary life in an otherwise hyper-connected world.

Iisaaq has come to Qeqertat because he used to live here and there is something of an emotional reunion as the 88-year-old man totters over the slippery ice to greet old friends. If you blinked, you might miss the place. There is getting away from it all, and then there is this. Walking up to the settlement, you can feel the peaceful karma wash over you. This is an oasis of calm, hidden away in the corner of a hostile environment. Life here is very, very slow. Although there are apparently twenty-two residents, I see no more than ten people. A small child comes to greet us. I wonder if he has any play friends. The school looks like a church but that is because it is the church. It is also the community hall and is just one room slightly larger than my living room. The dogs are sleeping, but open one eye and push their snouts towards us as we parade past. The arrival of two cars seems to have doubled the population of the place.

The Government officials disappear into a red A-framed house and I take a stroll to see if I can find any life. There are about twenty houses in the settlement, but like Haviggivik many of them are abandoned. I walk around for ten minutes, before looping back on myself and bumping into Arqioq. Neither of us has managed to find a single soul. The weather is good and people are no doubt out hunting. Then, an elderly man standing on the balcony of what looks to be a very modern, blue pre-fabricated Danish bungalow waves and beckons us over. Arqioq knows the gentleman, and in fact he is in some way related to him. His name is Miteq (the 'Eider duck'). Inside, we are offered tea, coffee and cakes before Arqioq helps himself to what is ostensibly lunch on the sheet of cardboard on the floor.

Frozen Greenland Halibut is eaten in small slices and rubbed in a slightly spicy, but moreish condiment. After my time in Greenland, I think I would probably say I prefer frozen fish to cooked fish. It just melts in your mouth and is quite divine. After the Halibut, we move onto the *mattak*. I have found it far too chewy in the past, but this is really tender and absolutely full of flavour and vitamins too. With the mattak, we have dried cod and some dried narwhal skin which is black and looks like charcoal.

It is not true that there is no electricity in Qeqertat. Some of the homes, this one for example, have a small private generator outside. In essence, if you want electricity, get yourself a generator. This very modern house has a flat screen television and a smart Hi-Fi. It is not what I expected at all. As always, the atmosphere is jovial with all kinds of jokes circulating, mostly at my expense. After a lunch of raw, dried and frozen fish, I am off to explore. I wish to find the graveyard, the resting place of the last shamans. Perched just up on the rocks, but immediately behind the settlement sits the minuscule cemetery. There are fourteen graves, most of them lost in deep snow and thus forgotten for much of the year. I also discover what seems to serve as a shop. It is closed, and is a tiny cabin about ten feet long with various bits of merchandise (loo rolls, dented cans of tinned fruit long past their sell-by-date and crushed cereal packets) stacked high in the dusty windows.

I find two gentlemen to speak to, both of whom I recognise and have seen in Qaanaaq before. One of them is a short, wiry man with high cheekbones, a wispy beard and smiling walnut-coloured eyes. The other is round-faced and thickset. They are doing some repairs to a sledge. Another gentleman sits on his balcony enjoying the sub-zero sunshine, holding a pair of binoculars vertically and peering through the only functioning lens at his dogs parked on the sea ice. Even though it must be months since he last saw an outsider, he does not look remotely surprised when I address him in his language. He has a kind, expressive face and looks like he might have been here forever.

After inspecting an impressive cache of Greenland Halibut, we saunter down the lazy slopes to the sea ice which shines with the sheen of desert varnish. The whole present population of seven follow us down, shake hands and wave as we disappear back to the real world, but not really. Qaanaaq seems like an urban jungle compared to the tranquility of Qeqertat.

It is April Fools' Day and gentlemen are joking around at the shop. I leave, thinking as per usual that I am on set with Benny Hill. I remark to incoming shoppers that the light is never-ending now. It seems to me as if it is getting slightly warmer each day too, but the temperature is still -18 degrees. It is all relative. With the sunshine, you can see patches where the snow is beginning to melt, revealing the slippery dark blue ice beneath. I remove all the bin liners from the windows and open the vents. Some have been concerned by the complete lack of ventilation in the house, especially given the problem of tuberculosis in the region. It feels like an historic moment.

Seeking my supper, I am on my way to the Polar Cod fishing ground when a slightly chaotic dog-sledge comes towards me. It is Ole Danielsson and his wife and they are coming right for me. The camera case, my gloves and Thermos are on the sea ice. The dog-sledge goes right over them. The case is fine, but the sealskin gloves are gone. The dogs have run off with them. I scout around, but only manage to find one. I try to follow the tracks of the dog-sledge, hoping at some point that the dog realised it was not food and would have spat out the glove. I walk very slowly, scanning the horizon looking for a small blob on a vast, endless white seascape sculpted by the wind. The sharp irregular grooves that the *sastrugi* form from the wind erosion of the snow on the ice make for a pattern of perfectly shaped, but ephemeral dunes like a snowy

Sahara. I see in the distance what looks to be a black bin liner and wander over in that direction. I realise that it is in fact a very dark furred dog splayed on the snow. I cannot think what he is doing here, so far from anywhere.

Approaching it, I immediately realise that this is going to be another one of those 'difficult Greenlandic moments'. It is a well-fed male Greenlandic dog with thick, dark fur. I get very close to him and he does not move at all. He is lying on his side with his head facing the snow. He does not stir, but is breathing. His hind legs point at an obtuse angle but the dog does not seem to be in any obvious pain. He has a harness on him and a piece of rope pulled tightly around his rump. The hunter has cut the line which is what they do in an emergency situation. The dog lies there completely motionless as I try to undo the knot of the rope. I do not have a knife on me, but do manage to get the rope off him. It does not seem to make much difference. It is all horribly futile. He can walk for two or three metres, but then just lies down. The dog is moving away from me. I wonder if he could make it back to Qaanaaq, but the answer is almost certainly 'no'. I am able to sit right next to him and stroke him, but there is no real response or reaction. He looks tired, but is not whimpering or in any ostensible pain. There is a tragic resignation in his eyes and that is all. I cannot believe that I have found myself in this same horrible dilemma once again.

The hunter must have realised that one of his dogs had been badly injured, but has apparently just left him here. I am out on the sea ice, about 45 minutes walk from Qaanaaq and this is a big dog. Without a sledge, I could not get this animal back to town. The dog is not freezing, but is lying in the sunshine. If I were to be able to get him back to Qaanaaq, there is nothing that anybody could do for him there. They would just see him as a useless dog and would shoot him. Worse still, there may even be an act of cannibalism. The dog is not in pain, and I will not therefore kill it myself with my shotgun at home. The dog killer would not dream of walking all the way out here to kill a dog that is not a threat to anyone. The suggestion alone would be laughable to him. I could perhaps get somebody else to do it, but once again the dog is in discomfort but as far as I can see no real pain. He does not respond to me stroking him at all. Unlike the last episode, the dog is not frightened or desperate. He just looks horribly discontented at his new disability.

He appears to want to be left alone. Perhaps he knows what his lot is. He is standing rather awkwardly with an arched back and I wonder if the dog has in fact damaged his abdomen, perhaps getting caught under the sledge which can easily happen. I stay with the dog for quite some time, stroking him and going through the options in my mind. They are all equally unattractive. In the distance at the Polar Cod ice-fishing ground, I see two hunters and decide to go over and talk to them. They have caught a great number of Polar Cod and tell me that they are now off to fish for Greenlandic Shark. I ask them how long they have been here, and they point to the sun and paint for me part of its arc in the air with an index figure. The movement of the sun is all you need to tell the time. It is nearly 5pm in the afternoon and the sun is just creeping along the horizon. One would guess it were midday.

I do not wish to give the hunters any instructions, but just mention the plight of the dog and see how they respond. They tell me that the dog almost certainly slipped and got caught under the runners of the sledge as the *qamutik* bounced over the rubble field. They look sympathetic, but do not wish to act on it. The gentleman is the smiley Uumaaq Jensen. I have met him many times before and he is always donning a great big grin. He seems happy with today's catch. They have a gun on the sledge, but we are not at that stage yet. I walk back towards the dog again. It takes quite some time to find him as he is just a tiny black speck on an immense sheet of ice that stretches as far as the eye can see. All I can remember is that I left him in the middle of a great big ice rubble field stretching for half a mile or so westwards, formed from fractured ice broken out of a moving ice sheet. He does not seem to have moved and is in fact dozing in the sunshine. Just a few metres away from him I see the other glove. It has been ripped to pieces by one of Ole's dogs.

After much deliberation and hesitation, I decide to do nothing. It is horrible leaving him here, but if I have read his eyes correctly I would guess that is what he wants. He does not appear to wish to be moved at all, but just wants to lie on the ice. From previous similar episodes, all the arguments and counter-arguments for the various permutations of different steps of action are well rehearsed in my mind. I might be able to get him back to Qaanaaq and could certainly keep him alive, but then he would only be shot once I am gone. I think it is best to leave him here in peace and quiet. I will go and check on him tomorrow to see if there is any improvement. With the tragic hopelessness and pathos of the situation weighing on my mind, it is a long, slow walk back to Qaanaaq on the sea ice. It is suppertime, but I do not feel terribly hungry.

The shape of the sea ice is changing all the time. Overnight, the ice rubble fields have more or less disappeared, reconfiguring the visual poetry of shade, light and line. The view is different from one day to the next. The snow on the ice (*aputeqqautaa*) has been largely blown off and the sea ice is now an almost flat sheet of ice. I look for the ice rubble where I left the dog yesterday, but most of it has just been smoothed out. There is a bitter cold wind and I do not have enough layers on. It takes me the best part of an hour, scouting my way along a vacant white sheet of ice before I finally see what looks to be a dog in the distance. The poor thing is dead, frozen solid; it looks like he has been dead for some time. His mouth is slightly open, showing a set of very sharp looking teeth. There is a look of terror in his eyes. I feel a pang of guilt for leaving him here. I had fully expected him to survive the night. The dog was probably exhausted and just lay down and froze to death.

With the plight of the dogs in my mind and the sun creeping over the solitary landscape along the rust-coloured gullies of Herbert Island, I go and visit Inge who is the only person I have met who actually keeps a dog as a pet. I arrive at Inge's tiny sky-blue coloured cabin at 3pm and am greeted by her beautiful male dog, Kuugi, who stretches his front legs on my shoulders. The strength of the dog is quite overpowering. He pushes into you, making you almost lose your balance. I have barely taken my coat off when Inge is showing me the pictures on the wall. They were all taken in the summer of 1953 in Dundas just before the move. Inge was 19 at the time and talks about her life 'over there' (*avanni*). With the stubs of her fingers, she points to every face in the picture time and time again, telling me who they were but more importantly what their name is and how they are all related to one another. Like everybody her age, she grew up in a semi-nomadic culture, moving from one settlement to another for the hunting. But, her real home is Qeqertarhhuaq and she loves to share her happy memories of the place. My ambitions and initial points of reference were all embedded in Herbert Island, and I can understand perfectly well the appeal of the place even if I have not lived there. Inge has photographs of Wally, Marie and Kari Herbert and remembers the family well. I leave feeling as if I have found a new friend in Qaanaaq.

Back in Qaanaaq in the month of April, I skied across the sea ice on various excursions out to Herbert Island. Wally Herbert, a British polar explorer who had lived amongst the Polar Eskimos in the 1970s had been an inspiration for me and it was therefore essential that I got to know the island which shared his name, but also the closed-down settlement on the island (Qeqertarhhuaq) where he lived and which remains to this day a box of precious and difficult memories for the local people.

I set the alarm for 6am, having decided to make a dash for Herbert Island if the weather is good enough. Hans Miunge confirmed that the weather would be good (*iriarnaqtoq*) today and that I should take my chance. After the first few bars of the alarm call tune, *Don't Let Go*, I peep my head around the thin pink curtain at 6am and can see through the frosted glass that it is a bit hazy again, but this normally means that the weather is going to clear up later in the day. It is light at 6am, but the early April sun cannot yet be seen from behind the mountain.

The tracks leading down to the shore are empty and lonely. I have the ice to myself, except for the sleeping dogs, curled up in tight balls of tan, copper and sepia and dotted along the shore ice stained deep amber. I set off at 7.05am with a stomach full of porridge and a mind fixed on my destination. The conditions are very good. There is a generous layer of new snow on the sea ice (*matsak*). It is -22 degrees. I breathe in the fresh, tonic air. Going out towards Herbert Island, I ski initially on the road heading westwards formed from the toing and froing of the articulated hauler. The jagged, angular mountain tops of Herbert Island that grope the sky are bathed in first pink, and then the soft orange light of the early morning sun. The folds in the mountains shaped like the hull of a boat catch and collaborate with the light. The island looks so tantalisingly close. The dramatic mountain gorges and the island's apparent whale shape have always been so very alluring. After having read so much about Wally Herbert and his life on Herbert Island at the beginning of the 1970s, this feels like a pilgrimage and it is important I get there under my own steam. Wally is fondly remembered by absolutely everybody in this community. The Inugguit are very proud people and it is difficult to win their respect. It was clear to me that Wally Herbert through his knowledge of the region and hunting skills had managed to do so. It is said that once he was out hunting and was five days late returning to Qeqertarhhuaq. The women and the elderly men asked the hunters to go and look for him. They refused to do so, thinking that the traveller would be insulted if it was suspected that he was in need of help. Only his death would have proved them wrong. This is typical of the Inugguit: there is a discreet code of honour to be adhered to. This now abandoned island was in a way one of the reasons for me coming here in the first place. I have had my eye on it since the day I arrived and having had to wait so long to make an attempt at it has been a fly in the ointment of sorts.

I have my first short break at 8am and look back at Qaanaaq disappearing from view in the distance. Ahead of me, a museum of ice with statues leaning like drunks on lampposts made of antique glacial water. I continue to push on at a steady pace. There is not a soul on the ice, but I scan the horizon nonetheless for polar bears or evidence of any other kind of life. After about two and half hours, I reach a trail of enormous pinnacled icebergs parked in the slow current zone running westwards from Qaanaaq; their transit through the Murchison Sound halted until the summer months. Their edges and grooves shine and glisten in the morning sunshine. These frozen guardians of the Polar North stare down at the solitary traveller and grin at his toil. Like a good poem, their secrets lie beneath the surface. The silence is very nearly absolute. Many people in the world will never experience this or know what it is to feel the power of this fragile, dazzling white wilderness. It feels like a great privilege to have all this to myself.

I have not seen icebergs this big before, and I never cease to be amazed how such immense lumps of ice, thousands of years old and the size of football pitches, can be calved from the glaciers feeding into the bay. When these walls of ice break off, containing millions of gallons of freshwater, they can be so large that they can cause mini-tsunamis, even if they look like insignificant parcels of snow when viewed from Qaanaaq. I measure my breaks by the icebergs and decide that I will stop when I reach the smallest, flat-topped tabular iceberg resembling a monumental frozen coffee table. It turns out this particular iceberg is colossal. It just appears small because it is so far away. An hour later and I have still not passed it. It is almost impossible to judge distances in the Arctic. As a rule, if you think an iceberg is one kilometre away, it is probably more like five kilometres in the distance.

Some of the icebergs I am passing are like prodigious independent mountain ranges or ancient turreted, frozen castles locked in the ice with lofty spires. One of them is a deep cerulean colour, a sign of its age and density, with few bubbles. Another is practically ultramarine. All have been moulded by the wind and the melting process, making their shape transient and ephemeral. The appeal is a spiritual one that goes beyond religion. I am navigating myself through an antediluvian snarl of thought-provoking shapes of ice. It is almost impossible to guess the height of the bergs as there is nothing to compare them with, but I would guess that some of these might be one hundred metres high. In the Arctic, there are icebergs nearly the height of the Eiffel Tower. I am unable to photograph them. The Canon EOS 1000D flashes a card formatting error and will not operate under these temperatures for any amount of time. It is infuriating.

Having passed the flat-topped iceberg, my progress becomes quite suddenly very slow and I am disappointed at how quickly I have started to fade. The rucksack is horribly heavy and I curse at having brought so much with me. I am stopping now every ten minutes or so, resting on my poles and the head is dropping down. I have 20kgs at least on my back and I am suffering from fatigue. The straps are cutting into my shoulders and the pain is always worst on the shoulder which I have the gun on.

The last hour has really taken it out of me. Beyond the largest icebergs, the smooth sheet of sea ice has turned into a major ice rubble field reflecting the strong current underneath; a chaotic frozen jumble of broken ice stretching for a mile or so. Instead of practically skating along, I am now clambering over sheets of collided, fractured ice jutting up about three feet high. Tired, I fall over on a ridge and it feels like a Herculean task levering myself up again. I know from previous cross-country skiing expeditions that a few falls with a heavy load can sap your energy at a disproportionate rate leaving you physically and mentally exhausted. Beyond the first rubble field, the ice is chafed and creased before becoming corrugated, and then another rubble field. The last few miles have turned into a godless, frozen obstacle course. This was never meant to be an easy journey. Scrambling over the broken ice, I think back to the stories that Qaaqqu Miteq told me about his trip to the North Pole in the 1970s when in an episode reminiscent of the Peary days, he was asked by a group of explorers to lead them to the top of the world. Qaaqqu was the 32nd person to make it to the North Pole. He spoke about the appalling rubble fields they encountered where multiple year sea ice trapped in the Beaufort Gyre revolves clockwise in tight circles around the pole creating extremely difficult dog-sledging conditions.

The Arctic light is constantly playing with my mind, flashing me tantalising distorted images of weather-beaten houses floating in the sky. The light is bending and I am not sure if I can trust my own eyes. Psychologically, the momentary confusion is a little dispiriting. Even with the use of the binoculars, I have trouble spotting the settlement. Then, I identify what I am sure is a cluster of houses a few kilometres down from the pointed tip of the island. I try to push myself harder, breaking the last stretch down into sections measured by the position of icebergs. With the determination and anger that I am attacking this final stretch of sea ice, anybody would think there were gold on Herbert Island. Instead, there is permafrost, rock and nothing more. The tiny unidentifiable specks barely visible on the horizon half an hour ago have indeed become the houses which were once homes for a few hardy people living there. Herbert Island looks so close when looking at it from Qaanaaq, but it is in fact so very far. After having championed a second rubble field, I make it finally to the shore ice. It is now 1.20pm and it has taken me over six hours to ski across the entire Murchison Sound. Having spent approximately two hours of that clambering over frozen pressure ridges the size of demolished office blocks, I am exhausted. I leave my skis and rucksack on the shore ice and do a quick recce.

The snow here is deep like in Haviggivik and I find myself disappearing into snow holes on the short walk into the settlement. The first house is a relatively modern red A-framed house with a ladder leaning against the side of the wall. It is almost as if somebody had been up on the roof, and then just decided to leave the island and not return. The house is all locked up. Standing on tiptoes, I can just about see into the living room. The house was vacated in a hurry, leaving used cups and plates on the dusty kitchen table. Most of the houses are tiny, weathered cabins. Some have been ripped to pieces by storms; three have lost their roofs; others are just shaky wooden frames. At the remains of one house, the polar bear fur insulation in the cavities of the wreckage can be seen. Georg Poulsen's house is tidy, red and quite modern with white blinds in the windows. It could only belong to a *kadluna*. Most houses have a small padlock on the front door, the kind of padlock we would use to lock a suitcase. Many of them look like they have not been lived in since the settlement was abandoned. There are thirteen abandoned houses in Qeqertarhhuaq. There used to be a shop, a school and a church here. It was a normal, functioning community.

Towards the western end of the settlement, there is a grey A-framed house which looks exactly like the one Adolf Qaerngaq lives in today. Before that and slightly to the left as you are approaching it stands a tiny wooden, derelict cabin which once may have been painted green. There is no lock on the door, but just a piece of string tied around the frame of the lock. I remove the string and enter into a tiny porch full of rusting tools and frozen paraphernalia. Inside, the place is dirty and in a terrible state of disrepair. There is a stained mattress on an old-fashioned sleeping platform (*iˀdleq*), a ripped black leather armchair and a small, scuffed table cradling broken glass. I wonder who used to live here and what personal narratives and histories are bound up in these four walls. A woman murdered her husband in the settlement, shortly before Qeqertarhhuaq was closed down. I am perhaps at the scene of the murder. According to Kari Herbert's description, the house with its leather armchair sounds alarmingly like that of the man who lost his life, Marius Qaerngaq. I have the picture of him in my head, sitting in the chair with his thick eyebrows and straight black hair, smoking his pipe. There are also quite a few books piled up, a disconnected Refleks oil heater, empty grubby jerry cans and the odd discoloured crucifix hanging lop-sided on the feculent walls. Next to the cross hangs a faded black and white photograph of a woman I recognise, sitting proudly on a crate of Tuborg beer. It has all the trappings of an old Inugguaq house. In the kitchen sits a pile of snow right in the middle on the floor and a filthy gas cooker caked in grime. Nobody has lived here for a long time, but stiff, frozen coats hang from rusting hooks.

I decide that I will go and get my rucksack, change my clothes here, have a cup of tea and then work out if I might be able to survive the night sleeping in the living room with the aim of exploring the island tomorrow. The temperature in the house must be the same as outside, -22 degrees. I have brought with me my sleeping bag and an Emergency Survival Heat Sheet. Trudging through the very thick snow, it is quite a long walk to get my bag and it is then that I realise I have made a major mistake. I have not yet changed out of my wet, sweaty base layers. When cross-country skiing, I have got into the habit of doing this immediately after having stopped, but I was shattered on arrival at Herbert Island and could not quite face stripping off outside in -22 degrees. I decided not to wear too many layers today, just four very thin base layers with the tatty red RAB coat over the top and that is all. I knew it was going to be a long day and that I would have to be working really hard and thus getting hot.

By the time I have collected my burdensome red and grey bag from the shore ice and made it back to the abandoned hut, it is too late. The sweat has frozen and I am completely unable to get warm. I jump up and down, bang my feet together and do everything to get some heat into my body, but the pins and needles in my fingers are getting much worse: I am losing the feeling in my fingers. They may as well be solid lumps of ice. The sweat in the inner glove has frozen in a matter of minutes and I cannot warm up my fingers. I try to pour myself a cup of tea from the Thermos, but can barely get the top undone with my frozen hands. I have experienced this before. It feels tragically disabling and you have to act quickly to prevent frostbite setting in. I try to eat one of my liver pate sandwiches by lowering my head onto the surface of the sideboard and eating on it without the use of my hands. I have that horrible episode in my head when Ranulph Fiennes lost his fingers in the Arctic. His pulk fell through the ice of the Arctic Ocean. All of his expedition equipment was on the sledge. The sledge had got trapped under the ice and he could not get it out with his thick gloves on. He salvages the sledge with his bare hands, but ultimately loses a number of fingers in doing so. He sawed off the gangrene fingers in his workshop at his home on Exmoor. He saw no reason to mention it to Ginny. That incident in the Arctic is one of the very few occasions in his life of adventure where he called for a rescue team to get him out.

It seems pathetic, struggling to get the zip open on the back of the rucksack with frozen fingers. Inside are the heat warmers which are small packs of a granulated mixture of natural ingredients that when exposed to air react together to produce heat. This is accomplished through an extremely fast oxidation (or rusting) process. The ingredients include: iron powder, water, salt, activated charcoal and vermiculite. By shaking the packet and getting the granules to collide, they ingeniously provide heat. I curse at the packet cover which shouts out, 'wait 15 to 30 minutes for heat'. With some discomfort, I have now stripped off in the cabin and have donned five fresh base layers, but it is no good as my body temperature is still falling. I just cannot get warm and realise that quite suddenly I am probably experiencing the first stages of hypothermia as I am now shaking rather violently. With my disabled hands, I try hopelessly to fold with much care my clothes into neat parcels before repacking the rucksack. The onset of mild hypothermia is making me confused, allowing me to forget the urgency of the moment. This is no time for tidiness and order. Then, a moment of sanity. I realise that there is only one option: head straight out and start skiing again. After six hours of carrying a 20kg plus rucksack with a heavy rifle cutting into my shoulder and skiing more or less non-stop in temperatures of -22 degrees, this is the last thing I want to do. I desperately need something of a rest, but this will surely be the quickest way of increasing my body temperature.

I stumble out of the hut, stooping to open the tiny, rotten door and a honey-coloured dog runs past me. Changing into dry clothes has given me some relief, but I am surely imagining this. The confusion is alarming. Then Ingaapaluk Qaerngaq appears, wearing his polar bear skin trousers, seal skin *kamikker*, traditional anorak and carrying a whip in his hand. His twelve piece dog-team sits obediently behind him at the bottom of the slope, watching every move the hunter makes, waiting for the *qimmeerriut* ('dog that has broken his lead') to come back.

Nobody has lived on Herbert Island for over twenty years. The occasional hunter comes here, but that is all. Here is a *kadluna* walking out of a hut, tens of miles from Qaanaaq in an abandoned settlement and yet there is no expression of surprise on Ingaapaluk's face. He asks me whether I skied here and where I am off to next. He says he is going to Qaanaaq and offers me a lift on his sledge. With chattering teeth and an unsteady voice, I tell him that I am cold, that I must go back to Qaanaaq and will see him on the ice.

The offer is tempting providing I can warm up first. I calculate that it might take me eight hours to ski back to Qaanaaq. After my shilly-shallying around, the time is now nearly 3.30pm which would mean not getting into Qaanaaq much before midnight. Fourteen hours of skiing in one day in these temperatures is rather a lot to ask of anyone. I make myself jog through the settlement and along the rocky shoreline covered in slippery ice. With frozen toes, I am stumbling all over the place, but I push myself as hard as I can and try and work up a sweat. I run as if my life depends on it. It seems to work and the heat warmers are slowly giving some warmth to my digits.

Not being able to feel my toes makes clicking into the ski bindings problematic to say the least. I am desperate to get going, to get the warmth back into my body. The feeling is coming back to my fingertips and I try to clench my fists. The survival instinct kicks in and I push aggressively on my poles, pushing up the tempo and ski as fast as I can. I am relieved to have turned the corner. To have suffered hypothermia alone on an abandoned island in the remote Arctic would be a miserable way to go.

After half an hour or so of intensive exercise, I hear the familiar sound of the panting of dogs behind me. There is a penetrating wind sitting on the sledge, biting into me, finding every tiny chink in my armour. I chat briefly with Ingaapaluk; our words freezing instantly in the frigid air. I thought perhaps that he had been out hunting walrus near Northumberland Island, but instead he has just been checking some seal nets that he had placed near Herbert Island. Ingaapaluk is quite chatty, and has a kind, very round face. Tears pour down his face from the bitter cold and freeze before they reach his nasolabial folds. Ingaapaluk knew the Herbert family and speaks very well of them. Wally came here to hunt and to gain the experience he needed for his polar expeditions. He was basically being one of them, not studying them in any way. We talk about Qeqertarhhuaq and the hunting there. Small oval footprints of the Arctic Fox were to be found everywhere, and towards the pointed tip of the island three polar bears have been killed this season.

The dogs are pulling hard and we are moving at a good speed. As always, they are jostling with one another, motivated by constant competition and the need to lead. Every ten minutes or so, one of the dogs tries to stop to defecate. The faeces are runny and doing one's business on the run is an unenviable skill. After a few moments of agonising discomfort, trying to eke out the tiniest of impossible pauses to excrete, they are back in the pack, pushing the other dogs out of the way trying to get to the front. Beyond the view of the twelve bouncing dog-tails are once again the impressive temples of ice. Ingaapaluk tells me that the ice near Herbert Island will not be thick enough for much longer because of the *aukarneq*, the fast current that runs around the peninsula. The ice that skirts the island is often the first to melt in May.

Whilst it is pleasant not to have to ski all the way back, I am feeling terribly cold on the sledge. I am dressed for skiing and not for sitting on a sledge. There is a wind chill of -25 degrees at least and if you are just sitting still for an extended period of time, that is unbearably cold. I am wearing cross-country skiing shoes. When you are skiing, they are warm enough but they are no good whatsoever if stationary for this amount of time. We stop halfway for a short break. The dogs are lying in the sun and I marvel at how they are just completely unaffected by the cold. Ingaapaluk is dressed in his skins and he is laughing at me jumping up and down, running on the spot, trying to keep warm. I ask him for a cup of his potato and leek soup. This is of course the classic *kadluna*-Eskimo encounter, and it is an opportunity for them to show their superiority, to show how they have adapted perfectly to the hostile climate. They know that the average *kadluna* could never do what they do, and that is quite true. We have not evolved in the way they have to endure these kind of conditions day in day out.

It takes two and a half hours to get back to Qaanaaq by dog-sledge and by the time I arrive I am shaking uncontrollably and feel almost hypothermic again. I should have perhaps skied the whole way. Approaching Qaanaaq, we are coming along the man-made road on the sea ice. There is a pile of snow standing about ten feet high on one side. Three of the dogs head for the left of the mound whilst the rest go to the right. Ingaapaluk screams *atsuk, atsuk, atsuk* at the dogs on the left and with his whip tries to guide them to the right. It is too late. We are headed straight for the mountain of snow. The sledge slams into the snow, almost somersaulting over itself. Ingaapaluk and I jump off the sledge at the last second. After much cursing and shouting of orders, he sorts the dogs' traces out and then we push back from the pile of snow and head into Qaanaaq. It did not make for the most graceful and elegant of arrivals. With my frozen toes, it is difficult to walk. My feet feel like planks of wood, but I make myself go at a steady pace up to the house to get the blood pumping, having thanked Ingaapaluk for the lift. I apologise for not chatting, and disappear in a shadow of despair with teeth chattering. I am hoping and praying that the house is warm. I left the oil heater running. It is 6pm and with the sun pouring into the house, this is the warmest part of the day as far as the hut is concerned. It is 19 degrees inside, but today that is not warm enough. I turn on the (emergency) electric heater, put on all my clothes, but am still freezing even when the temperature has risen to 22 degrees. I defrost my fingers and toes slowly over the oil heater, turning my hands over like toast on a grill. There is a tingling feeling and they are quite painful. The end of the little finger on my left hand is numb and currently of no use. It is a very long process, trying to get warm. I make myself a cup of tea and it is three hours or so before I eventually feel in any way normal. After supper, I retire to bed in a lovely warm house penetrated by the beautiful deep blue of the Arctic twilight. I am exhausted after a long and demanding day and fall asleep more or less immediately. The brilliant Arctic light and sunshine now feels never-ending and that is because it almost is. It will not get dark tonight, but I am too fatigued and languid to allow that to be a distraction. In this place where there are no trees and the light is so clear, space, time and energy have meanings here that are completely different from those you absorb in the delineated, evenly modulated temperate zone. I am living in another dimension. Time and space are not cut up into small, regulated parcels, but are open and fluid, merging with one another.

Back in Qaanaaq, I browse through piles of tatty, black and white photographs of Qeqertarhhuaq: eddies of memories that bring a tear to the face of the Inugguaq. It turns out that the house I went to was in fact Wally Herbert's and that Marius Qaerngaq, who was shot by his wife on the island was Ingaapaluk's father. They lived in one of the houses that has been smashed to pieces. Subsequently, his wife and killer took her own life.

Eva lived at Qeqertarhhuaq in the 1940s at the time of the Second World War. There were just five houses there then. There was no shop and they had to go by dog-sledge to Hiorapaluk to get 'oil, sugar and chocolate'. The settlement closed down because Pilersuisoq (the partially State-owned shop which is part of KNI) closed its business there, indicating that the society had become more consumerist by the 1980s. At the time Eva lived on Herbert Island, there was only one house in Qaanaaq. Qaanaaq was not a settlement at all at that stage. Qeqertarhhuaq lost its *bygde* status and became a *bosted* like Qeqertat. This means that the State has no obligation to provide transport services (helicopter) or a shop.

Even after the drama of my trip to Herbert Island, I am drawn inexorably to the ice. The allure of the harsh, frozen world is overwhelming and runs deep in my veins. The emptiness becomes obsessive. It is more than a physical setting; it is a state of mind with deep figurative significance. The polar desert and the sea ice invite solitude, but not loneliness as they are full of spiritual awakening. One can spend weeks or months in England without looking at the moon, but not here in this uncluttered place where the elements matter. I enjoy the risk; the tip-toeing up to the precipice. Danger is interesting and necessary for the human spirit.

The emptiness of this white world renders one's thoughts into poetry, discarding the routine, vacuous words and leaving pure, unjumbled notions. One is resensitised and words regain their initial impact for one hears their sounds and not just their tired, recycled meanings. In a place like this, language really can be the 'House of Being' (Heidegger, 178: 217) because here you can 'dwell' poetically through a new frame of thinking. One is returned to the poetic essence of language, the purely semiotic; language speaking of itself. This frozen place leaves me with nostalgia for the intrinsic tenets of 'Being-in-the-world' that are passed over by a wholly destitute, technical understanding of language. This is what it means to live fully, to 'dwell' poetically in the Heideggerian sense, learning how to live a worthy life and relate authentically to Being through this reconnecting with the natural environment.

It is only a matter of days before Ingaapaluk and I are venturing out on the *hiku* again. This time, we will be hunting walrus. We will be away for a while. At times, hunters are away for up to three or four weeks at a time when hunting polar bears. On occasions, hunters may hunt for up to sixty hours without sleep. Back at home, they might sleep for fourteen hours or so. Down by the shore ice, there is a small crowd of people to see us off. Their faces are all framed in my mind now as if that moment is paused and photographed in my memory. The word has soon got round that we are leaving, and there are a few jokes about the *kadluna* hunter. Then, the mood suddenly changes. There is always a moment of seriousness just before a hunter or party of hunters leaves the town. Everybody understands that with such a hostile climate you cannot afford to forget, mislay or leave things behind. It is a well-rehearsed routine for the hunters, but it is imperative that they get it right. *Ultima forsan.* Ingaapaluk's wife has prepared a big bag for her husband and makes sure that he has two whips with him, knowing that the whip is essential to travel by dog-sledge. She thinks that I am going to freeze and looks genuinely concerned. They have forecast -33 degrees tomorrow.

Our destination is uninhabited Northumberland Island (Kiatak), lying due west of Qaanaaq. Here, walruses forage from sea ice platforms. The first stretch of the journey is of course familiar and takes us across the now very smooth expanse of ice (*maniraq*) towards Herbert Island across the Murchison Sound where I first met Ingaapaluk just last week. We have three very short stops, stopping once at a tiny hunters' hut at a place called Ikardloq, some way past the Qeqertarhhuaq settlement. I am beginning to freeze. I make myself run on the spot to try and get some blood flowing into my numbing toes. I put some of the tiny heaters into my boots. It is bitterly cold once you are out of the sun and in the cruel penumbra of Herbert Island. The island seems to go on forever and it takes a full two hours to travel the length of the barren, snow-covered rock.

Ingaapaluk and I travel by dog-sledge for nearly ten hours under the halo of the brilliant sun and the insidious evening shadow of Herbert Island. Rubble fields to my left, pyramids to my right. A hidden world underneath us. We sit in silence for much of the time, listening to the comforting rhythmic sound of the sledge runners on the ice and looking out for polar bear tracks. My legs are a bit too long for the sledge. They keep sliding off the wooden platform, jabbing into the hard sea ice under the moving sledge, reminding me that I should not doze.

Ingaapaluk is constantly shouting orders to the dogs, expertly guiding his team around the thin ice that skirts antediluvian icebergs the colour of Carrara marble. The strong, heavily-built, double-coated dogs are pulling well and it is fascinating to watch them constantly challenge their respective social standings in the 'pack order'. In this organised unit, there is no room for manners. When they change position, they duck under their traces and just wrestle one of the other dogs right out of the way. The three dogs on my left are sandwiched together, the one on the left is pushing with all his weight the one in the middle whilst the one on the right is pushing the sandwiched one in the middle the other way. This constant tussle makes for an entertaining soap-opera. From where I am sitting, all you can really see are a row of dirty anuses pooping every ten minutes or so. A couple of tails hang down, wolf-like, but for the most part their tails are curled over their backs and bob along. They are pulling hard; their long tongues designed to pick up snow whilst running hang downwards from one side of their jaw and their small triangular ears covered in hair to prevent frostbite, are alert. The dogs' remarkable sense of smell leads the hunter to the breathing hole. The largest dog is eight years old. The Greenland Dog lives to about thirteen years. This older dog has a tremendous amount of fur on his head and he looks very bear-like. The formation that Ingaapaluk is using today is one lead dog, followed by one sub-lead dog and then a fan of ten dogs behind those two. There are ten males and two females. Ingaapaluk shouts *nuiliqaa-nauk* to the dogs all the time, not wishing them to get tangled up. It is quite easy for the trace to get caught between the hind legs of a dog. The dogs soon become aggressive to one another when they are tangled up and on a couple of occasions Ingaapaluk stops to sort out the spaghetti scramble of leads. Ingaapaluk's mood switches between the very angry, authoritative Arctic hunter trying to control the dogs and the laughing, slightly hysterical Inugguaq.

The size of Herbert Island seems almost mythical, constantly deceiving me, throwing up rock formations which look like the tip of the island only to reveal themselves as another gully. After several hours, we pass it and turn the corner into Ikerasak, the channel that runs between the two islands. Northumberland Island was inhabited at one point. The remains of a settlement on the southern side of the island suggest that those who came from Canada may have spent some time there. Now facing Northumberland Island, the evening sun in the western sky is still shining bright. Tonight (12th of April), we will have the first midnight sun of the year. Just two months ago, there was no sun at all. We are slipping and sliding through an otherworldly labyrinth of evocative, transmogrifying lumps of ice that look like cold treasures in *pietre dure* from the palaces of Europe. Past Herbert Island, we encounter a tremulous, shivering ice rubble field lying just to our left. Qaanaaq is now way out of view and it feels as if we are travelling to a borderless mythical place, the end of the world, in search of the elusive ice edge. Its simplicity, whiteness and perfection is bewitching, drawing me deeper into its emptiness, taking my thoughts elsewhere to a lost, forgotten world of unfenced austerity away from the world of objects, and towards the universe of sounds, where words are noise and not scribbles, where the raw beauty and inhospitableness of the Arctic share the same bed.

Desperately cold and practically anaesthetised on the sledge, I force myself to hop off every ten minutes or so and jog behind, holding onto the stanchions and trying to keep the blood circulating to my frozen toes. My limbs are numb. We have had a cold spring, securing the best sea ice conditions in years and even now in April, the thermometer is flirting with the minus 30 degree Celsius mark. Shortly after ten in the evening, we arrive at what Ingaapaluk flippantly calls the *hotelli*. The dogs clamber up a steep slope and there at the foot of a mountain is a tiny, weathered cream-coloured wooden hut which Ingaapaluk built in the 1980s. Most of the huts on Northumberland Island have been damaged or blown away by Arctic storms, but thanks to four massive boulders attached to the roof with ropes, this one is still standing. Once the dogs are tethered, Ingaapaluk retrieves a large piece of frozen walrus from what is called the *qingnivik* ('the subterranean meat store') – here in the frozen North, the outside is the natural refrigerator.

Inside the tiny hut there are two wooden sleeping platforms, and filth and rubbish scattered all over the place. Ingaapaluk curses the previous occupants and we are quick to clean up the mess. Ingaapaluk offers me a spare reindeer skin (*inguriq*) to sleep on. Exposed to the very low temperatures, my aluminium water bottle has split. The water in the bottle froze and then expanded, making my *kadluna* equipment the butt of jokes for the rest of the evening. Two days later, the glass inside my plastic Thermos also explodes. Strange things happen in very low temperatures. When I came back from Haviggivik, glass jars of pre-boiled potatoes had smashed under the pressure of the cold in my house in Qaanaaq. The kitchen worktop was covered in smashed glass, potatoes and salted water.

The frozen lump of walrus meat is suspended over the heat using a pulley system and slowly thaws. Strips of meat are cut off, but not completely. Then, he takes the hanging slice of meat with his left hand and cuts it into small mouthfuls and places it into the bucket. The dogs swallow the meat whole, keeping their eye on the feeder all the time. The Inugguit cut the meat for the dogs the same way that they cut meat for themselves. First of all, the starving dogs are fed, then we boil thoroughly some meat for ourselves. It has been a long day and we are both tired. The meat is excellent: very black, dense and nourishing. Few words are said, but contented grins are shared in the perpetual light.

After some aggressive pumping of the brass Primus paraffin pressure stove, it is warm enough for me to fall asleep to the sound of blood dripping from the thawing walrus suspended one foot to my left and to the glare of the first midnight sun of the year peering through the curtainless window at the consciousness dozing on the hard wooden sleeping platform. Outside, there is stillness, just stillness. Inside there is the occasional belch of the paraffin stove and then silence. This is the lost life of uncorrupted morals that civil society eschewed. I fall asleep thinking about the appeal of remoteness. But, what is remote for me, is not remote for them. Why do our words for 'remoteness' carry such negative connotations when crowded suburbia only suffocates thinking? Living in cities that spill over into towns and villages, our notion of remote in an increasingly urbanised world has become absurd. Remoteness is appealing to me, but not to the Inugguit. If I lived with it everyday, then I would probably feel the same way that they do about it. But it is there, living so close to the natural environment where unqualmish thoughts can really unspool from my mind. One can enjoy a dialogue with the environment. I am drawn to these places for their simplicity, elementality and rawness. They have a mental shelf life that outlives any city because you are continuously taken back to them in your mind. In your acoustic memory, the wind continues to blow, the snow continues to crunch and the past is reconstructed time and time again. These places may be small and insignificant, but it is the scale of these places relative to their surroundings that leaves the mental mark. One cannot forget these places; they enhance a sense of acoustic definition and reflexive understanding. They enable a reawakening to the world, a route to phenomenology.

People have forgotten that the essence of travel is *travail* (hardship). For many in the twenty-first century, travel has come to mean the polar opposite, the craving for the familiar. One commutes from one shopping centre to another via an airport which acts as another shopping centre. Many British travellers seek this absolute familiarity, but with just one difference – sunshine. The world is becoming rapidly less interesting, but for many the ease of navigating one's way through a familiar world is the great appeal.

My bed for the night is a reindeer skin on a hard, uncomfortable wooden sleeping platform. As I have witnessed from previous hunting trips, the Inugguit are not remotely fussed about potential carbon monoxide poisoning, sleeping in their zipped up tents and huts with the Primus burning much of the night. I have no choice but to take the risk and do as they do and try not think about it. Throughout the night, Ingaapaluk gets up and pumps the old heater to make the hut warmer still. He is probably used to sleeping in a warmer house than this, but I am certainly not and find it stifling.

My back is very stiff in the morning. We do not get up till 10am and then Ingaapaluk spends most of the morning sharpening his knives. That is no exaggeration. This seems like a strange use of our time and is quite puzzling. I climb up the slope, binoculars in hand, and look out for polar bears. The absolute silence and stillness of Northumberland Island will stay with me. It is a silence broken just occasionally by the howl of the visiting sledge dogs which echo around the place, ringing empty the sound of the wilderness. The memory of the echo lives on, circling in my mind like an ontological merry-go-round, taking me back to places I have been. Everything seems to echo, both past and present. Even if silence reigns, there is life here in this timeless, frozen heaven: the delicate, oval shaped tracks of the Arctic Fox criss-cross the snow and soon the slopes will come alive with the arrival of coalitions of squabbling sea birds. The Arctic Foxes live on lemmings and the sea birds when they arrive in the spring.

The knives as sharp as they could surely be, we are headed to the edge of the ice, travelling north-westwards in a torpid wind. We travel across the sea ice for about an hour or so before coming quite close to the end of Northumberland Island and the elusive ice edge. Hakluyt Island (Apparhuit) is visible in the distance, but is surrounded by open water. We stop just beyond the Kissel glacier and the dogs' traces are undone. The walrus is always hunted on foot at this time of the year, leaving the dogs behind. The walrus is ferocious and this is probably the most dangerous form of hunting for the Inugguit. Spikes (*pituqqamavik*) are screwed into the ice and the dogs are paired off.

The recent full moon has meant the lunar spring tide was high and has broken up the ice ahead. The sea ice that forms during neap tides is normally firm and smooth. At the times of the spring tides, it is rough and broken, and not actually suitable for walrus hunting. The ice is now thin with patches of open water in the distance, sitting in between major ice rubble fields (*maniiʹdat*). Clouds of smoke (*pujoq*), the shape of ogees, above the water in the distance show that we are near open water (*imaq*). This so-called 'sea smoke' occurs when still cold air overruns the warm, moist air at the sea surface. Leaving the dogs on the ice, we climb up to a vantage point, binoculars around neck and rifle slung over shoulder. The open water cannot be quite seen in the distance, but pools of water and major ice rubble stretch for miles. Ingaapaluk caught walrus here in March. In the distance, Ingaapaluk spots the prominent tusks of a walrus lying on the ice. It is a bull, probably measuring about twelve feet and weighing up to two tons. We stand in silence for some minutes on the sea ice, heads bowed, patiently waiting for the sound of the breathing walrus.

Strong winds have blown the old ice away and the new ice that has formed is squeaking and creaking like an old rusty door, indicating that it is thin and dangerous. His mind is, however, already made up. The 'squeaking' of the ice is a warning sign that the ice could break up quite suddenly and leave us stuck on an ice floe. We have no choice but to retreat with the dogs onto thicker ice, and are left scouting around instead for recent evidence of walrus in the area. It is late in the year for walrus hunting and the Inuit do not take unnecessary risks. We spot some *nakkut*, narrow leads in the ice which have frozen over again, and possible indications of the path of the walrus moving underneath towards land, but the herd of walruses that Ingaapaluk spotted recently here have long gone. The walrus has to surface to breathe at least once every ten minutes, and there are no signs of freshly broken sea ice.

We draw back and spend some hours scouring the ice with binoculars, looking to see if any walruses appear on the thicker ice before heading back to the hut. Having returned, we climb up the slope to the look-out-point. With his naked eye, Ingaapaluk spots a sledge way in the distance: a tiny minuscule speck on a white carpet. I cannot see the sledge at all, but Ingaapaluk thinks it is Iggiannguaq Kristensen. The hunters have a remarkable ability to identify each other from a great distance. Iggiannguaq turns up at the hut two hours later wearing polar bear trousers and a caribou skin anorak (*qulittaq*). Shortly after he arrives, he digs up a large slab of meat from the deep subterranean refrigerator. Great caches of walrus meat are kept under the ground. He makes a quick call on his 11,000 DKK satellite phone to his wife in Qaanaaq to let her know that he has arrived safely. It is a curious juxtaposition to see a hunter dressed in traditional clothing from head to toe, holding a satellite phone in one hand.

Back in the hut and over a pot of boiled walrus and blubber, Ingaapaluk tells me about some of his misadventures on the ice and the importance of working with nature, and not trying to fight against it, conquer it or convert it. *Hila* determines the course of the day, movement and sleeping patterns, but also the consciousness and mind. Nature is here not something observed from a distance, but is all-encompassing and self-defining. The Inugguit live so close to the natural environment, that at times they have difficulty in distinguishing themselves from it. Whilst so much has changed so rapidly in the Arctic, this feature does seem to be constant and sets them apart from so many cultures in the world which are thought of as 'civilised', but where 'nature', if it exists at all, is something alien and observed through a lens whilst on holiday.

It is gone eleven in the evening and we are dozing on our sleeping platforms in the blinding sunshine. The thawing walrus is dripping beside me when suddenly we hear the sound of dogs and a sledge. Iggiannguaq and Ingaapaluk jump up and run outside. Another hunter has arrived. He is the shortest man in the settlement and is missing part of his little finger on his right hand. Massannguaq cannot be much taller than five foot. As he approaches, Ingaapaluk tells me that he is not *kadluna* friendly and that I should keep quiet. He more or less ignores me. He has had a long day and sits down straight away to a pot of boiled walrus, alternating between meat and blubber in a familiar fashion. The hunters share their food with one another. Once he has eaten, the newcomer sees to his dogs immediately, cutting off strips from the suspended walrus next to me. Back in the hut, Massannguaq has brought with him several Danish pornographic magazines. It seems that he is not averse to all the *kadluna*. The three Inugguit, all dressed in their polar bear pants, sit on the edge of the sleeping pattern, browsing through the magazines, chuckling occasionally as they rotate the glossy pages.

Massannguaq seems to have a sensible way of feeding his dogs. He has tethered them individually to avoid the problems of fights breaking out between them. Ingaapaluk uses a quite different technique. He tethers them in two groups of six and puts the food in the middle, just out of their reach. Then, he throws each dog a slab of meat. He insists that each dog follows its turn. Any dog that tries to jump the queue is beaten quite hard with a wooden stake. There is a splendid chorus of snoring in the night and I wake up, wondering if it is the hunters or a bear outside. Various trips out to the edge of the sea ice over the next week are equally unfruitful. The tides have worked against us, and thus we are headed back to Qaanaaq. Throughout the year, I was shown in many occasions just how difficult hunting was.

Early one morning, we load up the sledge with walrus meat from the *qingnivik*. Ingaapaluk is not convinced that it is worth looking for walrus again. The spring tide has broken up too much of the ice. It is going to be a very long day, travelling back to Qaanaaq with a heavy sledge. Much to Ingaapaluk's amazement, I put on all my clothes for the journey home. I have ten layers on in total and am blown out like a balloon, but hopefully I will manage to stay warm. On my feet, I have five pairs of socks, but even that is not a proper defence against the cold. I do my duties as the passenger on the sledge, holding the sledge from the stanchions and leaning back down the slope to prevent the dogs pulling the sledge at high speeds across the hummocky shore ice. Then, we are quickly and quite suddenly on our way again. On the way back, we see polar bear tracks that lead from Herbert Island northwards across the Murchison Sound.

We take a small break at Qeqertarhhuaq, situated at four miles west of Bastion Point, the eastern tip of the island. Ingaapaluk walks up to his small, red hut which is towards the back of the settlement, to the left of the church. The cabin is tiny, but homely. It is perfectly Inugguit with a pulley system to hang up sea mammals, large bowls for meat, faded pictures of Christ, family photographs and a crucifix on the wall. There is a picture of Ingaapaluk with his brother and twin sisters, his father in the background. Stories and narratives almost speak to you through the whispering winds in this abandoned settlement. Memories sit on empty shelves in Qeqertarhhuaq, and therein lies somehow its appeal. It is a closed-up settlement that feels spiritually alive.

Ingaapaluk has come into the house to pick up a *tarhaq* ('a white shooting screen used in the spring to shoot seal that are basking in the sunshine on the ice'). He tells me that Wally Herbert's old cabin where I got changed on that freezing day was also the home of the famous Polar Eskimo that travelled with Rasmussen across to Alaska. Walking past three houses ripped to pieces by storms, we head up to the newish looking church with the school attached to it at the back.

There are six white crosses in the silent, forgotten graveyard. Behind the church, the slopes are steep and rise to 890m metres, about 300 metres higher than the cliffs behind Qaanaaq. Inside, the church is very neat and tidy, and in stark contrast to the nearby roofless properties that are barely standing. The red interior looks almost freshly painted. The room is tiny. Through a door at the back is the school which is the smallest school I have ever seen. It is one room about the size of my living room. There is a blackboard with various scribbles on it, a tiny table with two chairs and four beds. Children must have boarded here. They slept in the school or rather the room annexed to the church.

It is another three hours before we are back in Qaanaaq. The journey seems never-ending at times and the dogs are tired. When we arrive, it is as if we never left. Tall Masautsiaq is standing there with Ingaapaluk's wife. He calls me *piniartoq nuutaq* ('the new hunter') and everybody laughs. The flags are flying at half-mast in the town. There has been a suicide. Careful to avoid the name, Arqioq tells me that his girlfriend's mother's older brother has died. Inuuteq Kristensen hung himself. He had a long-term problem with drinking and had tried to kill himself previously. He leaves behind an 18-year-old daughter and an adopted son. My house is cool, but not freezing and that is quite a relief. It does not take too long to warm things up. I am exhausted and get straight into my sleeping bag. I am grateful for not sleeping on the *i'diq* ('sleeping platform') tonight.

In the mid-April sunshine, Qaanaaq seems to be deserted, except for the odd elderly woman staggering around. I go for a walk in these days of exceedingly bright, sempiternal Arctic light. It feels like I am sitting under a spotlight. Breaking the angelic light for a moment is the enormous belly of the Lockheed C-130 Hercules which flies over my head in the company of smiling Qulutannguaq who is visiting briefly from Hiorapaluk; the machinery of the West dwarfs this tiny town and makes for a surreal juxtaposition.

I leave all the ventilation flaps open, but it is getting hot in the house in the afternoons now. The contrast with the temperature on the sea ice is mind-boggling. It is still -20 degrees out there. On the way back up the slopes, I notice that there are two dead dogs, one having been half eaten by Ravens, sitting by the red Arctic Line container.

Spring has arrived and it is now time to move to Hiorapaluk. I have got through the winter storms and the howling *nigeq* reverberating down the chimney, scudding from East to West, finding every chink in the skirting board, every cranny and cleft in the ceiling. Sibelius no longer plays to quivering curtains and twisted walls that speak. I am no longer lost in a swirl of amaranthine confusion and have awakened from that *langsam, schleppend* existence that characterised the dark period. I am looking forward to life in the settlements again.

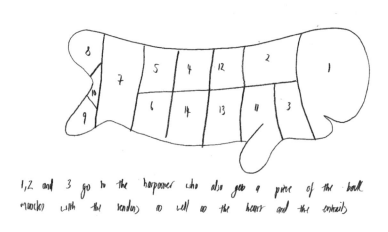

1,2 and 3 go to the harpooner who also gets a piece of the back muscles with the tendons as well as the heart and the entrails

Author's drawing of how a walrus and beluga are divided up between hunters. Sections 1, 2 and 3 go to the harpooner who also gets a piece of the back muscles with the tendons as well as the heart and entrails

8: Hiorapaluk

And there sits Hiorapaluk, the northern most permanently inhabited settlement in the world, timeless and silent in an immaculate white wilderness, in a never-ending winter. From the air, the settlement looks rather like Haviggivik with a similar number of buildings but much more compact. The distances between the houses are quite small. There is the same large, blue warehouse housing the water works and the same longish red house with a flag outside, marking the Pilersuisoq shop. It does not look nearly as derelict as Haviggivik; there is a functional feel to the place. Haviggivik feels much more peripheral. Behind the settlement, there are two mountains and a narrow corridor of shadows running between them. The settlement has electricity, but no running water. The shop is more or less the same as Haviggivik. There is a community hall here, between the church and the school and Bingo is played on a regular basis. It is a familiar model. Places in north-west Greenland are often defined and described in terms of their location relative to various winds. Hiorapaluk is considered *oqquatdi*. The rich repertoire of winds have very special significance in this part of the Arctic. The area of the Inugguit is split into two according to which side of the wind shelter you live. *Niger'di* means on the side of the *nigeq*, the wind that blows from the East, and typically means the area south of Herbert Island. The back side of Herbert Island furthest from Qaanaaq is *niger'di* whilst the front side is *oqquatdi*. *Oqquatdi* means the area behind the shelter or the area behind the *nigeq*. An *oqqua* is a calm shelter from a wind or the leeside whereas the *aggua* is the wind side.

Ane leads me to a tiny, red, rather dilapidated cabin with rotting window frames and cracked panes holding captive a grist of flies. I remind myself that it pays to live in a small house here for heating reasons. The cabin is on the other side of the settlement from the helicopter landing site, and sits in front of a small blue house which is the Nukissiorfik. The four rotten steps are caked with large amounts of snow and it does not look like anybody has lived here for a long time. I discover that the house is basically a spare room that has been used as the school in the past. The cabin comprises two small rooms. The first one is the teaching room, a room about 11 feet by 9 feet with a tiny table and two children's chairs. On the blackboard are written the words: *Illegitimi non carborundum*. I was certainly not expecting to find any Latin written on the blackboard. The second room is a room seven feet square. There is a narrow kitchen surface with a sink, a loo in the corner behind a cupboard door and a mattress in the corner. I will be sleeping in the kitchen.

I have not been there long when I hear the sound of heavy footsteps crunching in deep snow outside the house. It is Aki Himura. He has kindly brought me some musk-oxen meat which he leaves in the porch. He hunted it himself up at Etah. He comes in, but I have absolutely nothing to offer him. He rushes over to the humming oil heater and turns it up, complaining of the cold floor. It is a familiar routine which I have observed many times before. He is a very likeable man, full of energy and stories. I had heard a great deal about him prior to this meeting. For Aki, a way of life started to change in 1991 when the settlement got television. It was at the time when many of the older people died. Suddenly, everything transformed. When you went to visit somebody, they would be watching television. Previously, the *pulaar* ('visits') had been a means of passing on knowledge. Aki is very grateful for the fact that they voted to keep the settlement 'dry'. It is reviewed on a regular basis, and he is concerned that the settlement might decide to sell alcohol again. Aki says that the drinking situation was terrible in the settlement at times in the 1980s and 1990s. The community became very violent, so much so that he and his wife moved to Herbert Island and spent the winter there to get away from it all. Since there has been no alcohol, the community has saved a lot of money in social welfare, the school has begun to function again and the children are not frightened of going home. Hiorapaluk is a success story. That much is clear. The children are happy. They have got an educated teacher at the school and the hunters are very active. This is a well functioning settlement that will not accept any of the criminal exiles.

Aki is every bit the product of the Arctic nature and all its harshness. He has lost part of his little finger on his left hand and his face with its three large white patches bears the scars of frostbite which he contracted on Ellesmere Island in the 1980s. It is often said that it is much colder in that part of Arctic Canada than here. In Greenland, he has been as far north as Washington Island. He speaks very good Qaanaamitun, but with a strong Japanese accent. He first came here in 1972 as part of a Japanese expedition (he was working for a museum at the time) and decided to stay because the freedom that the life of the Arctic hunter offered was so appealing. He has only been here a few minutes when we are writing words down. This was the person that I needed to meet right at the beginning, but of course he is not an Inugguaq and it shows. It will be the ultimate irony if I end up learning more of the language from a Japanese person than anybody else.

Aki thinks that the Inugguit way is very similar to the Japanese. They like to hold back. They do not like to be assertive. They find Europeans too direct and pushy. Aki even points out that the tools that the Europeans have made are all about pushing (scrapers, planes, etc.). On the other hand, the people in the south of Greenland are quite different. They have exact opinions like the *kadluna*. It is so refreshing to speak to somebody who is part of their culture but who was not born into it. It is a chance to test my various views, theories and hypotheses. When Aki first came here, he was struck (as I was) by their ribald sense of humour. Surely, in this respect at least, they differ from the Japanese. Lauge Koch, the Danish geologist, was here drawing maps in the 1920s, and he and the Inugguit went up to Kap Alexander. Not far from the point, Koch spotted an island and asked the local what was the name of it. They told him the Inugguit name which translates as 'erection'. It was a pointed island. Koch saw no reason to question it and so it appeared in a map published in the 1920s as 'erection island' *tiggarniq*. Aki has seen this map in Denmark. It was some years before the name was changed on the map.

When Aki first came here, the settlement was very focused on walrus hunting as subsistence. That remained the case up until 1995 when the climate changed very significantly and very quickly. The hunting season became much shorter, the ice much thinner and walrus hunting became even more dangerous. A male can weigh up to two tons and can easily drag a man down under the ice. The thinner the ice, the more dangerous the task of hauling the animal onto the ice. Sometimes, with three men, it is possible to lift the animal out of the water, but more typically a dog team is used to tow the animal out of the water. Aki has been out hunting Arctic Hares, but that has become much harder too. Food was very scarce for them in the months of November and December. The unusual rainfall meant that there was a thin layer of ice over the lichen (the black moss, *qujauti* and the light green moss, *orhuassak*) preventing them to get at their food. Many of them died of starvation. The movement of the Hares appears to have changed too with them travelling further and further to find a mate. Talking to Aki, he constantly has one eye on the ice, the weather and his dogs. That is his world. He tells me that he has to prepare some skins and disappears. He cannot be kept away from the hunting life for long.

The weather deteriorates in the evening with snowfall. It is late April and I wonder whether the winter will ever actually end. On the disconnected, outer part of the settlement known as Itsaktak where there are five more houses (four of which are abandoned) practically lost in snow, an Arctic Hare, large and almost completely white except for its black eyes and black tipped ears, shoots past me. A flash of white on white. Through the slow-falling, heavy and tired snowflakes, a man waves me in from his window. Inside, there are two women giggling and I am intrigued to see what I will discover. These moments are unforgettable. The door has been left open and it is almost as if they were looking for a visitor to fall into their happy household. I recognise the gentleman. It is the hunter I was speaking to in Qaanaaq the other day as the Hercules flew over. His name is Qulutannguaq Olsen and he is married to Stinanguak.

There are six hunters in Hiorapaluk and Qulutannguaq describes himself as a *piniartoq mikihoq* ('small hunter'). He is one of ten children and has nine himself. Five of them live in his tiny one bedroom house in Hiorapaluk, two are in Qaanaaq, one is in Illulissat and one is in Nuuk. His wife no longer works as the cleaner at the school because she has injured her shoulder. The other woman here is their daughter who is great fun, laughing at everything I say. This makes a great change from the moody teenagers in Qaanaaq. Once again, the difference between town and settlement cannot be lost on the visitor. The dynamic of Hiorapaluk is quite different from Haviggivik too. There are thirteen bachelors in Haviggivik, but Hiorapaluk is about young families.

There is a wonderfully warm, jovial atmosphere in the house that characterises life in the settlements: a never-ending circus of smiles and banter. Everything is more immediate here than in the town, the natural and social environment included. The size of the community means that there can be no social probation period for visitors. Instead, young children walk into your cabin on the first day, hoping that they have found a new playmate. Qulutannguaq is keen to learn English and wants to help my Inuktun. They insist that I come and visit tomorrow to drink coffee with them.

In the morning, the view over the fjord and the creases in the mountains is spectacular. One can see Northumberland and Hakluyt Island quite clearly in the distance. Qulutannguaq tells me that they are going to Iihaaq Himura's house (the Oxford blue one immediately next to Heidi and Aki's with the skins hanging up). There is to be a *kaffimik*. Iihaaq is Aki's son and his daughter turns six today. The smell of pungent *kiviat* hits me as I enter the house. A family of four are feasting on fermented Little Auks and dried Greenlandic Halibut. The Inugguit are the only people in Greenland to eat fermented Little Auks. The wings are removed first and then the feathers are plucked. Then, one bites into the pungent, dark red flesh. All the organs are eaten and the bones are sucked dry. The longer the birds are left to ferment in the blubber outside, the stronger the taste. Once Ane has finished eating four of the little black and white birds, she looks down at the bones of the bird and says *qujan*. Eating blubber and fermented birds in a house in Hiorapaluk is no different to eating on a hunting trip. The only difference is that the meat is entirely fresh when the animal has just been killed. When the hunters kill a seal, they first eat the liver when it is still warm and raw. No time is wasted.

An elderly lady hacks at a piece of frozen caribou meat with an axe. Sitting on the kitchen floor with legs at 120 degrees and sleeves rolled up, they bite into the bird's red flesh with an offal-like texture. Conversation is about a ghost that the children have seen in the school. I join the small group on the floor. Soon, my lower arms and wrists are stained in blood from eating fermented birds. I take the bird in my left hand and with my right hand remove the small black and white feathers and the legs. The smell is overwhelming. The flesh is a dark red colour soft and chicken-like in texture; the meat is very bloody. All eyes are on me and they can see that I am struggling a little with the concept of just biting into a bird. It is not the taste of the birds that is unappealing, but is more the smell and the fact that one has a bird with its head, beak and legs in one's hand. However, it would not be long before I would be eating the birds on a regular basis.

Iihaaq looks different from the other Inugguit with quite dark skin and a fashionable, Western dress sense. He does not speak Japanese, and has only been there once. He thinks the sea ice in Hiorapaluk has been good this year and much better than last year where there was open water appearing at this time. He has been fishing Greenland Halibut with his older sister, Rosa Jensen at Qeqertat. They caught 1.2 tons of fish in five days. That is extraordinary and surely the future for the community. He is convinced by it too and especially likes the fact that you do not have to worry about finding food for your dogs all the time. There is always enough fish for the dogs. They can sell it to southern Greenland for good money. The only problem is the very high transportation costs. Iihaaq is of course an Inugguaq, but his attitude and approach to life is perhaps more Japanese. It seems that the Himuras are the most successful hunters in the region. They have played the Inugguit at their own game and beaten them. The best houses in the district all belong to the Himuras. I think that is rather telling.

Rambling around the settlement in the afternoon, I hear somebody call *kinatin*? ('who are you?'). It is Inukitsoq Dunneq. I recognise him immediately: diminutive and impish with a strange haircut and a big smile. Standing outside a green house in the middle of the settlement where his younger brother lives, he saws up frozen walrus meat as if it were firewood. Somewhat disconcertingly, he does not seem too inter-ested in me visiting him nor does he wish particularly to tell a story. His work keeps him too busy: his job is to collect the waste in the quad bike once a week and to ring the bell at church. I have been told previously that he is a fickle, slightly difficult character, so I should not give up on him just yet.

It is Good Friday and I manage to make it to the church in time. This building used to be both the school and the church, but now the school is housed in a larger, modern building immediately behind. It would explain why there is a playground outside the church. Inukitsoq Dunneq rings the bell and takes his seat at the back of the church. There must be twenty people in the church at least, which is over a third of the population. Padlunguaq (Qulutannguaq's sister) sits behind me with two wild children who are coughing, snorting, sniffing and hawking up phlegm right through the service. The lay-preacher is a young, plump lady with a sad face and not a lot of confidence. She is mumbling the words of the readings to herself, not once caring to look up at the Congregation. She stumbles over the long words. It is a pitiful and an ultimately pointless affair. Nobody can hear anything and nobody seems to care. I think people come to church to meet people, exchange gossip and that is probably about it. One of the hymns, no. 195, is not sung at all. People just read it through. As for the others, one might catch the odd syllable or two.

Afterwards, the Congregation rushes outside and lights up cigarettes. Clouds of cigarette smoke linger in the cold air. In the foreground are brightly coloured swings and see-saws, behind, the *kangerduks* ('fjords' or literally 'empty space') are devoid of icebergs and in the distance, fifty or sixty miles away, Northumberland, Herbert and Hakluyt islands are a reminder of recent journeys. The clarity of everything seems conspiratorial; the view seems almost too perfect to be real. It does not matter how many times I check the map. The fact of the matter is you can see for one hundred miles. The sea ice is very neat and flat like a perfectly fitted white carpet, stretched and tacked to the stony edges of the bay. Only with the recent full moon has the shore ice begun to break up.

After the service, Qulutannguaq invites me to join his family who are having coffee at Nivi's house. The house appears to be just one largeish room. The table is decorated for Easter. There is a yellow tablecloth and a few small seasonal decorations, but no sign of Easter eggs or chocolate. The normal montages of family photographs populate the wall behind me. She is related to the wife of Avigiaq Karlsen who lives next door to me in Qaanaaq, and they are quite alike: both portly and quiescent. The atmosphere in the house is jovial, and there are various jokes at my expense. Nivi makes some coffee and fills up the rather dysfunctional Thermos. Coffee is never served here. One has to help oneself. We chat for a while, or rather they do. I think to myself how odd it would be, the parallel situation in the UK. One goes to church on Easter Friday, and then a complete stranger follows one's family back to one's house and drinks one's coffee. It is useful to think of it like that sometimes to put the Inugguit kindness into perspective. Quite suddenly and in a paranormal like fashion, they decide it is time to leave and we part having said 'thank you' many times. I am reminded to thank the host again, even though I have just done so. There are occasions when then can be never enough *qujan*.

At 5pm, there is another service at the church. It is much the same as before, but this time there are just three hymns. The children are even more boisterous and out of control. It is an absolutely farcical scene and even Naaja sitting in front of me is annoyed that the mothers are doing nothing to rein in their children. Thirteen people turn up for this circus which is extraordinary given that this is the second service of the day, that you cannot hear a word and that nobody sings the hymns. It is significant that the only priest in the settlement, Ane, does not attend. It is obvious that their whole universe revolves around children. Houses that do not have children (like mine) are to be avoided. The Inugguit know that the *kadluna* tend to govern their children and think therefore that we are harsh. They cannot understand how we can show affection to animals instead. This society's attitudes are diametrically opposed to mine in almost every sense. The Inugguit are less inclined to rush to formulate opinions or talk things through. Actions come before words for them, children way before animals. Often when I was out on the sea ice, hunters would act quickly and in concert without any discussion. Once, they were concerned that their boats would be trapped in drifting sea ice. In a tele-pathic manner, they got up and ran down to the shore to rescue their boats.

In total, there were nine church services over the Easter period for a community barely numbering fifty people. There is no doubt that this community is much more religious (or church-going at least) than Haviggivik. There were thirty-five to forty people at church on Easter Sunday. When I speak to Stinanguak in the afternoon about it, she talks about church going as an unquestionable obligation. She shows me the calendar and all the dates that she needs to attend. It is almost as if a higher authority has told them that they need to attend on the following dates, and it has been just accepted without questioning it. It does not mean that one engages with it; one just turns up and does one's duty unthinkingly.

I take a stroll along the shore ice (*higgat*) in the evening. Large, deep cracks are now appearing in the ice on the tidal zone. Arctic Hare tracks criss-cross the snow-covered slopes to my right. The sun disappears behind the mountain at 9pm, casting a shadow over Hiorapaluk. I circumambulate the frozen shoreline to the other end of the settlement, following Arctic Hare tracks and watching the sun's trajectory. Untainted shadows spread rapidly across the fjord like water spilt on a white carpet. Here, the chaffs of the day are unprolific, sighing and groaning like the ice under my feet, serving up time and space to think, cogitate, ponder, reflect upon and think again. This uncrowded vista takes your mind away to an other, lost, forgotten existence of silent rooms without verbiage and all the lost credos of a former, but recent time. I marvel in this antidote to modern civilisation. When the sun inches behind the mountain, the temperature drops quicker than one can imagine. One minute one is enjoying the sunshine; the next one is fighting frostbite. The Far North serves up a harsh, but splendid form of Romanticism.

At this time of the year, the shop is almost empty and I am increasingly dependent on the hunters' food. In the cabin that houses the laundrette, seal skins sit in buckets and hanging up to dry are four skinned Arctic Foxes. These animals are all fur. The body itself is extremely slender, and it looks like a small dog. Fortunately, I do not have to survive on a diet of Arctic Fox and am able to buy a number of Greenland Halibut off Aki who stores a great big cache of them outside. The frozen fish with the *Aroma* (a salty, garlicy condiment made by Kraft) is delicious. I have gone quite native with my tastes and prefer now frozen and dried fish to cooked fish. Here in Hiorapaluk, my diet comprises musk-oxen meat, frozen Greenland Halibut, out-of-date Lithuanian condensed milk which sells under the unfortunate trademark of *Pienas* and the divine *Marabou* Swedish milk chocolate.

I am made to feel so welcome at the Olsens that I spend most of my time there. I do not wish to impose, but they have practically adopted me. I relish my visits as I am learning so much from them. If only I had known about them when I first came to the region, I would have spent less time in Qaanaaq. The children are lovely, always smiling and laughing. There is a tremendous spirit to the household. On each visit, I am asked whether I am married. I tell them I am a bachelor and they roll around laughing. Stinanguak insists that I need a wife to do my washing and sewing. They find the subject of the bachelors in Haviggivik particularly entertaining, perhaps for the reason that they appreciate the fact the outsider is able to talk about an issue that for them might be a sensitive topic. I would only have to offer *Haviggimmi angatsuduk pa...pa...pa* ('there are a great number of bachelors in Savissivik') and they would scream with laughter. This phrase proved so popular that it became a greeting in itself. When I enter the house (I have finally managed to get into the habit of not knocking), I sometimes say: *angatsuduk pulaarniaralinga?* ('May the bachelor come and visit?') They find this salutation extremely amusing and cheer my arrival. Valediction is more problematic. Often after having spent several hours in their house, I will take my leave. Not because I have anything else to do, but simply because despite their protestations, one feels as if one must surely be imposing to some degree. This is followed by a quick succession of *hiuq, hiuq, hiuq?* ('why, why, why?'). If the pace of life were any slower here, it would stop. This kind, relaxed family do nothing really other than the basic chores and they have all the time in the world.

Marriage here is more than anything about convenience. Once you have a dog team, you are a *piniartoq nutaaq* and an eligible man having acquired a level of status. A woman needs a man to hunt and get food for the family and dogs. A man needs a woman to make him clothes, cook for him and look after the household. There is a clear division of labour and little question of either party crossing the threshold. I am not sure love really comes into it. I am advised that their oldest daughter is not married, but also that the woman who works at the shop and lives next to Ane is an *arnaduq* (an 'unmarried woman'). The various possibilities and permutations provide much mirth to the family. *Angatsuduk* and *arnaduq* are an anomaly in a small, coupled place. I am the fourth bachelor in Hiorapaluk: there is Inukitsoq Dunneq and Navssaaq who lives in Itsaktak – the tiny settlement of one house next to Hiorapaluk. He lives out there on his own. There is a path with a rope to get out there. When the weather turns nasty, it can be dangerous walking even a few hundred metres to his house. And, finally, there is their son Ingaapaluk who aged 17 can surely not be considered a bachelor.

They joke that Inukitsoq and I will *iviriihaq*, i.e. will compete with one another. I jest that I could start ringing the church bell tomorrow, *hianeqtaqtunga*. The *iviriik* is a reference to how men used to drum-dance to compete for a woman. At that moment, I pull the drum out of the bag. The skin is made from a polar bear's stomach, the rim is walrus and somewhat shockingly the beater is a polar bear's penis. Qulutannguaq stands up and gets me to stand opposite him. He hands me a small stick called an *aviorut*, and tells me that I have to sing in a high pitch. I have to twirl the stick clockwise and relatively fast. This seems to set the rhythm for his tapping. The children enjoy the performance and *qujan* is said repeatedly afterwards. For a moment, I feel as if we have turned the clock back one hundred years and that I am a participant in a shamanic dance. The old shamanic traditional beliefs have gone, but in a sense they still linger in the mind and consciousness. That is obvious to me although it is more apparent here in the settlements than in Qaanaaq.

In such tiny, remote communities there is a social pressure to conform in every respect otherwise one's eccentricities and idiosyncrasies will be put on public display and become the fuel of gossip. The scale of the place means that movements of people are easily monitored and that all social interaction is public. These movements form the ingredients of conversation: so and so has gone to Qaanaaq by dog-sledge or helicopter. The question of when they will return is less certain and dependent on the weather and thus has to be answered by *ammaqa*.

On subsequent visits to the Olsens, I would be asked as I entered the house: *Stiffi, ningauhaqtutin?* ('Have you got yourself a brother-in-law?'). Qulutannguaq would want to know if I had married Nivi. There are only two available women in Hiorapaluk, her and their teenage daughter. The mother then offers in earnest her daughter. I think if I had said 'yes', they would have just got on with the arrangements straight away without making any fuss. At twenty-five, they need to find a husband for her daughter. I manage somehow to change the subject to hunting, currents, movement of ice floes and polar bears. In April, the bears leave this area and go north as the ice begins to disappear. They go up to the Kane Basin and the Nares Strait area where there tends to be some ice all year round. At this time of the year, hunters wait at the seals' breathing holes (*a'du*). The hunter works out which way the wind is blowing and stands facing the wind, so that his scent is not blown towards the breathing hole. The hunter waits with a gun for anything from five minutes to an hour. He will crouch and listen to the seal coming up to the breathing hole. When he does so, he will shoot at the hole and retrieve the animal using his *niggiq* ('a rod with a hook on the end'). Whilst the ice might be still quite thick at this time of the year, the seal is constantly eating away at the ice at the various breathing holes ensuring that it can quickly get access to oxygen. In May and June, the seals are shot when they come out of the breathing holes to bask on the ice. This is when the hunter wears his white anorak and shoots from behind his *tarhaq*. For this, one needs to be a good shoot. In July, August and September, seals are shot in the open water from a boat with a gun.

Throughout the afternoon and between various visits, endless handshakes and constant repetitions of 'Happy Easter', Stinanguak is again complaining about the terrible pain in her shoulder. Quite suddenly, I realise that she must surely be the woman that tried to shoot herself in August 2010, shortly after I had arrived in Qaanaaq. She missed and the bullet went through her shoulder. I cannot believe it is this kind, happy woman, but it must be as she fits the policeman's description exactly: a woman in Hiorapaluk, married with five children. It is chilling to think that this woman who is constantly laughing tried to take her own life just a few months ago. Like the weather, everything changes rapidly here.

The sun disappears behind the mountain at 9pm, plunging Hiorapaluk into the shade. The temperature drops rapidly but the surface is really warming up during the day now. Before returning to the cabin, I go and visit the caramel coloured bitch that I like very much. She is tied up just behind Qulutannguaq's house. I make a fuss of her and she loves it, rolling on her back. The good thing about going to see her is that I am out of the sight of the Inugguit as she is behind all their homes. For a moment, I can be the *kadluna*.

It is getting warmer with each day that passes. For the first time in months, I have discarded the trouser base layer and am now just down to three layers on the top (minus coat). It is difficult to know what the temperature is today, but in the sun it feels significantly warmer than it did just a week ago. It gets very warm in the cabin in the afternoon with the sun on it. The heater is on '1', but I could almost think about turning it off. That would be something. It has been a very long wait, but the winter is now over and May is almost upon us. For a number of reasons, May is probably the best month to visit the Arctic: the sea ice should still be here, the birds will come back, it will be a pleasant temperature but there will still be snow on the ground. With these temperatures, the sea ice will surely begin to melt quite quickly.

Down at the dump (*aktat*), I meet Kuulut Olsen. The dump is situated behind the settlement, in the Robertson Fjord down by the shoreline. It is quite a long walk from the settlement. There are various white goods, mainly washing machines, and the ubiquitous black and yellow bags. The remains of dogs' bodies peek out from piles of rubbish. Ravens circle overhead. Kuulut races around on a push scooter on skis. He is a very kind, gentle boy with a nice personality, telling me that he does not want to be a hunter because he does not want to shoot a gun. I ask him whether he would like to live in Qaanaaq, but he says that he does not like it because he says it is full of drunks. It is rather tragic to see him impersonating a drunk falling over, just the way so many children here do. The Olsen family are the highlight of my trip to Hiorapaluk, but also my stay in the Arctic in general. Qulutannguaq teases me the whole time; all the jokes are based on my bachelorhood. He asks me whether I am going to marry the Korean woman that is visiting, whether there is a wife on the helicopter on the way to me this afternoon. It is all tremendously good fun. He likes nothing more than to jest with the *kadluna*. Being able to accept this ridicule is, I think, a key criterion for acceptance in an Inuit community, and on that score at least I am doing rather well. Qulutann-guaq loves to tell me that he is a shaman and that he has special powers before rolling around laughing. He jokes that his special abilities enable him to spot a helicopter before anybody else. Every week we would play this game. He would always see and hear the helicopter a good five minutes or so before me. Eventually, I would spot a tiny fleck in the sky. He had won.

Laughter and tragedy are always mixed up with one another in Inugguit society. Qulutannguaq would tell me about walrus hunting, reminding me that the Inugguit are exceptionally strong people and that they can pull walruses out from the water with their arms. Then, he would chuckle before telling me that actually they attach a rope through the animals' mouth and tie it to the sledge with the dogs pulling it out of the water. The account would end with a reminder of how dangerous

walrus hunting is and the fact that he lost his son to a walrus hunt. Death
is never far from their thoughts. Then, it is immediately back to the
Inuktun terms for the different parts of the sledge and his delightful,
ribald sense of humour. The jokes are based on the name for the ropes at
the back of the sledge which are derived from the word for 'buttocks'.
Qulutannguaq is reluctant to teach me how to hunt because he says I will
soon leave and that he will not see me again. This is of course their experience with most *kadluna* that they meet. Interestingly, he tells me that I
can come back but that he might be dead. He utters *toquhuq* and draws
the line across his neck, as people always do here.

I have had disturbing dreams and nightmares every night since
coming to Hiorapaluk. This is not like me. Stinanguak insists it is
because I am living in an *i'ddu ajorpoq* ('a bad house'). She says that the
house is haunted. She looks very concerned and insists on speaking to
Ane immediately about it. It is not as if I am having any problems
sleeping though; I fell asleep to Bartok's piano concertos last night. I
didn't know that was possible. Over coffee and 'Inuit cake', there is much
discussion about my nightmares and what the reason might be. Ane is
worried that the house might be haunted too. She did not mind that I had
to tolerate near freezing conditions in her house in Qaanaaq for weeks on
end, but the idea that there might be a ghost in my Hiorapaluk cabin is a
different matter. She asks if I have seen any ghosts. The consensus is that
the mattress is the problem. Louise Simigaq slept on the mattress before
and had nightmares every night. Naaja Simigaq had a 'bad' (*ajorpoq*)
mattress and had problems with nightmares too. When she lived in her
old house, she told me that there was a problem with ghosts. In the night,
she would hear a knocking at the door. She would go to the door and
there would be nobody there. There is a tremendous appeal to supersti-
tion. Ane comes round later in the afternoon with a new bed. She wants
to take the old one away, but we cannot get it out the house. She is quite
unsure about me using it as a sofa. The children have heard about the
cursed mattress and insist on jumping up and down on it, before running
away screaming. Everybody assumes that somebody might have died or
been very ill on my mattress. The mattress is spoken about in the same
terms as the empty house on the other side of the settlement. The house
is let out to the occasional visitor or tourist wishing to go to the furthest
north settlement, but is on the whole avoided because it is alleged that a

woman killed her husband there and that the house is haunted. There is a belief here in *anerhaat* or 'pure spirit forces'. The Inugguit might use this word to refer to supernatural events such as ghosts, etc. People go to Church, but have alongside a belief in *anerhaat*. Ane, the priest and my landlady, does not see any contradiction and subscribes to it herself. She had a supernatural experience whilst at a conference in East Greenland and was terrified by it. A human-like person came towards her and chased her. Most Inugguit still believe in spirits of some form.

Qulutannguaq is the only one with a different theory. His explanation for the nightmares had been that I had bad blood circulation because I did not eat enough. He thinks that men should have big bellies. For him, that is a sign of their manliness. He looks at my hands and compares them to his. He tells me that I do not have enough veins in my hands and that I should eat more meat. He has seen on television, *kadluna* eating what he calls plants and that that is no good. This is probably Jamie Oliver on KNR. He points to the plants in Iihaaq's house, but he surely means 'salad'. We must eat meat. This is a familiar story that I have heard many times before. One does not want to be a vegetarian here.

With the new bed, I sleep without nightmares for the first time since my arrival. That is quite something and exactly as the local people predicted. I left the heating off overnight and with hindsight that was bit of a mistake. It is cold in the house in the morning and takes a while to warm the place up before the sun has come around. It is -13 degrees today which is fifteen degrees warmer than it has been, but what kind of man sleeps in a house without heating on when the temperature outside is -10 degrees? I now realise to what degree I have acclimatised.

In the evening I decide to go for a walk and end up crossing the entire Robertson Fjord (Hiorapula Kingua). The fjord is an *ilulidoq* ('the place where there are no icebergs'). There are few icebergs in Hiorapaluk because the glaciers do not calve big bergs when it is relatively shallow. This fjord is about 200 metres deep. I walk up behind the settlement and across the frozen sea, hoping that nobody will see me as such excursions only lead to gossip. It takes three and a half hours to get there and back. The pith and gist of the endless summer sun circles above me in a sky without contrails, before twisting into a rictus of anguish.

It feels good to get some fresh air, much needed exercise and time to myself to digest the aphorisms and *Lebensphilosophie* circling in my head. A few Arctic Fox and Arctic Hare tracks zig-zag the fjord. There is no reason to cross the fjord; it is just there, staring at me, but is almost impossible to assess how far away it is. That fact in itself seems reason enough to go, and has motivated more than one Arctic excursion. The ice is thick enough, but my mind keeps returning to various conversations with Aki about thin ice. Dark ice is thin, thick ice is white. If one suspects the ice is thin, one should test the ice with a pole. If it goes in very easily, then it is thin and not safe to travel on. Salty ice is very flexible whereas freshwater ice such as that surrounding the icebergs is very brittle and can suddenly break up. If the ice breaks beneath, one must move slowly and spread one's weight across the ice like a polar bear does. Moving fast risks causing waves underneath the ice which will break it up. One should not travel on ice that is less than five or six centimetres thick. When dogs fall into the water, one should fish them out and get off the sledge as quickly as possible. The ice will be very thin and there is a risk of going in with the sledge. Aki fell through the ice and I got to hear about many close shaves. The sheer fact that he told me that reminds me that he is not a Polar Eskimo; an Innuguaq would not be so forthcoming about his mishaps to a *kadluna*. Having fallen through the ice, one should try and get out by pushing oneself up on one's back rather than go out frontwards. Put your legs on the edge of the ice opposite, push against it to lift yourself out of the water. If one climbs out frontways, one will put too much pressure on the ice, breaking it up and one will then have to get out of a bigger hole. Aki was told this by an old hunter and luckily remembered it the first time that he fell in. Once he was lying on the ice, preparing to shoot a seal basking in the spring when the ice broke up beneath him, plunging him into the freezing water. It is 'midnight' by the time I get back, but that term is meaningless at this time of the year in this part of the world. The sun has disappeared behind the mountain and the temperature has plummeted. This settlement of lost digits and private existences is deadly quiet. Sleeping dogs stir as I walk past, trying to assess the chances that I might have food for them. Others munch on their own excrement. My hut is warm, but full of flies that seem to have come back from the dead.

The following afternoon, I take some coffee and cakes round to the Olsens. Qulutannguaq is asleep on one of the beds in the living room, but I am told just to go in. At some point, there is always one member of the family asleep on one of the two single beds in the living room. In this way, a family of seven can sleep in a one-bedroom house. Qulutannguaq has just eaten walrus meat and is resting with a full belly, replete, satisfied and lethargic. I am invited to eat, but am then chastised for eating like a *kadluna* and he takes my fork away, telling me to eat like them and to do as his nephew. The walrus meat is very good: tender and nutritious.

Qulutannguaq informs me that I did a bad thing yesterday, but I have no idea what he is referring to. He says that I made a mistake (*kukkuhunga*). He looks very unhappy and I feel as if I have insulted him, but do not know what I have done. I ask him for an explanation and he reports that he saw me walking out on the ice. The children spotted me, told their parents and suddenly the whole community was watching me through telescopes and binoculars. Phone calls were made and everybody was informed. He talks to me like a four year old boy in front of every one. It is very embarrassing. He says that I was stupid, that there are polar bears out there and that I should not take those risks. Earlier in the week he had told me that all the polar bears had gone north, but now he is changing his mind. Then, he wishes me to believe that the Arctic Foxes are dangerous too. I do not know if he is joking and try and suppress my laughter. He is definitely not joking and is now claiming that an Arctic Fox will jump at you, plunging its teeth into your neck. This sounds just too ridiculous for words, but he is sure that *kadluna* have been killed like that. The few Arctic Foxes that I have seen on previous trips disappeared the moment they picked up my scent. Of course, no Polar Eskimo would die like that. He then discloses that a *kadluna* was 'eaten' by a polar bear not far from here. It is all a bit too much, but the point is clear. I have provided the fodder for the Inugguit to demonstrate once again why they are superior. Afterwards at the Bingo, which in my opinion, is no game for an intelligent adult –which is perhaps why Qulutannguaq does not go – I am told quite the same thing by Inukitsoq and Stinanguak. They firmly believe that only the Polar Eskimo can survive in this part of the world, and that it is not meant for anybody else. The Inugguit like to postulate that in the event of a major world disaster, they would be the only people in the world who would be able to survive because they have not forgotten the skills of their ancestors. I am bored of the Bingo and leave early which is sure to leave somebody insulted. As is invariably the case with these occasions, I spend most of my time thinking about how I can abscond.

On the 5th of May, a screech of gulls sits on the sea ice in grey and white plumage, congregating and making plans, looking cold, lost and ill-at-ease. Early in the afternoon, I decide to go and visit Inukitsoq. On the way, I am delighted to see the first Snow Bunting (*qupanuk*) of the year perched on Qulutannguaq's store house (*iliuqqaivik*). I shout out *ihiigu* to Miggoq's wife who carrying her baby in an *amaut* is on her way to visit a relative, but she just shrugs her shoulders. I remember very well when I said 'goodbye' to these small, cheery birds. I was sad to see them go and knew I would miss their friendly, familiar chirp. There is just one, but they are not solitary birds and there must be many more. Spring has arrived at last.

Inukitsoq lives in a small, green derelict cabin, very similar to mine with a stable-like door. On the front door there is a Danish sign saying *lukket* ('closed') which does not look very inviting. I knock on the door and I hear a groan. As suspected, he is sleeping. It is 2.30pm in the afternoon. Inside, it is obvious that the cabin could only belong to an *angatsuduk*. It is chaotic and filthy. Inugguit homes are normally clean, but untidy. Qulutannguaq insists always that I do not enter their house with dirty clothing on, examining my coat for the slightest evidence of *ipeq* ('dirt'). Entering the abode of a bachelor is a different story. The cabin comprises a living room and a tiny bedroom. In the living room, there is a standard oil heater, but also one of the big old paraffin heaters that we used out hunting on Northumberland Island. This is essentially a hunting cabin used as a permanent home. He is living the simplest life possible with no electricity and thus no electric lighting in this most northerly of places. His life is absolutely simple; ownership seems to have little meaning for him. When he first came to the settlement, he was described as *nujurataq* ('wild, untamed'). This is a word that is normally used to describe animals.

I said at the beginning of this trip that if I could understand Inukitsoq, then I could understand anybody. I still hold that view, but I certainly understand much more now than ever before. He is one of six children and moved to Hiorapaluk in 2000. Previously, he lived in Qaanaaq where he was born and Qeqertat. Flat Qeqertat offers no escape from the endless summer sun, the ethereal daze, and it became apparently intolerable. He sits in his armchair with his dirty black *salopettes* and clogs on, smoking a roll-up cigarette, playing the cat's cradle string game (*ajarraaq*). It turns out that he is exceptionally good at the cat's cradle, and with one piece of string wrapped around his hands is able to make the shape of a walrus, dog, seal, seagull and practically any animal you care to name. Laughing and grinning, the show then works up to the grand finale of producing the genitalia: the anus, vagina and penis. I can see this is a well-rehearsed party-trick for the visitor. There is a fixation with genitalia and this is an absurd example of that. It is a bit difficult to work out some of the shapes, but the speed with which he twists the one piece of string around his hands and figures to make all these very elaborate figures is very impressive. The best thing about this perform-ance is how easily he is entertained by it.

The cabin is very smoky and the door is closed. He puts a saucepan of water over the paraffin heater and prepares some coffee, allowing us to inhale the carbon monoxide. The electricity unit in the cabin blew up in 2007 during a storm, and he has not been able to afford to repair it. Throughout the dark period, he is dependent on candles for light. The simplicity of it all is very appealing, but the romance must soon dissipate when the gritty reality of darkness kicks in. He admits that it is quite difficult stumbling around in the winter. The winter must seem endless for him. Inukitsoq laughs and jokes about me and Qulutannguaq having become close friends (*kammak angihoq*). Cigarette hanging out of his mouth, he then stands up and pulls his pants down, urinating into an empty fruit juice container.

It is 3pm and he insists that we listen to the news in Greenlandic and Danish: the radio fuzz blows around the cosy, smoky cabin; Inukitsoq shrugs his shoulders when the Danish newscaster comes on air. Then suddenly, he tells me that he is going out and that is my sign to leave. I have tried the same trick in my hut in Qaanaaq, but it does not mean that the visitors will always leave. When I leave, he asks me *kinamut*? (literally 'to whom'?). One does not just saunter around the settlement; one has to be always on the way to visiting somebody. This local knowledge of who is visiting whom is important as people need to be able to position you socially and understand with whom you are interacting. Movements within networks are registered in minute detail. There is little room for outsiders in such a tiny community. *Kinamut* is a common greeting here in the smaller settlements. It will be strange to return to a world where one is not constantly visiting people for no reason whatsoever, other than to be with them. It is surprising how quickly one adopts their ways.

In the afternoon, there is a small gathering in the community hall. A Government notice about an alcohol awareness campaign is read out by Stinanguak in an inexpressive monotone. It seems like a strange undertaking given that the settlement is 'dry'. The residents voted to keep alcohol out of the settlement which will surely mean that none comes on the supply ship, but that some alcohol gets into the settlement via the helicopter. Riotous children run around and it is the normal mayhem. Nobody listens to a word that is said, even if the lady reading out the notice tried to shoot herself under the influence and has since then given up on the alcohol. Hiorapaluk is a strange place. It is a settlement of children and a few women. Most of those that live here do not want to be disturbed by visitors. They want the peace and quiet of the settlements. That is all. Many of the men are away hunting for much of the time. Either that or they are in Qaanaaq, enjoying the social life of the town.

Talking to Ane later in the day at her cabin, I get the true story about Qaanaaq and her relationship with the place. As suspected, she was more or less forced out of the town. The catechist who is there at the moment is apparently quite vicious and a back-stabber. She was telling horrible lies about Ane and was extremely unpleasant to her: the people of Qaanaaq can turn against outsiders. Ane agrees that there is a tense atmosphere in Qaanaaq and that alcohol abuse is destroying the town. She used to write letters to the newspaper about the problems in Qaanaaq, particularly the problems that the children have growing up in households of alcoholics and the locals turned on her. When they stopped selling alcohol in Qaanaaq, people started to demonstrate. The other disagreement she had with the people of Qaanaaq was about animal abuse which she thinks is rife. She has contacted the police and the Government, reporting various offenders in the town. In her view, most hunters in Qaanaaq should not be allowed to keep dogs. In the summer, she says dogs have died of thirst in Qaanaaq simply because their owners could not be bothered to give them water. This confirms what I had suspected. It is clear that the bond is quite different between those people that live in the settlements, and there is a respect for those who have managed to avoid the allure of the town.

The basis of the network here in Hiorapaluk is family; much more so than in Haviggivik. If you are not related to them (as Ane clearly is not), then you might still be accepted, but you are certainly not one of them. Life in Hiorapaluk is based on two families and that is all. Haviggivik is friendlier and more open. Historically, there have been more outsiders with families moving up the coast. Ane is a teacher at the school in Hiorapaluk. Previously, the children of Hiorapaluk did not have a teacher for two years. A layman would go up to the school and read to them.

In the evening, I go and visit Qulutannguaq and decide to ask him about recording his drum-songs. He has often alluded to the fact that he knows a great deal of songs, and he is fully aware that I am here to document their oral traditions. We skirt around the issue for a while and then I come straight out with it and ask Qulutannguaq whether he would let me record him. I sense the whole family who are perched on bits of furniture around the room have been waiting for this question. The atmosphere changes. Suddenly, they are all ears. The conversation is going to be delicate because of the issue of how much to pay for data.

He tells me that I can record him but it will cost 5,000DKK for about half an hour of songs. I feel very insulted. That is many multiples of what I would pay his father. I feel very uncomfortable about it and it makes for a difficult atmosphere. He performed an impromptu drum-dance for me the other day and I think he is unhappy that I did not pay for it even though there was clearly no reason to do so as I had not even asked him to sing. According to him, two Finnish women came to visit him in the late 1990s and recorded a great number of his songs. He says that they paid 5,000DKK. I hope that is not correct for their sake. A drum-song is less than a minute long and to pay that amount would have been scandalous. But, I have heard many such stories. I tell him that I am interested in the language and that I would wish to write down the words of the songs that he knows. Then, the price doubles. The Inugguit feel very strongly that previously researchers and anthropologists have taken their oral heritage and intangible culture away from them without paying for it. Now, they are out for revenge. Qulutannguaq claims to know thousands of these songs and that they are all in his head. He has never written them down. He just remembers them. I am suspicious of this as

most of them do not have words, and those that do have very few words
that people do not even understand. It is a very fragmented spoken
tradition and to put a price on it in this fashion is meaningless. Contrary
to what they might think, there is of course no chance whatsoever of me
recording these songs and then producing a CD with them on and
getting rich on the back of it. That is sadly their misplaced expectation.
There is a short silence after this discussion. One cannot help feel that it
has soured the relationship a bit. The line between joking and making a
serious point seems to get thinner.

I wake up to what I think is the sound of seagulls. The sound is so
reminiscent of waking up in the back room at Cliff House, Eastbourne,
as a child that it is almost as if I am dreaming of former days. I peek out
the window to confirm that I am indeed still in the Arctic, and not on the
Sussex coast. I left the heating off overnight. The temperature is about 0
degrees outside and I have not found that I need the heating on in the
cabin with these mild temperatures. After nine months of living in
freezing conditions, it is perhaps not so surprising that I have adapted to
the cold in this way. The sky is thick with snow. It falls incongruously, like
manna in small, angry flakes. There is limited visibility with the low
cloud, and the white sky merges with the sea ice, blanketing the place in a
contourless whiteness. The vista is blurred and puffy and once out of the
settlement, almost universally white. The *huuviataqtoq* or 'slight wind'
redistributes not quite indiscriminately handfuls of *pilaaq* ('powder
snow'). My eyes focus on the *natserivik*, the 'snow that blows across the
surface of the sea ice', and the mesmerising patterns that it creates,
reshapes and then erases.

The gulls are clustered on a patch of sea ice in the middle of the fjord.
Announcing their arrival, they work their way through a melody of bugle
calls starting with the Reveille. After months of silence and no birdlife at
all, except for the occasional Raven, the Arctic has suddenly come to life.
Within a few days, the Snow Buntings have arrived and now there are
gulls too. The snow is still falling, but this must be spring. The terror and
hardship of the winter is behind me. Everything happens so fast in the
Arctic. The light comes back in a flash and disappears just as quickly. The
ice on the tidal zone is now bearing large cracks and with the fresh snow
and reduced visibility, it looks rather hazardous getting onto the sea ice at
certain uncrossed points. Qulutannguaq tells me that the gulls are tasty,

but that there is no need to shoot them as they have enough food. That is reassuring on both counts.

At the Olsens, Abi is asleep on one of the single beds in the living room. Stinanguak is playing a hand-held computer game whilst Ingaapaluk watches an Irish soap-opera without the sound. Qulutann-guaq is trying to sleep in the adjacent room, complaining of a headache. The time is 3pm. I remind myself of the fact that there is no real generic word for time in the Qaanaamitun dialect. Stinanguak tells me that she feels very tired and that this kind of weather puts the Inugguit to sleep. The link between weather and mind (*hila*) is tangibly strong, as I have witnessed so many times in the past. Today is not a day for visiting, but there is really nothing else to do. Weather determines everything – the prospects for the day, sleeping patterns and their state of mind.

There has been nothing but feverish conversation about the Little Auks ever since I arrived in the settlement. The first few have now arrived and soon the sky will be black with migratory flocks of laughing birds as they arrive in their millions in acrobatic murmurations. The spectacle of such large numbers of tiny creatures moving perfectly in unison across vast distances to a tiny, specific place at the same time each year is enigmatic and something that only nature can comprehend. They come to Hiorapaluk the same week in May every year and then leave again on the 7th or 8th of August. Now, the Inugguit are getting their nets ready. The nets are attached to very long poles (*ipoq*). As the birds fly over, the wrist is twisted. Once the bird is caught, the wings are rotated so that it cannot fly away, and then one presses hard onto the heart, slowly pushing one's finger up towards its neck. This method causes internal bleeding and the bird soon dies.

Qulutannguaq stirs and moans about the weather. Suddenly, he picks up his gun, races outside and shoots twice at a dog that is running past, missing on both occasions. This is the very shy dog that used to be chained up next to one of the outside meat stores. The terrified dog pelts it across the ice. Qulutannguaq does not seem very happy and will not answer me when I ask him why he tried to shoot the dog. Subsequently, Ane tells me it is because the dog is very shy, is on the run and no good to anybody. Timid dogs are no good to a hunter and are normally shot. It is cruel, harsh and unnecessary, but I am much less shocked by it now than I would have been nine months ago. Stuck in the settlement looking for food, the dog must live a life of appalling terror, dodging bullets and never being able to relax for a single moment.

Qulutannguaq has apparently lost interest in 'teaching' me. He is no doubt insulted that I did not wish to pay a fortune to record his drum-songs. Equally, it might be just the effect of the weather. I think he has lost interest in helping me because he knows that I am leaving. It is true that the Inugguit always ask when you are leaving, but that is probably because they just want to know how much time to invest in you, and not because they want you to leave. The only difficulty with that is that when I arrived and told people that I would be here a year, they still showed absolutely no interest in me. And then shortly before I leave, I am told that they will not help me because I am leaving soon. These are some of the many frustrations of doing fieldwork in an Inuit community. Without the Olsens, there is little point staying in Hiorapaluk as most other people are so closed and much less willing to help. Ironically, for a people living so far North, I think they have seen it all before: researchers and tourists staying for short periods of time before moving on. Some have certainly made a beeline for Hiorapaluk in the past simply because it is a place of superlatives, a sort of John O'Groats or Land's End.

It is mid-May and soon it will be time for me to leave the settlement. There is bright blue sky, sunshine and the Snow Buntings chipper and chatter to one another outside. A strong wind from the north (*avanngaq*) makes it unlikely that the helicopter will come today either. I have been waiting several days now. It makes little difference, but I am all packed and ready to go. Angutdluk shouts out that the helicopter will not come and then laughs, muttering under his breath as per usual.

I go to Qulutannguaq's house to see if I can have a look at their teletext screen. Ingaapaluk is asleep on one of the beds in the living room. It is 11.30am. Qulutannguaq exclaims that the flight is cancelled without turning the television on. Then, the phone rings and it turns out that it is the shop looking for me. Qulutannguaq insists that I go down to the shop immediately and check my bag in. I assume that this is another practical joke, but then I realise it is not. I trot back to the cabin to pick up my bag and take it down to the shop. It is seven kgs over weight, but nobody cares about that. The helicopter is coming in ten minutes. For once, I see the Inugguit get into action. I collect my luggage, leave the haunted 1950s cabin and have just time to go over to the Olsens to say one last goodbye and thank you. They are eating and tell me to come in and stay a while, but there is not really time. The helicopter is approaching the settlement. Even now, its familiar thud is somehow ensconced in my acoustic memory. It symbolises arrival and departure and its power and metaphorical presence has not diminished in any way. Shortly after leaving the Polar North, I would lie awake at night with that sound in my head.

There is a quick goodbye (*inudduarit*) and then I am left climbing the steep slope up to the helicopter pad with the wind in my face. The children have gathered and collectively shout out 'Stiffi' from the school window. I do not have time to say goodbye personally, but give them a very hearty wave. Once the helicopter has landed, they like to leave as soon as possible as the conditions can quickly change. There is now a strong wind and so Steffen flies very low over the sea ice, probably just twenty feet above it or so. We fly right over the head of Aki and his dog team. He waves and grins. The ice is thin at Kangeq, but there is no sign of open water.

9: Ways of Belonging

A narrow channel of cloud runs right across the horizon dividing the panorama into wafers of different shades of blue and grey – the seascape and landscape becomes one. A small pod of beluga whales pass through the bay in August, escorted by a colony of obstreperous Arctic Terns. Down at the shore, a silent hunter has killed five Ringed Seals (*puihi*) and two Kittiwakes (*taatiraaq*). Lonely cathedrals of ice turning blue sit like moored ships in the bay. Their west-looking escutcheons are amphitheatres of light under the supine sun. It is a floating island of ice with frozen peaks, valleys and escarpments. With just one tenth of its ice above water, I contemplate how this visiting, eroding nation must appear from below the sea level. In the treeless Polar North, the visual field extends so far that it prevents space from being boxed in and organised into different distances and perspectives. Size and distances can only be ascertained by movement. A motorboat passes in front of it, like an insignificant fly buzzing across a whiteboard, and I can begin to appreciate its vastness. This one iceberg must be the size of Qaanaaq alone. Hungry glacial tongues lick the opposite shore. In the foreground, tufty-headed cotton grass sways in the breeze.

On the way back from the shore, a woman waves at me from a window of one of the red A-framed houses beyond the bridge. A disfigured grin beckons me in; florid complexions through the *fenestra*. I open the porch door and clamber over a jumble of clothes and tools strewn all over the place. A dirty bowl containing prawn shells sits in the corner, nestled between various pairs of sandy boots. The pungent smell of sea mammals is overwhelming. I am greeted by her husband, Henrik Dunneq. He is in his early fifties and wears a filthy orange T-shirt which barely covers his huge, swelling bulk. In the living room awaits a festival of glazed, almond eyes. Still, I cherish these visits to these old traditional, chaotic hunters' homes towards the shore. Their simplicity, smells and air of *ammaqa* pervade the place, defining Greenlandicness. It is a world apart from the tidy, modern homes where many younger people live at the top of the town which with the exception of the loo facilities could be anywhere in Scandinavia. Here, at one of the Dunneq households, the sitting room is complete mayhem.

Marmarut Eipe, one of those in the town who suffers from mental illness, is sitting next to me. Today, he wears a swollen and cut black eye – the result of a fight at the weekend. The slurred drunken colloquy is an unfortunate series of misunderstandings, garbled non-sequiturs and high-spirited laughter. He insists on writing his name, age and address in my notebook, as so many have done. Then, he gestures to me to put the book away immediately as it can serve no other purpose. Sitting on the tatty sofa is a toothless, tracksuit-clad woman in her early fifties who seems relatively coherent. There is a programme on the television showing a hunter skinning a caribou in graphic detail. It occurs to me that it would be quite unacceptable to show such a programme on British television.

Henrik is sprawled out on the sofa, shouting and screaming like a mad man. For a moment, I feel as if I am in some sort of Siberian psychiatric hospital. I try and stay calm and not look remotely perturbed by his hysterical outcries and guttural imprecations, some of which are increasingly directed towards me. More red wine is poured from a polythene bag into cloudy, stained receptacles. They insist that I join them and a glass is encouragingly raised to my lips. As is invariably the case in these situations, I am invited to peruse the family photograph album.

Henrik's wife asks me repeatedly why I do not have a wife and she seems genuinely upset about the matter. Using her hands and figures, the woman tells and signs me that she is 50 years old. Holding up two more figures and feigning a noose pulled round her neck, she relates that in two decades she will be dead. She drops her head, looks tragically solemn for a moment and tells me that I had better get on with it. The message is clear. To be unmarried and childless at my age is inconceivable in this community. If a man has a family, the only way that he can hunt is if his wife works. This process risks creating what one might call a 'disjunction of belonging' whereby the demands of modern life risk fracturing their networks of belonging as the culture of sharing the catch amongst family networks is increasingly threatened by a new paradigm of individual salaried employment and by the fact that it is increasingly difficult to find the sea mammals as the ice-edge retreats. The discussion moves on to *kiviat*. They are eager for the foreigner to try the same delicacy that ended up killing Knud Rasmussen, and Henrik stumbles off into the kitchen to procure some. There are no *kiviat* to be found, and the conversation is beginning to pall. A few sardonic smiles, and then I take the opportunity to try and leave.

Merleau-Ponty (2002: 530) in the last line of *Phenomenology of Perception* says: 'Man is but a network of relationships, and these alone matter to him'. The desire to belong is universal and was implied in encounters like this time and time again during my year in the Polar North. The idea of belonging is central to the notion of how we give meaning to our lives. Our sense of identity is based on our interactions with the people that surround us through shared beliefs, traditions and language. Belonging is about belonging to a particular group of individuals. We define ourselves to a large extent by the communities we belong to. In small, homogeneous societies in very remote locations, the parameters of belonging are so well defined that to be an outsider in some way may even be dangerous and will soon lead to gossip. Social life is governed by a rigid, unwritten code.

Changes in the natural environment will have ramifications for the notion of 'belonging' in the sense of social inclusion and 'interpersonal attachments' (Baumeister & Leary, 1995: 522), and in the way one relates to and corresponds with the immediate natural environment. Here, pseudo-subsistence hunting represents still a tightly intertwined human environmental system in which indigenous people interact symbiotically with an ecosystem upon which some still depend for their way of life. Affected by dramatic social change over the last fifty years and recent climatic change, indigenous ontologies of place in this Arctic community are now at risk of being redefined by new cosmologies.

With the onset of very rapid climate change since the late 1980s, the Inugguit sense of place and their need to form associations with their environment has begun to mutate, suggesting that the two inter-related themes of place and belonging might be reassessed in the future as new identity paradigms are formed by the younger generation. With the disappearing sea ice, 'experienced' space is shrinking and this is reflected in new mindsets – the product of a more urban, sedentary lifestyle. Indigenous conceptions of place and environment are beginning to be revised as the remnants of animist and spiritual beliefs disappear completely, the transmission of stories dies out and as the sea ice struggles to form.

The young people of north-west Greenland have today a fraction of the knowledge of the older hunters and the landscapes of the older hunters' stories are losing their narrative significance: a sensuous world is being replaced by a Cartesian cosmology of empty objects as the space is no longer 'lived' in the same way. For the older people, a mountain is not just a mountain, but is a confluence of historical events tracing their previous peripatetic lifestyle. Even if their stories' principal function is a 'humanising' one (Willerslev, 2007: 172), knowledge is passed on through *hiku* ('sea ice')-based stories. Without the sea ice, the stories would lose their essence as the journey to the places where the 'storied' events took place would be a different one (by boat) and thus the experience would not be the same. Disappearing sea ice will inevitably result in cultural shift because the sea ice is so fundamental to the Inugguit way of living and always has been.

Despite extreme isolation over an extended period of time and despite living in an age of globalisation, the Inugguit of north-west Greenland have a tendency not to look at the outside world for contact or future cooperation of any kind. Instead, they are more concerned with maintaining what one might call their own dense 'networks of belonging'. By a 'network of belonging', it is meant a network with a few nodes representing branches of an extended family (typically) that constantly reassert their kin links with one another through various modalities and practices of social belonging. These include intensive visiting and other mechanisms such as naming, celebratory *kaffimiks* and the toasting of shared birth years. To not belong in such a community is akin to committing a form of social suicide, and is avoided at all costs. It is likely that this has always been the case, and it remains so today.

When meeting the Inugguit, the first things they will want to know is your name and age. The latter, and more frequently the date of birth carry great significance. It is a means of creating links and bonds in the dense familial networks, but also beyond. If they are not able to remember your name, one can be sure that they will remember the year of your birth. For those that share a birthday or year of birth, a special bond is quickly formed. When I was living in the settlements, the revelation that I was born the same year as somebody else was a cause of celebration. Basic personal statistics such as this are important in this society.

The geography of Greenland is conducive to what one can call unique networks of belonging because places are 'bounded'. Unlike any other country in the world, this peculiar topography enforces certain patterns of intensive community interaction because it is relatively difficult to leave these thinly populated settlements. On the largest island on earth, 55,000 people live dotted around the edge in small, unconnected towns and settlements. In the more remote, road-less settlements of north-west Greenland, all of which are skirted by the Greenland Ice Sheet, the only way out is either what is for many the unaffordable weekly helicopter, dog-sledge providing there is sea ice or in the months of July and August, a small motor boat. For Haviggivik, none of these options are often available: storms in the winter months prevent a helicopter landing for weeks on end, and the thinning sea ice means that it is now too dangerous to negotiate the Cape York archipelago.

Living in a settlement where there was effectively no way in or way out (during the periods when the sea ice had not properly formed, but when there was sufficient sea ice to make it difficult to go out in a boat) was to become a curse during the initial part of the dark period. To live in such a bounded place was a double-edged sword: it was suffocating at times and led me looking for an exit, but it was also remarkably conducive to intensive contact and visiting which in itself had its advantages and disadvantages. Rather than the Inugguit feeling like the object of anthropological enquiry, it was often myself that felt like I was living in the fish bowl.

At times like this, it was clear to me, however, that the need to 'belong' is undoubtedly compelling in all societies. Erich Fromm (2004: 17) says that the reason for this is our subjective self-consciousness, the faculty of thinking by which man is aware of himself as an individual entity, different from nature and other people. Fromm believes that unless man 'belongs' somewhere, he feels as if he is overcome by individual insignificance. Fromm thinks that there is a human imperative to avoid isolation and moral aloneness. The Inugguit are in agreement with this. To be without a wife for instance is the greatest misfortune that can befall the Arctic hunter.

The process of the emergence of the individual from his original ties, a process which Fromm calls 'individuation' seems to have barely begun amongst the Inugguit. In my case, the process of individuation was furthered by education. If the *inuk* has gone through the process of 'individuation', this might mean that he has been rejected from society for there is little space for 'individuals' in a society that historically has only managed to survive by sharing and working together. If an Inugguaq has gone through the process of 'individuation', this might mean that he has become a *qivittoq* for there is little space for 'individuals' in a society that historically has only managed to survive by sharing and working together. Recently killed or raw foods are shared community wide in the small settlements and between the family group in the town. Those who do not share their food soon gain a reputation.

As is the case with many members of 'small' societies' that share common bonds and history, the Inugguit feel a tremendous sense of rootedness, expressed through their relationship with the *nuna* and through their ties with one another. They take comfort in the tiny and unchanging circles in which he moves. It was obvious that this sense of rootedness was alien to me, not in the place where they come from, but the place where I come from. One could say that the Inugguit are living a pre-individualistic existence. Individuation leads to a new kind of relatedness to the world.

During my stay in the Polar North, I felt a very strong sense of the self and the other, but wondered initially whether this was just because I am the product of a society where there persists a lens of dualism. This dualistic problem lies at the centre of the environmental problem, but the perception of dualistic categories when it comes to humans is more prominent in the Polar North than it is in Europe. The Inugguit can be deeply racist (racist towards white and black people) and xenophobic. It is in fact clear that the Inugguit have a very pronounced sense of the racial 'other' (perhaps stronger than the 'white man') in the way that they refer unnecessarily to *kadluna* all the time.

In Inugguit society, identity with family and kin gives them tremendous security, rooted in a structuralised whole where their place is unquestionable. This whole is the meaning of life. Being a part of this social order gives the Inugguaq the feeling of belonging and security. They may be seen as marginal people, but they may sees us (*kadluna*) as marginal in a different sense because many multi-cultural societies in the West have lost their group cohesiveness, indulging in a confused sense of Self. To suffer aloneness in Inuit society is surely one of the worst sufferings for an Inugguaq. Alienation in an Inuit settlement requires an exit strategy – normally moving to another settlement or suicide. In my stay in the Polar North, I witnessed cases of both. In the case of the former, a friend of mine had been accused of having an affair by the mother of his girlfriend. He was physically attacked by the mother. He managed to leave, getting on the next flight to Upernavik the following week leaving his girlfriend and son behind. In his opinion, his life was in danger. The mother had organised a gang of men to attack him. He has not returned to the town and now lives in Denmark.

There is often little concern with abstraction, and they would no doubt find it strange that many of us sit around thinking about abstract things. 'Of what are you thinking?', Peary asked one of his Eskimo guides. 'I do not need to think', was the answer, 'I have plenty of meat'. The hunter-gatherer lifestyle is conducive to couching thoughts in concrete terms. The Inugguaq is conscious of himself first and foremost as a member of a kin group. The Inugguit existence is so communal by nature, the safety net of kin is so secure that there is little reason to pose these questions. What matters is the security of the group, not the individual. The sense of being an outsider is therefore especially strong for a newcomer to a pre-individualised society where the bonds of kinship are so strong.

Individualised man seems to have lost his relationship with nature. Fromm thinks that individualised man is alone because he has severed his relationship with nature, but that he cannot return to it. Fromm thinks that the individualised man wishes to return to the security of the pre-individualised existence, such as that of the Inugguaq. Fromm (2004: 34) believes that it is this lack of individual freedom that characterises medieval in contrast to modern society. Individualised man has become detached from the world. He lacks the oneness with nature and the world. In Fromm's opinion, individualised man wishes to 'flee from freedom' because he cannot cope with the 'aloneness'. Fromm seems to be suggesting that the paradox is that the modern man wishes to achieve

freedom, but having attained it he feels isolation and personal insignificance. At that point, he wants to return to the comfort and security of the
pre-individualised existence, but is unable to do so. He wants to return to
the oneness with nature, but does not know how to. To achieve personal
freedom, he had to sever that bond.

This is not my story. My story is one of individual freedom and the
contentedness of having obtained it in the Arctic where I discovered a
complete absence of restraint that was mirrored in the impressive
stillness of the empty landscape. For me, it was not about the feeling of
individual significance that Fromm claims is the ultimate result of having
obtained personal freedom. However, I do understand that the individu-
alisation process has led to the severing of the bond with nature. It was
that bond that I was seeking to recreate, and the Arctic was the vehicle for
doing so. I cannot return to nature, as Fromm says, but I can still learn to
appreciate it again nonetheless. I am not fleeing from freedom, but I
came to understand that complete personal freedom in Inugguit society
would be an unattractive prospect and would imply alienation from one's
community. Herein lay the ingredients of a clear clash of cultural values.
I esteem personal freedom; the Inugguit think it is a curse. That is not to
say that they do not enjoy the freedom of travelling by dog-sledge out on
the sea ice. They most certainly do, but once back in the settlements they
crave company.

Paradoxically, the Inugguaq's position in society can be put in doubt
through the 'achievements' of the individual himself. Outsiders would
speak of the problem of the *jantelov* in this community, the idea that
those who stand out as achievers should be punished because success is
due to the collective and not the individual. Visiting academics and
researchers are not respected for the reason that according to *jantelov*
nobody should think they are better than anybody else, but one suspects
that this perverse piece of thinking applies more to insiders than
outsiders. Those Inugguit who had been successful would typically leave
or be the source of much gossip in the town. Having these kind of people
around seemed to upset the balance of things and led to people developing inferiority complexes.

My distinct impression was that in the settlements where I worked,
everybody was engaged in the search for belonging, and not just the
outsider. 'Belonging' was a social imperative. To belong is to be part of

the collective consciousness that defines the community which is the permanent and perpetual condition of things. The problems of not being 'accepted' do not, however, just concern genuine outsiders like myself. For some, being 'accepted' was a perennial problem. Inuit society is very unforgiving in terms of who is 'in' and who is 'out'. Members of society can be 'forced out' by being subject to cruel and merciless ridicule. Even having a patron in advance who will promote one's interests might be a risky strategy as if this person is not widely liked in the community, then by associating with him or her, one risks being tarred by the same brush of social exclusion. Being socially excluded in an extremely remote Inuit settlement where there might be no way in or out (as in periods of bad weather when the sea ice has not formed properly) would be for some an equivalent of a death sentence, a form of incarceration – the greatest fear of the *inuk*.

As it happened in my case, the two contacts I had in the community prior to my arrival both turned out to be *persona non grata*, but for two different reasons. Apart from the West Greenlandic priest, my other contact had left the Polar North many years previously to become a 'professional Eskimo', cashing in on the Peary name. He had tried to return, having lived in Europe for many years, but was not accepted. It was perhaps not so surprising therefore that my integration into the community was a particularly tall order. In my case, it was obvious that if I were accepted at all, it would be purely for being the person I was and the help I was giving them to promote their language, and not because of who I knew. I had spoken to this particular Peary twice on the phone before leaving for Greenland. I met him in Copenhagen, bought him dinner and had an enjoyable evening. That was it. On the 2nd of January 2011, I received an invoice from him for 'consultancy services'. The amount was 3,000 Euros. I was advised that he was depressed and deep in debt. I ignored the invoice and he sent me various letters telling me that he had reported me to the Cambridge Constabulary. It is perhaps no wonder that he had been rejected from Inugguit society.

The discovery of Kap York Radio which broadcasts in the Polar Eskimo language helped to some extent with my integration. The disc-jockey at that time was Arqioq Jensen – a man whom I could trust and rely on as a friend from the beginning to the end. Going on the radio (with an interpreter) gave me a sense of authority. Towards the beginning of my stay and through the words of an interpreter, I could explain to the community what the purpose of my stay was and how I had hoped to go about it. The radio helped to legitimise my presence. The radio gives the Inugguit a voice in their own language and helps to shore up a separate identity. It also reinforces the strong bonds that connect the members of the community. When people call up on the radio, everybody knows who the speaker is and how exactly they are related to him or her. The radio offers a means by which people can discuss things, which is not something that has happened historically.

Social (or familial) connectedness and spatial attachment converge in the notion of 'belonging' which is inherently tied to identity and the differentiation between 'us' and 'them'. The Inugguit sense of belonging is composed of an affinity to the local cosmos *and* 'membership' of the community. Active membership and participation in the environment is the experience of place and culture. This rootedness in their surroundings creates an existential framework which governs large parts of their lives and their overall philosophy. The Inugguit belong to the landscape around them more than it belongs to them. It is not a relationship expressed in terms of ownership and certainly not in terms of personal ownership. Personal ownership extends to clothing, but not much else. For all of us 'places nurture a feeling of belonging' (Nuttall, 1992: 40), but place identity for the Inugguit does not mean belonging to a specific settlement. The sense of 'belonging' is anchored to the *nuna* (for the occasional one with political ambitions, the *nuna inugguit*) and the shared experience of hunting.

There is a deep communal bond with the natural environment, but you have to be born into it or earn it. The bond can be broken, and once it is broken it is difficult to mend. As sworn to me by a number of Inugguit, the bond is so strong that one should not leave the place for the long term. If one does so, one is severing a more fundamental, irreversible bond to the *nuna*, and the result is that one might not be accepted back when one tries to return. A young man, Mikkili, told me: 'They would have to kill me before I move'. 'I would not leave Qaanaaq for any amount of money', he continued. He had such a strong bond to the *nuna* that he spent his whole time in Copenhagen with his father wanting to get back. Now, that he is back he does not plan on leaving again. The relationship Mikkili has with his primary place of upbringing could not be more different from my own. His sense of 'belonging' is so strong, enforced by a dense network of extended kin and a semi-spiritual link with the *nuna*. There is absolutely no doubt in his convictions.

Nuna is more than the land. It is the surrounding physical and spiritual environment including the sea ice, the mountains, the air, the animals, fish and even souls and memories of events and people who lived in the past. It is the place where men and animals share the same breath, and might even include future generations. Its associations are both spiritual and physical and the nature of the bond reflects this. It is not a relationship expressed in terms of ownership, a defined territory or an object; it is a home for all the Inuit where historically they have always found food (animals). There is an intimacy with the *nuna* and all age groups expressed sincere respect for it. It should always be possible to travel over it 'freely'. If it were misused, the caribou or the narwhals may not return the following year. Implicit in *nuna* is a strong sense of the inter-connectedness of human and natural communities and great pride is taken in this primordial relationship with nature.

For the Inugguit, the Arctic wilderness which is of course for them not a wilderness at all, is first and foremost a hunting ground, their back-yard, a source of food and not a 'beautiful' landscape. The wilderness for them is the *hermeq* which covers 88 per cent of the country and where man cannot survive as nothing lives there. As far as I know, there is no word for 'wilderness' in Polar Eskimo. The *hermeq* would be described as *inukanngitsoq* which means 'a place where nobody lives'. This word might be used to describe a closed-down settlement too.

It is the spiritual value of the *nuna* which their ancestors have occupied. It is something that has been shared and passed down. This identity is also socially constructed through the identification of certain characteristics seen as particular to that region and embedded in the *nuna*. These would include hunting practices (hunting narwhal from kayaks using harpoons), eating of certain traditional foods which are peculiar to the outer settlements (polar bear, narwhal and *kiviat* in particular) and of course their language whose aberrant phonology makes it inaccessible to most Greenlanders. Eating this food is a way of reinforcing the oneness of the group and the sense of relatedness, connecting oneself historically to a specific cultural landscape inhabited by one's forefathers and to the shared culture of hunting. Hunters share game amongst one another according to complex rules depending on the hunter's level of involvement in the catch. No hunter is left without in a society where there is a clear disdain for unshared, individual wealth. The Inugguit subscribe to an egalitarian ideology and are reluctant to make moral judgements on other people which might be seen as individual criticisms.

Belonging has an important social dimension too, and is even arguably the basis for the penitentiary system. There are detention centres in the capital where inmates are tagged, but have almost complete liberty, holding the keys to their cells. The system represents instead something resembling the model of punishment in medieval Iceland. The punishment for a serious crime might be exile to another settlement where one is given a job, a place to live, but where one is importantly an 'outsider' and where one's status is known to everyone. The peculiar topography of Greenland enables the system of exile to act as a *bona fide* punishment in a place where the links to the local community and the local cosmos are of paramount importance. There are many stories in Greenland of murderers fleeing from the scene of the crime towards the Ice Sheet behind the settlement. Knowing that the criminal cannot survive in this hostile wilderness, the police take no action. Either he dies in the wild, or more typically returns to the settlement where he is arrested.

There are no lawyers in Qaanaaq, but there is something of a justice system. The large, blue house behind Inge's is used as a court where video evidence is given to judges in Nuuk who decide on cases. There is one tiny prison cell in the hut which houses the police station. During my stay, there was a man there that was held for the maximum period which is four weeks. The gentleman was held on suspicion of GBH. Without any roads, criminals and prisoners are flown around the country with a police escort. If one sees a policeman in uniform on one of the turbo-props, it is likely that he is sitting next to a criminal who awaits sentencing. It is these small things which make Greenland unique. It is especially punishing for a Greenlander to be sent away from the community where he grew up in. In some cases, this means ties are severed with their family, their home and their community. In Greenland, that means everything. As Greenland is such a tiny society, almost everybody will know about your crime and your name and reputation will be destroyed.

A tiny number of criminals are actually sent to prison in Denmark.

On a number of occasions, I was told by the Inugguit that I must be very brave to live so far away from home for such an extended period of time. The children that go to Nuuk or one of the other towns often have problems of cultural integration (in Qaanaaq, most of the children leave school at 15 and almost none of them will get any further education). Often, they return home early, not having finished the course. It would be probably easier if they were to go to the Baffin Island region of Canada as they are closer to them in terms of cultural identity. In many respects, the Inugguit perceived my stay in the Polar North as a sort of exile. Such a voluntary detachment of kin, albeit a temporary one, would have been intolerable for them. Throughout my stay I was continuously asked if I was feeling homesick, *angir'dlarhiqtutin*? Their sense of belonging is related to a sense of place which has been internalised, intertwined with hunting practice. It is common to return to their birthplace to die, underlying the sense of continuity between personhood and land. This special, spiritual bond and loyalty to land and place, which for many of us is so alien, is felt at all ages. Through networks reaffirming belonging and through the culture of hunting on the ice, the Inugguit have created a fixed, non-negotiable identity for themselves which only now might begin to be tested.

The reasons for feeling 'invisible' puzzled me for much of my stay. Predominantly, it was something that I experienced in group situations. There is certainly an inherent shyness to the Inugguit which is rapidly overcome with the effects of alcohol. They are very friendly, but very closed at the same time. They can be particularly unengaging, and there is often very little eye contact, especially between myself and the local women who in the company of their husbands will turn the other way when I talk to their husband. The Inugguit women are attracted to the white man as they would always tell me. It is not surprising that the men see therefore a white, male 'outsider' as a threat. Once I understood their language, I could sometimes hear the male telling his girlfriend to look away as I approached.

There is a clear sense that close kin provides the most reliable support network and that ideally one should be surrounded by close kin all the time. To belong is to be able to boast a group of kin relations. 'Strangership' is something unsettling for them. Inugguit who left the community for other parts of Greenland spoke of how uncomfortable they felt to be surrounded by 'strangers', i.e. people they did not have any kin connection at all. I was often asked how it was that I could live among strangers at home. A special kind of hostility was felt towards those who they felt were maximally 'strange', such as Muslims. Even though they had never met a Muslim, they considered them, perhaps due to representations in the media, to be terrorists. Their knowledge of current affairs might be fairly minimal, but Osama Bin Laden's name would frequently be mentioned.

It does not matter much how well one speaks the language, what one eats and what kind of house one lives in, one cannot *really* belong unless one can boast the right kin relations and genealogies. Those most likely to commit suicide are those who might feel they have become 'outsiders', when a network has been fractured, perhaps because a personal relationship has broken down. Belonging can connect, but also exclude. Previously, if one were an 'outsider', one might become a *qivittoq*. In a recent school exam in Qaanaaq (north-west Greenland), teenagers were asked to write an essay on 'why there were no more *qivittoq* in Greenland'. Almost every student said the reason was that people had learnt to commit suicide. It is significant that the word for 'commits suicide' *imminortoq* refers to somebody 'who goes away from home' (and thus breaks the bond of belonging).

There is little doubt in Frederik's mind why this community has one of the highest suicide rates in the world. People here do not talk about their problems. They are paranoid talking about a difficulty they have for fear that they would be the subject of gossip and ridicule. The community is very closed, but at the same time it is very troubled. The Inugguit do not want to seem weak and vulnerable by exposing their own problems. In the case of the suicides of younger people, these are often problems of love. Rather than have their rejection exposed to the wider community, some prefer to take what is for them the easier way out. The ingredients seem to be therefore a combination of proud and very emotional characters living in a closed, gossipy community. For a variety of reasons, leaving the community is simply not an option for many people, but being locked in a small society and being the object of gossip and ridicule is understandably not an option either.

Strolling around town, I am delighted to see my cheerful friend from

Church with the dark wrap-around sunglasses. He stands on his rickety balcony, wearing unzipped, heavily stained trousers. His flaccid biceps grip the decaying wood. I see him for the first time without his glasses on. It looks like he had a bad accident, or at least his vision is seriously impaired. His face is withered from living a life in the dry, polar desert where the relative humidity is so low that snow can evaporate even in the coldest months. He speaks very slowly, articulating very carefully for my benefit. His green, weather-beaten cabin is not far behind the large, shiny cylindrical water tanks. He insists on inviting me in.

His entire living space is one room, about 11 feet square. The bathroom is a bucket on the right hand side as you enter. There is a sink, but very limited cooking facilities. Used pots and pans cluster around the oil heater. The hut is very dirty and shabby. As is often the case, the bed doubles up as a sofa. The walls are adorned with all kinds of faded photographs of family members and friends, a very dated aerial photograph of Qaanaaq which looks almost sepia-like, dowdy Christian iconography and damaged vernicles. There is a small television and clothes are piled up, spilling out of black dustbin liners in the corner of the room. Walking into the cabin is like entering another world. There is a faint smell of tobacco. The oil heater belches occasionally. It is warm and welcoming.

Appalersuarsuk lights a candle as tradition here dictates when one receives a guest. I am offered a cup of tea from a grimy Thermos. The glass seems relatively clean, but I try not inspect it too closely. On the table sit his cracked wristwatch which he keeps tapping, a faulty Nokia mobile phone held together by sellotape, roll-up tobacco and a spare candle. Appalersuarsuk Qaerngaq is an 80-year-old former hunter. He is a very kind man with whom I instantly felt a close bond shortly after I arrived in the town. He is constantly smiling and laughing. He has almost no material possessions, but seems contented and the simple life is all that he knows. He has five sons, two of whom live in Haviggivik which is his real home. He moved to Qaanaaq in 2003. Although at the beginning of my stay, we only had the smattering of a common language, we manage to communicate now quite well and the silences are never awkward. He is patient with my faltering Inuktun. Energetically, I write down words and phrases which he repeats time and time again.

At the beginning, I made inevitably a number of cultural faux-pas when it came to the protocol of visiting or being visited by people like Appalersuarsuk. The correct *modus operandi* is to walk into their homes without knocking, pour yourself a coffee from the Thermos and then cut yourself a piece of caribou or narwhal meat. Then sit down and say *qujan*. It is often said that only the policeman and *kadluna* knock. The reason for not knocking is presumably that the old igloo style houses had no door to knock on, but just a narrow tunnel as an entrance. Modalities of 'belonging' are practiced through various mechanisms, but principally through networks of *pulaar*. The word *pulaar* means 'visit', and the Inugguit spend their days going from one hut to another, sometimes visiting the same family member four or five times in the same day, even if there is absolutely nothing to say, no news, no gossip. Sometimes, after having spent the entire day ice-fishing with Magnus and having exhausted all channels of conversation, the moment I got back to the hut, he would come and visit. Apparently, the Inugguit never need time to themselves. The pulaar is a kind of formalised way of sharing. Once one begins pulaar relationships with people, there is an unsaid obligation to maintain the visits. It took me a while to appreciate this and I would at times get a very frosty reception if I visited somebody after an hiatus.

The *pulaar* is the most defining social institution in this part of the Arctic and in the smaller settlements this intensive socializing can become overwhelming. The smaller the place, the stricter are the parameters of belonging, the more suffocating these reaffirmations of belonging can become. The important point to remember about these visits is that there is no point to them, other than the objective of co-presence which is essential and underpins Inugguit social organisation. In particular, there is a need for very regular face-to-face contact between members of bilaterally extended families where there is a high degree of mutual assistance and which are the cultural and social units of productions.

These visits are a means of exchanging gossip and news, but often in the smallest of settlements there is little of importance to report and never enough material to cover three or four visits from the same person in one day alone. The Inugguit are the ultimate social beings, and many live in fear of being alone. The number of visits an outsider receives is the barometer for how well his efforts at integrating into the community are succeeding.

Shortly after arriving in the settlements, men would enter the house, sit down, smile and grin. Initially, the very shy Inugguit can be circumspect about contact with strangers. For the most part, they wanted nothing. They just wanted company, even if that meant not saying anything for what seemed like intolerably long periods of time. Conversation turned invariably at some point to kinship and the complex familial genealogies which are recited to the visitor in great detail. The mutual familiarity and inter-connectedness is a matter of pride. By making kinship the key subject matter for conversation, the sense of relatedness is constantly reinforced and the need to be part of this familial web is overwhelming.

A visit might last for anything from a few minutes to several hours. Houses are left open and visitors come and go all day long. It would be frowned upon to lock a door and might suggest a lack of trust on the behalf of the occupant. A locked door during the day would normally imply sexual activity or a serious drinking bout was taking place in the home. On occasions when I visited women living on their own, the door would be quickly locked behind me and this meant that they would shortly make a pass at me. By locking the door, one risks one's social reputation. Initially, the protocol and the mechanics of these visits were difficult to determine. It was easy to make the mistake of waiting for an invitation to 'visit' people; of not reciprocating the 'visit'; and of committing minor cultural faux-pas such as knocking on the door, forgetting to light a candle when somebody visits, not having pre-prepared coffee in a Thermos, asking direct questions, etc. I was coeval with the Inuit lifeworld I inhabited, but the exchanges, reciprocities and interdependencies were sometimes misunderstood.

I was curious to know how I would fit into this entangled web of visits. Not being related to anybody or having any 'sponsors' to whom I could fall back on, and being most obviously an 'outsider', I did not have a clear peer group. Typically, it was the children that came to visit who had sometimes been sent by their parents to spy on the outsider. Others that came to visit were the *angatsuduk* ('bachelors'), some of whom did not for various reasons belong properly to an extended network of visits. Not having a wife and children is socially frowned upon, stigmatised and the subject of endless jokes. The single men are single for a reason. Whilst it was taboo to discuss it, the reason they did not have a wife would have been known to everyone. In the case of those that visited me, some had previously wives who had left them due to domestic abuse, some suffered from schizophrenia or minor mental illness, others were criminal exiles and one just had severe learning difficulties.

In the settlement of Haviggivik, social integration took on a fascinating dynamic with the number of visitors one would receive on some days reaching absurd proportions. As an *angatsuduk*, these bachelors had become my peer group and my network of belonging. Unsurprisingly, many of these visits were simply spent discussing who had been visiting whom. It is in these most remote Inugguit communities with one cultural setting where there is a particularly strong tendency for people to monitor each other's sociability. Close observation of each other's behaviour is facilitated by the spatial arrangement of houses dotted around the shore. Movement in such a place is recorded and reported first hand, or more commonly second or third hand in encounters in subsequent days. All the houses face the frozen sea and thus these visits are in public view and one is seldom granted privacy of any kind. With binoculars sitting on every window-sill and with 24 hour daylight for four months of the year, any form of clandestine socializing would be more or less impossible in this treeless environment. It is in this context that a small, but intense social world develops fuelled by incessant gossip often insinuating sexual relations between local people, obscene jokes and ridicule. The Inugguit take comfort in the localness and total familiarity of their lifeworld where everybody knows everything about his neighbour.

When the outer settlements close down, a form of urbanisation takes place and inevitably the way people relate to the land and surrounding people changes with it as their interaction is less immediate and the need to belong is less of an imperative. Many young people in Qaanaaq see no reason at all to go out on the sea ice, for example, the physical platform for the culture of the Inugguit. Practices of belonging continue in the town, but in a less intense way.

The dynamic of social movement and inter-connectedness is quite different in another settlement, Hiorapaluk. Here, there are just two families and one bachelor. He lived in a tiny hut without electricity, and was known as *hiuliqatuk* which means 'somebody who likes to live as in the olden days' (*qanga hiur'du*). In this closed, inward-looking community, there is no space for an outsider at all and it would be difficult to imagine more dense social networks of belonging than in these settlements. The options for visiting are no more than a handful of households, all of whom represent two extended families.

People are consistently and directly dependent on one another. Historically, one could not survive in isolation in such a hostile climate. Thus, the personalities and behaviour of the people living in the settlements in particular are important to their own interpersonal lives and as communitywide concerns. Locally criticised emotions such as anger and jealousy which play an important role in Inuit society, are negative 'emotions of place'. They are sentiments that people do not want strongly associated with the local environment (but that is not to say that they are not). Evaluations of others' emotional dispositions are assessments of others' positions in societal space, of others' connectedness to the community. Those who are not 'accepted' in the smaller settlements would normally leave.

Life in the settlements is characterised by this very small scale of life, constantly reaffirming family inter-connectedness through a discourse of kinship and relatedness. The social ingredients of life in the settlements are collectivity, solidarity, hunting culture, eating of sea mammals, a pseudo-subsistence way of life and proximity to nature. This is a place where one might expect to encounter a strong sense of belonging, but perhaps not the apparent need to reaffirm it. To be alone and not surrounded by children is for the Inugguaq 'not to belong' and constitutes the worst possible scenario. It might either arouse suspicion or feelings of sympathy.

Belonging is forged through the reaffirmation of almost impenetrably dense networks of kin relations and through the constant use of kinship terms where one might expect to hear a personal name. To an outsider, the use of some of these kinship terms can be quite puzzling, such as when a boy is named after a dead relative – another means of maintaining the continuity of the sense of belonging, but this time between the living and the dead, the people and the *nuna* where the deceased are buried. The name (*ateq*) is the most important cultural identity marker of the Inuit, connecting the *inuk* to ancestors, and the cycles of the living and the dead (Bodenhorn, 2009: 139-57). The *ateq* is closely linked to the issue of 'belonging'. It is clear from every encounter that the *ateq* has a very special significance in this society. It is believed that a child does not become a person until he or she receives a name. The name is the link to the soul (*tarneq*) (Alia, 2008: 21) and the namesake name can be recycled lots of different times, creating lots of different embodiments of the same ancestor. As Alia (2008: 35) explains, the naming procedure is part of the grieving process and creates a whole new web of bonds when a mother embraces her child and calls her 'mother' or when a child gets a new sibling because the new born child is the embodiment of the ancestor who was the sister of the girl the other girl is named after. To an outsider, the complexity of these kin relations which are as much socio-cultural as they are biological, can be rather challenging especially so as the link between name-soul and identity is so intimate that new names seldom develop. In addition to the recycling of names and multiple usage of kinship terms which conjure up previous socialities, the Inugguit tend to have six names and will frequently use them.[2] These other names bring with them another bundle of complex relationships and this is before one considers the issue of descriptive nicknames which the majority of people have. These names aside, if the *ateq* is not passed on, the soul wanders around with nowhere to rest. It is taboo to mention the name of a dead person until the name has been recycled. Name avoidance rules are strong as I discovered subsequently when there were suicides in the town.

Being the embodiment of the dead ancestor, the boy not only assumes the name of the deceased, but also the kinship term so that for example his father will refer to his son as 'father' if his son is named after his paternal grandfather. In turn, the child will call his father 'son'. There are about six families in Qaanaaq and the kinship ties are enforced, and even exaggerated, through the use of a micro-system of kinship terms whereby first cousins of the opposite sex refer to each other as 'younger brother, older sister', etc., and male second cousins once removed are called 'paternal or maternal uncles'.

To take an example of this micro-system of kinship terms, Peter Frederik Sadornana is Frederik Kristensen's paternal grandmother's grandson. In the rest of Greenland, this would make him a cousin, but

---

2 Danish teachers at the school in Qaanaaq would frequently have problems identifying exam candidates because they would use different names on their scripts.

here he is Frederik's *akkak* or uncle. Families are so close in Qaanaaq that second cousins once removed are referred to as uncle (paternal) (*akkak*) or maternal uncle (*angak*). Frederik Kristensen refers to Peter Frederik Sadorana as his uncle, but he is in West Greenlandic terms his second cousin once removed. Frederik refers to Mina Avike as his *naja* ('younger sister') even though she is the daughter of his maternal aunt. First cousins are referred to using the sex and age specific terminology for siblings.

In the Polar North, there is a pronounced need for a collective onto-logical security. This is expressed through a system of genealogical reaf-firmations of belonging, but also through a shared holistic philosophy. The upbringing of a child is a collective responsibility for the members of the extended family. Parents might give one of their newly born children to an uncle because they already had two children and the uncle was not able to have any. Without this sense of belonging that comes from these genealogies, the Inugguit believe that their lives would become desperate and meaningless. The framework for this ontological security is the dense family network. During my time, I discovered that each family network had its own, separate identity, characteristics and personalities. I would often speak of the 'Qujaukitsoq difference'. One could soon tell if you were talking to a Qujaukitsoq: they tend to be relatively engaging, open and outward looking. They have drive, ambition and are perhaps the proudest of all the Qaanaaq families. One justification for their pride (in their terms) is their size – this is the largest family in Qaanaaq.

One cannot consider 'belonging' in such small, well-defined commu-nities without considering its interaction with the notion of place because place is a set of spaces converted into meaningful locations through people's ideas and experiences with them. In recent years, there has been much written on the 'sense of place' as socio-spatial interrela-tions change in the context of globalisation (Massey, 1994; Rose, 1995: 87-132). Place implies a sense of 'attachment': an amalgam of social and cultural interactions and associations. Conceptions of place and indeed nature are socially constructed in accordance with local ontologies, and through daily spatial activities of people (De Certeau, 1984). The ontology of an existential man-nature enmeshment or intertwinement is characteristic of the Inugguit. The use of the word *hila* is indicative of this refusal to separate mind and nature. In other words, the human-environment relationship is lived existentially as one, but is also assumed conceptually to be one. For the reason of this always-already-lived-togetherness of person and world and people and environment, one cannot phenomenologically assign specific phenomena to either self or world alone. At the same time, the dualistic ecological perspective of people environment is more pronounced than ever before with the current discourse of climate change and sustainability.

When the weather was bad *hila naammangitsoq* which in their terms typically meant when there was mist, fog (*pujoq*) or low-dense cloud giving a feeling of oppression or closeness, people would often complain of headaches. On more than one occasion, I was advised not to visit people during periods of bad weather because people might be feeling depressed or not well. For the Inugguit, the conceptual distance between nature and humanity is in fact very narrow and the environmental crisis is a philosophical crisis. Their mindset is a challenge to the anthropocentrism of the West, and questions the supposed moral superiority of human beings over other species on the planet.

Environmental degradation is particularly painful for the Inugguit because they do not feel the separation or estrangement from nature that is so grounded in Western culture. Their respect for the environment comes from a genuine feeling or being part of it. This does not mean to say that they are overtly respectful in their dealings with nature. Rubbish is thrown on the floor and often out on the sea ice. I would find the omnipresent green beer cans scarring the sea ice. Many pre-modern and preliterate societies are bound to their environment in the sense that they and the place seem virtually one. In this society, there is a strong sense of oneness or unity with nature which at times almost becomes an ideology, at least in discussions with Westerners. Their environment is not for them the 'empty place' that Westerners perceive it to be. My perception of place expressed in terms of wilderness, vacuity and vastness was surely shaped by the Cartesian 'detachment' from the world which tends to characterise Western thinking.

Conceptions of nature are socially constructed and I was trying to project my dualistic notion of the universe as an ontological paradigm. Their vision of reality would appear to be a universe where man is at nature with his environment, where everything is interconnected and interdependent. Their life-world is one where there is no space between

society and nature. Not only are man and nature to an extent co-
terminous, they are mutually dependent on one another, bound up in
one sentient worldview. The natural environment or *pingortitaqaq*,
literally the 'nature that has been created' determines mindset and
thinking. When I was living in Hiorapaluk, the northernmost permanently inhabited settlement in the world with a population of fifty-nine, I
spent many an afternoon chatting to Aki Himura. One afternoon, he
came round with a gift of some fresh musk-oxen meat and over a cup of
coffee, I asked him why he chose to stay. He looked out of the window,
eyes fixed on his dog team skulking on the sea ice and after an unfeasibly
long silence, Aki uttered one word with a great sense of purpose,
ihumaninahorjamahunga. The word *ihuma* means thought and the
expression would have to be translated as 'I wanted my mind to be open
to thoughts'. In his view, the Arctic wilderness offered the best means of
keeping one's mind open. This line strikes a resonant chord in my own
soul, and the word kept circling in my mind even after I had 'come down'.
By belonging to the landscape, one can hope to obtain a clarity of vision
and a sense of harmony. This is why the move from Dundas was so dis-
ruptive. The move meant that the crucial bond of 'belonging' with both
the ancestral land and the kin that lie beneath the land was severed.
Qaanaaq, the hunting camp they moved to in 1953, is still today a
metaphor of dislocation for the elderly residents.

Some, like Aki, might argue that a link to their oral traditions was also
severed with the arrival of television. There are no subtitles –
Greenlandic words are too long to subtitle – and some understand very
little of the programmes on television. The rich indigenous culture of
storytelling has been replaced with the idiotic television of our Western
culture. No longer reciting stories and myths, adults are glued to the television watching cartoons aimed at small children in Denmark and not
adults in Greenland. The loss of cultural richness seems so sudden and
the misfit between their previous rich, indigenous way of life and the
trappings of a Western benefits culture is jarring and painful to observe.
There are a few exceptions to this.

In a plume of choking smoke, Iisaaq Jeremiassen sits on a settee in his
cosy room, humming a tune on the local radio. He has a smiley, round,
boyish face, engraved by the cold. His sunny room is full of assorted
memorabilia, but no curios: various hunting certificates signed by

members of the Danish royal family, the normal discoloured pictures of Christ, and a wall full of photographs of smiling friends and family. In one of the photographs a younger, beaming Iisaaq stands next to Frederik, the Crown Prince of Denmark. It is obvious that Iisaaq is a natural storyteller and we have barely sat down before he starts talking about life in the old days. He utters a mêlée of creaky fricatives mixed in with a series of long, drawn-out sighs and groans, delivered from a near toothless mouth. His voice is deep, a vehicle of gravitas and presence. As with many elderly people whose speech is so slow and purposeful, once he starts talking one feels as if one cannot and should not interrupt. His eyesight is very poor, he is a little hard of hearing, but otherwise he is in good health. He sits there, smiling and grinning, his narrow eyes practically disappearing into the folds of his skin. He tamps the tobacco in his pipe before wadding it up and sticking it in his pocket.

Anxious to sort out issues of payment in the correct manner, we agree that I will pay per session and not on an hourly basis. Interestingly, they refuse to discuss money and how much I should pay. It is for me to determine, *i'ddi naalagat* 'you are in charge (literally, 'you are the Lord')'. Else tells me that I can give what I think is appropriate. Prior to the meeting, I did my research and was advised that a figure of about 250 DKK (approximately £32) would be the right amount for a one hour recording. As I am getting a translator as well, I offer them considerably more and they seem happy with that. It is obvious that storytelling has been commoditised, but not to the point that a particular story has a certain monetary value.

With the absence of a written culture, the Polar Eskimo language has historically been the vehicle for a rich tradition of storytelling. Historically, there were two different categories of stories: *oqaluktuat* which were the old tales, legends and myths and *unikkaat* which were factual accounts. Today, the former have all been forgotten, but many of the legends and myths were recorded by Knud Rasmussen and Erik Holtved in the first half of the twentieth century. All the stories that I recorded fell into the category of *unikkaat*. Among the Inugguit, Amaunalik Kavigaq is often considered the best storyteller of the twentieth century. She was Erik Holtved's lead informant. Erik, a Danish anthropologist, worked in the region in 1937. Amaunalik had learnt her stories from her grandmother, Itugssarssuak. Itugssarssuak was one of those that came in the last wave of migration from Baffin Island in the 1860s. By tracing the families of the last storytellers, it is clear that there must have been a very strong tradition of storytelling in that part of the Canadian Arctic and that this last wave of immigration from Baffin Island enriched the Polar Eskimo culture considerably. From the 1970s onwards, it seems that the tradition of grandmothers telling their grand-children the old tales and myths broke down quite suddenly and then the old stories, lullabies and creation myths more or less disappeared in a generation.

The whole traditional culture of storytelling is now vanishing as glob-alisation, modernity and rapid socio-economic change expose the community to complex pressures. Over the last three decades, the story-telling transmission process has begun to break down for the first time and the spoken forms and traditions by which place-specific knowledge had once been preserved and disseminated are rapidly becoming no longer operative. The introduction of television in the 1980s and more recent digital entertainment has eroded this ancient cultural practice. One settlement, Hiorapaluk, only got television in 1990 when the tiny power plant was built.The stories are testaments of perhaps the last Arctic hunters. They were always a social activity, not a reified product. Nowadays, the stories still told are primarily life stories, sometimes life stories as travel narratives. Typically, the men tell hunting stories whilst the women speak about domestic life at home. They are both extraordi-nary records of survival. The men's hunting stories are significantly stories about animals that are hunted on the sea ice or *hiku*, and not fishing or land mammals. The practice and drama of hunting polar bears is for obvious reasons particularly conducive to storytelling. Polar bears hunt on the sea ice and in a world where there is no Arctic sea ice, it is difficult to see how either polar bears or the stories can survive.

The stories are not great works of literature, but are more of a 'way of speaking'. They show how extended family connections are foundational to life in the region. The stories are records of prodigious memories and social history. With extreme precision, storytellers talk about events that happened seventy or eighty years ago. One gentleman told me that he could remember the day he was born. In the absence of a written tradition, all knowledge is stored orally. One friend and informant, Josef, told me shortly before I left, the exact day and time that he first met me down by the shore eleven months earlier. The telling of stories takes you to places: old hunting grounds, now abandoned settlements, the icy wilderness, but also away from the edge of the shore (some children are told stories about creatures living in the sea to prevent them going out onto the sea ice when it is thin). For narrated events always happen somewhere. And for an oral culture, that location is never merely incidental to those occurrences. The events belong, as it were, to the place, and to tell the story of those events is to let the place itself speak through the telling. The Inugguit have a very 'visual' memory and the landscape for the Arctic hunters is mnemonic, a trigger for the telling and preservation of the stories, and memory is a way of articulating the relationship between community and landscape.

The storytellers I worked with spoke of the land and sea ice as boundless. The sea ice symbolised travel and mobility, the highway that connected all the Inugguit settlements. Hunters used to hunt bears and musk-oxen on Ellesmere Island and one of my informants spoke of the horror and disbelief when he encountered for the first time the Royal Canadian Mounted Police who prevented him from travelling across the Smith Sound to the land of his ancestors. The concept of formal boundaries seemed incomprehensible to him. This sense of mobility has changed radically in the last thirty years as the smaller settlements have closed down, people have moved to the town and the area of sea ice has diminished.

Iisaaq wanted to tell me his life-story. He spent the first thirty minutes explaining in great detail what he did for his third birthday. He killed his first seal when he was just five years old – a significant event for a boy growing up in such a hunting community. The cultural expression of respect for animals is manifest in first catch celebrations (Nuttall, 1992). When a boy catches his first seal, friends and family are invited to his parents' house for coffee and cake. The first catch celebration is a recognition of the boy's development. When he was ten, he got the message that his mother had died in another settlement two weeks previously. He got the message from a hunter who visited Hiorapaluk to tell him the news. At that time in the 1930s, travel by dog-sledge was the only means of communicating such news.

Iisaaq was subsequently brought up by his uncle and aunt who had lost a child of their own. This is a common arrangement in Inugguit society where the upbringing of a child is a collective responsibility for the members of the extended family. One of my friends gave his newly born child to his uncle because he already had two children and his uncle was not able to have any. He enjoyed living with this aunt and uncle and talks of how his aunt showed Iisaaq how to make a tent out of sealskins. At the age of 12, Iisaaq got his first dog team whilst living in Haviggivik. Iisaaq talks about how he made cups out of the skins of Little Auks that he caught in the summer of 1931 in Hiorapaluk. What comes out in his story is the complete freedom that he had as a child. Also, Iisaaq told me how on a long polar bear hunting trip, his brother fell seriously ill. He had got trichinosis from polar bear meat that had not been properly cooked. His brother's condition deteriorated and they were too far from a settlement to get any help. During the night, his brother died and Iisaaq could do nothing to save him. Iisaaq sat next to his body and prayed throughout the night. In the morning, his brother came back to life.

He also talks about how he travelled from Hiorapaluk to Haviggivik by dog-sledge in the spring to marry his wife. On the way back, the newly-weds fell through the thin ice, but managed to clamber back onto the ice by pushing themselves up onto their backs. Once out of the icy water, he and his wife spread their weight across the thin ice, as a polar bear does, and pushed their way over to the thicker ice. Iisaaq told me repeatedly that he had met his wife many times in his dreams some years previously, and knew exactly who she was when he met her in real life. Peeking out of the window, he reminds me that time is told with the seasons, sea ice and the wind. He wants to tell me about the winds: the *nigeq* blows from the east/south-east, bringing snow and low pressure; the *avannaq* is a strong wind from Etah (north of Hiorapaluk); the *pavanngainnaq* is a wind that comes from the north and makes the water flat; the *anilatsiaq* blows the icebergs and incipient sea ice away in September/October/November; the *koororranertoq* is a mild wind that blows alongside or down a river; the *kanannaq* blows in from the sea and brings fog or mist; the *pikannaq* blows down from the mountains, pushing the fog or mist away; the *atuarnaq* blows down the Nares Strait, between Canada and Greenland, damaging edges of sea ice where walruses lie; and the *pigguahoq* is perhaps the most dangerous wind for hunters bringing fog and reducing visibility to zero.

The stories show how the Inugguit see their own relations with the environment in terms of generalised reciprocity: interactions between themselves and their environment were mutually beneficial. Historically, this has been a community of storytellers and their stories represent another modality of belonging, tying the phenomenon with that of place. The stories tend to be *hiku*-centric. In these stories, the *hiku* or sea ice represents travel and mobility. It is a connective, geographic entity that reconnects kin in the settlements. In the recorded Inuit lunar calendar, the formation of the sea ice is known as *tuhartuut* ('hearing news from other camps') – a time in which the sea ice is solid enough to permit travel and enable people to visit relatives in other camps. The *hiku* is the platform for their hunting culture. Sea ice features are associated in the collective and individual memories of most Inugguit. Trails on the sea ice are similar to land trails in their remarkable historical continuity. They usually follow similar courses along or across seasonal ice features, avoiding recurrent dangerous spots, and aiming at precise destinations. The *hiku* enlarges the Inugguit territory and offers access to essential dietary resources for the community.

It is clear that the Inugguit feel strongly that *hiku* is their domain and not that of the *kadluna*. Their sense of place has a proprietorial exclusivity to it that has been fostered over the course of centuries in a climate more hostile than today, in an age when survival was the only concern. Looking at a map of the area, every fjord, bay, island and land is named after an eighteenth, nineteenth or twentieth century explorer, geographer or geologist. All of them are English, Danish, Dutch or American. The Inugguit would not take a map with them whilst out hunting. Indigenous cartography works in different ways. Every contour of the landscape is etched on the mind of the Arctic hunter. The Inugguit place-names are absent from most maps, but complex mental maps with indigenous, local names are stored in their minds. The Inugguit did not traditionally use maps to represent their territory. Some of these indigenous place-names are being forgotten because it is no longer possible to hunt in some of the former hunting grounds due to the *imaq*. Inugguit place-names often inform you of land and sea use. So, *qammavik* means the 'place where hunters lie in wait for sea mammals' or *ukalerhalik* 'a place where one finds Arctic Hares'. As Keith Basso (1996: 47) says 'place-names are important in storytelling because they are situating devices, as conventionalised instruments for locating narrated events in the physical settings where the events have occurred'. The proper name and the geographical feature or clues to hunting merge in the conscious-ness of the people.[3]

Over the last three decades, the storytelling transmission process has, however, begun to break down for the first time and the spoken forms and traditions by which place-specific knowledge had once been preserved and disseminated are rapidly becoming no longer operative. The disappearance of traditional spoken traditions might have conse-quences for the relationship between the Inugguit and the notion of 'place'. In this part of the Arctic the primacy of *place* is being forgotten, superseded by a new, more abstract notion of 'space'. The hunters are no longer nomadic, but rooted to a town. As the stories disappear, the land and its particularising stories begins to lose its multiplicitous power. The human senses are no longer as gripped and fascinated by the expressive shapes and sounds of particular places. If place-names are forgotten, the social experience of the shared existential space is lost and the landscape returns to a blank environment.

A place-based, vernacular culture of face-to-face storytelling is now being replaced in part by the automated video game where the interac-tion is with a consol. The result is that some young people are losing the pulse of the place and are becoming impervious to the sensuous world. Young people's conceptualisations of space are expanding in size, but diminishing in depth and detail. Horizons of knowledge are diminish-ing. For those with a lack of consciousness of local history and culture, the land is becoming less of an animate, expressive power. The sense of geographic embeddedness and collective memory of place that was passed on through stories is fading. Place-names are focal points of human attachment, often providing clues to what can be hunted there. In any one locality, an individual is surrounded by a relational network of marked places that identify potential resources, stored supplies, stories and historical events in the record of the land. Place-names can become active agents of identity, creating contextualised feelings of 'attachment'. The loss of storytelling may have implications for the very strong sense of 'belonging' to be found in this corner of the Arctic. From the stories, one

---

3   In a seminal article, Tuan (1991: 684-96) discusses the role of language in place-
    making.

can infer that for the Inugguit, land and kinship are the most important attachment points for memory. Stories manifest different modalities of belonging, tying families together and reaffirming kin relations and genealogies in complex ways through narrative accounts.

Despite the very significant changes that have impacted the community – the demise of hunting, the disappearance of the semi-nomadic lifestyle, the effects of encroaching globalisation the local urbanisation – the Inugguit still engage in the same practices of belonging. The animist beliefs have for the most part been lost, but those traditional beliefs that are conducive to a sense of belonging such as the use and recycling of names are still upheld. Belonging is not reinforced by collective rituals, but naming remains an essential part of Inuit culture even in regions more subject to the forces of modernity and globalisation than north-west Greenland.

But, belonging is two-dimensional: social (or human) and environmental or cosmic and in terms of the interaction of the dynamic of belonging with the sense of place, it would seem that new paradigms are beginning to form and that old ontologies of place bolstered through the art of storytelling are beginning to diminish. It is not surprising that the Inugguit show such connectedness to the land as most other indigenous peoples who have resided in a particular place for centuries and have been directly dependent on their environment for survival, are likely to have done the same. The way that the Inugguit embed knowledge in stories that are linked to the landscape is not surprising either. However, if hunting dies out altogether because of the lack of sea ice, there will be little need or occasion to activate this knowledge which will ultimately be lost. Knowledge is rooted in place, and having this knowledge or at least being able to tap into it enforces the sense of belonging with the local cosmos. In the light of social and environmental change in north-west Greenland, there is evidence of an indigenous perceptual remodelling of the relationship between man and nature, but the traditional modalities of belonging are hitherto unchanged. Relatedness and belonging are constantly being reaffirmed, and it is this constant reaffirmation through these practices of belonging which creates the requisite social cohesion which this society lives off.

It is significant if this intricate knowledge of the natural environment begins to disappear because this 'nature' as it has been perceived historically by the Inugguit is not something externalised in the way that it is for us (to an extreme degree with special demarcated areas called 'nature reserves', 'national parks', etc.). Nature is not a separate ontological category, but it is part of who they are. The two are seamlessly bound together. This holistic indigenous epistemology is sometimes known as *inuit qaujimajatuqangit* and is a reference to the Inuit body of traditional knowledge passed on orally and concerned generally with the life and value system of the Inuit. With this loss of knowledge, the Inugguit's own emotional landscape and sense of Self will therefore be impoverished (but perhaps also expanded) in some way. One can see therefore how identity, language and landscape are all drawn together as this sense of 'belonging' is rooted in the *nuna* which is the subject matter of the endangered oral traditions and the extension of the indigenous mind. Identity paradigms are beginning to shift and will presumably transmute further as indigenous ecophilosophies clash with other perspectives on the world:[4] the mechanistic Cartesian philosophy of the West has of course a quite different perspective on the human-nature interrelationship. This latter mode of thinking is becoming increasingly familiar to the Inugguit and arguably lends itself more to a sedentary lifestyle where the level of engagement with the natural environment is much less intensive, where land and people are separated. Many of the Inugguit are now dependent on supplies from the south which must have the effect of slowly distancing them from the concept of their immediate natural environment being their source of provisions.

Bender (2001: 7) talks of the 'opposition between a rooted sense of belonging and the alienating forces of modernity'. At a personal level, I felt this very strongly. The Inugguit sense of embeddedness to place was something alien to me because of its spirituality and magnitude of feelings that it aroused. What it means to belong is what it means to be human and is embedded in the existential experience of living with others. It would be difficult to find a subject which was more important to the Inugguit than that of belonging to your local community. Historically, the issue of belonging has always come with a sense of imperative for the Inugguit. This community was just 'surviving' up until

---

4   The indigenous philosophy of the Inugguit is akin to Næss' ecosophy (Drengson & Inoue, 1995: 8) which is a philosophy of ecological harmony or equilibrium.

recent times (1950s approximately) and one can only survive in a group situation. Social exclusion would often result in death, voluntary or otherwise. Unsurprisingly, these remote Inuit communities have not been 'deterritorialised' (Appadurai, 1997: 38), i.e. the objects, traditions and beliefs that define their culture have not been detached from their physical space. The Inugguit are still very much anchored in their physical environment, even if it is changing rapidly. There is no immediate threat to their cultural identity. The interaction of modernity and tradition in these twenty-first century pseudo-hunter-gatherer communities has brought great social change, but little has changed in the sense of 'belonging'. People still need to belong in the same way that they always have, and use the same mechanisms to reinforce this.

10: Back to the Beginning

Arriving back in Qaanaaq is a strange sensation as one feels like one has jumped a season. It is milder and much of the snow has melted on the slopes of the town. Ice and snow has been replaced by sand, soil and mud. Water is pouring off the slopes and picking up dirt and mud on the way as it leads onto the sea ice. With all the dogs on the ice, the settlement is eerily quiet. There is now no snow for them to eat, so hunters leave the sledge dogs on the frozen sea to avoid having to give them water. The ice on the *aukarneq* surrounding Herbert Island is now very thin, decorated with a series of *nakkut* which will soon become leads and it is no longer thick enough to travel there by dog-sledge. The constant sunshine and wind is wearing it down and the coming *avangnaq* will damage the edge of the sea ice where the walrus are.

It is 7.2 degrees in the house. I try lighting the heater, but there must have been a patch of oil at the bottom of the heater. The flame shoots up, burning my right hand and taking the hair right off. The temperature in the house rises to 11 degrees in the afternoon and that is good enough for me. I have an appointment at 2pm with Inge. I open the door and the door handle comes off in my hand. Not a good start. She welcomes me in and I can tell that today she is in storytelling mode. Angry that drunks stagger past her cabin, knocking on her door looking for money and kicking and throwing stones at Koogi, she notices that I am quite different, being so affectionate towards her dog. With Inge, a kind, tiny woman in her seventies with a clubfoot, I have found a soul mate of sorts. The session begins with Inge telling me that she has a headache today and that she has often suffered with headaches since the American B-52 bomber with four nuclear bombs on board crashed into the sea near Pituffik in 1968. The explosion was of such a magnitude that an enormous ball of fire could be seen from Qaanaaq.

She knew the Inugguit that worked in the clean-up operation and says that lives were lost. It happened during the dark period and the Americans had to bring back the Inugguit that they relocated as they were the only people who knew the region well enough. The food tasted bad after the accident and many people suffered with various illnesses. The story was covered up for years and one of the unexploded bombs still lies on the seabed today. Inge gets out hundreds of old photographs from the Geological Survey of Canada (May 1953) and wants to have a look at my maps. As with all the Inugguit, she is fascinated by maps and it makes me realise how popular the first cartographers must have been who worked in the area. *Taku, taku*, she would say before pointing to a tiny, former settlement on Washington Land, Inufissorssuaq, where there were just two houses. She sits next to me and makes quite suddenly a pass at me. She puts my arm around her, kisses me on the cheek, shows me her prosthetic knee and then guides my left arm which hangs around her neck down to her sagging breast. She is such a kind and very loving woman. No wonder they find the *kadluna* harsh and cold; they are so forward with their love and kindness compared to us.

Greenlandic flags fly from people's windows; there is an early morning silence in the town. Today there are confirmations right across Greenland. It is a public holiday. There are thirteen children being confirmed in Qaanaaq alone which means thirteen *kaffimik* outside on what is the warmest day of the year so far. It will be the equivalent of an English street party. People are gathering outside houses. Tables are being laid and food is being prepared. There is *mattak*, seal, narwhal, frozen caribou, *kiviat* and polar bear soup. Inside, coffee and cakes are on offer.

Stiffi, Stiffi, Susanne runs towards me wearing her *arnatut*, the outfit worn on confirmation day by girls, comprising very long white *kamikker*, a fancy belt garment made of Arctic Fox and a pink blouse. She is very excited about her confirmation and tells me that she has received over 1,000DKK in gifts. It is all about money, and nothing more. I find it most unattractive and almost Catholic as a concept. Susanne has a great pile of presents: most people give cash (including myself), but she has a new mobile phone and is absolutely delighted with it. I am of course pleased for her.

In subsequent days, the flat sea would become perfect for skiing. One day, I ski directly south towards the other side of the fjord, excited at now finally being able to lord over the ice. After twenty minutes or so, I encounter a very large rubble field running east to west and surrounding the small family of icebergs frozen into place. It is not long before I see twenty or so Inugguit fishing. They are not ice fishing, but fishing in an open lead which at this point is about 5-10 feet wide. I had not expected this. I ski northwards along the length of the lead and it seems to cross the entire fjord and gets wider the further southwards one skis. I could probably get across, but I am not sure I want to risk it and it would certainly mean getting wet. With these mild temperatures, the sea ice is going to soon start breaking up now and the white, frozen world will become fragmented. I travel back the length of the lead towards Qaanaaq and finally find a place where you can cross, but I am not sure it will be possible in a week's time. The excellent skiing in the afternoon has made up my mind. I need to ski up to Hiorapaluk or Qeqertat next week whilst I still can. It is not at all necessary, but the urge is incontrovertible. I borrow a pulk, satellite phone, Thermos and Primus off Arqioq and begin to make preparations. He also insists that I take his gun.

In the afternoon, I pack the pulk up and have a dummy run on the ice. It is very warm in the sunshine and I soon realise that I have too many layers on. The ice is quite different from two days ago. Areas of open water are now appearing on the ice. It is icy and the thin layer of snow has turned to slush. The conditions are deteriorating rapidly and I cannot wait much longer. The pulk seems to run quite well and I think I am almost ready to leave tomorrow.

For the first time, I sleep with a blindfold. The thin pink curtains are useless and it is becoming difficult, sleeping with the sunshine cascading into the room 24 hours a day. My sleep is becoming increasingly disturbed because of the non-stop light. I set the alarm for 7am. In the morning, I wake to a sallow light; a few strands of wispy, feathery cirrus cloud paint the sky in the East. I have breakfast and check once more that I have everything. It is a Sisyphean task carrying two rucksacks, skis, a pulk and a gun on my own down to the shore. By the time I get to the shore ice I am rather worn out and in a foul mood. Standing outside Arctic Foods and next to dried halibut hanging on lines is Piuaattoq, Masautsiaq's brother. He wants to know where I am headed, with so many bags. We chat briefly. There is a tinge of gloom in his meditations. He can see that I am exhausted, but does not offer to help. They like to see the *kadluna* suffer a bit. There is a sense that life is a struggle, that it has to be that way and that there is no point in helping each other. Once on the sea ice, I leave the skis and gun behind and shuttle my stuff out to the flat sea ice in two trips. There are now pools of water on the shore ice and the cracks in the leads are getting wider by the day.

The spring sea ice is horrible. There is no snow on it. It is just very hard, but rather slushy in places. The conditions are not good at all and it is going to be slow going. A new lead has opened up. It is not a problem getting across it, but I can see that it soon will be. I cannot help wondering whether I have left it too late. After no more than half an hour of skiing, Herbert Island disappears in cloud. A soufflé of melancholic-looking cloud coming from the east sweeps across the bay. In a short period of time, it has gone from being almost clear to quite thick fog. This does not look good. I am barely beyond Qaanaaq, but within minutes am no longer able to clearly see land and am at risk of being lost in such a self-similar terrain. Without much hesitation, I decide to abandon the trip. I could find my way up to Hiorapaluk but this is not going to be any fun. If leads are opening up, visibility is quite important. I am soon back in Qaanaaq and pleased that I made the right call. A small crowd stands outside Arctic Foods in their overalls. They had all been watching me and suspected that I was making a mistake, but of course wanted to see me find out for myself before telling me.

I spend some time looking at the map, trying to work out what can be achieved over the next few days. Hans, the policeman, has advised me not to ski to Hiorapaluk which makes the whole idea problematic. If something were to happen and I ignored the advice of the police, that would not look good. It is no longer possible to get down to Qeqertat either because a very large lead has opened up by the Hubbard glacier. Suddenly, everything is changing very fast. The only option is to head due south and stay the night at the hut at Kangeq, the promontory to Olrik Fjord.

The constant light is making me feel slightly disorientated; a sort of metaphysical unease. I go to bed at 1am, not feeling particularly tired but do not fall asleep until 3am. I set the alarm for 7.30am. Just a few strands of cirrus cloud garnish the sky. The sun is shining, but there is a cold, stiff wind. The sun appears from behind the Ice Sheet at about 6am now, and does not disappear until gone 1am. It is the beginning of June and there is still 50 kilometres of sea ice. The supply ship is due on the 11th of July but at the moment I cannot see how she is going to get in. She is not an ice-breaker. The flat sea ice is conducive to very fast skiing, and the appeal of the empty, white world is now embedded in my mind; its inhuman silence and emptiness lurking behind its ice-arches formed during the winter fill me with awe. In Greenland, one just has to step outside a settlement and one finds total silence; in overcrowded UK, it has become almost impossible to find. Hemmed in by solitude in this severe land for so many months, I intend to make the most of my freedom. Some of the patches of ice are like glass. I am poling my way across them, just using my shoulders. Where the ice is thinnest, it is a greyish colour and is completely flat. One can move very fast across this ice. There are a few rubbly patches, then it turns very smooth, then a bit of rubble again, and so on. The sea ice is still thick enough, but is thawing fast. When this happens, ledges form. It is easy to miss the ledge and fall into water which is not always visible if there is a layer of snow on it.

I am pushing on and soon have the now very familiar Herbert Island on my right. I am on the look out for seals at their breathing holes, but there have been very few seals in the bay this year and nobody knows why. I have been skiing for nearly two and a half hours and can now see Northumberland Island behind Herbert Island. This is extraordinary. I could slash the six hours it took me to get to Herbert Island last time. Then, I hit a strong westerly wind blowing right down the middle of the Murchison Sound. With the strong wind, the temperature plummets and it is quite hard going. There is a short snow flurry which makes travelling on the ice more dangerous as one is unable to spot the thin patches of ice which are darker. Suddenly, I slip on the ice. I land on my pole. I look around and know immediately that the trip is over. I have bent the pole in half. I try to straighten it out, but the damage is done and it just splits in two. It happened so quickly. Qaanaaq is barely visible in the distance. I am about thirty miles from home and now I only have one pole. I turn round straight away and head back. I have visions of me taking hours and hours to get home, but nothing could be further from the truth.

I soon develop a technique whereby I use the pole as a sort of paddle, taking strokes on either side and propelling myself across the ice. The ice is so smooth that this proves to be very effective. I am going nearly as fast I was with two poles. Icebergs are exploding with the sounds of gunshots behind me in the summer sunshine and I am minded not to get too close to them. I cover the distance in just under two and half hours. It is of course thanks entirely to the conditions.

Each day it gets slightly harder to get onto the main part of the sea ice, i.e. the bit beyond the tidal zone, and it now requires larger and larger leaps. The ice of the tidal zone is constantly being moved about by the tide underneath. Some of the hunters are now using extra long sledges designed especially to travel across the wide leads of the spring. The meltwater from the Ice Cap, my source of drinking water, pours now down the slopes all day long, forming a pool of water or *imatsinaq* on the ice, growing in size by the minute. The cleanest, finest drinking in the water available anywhere runs straight into the sea when they could be bottling it and selling it to the Chinese.

Despite the difficulties of the tidal zone, there is now perhaps more sea ice traffic than before with the narwhals arriving in the fjord. A few hunters have gone out to the ice edge with a group of biologists to put transmitters on these unicorns of the sea and study their movements. Their tracks are still visible in the slush, but they will make sure they are back for Friday morning when their wives get paid. Before climate change, it must have taken days to get to the edge of the ice. Global warming has at least reduced the commute. Remarkably powerful dog-teams now pull sledges, with kayaks tied on the side, which tow rakish motorboats out towards the edge of the ice. It does not look like it should be possible, but somehow it is.

The Arctic is coming to life with new visitors returning from the autumnal exodus. The first migratory wader bird has arrived in the tundra, feeding on the lichen. First one, then several medium sized waders with orange-brown rumps trumpet their arrival with their male display song, a sort of poor-me, repeated time and time again. These Red Knots (*calidiris canutus*) have one of the longest migrations of any bird, flying from Tierra del Fuego to here every year, a distance of 15,000 kilometres. Small flocks of Lapland Buntings (*narharmiutaq*) peck at the ground amongst the Cotton Grass, blooming Arctic Poppies and the roots of the Arctic Willow: this small bird, about the size of a sparrow is a mottled, chestnut colour with a streak of yellow on its face. Little Ringed Plovers with distinctive yellow eye rings fly at great speeds along the shore, banking from one side to the other with their forked wings. Tiny puppies play in the shaded shelter, chasing their tails under forgotten, up-turned boats. Old scars hidden by months of snow are reemerging too. Walking along the shoreline, the melting snow reveals any manner of scars of consumerist society: empty beer cans, crisp wrappers, discarded furniture and cigarette butts. A woman urinates by the side of the track to the airstrip.

Harbingers of the changing season, half a dozen snow geese (*kanguq*) fly over in honking U-formations looking for breeding grounds. These birds which are not allowed to be hunted sweep over towards the cemetery. I try to pursue them. It is snowing now and on the way to the cemetery, I meet two ladies. I mix up my vowels and ask them if they have seen the 'promontory' (*kangeq*). They point over to the east, across the fjord and I tell them that I am going there. They must think it is very strange. At the cemetery, I see Inuuteq Kristensen's grave who committed suicide last month. There is also Jonas Imiina's tombstone, the thirteen-year-old boy took his life in March of last year.

Putsaq or low-lying cloud hanging over the sea or the sea ice makes for a grey and slightly bleak start to this cold, June morning. Old men sit at their windows, grinning, looking through binoculars. The old, rusty blue Toyota pick-up truck that serves as the ambulance rattles along the sandy tracks. Josef waves to me and I join him on his round, driving very slowly around the town, smiling and waving to everybody we pass. We meet an old man with a wispy beard called Taitennguaq who is carving *hakiagut* which are shaped pieces of wood put on the rim of the net used to catch Little Auks. As with the police car, the ambulance operates more as an informal taxi service for much of the time. Josef is clever as well as funny, predicting exactly when the *pujoq* will hit the town and planning the future of the settlements. Having declared this, he would say *uanga, angakkoq mikihoq* ('I am a little shaman') and then laugh. Over the following weeks, I would enjoy my frequent visits to his house to discuss all the Inuktun words that I had collected. Visits would invariably start with a practical joke. Hearing my familiar gait on the wooden steps to his house, the family would sometimes hide or pretend to be asleep, and then scream with laughter after a few moments of silence. The non-stop japing of those visits brought life to otherwise quiet and uneventful after-noons. They would often invite me to eat with them and all stand up and say *qujan* at the end of the dinner to thank the animal for giving itself up. Josef sits on the settee in his familiar Thule Base T-shirt, patting his bulk, knowing that he is the king in this world, a man's world. A man has a guest and the woman disappears to work through a small mountain of washing up. Then, she prepares dinner. After dinner, we sit on the settee and Josef would break wind audibly, giggling and shouting *Produkt*. He vents the fumes in the direction of his wife and daughter and reaches for yet another beer. The women drink soft drinks.

Through the curdled mist, I see something that I thought I would never see: the Inugguit are out in force, collecting all the rubbish from all over Qaanaaq. Her Majesty the Queen of Denmark is arriving on the 11th of June. The Danish Royal Family is the glue that keeps Denmark and Greenland together. The Royal Family are extremely popular in Qaanaaq and this is such a big occasion that all public buildings and many private ones will get a lick of paint before her arrival. Now, suddenly, there is talk of nothing else.

Girdled in incessant sunshine and beginning to miss the evening sunset fiesta, I am now suffering from insomnia. A prisoner to light. Despite wearing two blindfolds, I am awake much of the night wondering how such incandescence can possibly be conducive to sleep. I close my eyes and I see the lamp of my soul burning in a sleepless delirium. There is no escape from the endless light; there is no dusk; there is no dawn; I feel as if I am trying to sleep under a spotlight. The sun goes behind the Ice Cap at about 3.30am, but about three hours later it has reappeared on the other side, ready for its next ecliptic. I am up early; Susanne comes to visit and we spend the morning cleaning the house. At last, I have got my *kiffaq*. As an award, she finishes off the dreaded and impossible to eat *skipskiks*.

From here on in, it is endless, blissful Arctic sunshine all day long, every day. The natural environment was growing more and more inter-esting. The slopes are now alive with wild flowers, fledgling Snow Buntings and Ringed Plovers that dance the cha-cha-cha by the shore. Out in the bay, there are flashes of black and white as the more pelagic Black Guillemots fly past. The following days were average, unexcep-tional, but perfectly typical in every respect. I felt like a disillusioned

Romantic. I might spend the morning reading Auden and Blake in silence and perfectly content, and then go on my visits and find the most intelligent members of the group playing video war games, packed with foul language, explicit violence and rebarbative noise. Teenagers walk the tracks with music blaring from their mobile phones or sit on their couches in shorts and T-shirts, sucking lollies, transfixed by Playstation games set in Tajikistan in 2016 where the Americans are fighting the Chinese using all kinds of ultra-modern weapons. The language is appalling, packed with expletives and euphemisms such as 'pacify' him, meaning 'kill him'. The appeal of these games is lost on me. I have discovered the face of modernity in the twenty-first century in all its ugliness. I had hoped to find poets and storytellers, but instead encounter empty minds glued to television screens, surrounded by half a dozen children sipping Coca-Cola amidst clutter. It is my house that is the house of books and poetry. The irony is perhaps that it is me who comes from the West, but it is me that is apparently the anachronism. Here, people have skipped the book generation and gone from the cat's cradle and wooden toys straight to Playstation. Like anywhere else in the world, the Inugguit are hungry for the latest technology, be it mobile phone technology, social media or gaming.

Fortunately, visits to Eva were always of a very different nature. The door is open and she welcomes me in. She sits me down and tells me that I have to try some Greenlandic food. We sit together by the sink with a plastic bag on the floor, and she produces four boiled Little Auks (*amiliq*). Boiled in salt for just over an hour, they are now ready to eat. The wings are first removed. The feathers are taken off and the bones are sucked dry. Then, there is the meat on the breast which is a dark brown chocolate colour, not dissimilar to seal. The taste is quite similar too, a sort of slightly fishy chicken. It is delicious. The whole bird is eaten: the two livers, the heart, the entrails and the head which is Eva's favourite is eaten last. She shows me how to suck the juices out of the bird's anus and we lick our lips. *The Persuaders* plays on the television in the background. Then, the skull of the bird is cracked open with the teeth and the brain is eaten, along with the tongue and the eyes. There is almost no waste whatsoever. Previously, they would eat far more birds and birds' eggs. The birds are still readily available, so this must have been a conscious shift in their diet amongst the younger people. The Inugguit used to collect Eider Duck eggs, put them in a seal skin along with meat and fish, sew it up and leave them over the winter when they had matured, but this is no longer done. In my opinion, fermented food is rarely good, but living in a period prior to the shop and the supply-ship, it would have been essential to be able to ferment food as the future supply of food was never guaranteed.

On the table is Malaurie's book, *Les dernier rois du Thule*. He gave the book to Eva when he last returned to the community in 1991. Eva was afraid of him when he was first here in 1951 because he would not leave her alone and was a ladies' man. On a sledge journey to Haviggivik in 1951, he proposed to her having slept with her. She was just 16 years old and was very embarrassed. Nonetheless, she remembers him as a very kind, friendly man with a good sense of humour. I tell her about the episode with Ingeborg Frederik when she walked out of the room when I mentioned his name. She cannot understand that. Her younger sister was for a while in a relationship with Malaurie and they lived together. Eva tells me that over the years most of her friends have been men simply because women become so jealous. It is a familiar story in small Inuit settlements. Eva is a kind, intelligent woman who understands instinctively the value in knowing other cultures which is why she is always so warm and welcoming towards me. She is also anxious to address the many misconceptions held by Greenlanders and others about the way the Inugguit live.

It is approaching the end of June. *Avataqs* hang up outside people's homes and the narwhals are now eagerly awaited. Streams of imperatives spew from open, summer windows: *ihiigu, iherit, akgerit, nirigit*, etc. With the perpetual sunshine, boundaries reappear and calligraphic leads now wind through the ice. Open water circumscribes Herbert Island and a blackish iceberg has been liberated in the annual metamorphosis. The iceberg is black because when it calved it must have come into contact with the sediment and rock on the ground beneath. Eider Ducks fly over the splintering *hiku* in the diaphanous light. The melt season is in full flow; the lake of glacial meltwater that sits on top of the sea ice grows by the day and horse-shoe shaped leads are now rapidly forming near the tidal zone ice. There are just a few remaining dogs left on the ice. The Inugguit will not abandon the ice until the very last moment; dog-sledge is their preferred mode of travel. Most of the dogs lie on the grassy slopes, panting excessively, often short of water. Occasional *uuttoq* are emerging from the melting ice and basking in the sun sufficiently close to the town that some hunters in the evening are now on foot. Moving like fianchettoed bishops on a chessboard, they hop diagonally across small squares of chittering brash ice in squelching wellies; their transit to land becoming increasingly more circuitous and implausible by the hour.

Some of the hunters are now camping on the outskirts of the town, shooting Cormorants and Eider ducks. Others have gone to Iterdlagssuaq where they fish for Arctic Char. It is clear that in the summer months, they are more inclined to revert to semi-nomadism following the animals around. By the beginning of July, the sun is visible in Qaanaaq 24 hours a day. At 4, 5 and 6am the sun is just visible behind the town above the Ice Cap. Over this period, smiling Susanne would come to visit me every day, often getting more and more upset, counting down with her fingers the number of days I have left in Qaanaaq. Typically, she would turn up and tell me that she was starving and so I would cook for her. I had been very concerned about leaving her, but she seems to have found some new friends and I think she is going to be fine. However, I have always in mind how sensitive this community is, and how even quite small events can trigger cycles of negativity, depression and, of course, suicide.

On the 4th of July, I wake up to quite a different scene. Quite suddenly, there are now large areas of *imaq* dotted all over the bay. The ice must now be very thin right across the Sound and the constant sunshine is melting it very fast. It might just be possible that the supply ship could make it in next week. Small clouds of *pujoq* sit above the open water, a reminder that these parts are now fully open and that it is not just surface meltwater. Unbelievably, there are still three dog teams left on what must be very thin ice. Constantly monitoring the ice conditions has almost become an obsessive habit. The speed of the seasonal changes in the Arctic natural environment is mind-boggling to the visitor from lower latitudes. It is like having a front row seat on a David Attenborough documentary where the cloud movement is all speeded up to give the impression of an incoming storm on the African savannah.

Not being able to escape from the incessant sun, it is unbelievably hot sitting by the shore watching the last few hunters bring in their dog teams off the wafer thin ice. The temperature rises in the coming days, and at one point reaches 16 degrees. It feels significantly warmer beneath the 24 hour sunshine. It feels so much hotter than it actually is because of the lack of moisture in the air. The hut that was barely above freezing for weeks on end has now turned into the most outrageous suntrap. If I were out all day and left it closed up, I might come home and find it 27 degrees inside. In groups of three, the dogs are brought in hastily by running quickly across the remaining patch of ice. The heavy sledges are transported in a quite ingenious fashion: they are tied to two motor-boats (one in front and one behind) and allowed to float across the water between the two, slow moving vessels. The period between when the hunters come off the ice and when they are out in their boats might be as short as a week.

The ship is due to arrive next week and it cannot come soon enough. Most of the shelves in the shop are empty now and much of the remaining produce is about three months out of date. At 1pm, I am preparing luncheon when to my amazement I spot a ship coming towards Qaanaaq. It is the first ship I have seen in ten months. I have no idea if she is an ice-breaker, but she has no trouble pushing the thin ice out of the way. It is not, however, the supply ship. Her futtocks were blue and not the distinct blood-red of the supply ship. She has none of the Arctic Line markings and most obviously no cargo. We were all at our windows with our binoculars and then she just stopped, a few kilometres from Qaanaaq, spun and went out of the bay again. The reason it is so puzzling, of course, is that we are hundreds and hundreds of miles from any port. She must have come from Nuuk. I can only surmise that this is a ship that Arctic Lines sent on a recce to see if the supply ship will be able to get through the ice. There is some speculation that the ship turned around because it could not get through the ice.

The following day, there is a strong breeze from the north and just as the hunters predicted, this very quickly blows away the very thin ice. Over the course of the day, very large areas of open water appear and in the afternoon I see the first motorboat on the water. After nearly ten months of sea ice and ice floes, it is actually quite a strange sensation to see the open water again. In my mind, the sea ice was permanent, but in the end it disappeared in the course of about 24 hours. Everything in the Arctic is transient and in a state of flux. Nothing stays the same for long. With such a hostile climate, nothing can afford to. The wild flowers are the fastest growing in the world and even the dogs seem to grow up incredibly fast. Icebergs are convulsing and rolling into the deep blue sea. *Pujoq* rises in surreal puffs above the millpond still water. Down by the shore, three pups are playing and follow me down to the water's edge. They taste the sea water and play in it for a while before clambering over the lumps of ice on the shore, frolicking together and making ampersand shapes with their tales. Puffing on cigarettes and with lost glances, couples walk their clans of toddlers around the town.

Her Majesty the Queen of Denmark has arrived in Nuuk, aboard the Dannebrog and will work her away up the coast over the next few days. She will go and visit an ice drilling project on the ice cap before coming in a navy vessel to Qaanaaq. During these hot, summer days, I spent many an hour on my hot balcony with Susanne. Sitting outside for much of the day, one can see exactly the scope and exact dynamics of the *pulaar* amongst member of the same kinship-visiting group. One cannot 'belong' in this community without these ties. Kinship is a self-enforcing safety net from the unknown, the outside world. By making constant reference to these networks, they have created a tremendous ring of security. The Inugguit typically only leave the area if they are paid by the Government to do so, normally to Nuuk or Copenhagen for any number of health reasons or to continue their training.

On the 10th of July, I look out of the window at 6.50pm on the way to the kitchen and there she is, *Arina Arctica* – the 110 metre-long ILUMAX container vessel with a cargo capacity of 7,000 tons, a crew of 14 and a service speed of 15 knots. She was built in 1984 and has come from Nuuk. Her hull is bloated with 7,000 tons of cargo. Everything comes on the supply ship – cars, lorries, boats, furniture, houses (flat-packs from Denmark), food and drink. With her familiar red hull and white text, it is as if the colours of the Greenlandic flag have arrived. We have not seen her since the beginning of September. It will take several days before the cargo is delivered to the shop, but she is a most welcome sight. Pulling up alongside icebergs, she sounds her horn four times and the children run down the grassy slopes towards the shore. There is no need to rush; the parents remain at the window with binoculars in hand.

The arrival of the supply-ship coincides with the visit of Her Majesty the Queen of Denmark with whom I met this afternoon. She is in her seventies now and my first sighting of her was wading through icy water towards me. It is bitterly cold waiting for Her Majesty down at the shore with a howling wind whipping the water, turning the messy waves into white horses that bludgeon the shore. The weather has changed very suddenly. Eventually, HDMS *Ejnar Mikkelsen* (P571), the 61 metre Danish patrol vessel that came to Qaanaaq last September, pulls into the bay. This vessel patrols Greenland the whole time. A dinghy from the vessel comes towards the shore, but has trouble getting through the remaining ice. On the dinghy are a group of Navy officers, but not Her Majesty. They are here to do quick security checks before she comes ashore. They all have cigarettes in their mouths and do not look like a very serious operation. Subsequently, a second dinghy arrives with Her Majesty on board. The dinghy struggles and skirmishes with the floating sea ice, making the Royal Danish Navy look rather amateurish. She is accompanied by the Prime Minister of Greenland, Kuupik Kleist. I doubt if they had much to talk about aboard the P571, considering his party was elected on a platform of a policy of independence from Denmark.

Her Majesty arrives wearing a wet-suit and non-figure flattering protective clothing. It must be freezing out there on that boat. Once ashore, she is driven by Kim Fritz in a polished pick-up truck with Greenlandic flags flying from the wing mirrors. The Prime Minister, Kuupik Kleist, travels with Jan in the next pick-up truck. She has one security person with her, but no more. She goes into the *kommune* to get changed and then reappears and is driven a distance of no more than twenty metres to the sports hall. A group of people in traditional dress line up to meet her: Ole Danielsson, Aeruna Qujaukitsoq, Iggiannguaq Petersen and a few other people. There is a speech by Paulus Matthiasen welcoming her to Qaanaaq. Else Dunneq performs a drum-song and the dignitaries are served a special cake. There is cake for us too. Susanne is starving, as always, and helps herself to a great big portion. One cannot blame her. The Queen makes a very short speech telling her how happy she is to be here and it is amusing to see the Prime Minister act as her translator. There is a bit more music and the Queen is given a variety of presents. Then, it is time for her to leave.

The local people spent weeks preparing for this visit. Her Majesty has a busy schedule and ends up spending less than two hours here; I think the Inugguit must be very disappointed. Their real love is Crown Prince Frederik who lived in Qaanaaq for two months. In tears when he left

Qaanaaq, he told the Inugguit that when he was in Qaanaaq, he could be himself and live like a normal person for the first time in his life. There was no special treatment.

In the second week of July, a committee of unruly Arctic Terns, black napes and white cheeks, visit Qaanaaq, diving into the water intermittently, constantly bickering and quibbling after an exceedingly long migration. The sounds of summer in Qaanaaq comprise the squabbling Arctic Terns, the exploding icebergs, the Greenlandic rock music in the background and the sound of the small outboard engines coming and going. A mischievous, piratical Arctic Skua is developing a strategy in the background to steal the catch from his noisy neighbours. The Arctic Rhododendron with its tiny, pink flower and the yellow and white flower of the Mountain Avens (*qaqudluuhoq*) are now in bloom turning the tundra into a quilt of ephemeral colour.

After much discussion, the final preparations have now been made for the narwhal hunt. We travel east from Qaanaaq into the Bowdoin fjord by motorboat. At Kangerdluarssuk, we stop at the hunters' hut on the left as you enter the fjord. It looks like the sea is going to be too choppy to hunt narwhals today. The conditions need to be absolutely calm and then one has to simply wait; not a skill that the *kadluna* is endowed with. Ringed Seals pop their heads above the water level to catch a glimpse of the new arrivals. The hunters shoot in quick secession, but the seals are too quick for them. Fulmars, Kittiwakes and Black Guillemots fly overhead, mocking our slow progress; sitting low in the water, curious Black Throated Divers appear, then disappear. We approach the Bowdoin Glacier. At the point where we are sitting, there used to be a glacier just two years ago. Now, it is just open water. Arqioq has never seen open water at this point before, and you can see the shock on his face. Things are changing. Memories and descriptions of landscapes and seascapes transmitted from one generation to another are becoming redundant.

Huddled together in three motor boats, a coterie of bashful hunters and myself speed down towards the end of the fjord in search of calmer waters, dodging large lumps of ice bobbing up and down in the swirl. The trip to Qeqertat seems never-ending and the *ad nauseum* repetition of the boat crashing on the waves rocks me to sleep. Then, a sudden crackle on the radio, harsh and obnoxious. Nukappiannguaq in Qeqertat confirms that there have been sightings of narwhals today. The mood ticks up. As we approach Qeqertat, the fog lifts and the clear blue water is perfectly still. The setting is sublime. The azure sea is studded with icebergs the size of housing blocks, broken off the Tracy glacier and flaunting their freedom. Some of them I have seen before, locked in sea ice.

After a few hours of relaxing in our outboard engine motorboats, waiting and listening, we decide to go ashore. The setting is as peaceful and tranquil as you could hope to find anywhere in the world. Icebergs groan, inquisitive seals with their heads just above the perfect, still blue lagoon like water spy on the visitors. Soon, the whole community is sitting on the rocks, a handful of rugged, indefatigable individuals with wind-burned skin, confabulating and looking out for narwhals occasionally, very occasionally. One man eats a boiled Guillemot. There is Miteq, Tunkutaq (and his wife), Angaangaq (the bigger gentleman whom I met before), Preben Dunneq who is the lay-preacher and Hans Sadorana. There is a small lake behind the settlement, a carpet of magnificent purple Arctic Rhododendrons, a few flies, mosquitoes and Arctic Terns that dive into the water with enviable precision. Flustered by the insects, jaded sledge dogs sit around the lake in the thick grass. Down by the shore, I walk pass the abandoned yellow house and discover piles of rubbish which were hidden beneath the snow on my previous visit. Broken bottles and tins shatter any notions of a pristine Arctic ecosystem. If you spend any amount of time in an Inuit community, the idealised notion of indigineity where indigenous people live in harmony with their environment is soon tested. This might be their ecophilosophy or ideology, but it will not stop them leaving litter everywhere.

With gentle-faced kittiwakes in close pursuit, we travel south into Academy Bay or Kangerdluarssuk. Ahead sits a magnificent, glaucous iceberg the shape of the Bridge of Sighs. On the right of the fjord at Qarungahhuaq, we stop and Iggiannguaq and Ittukusuk, the cruel jester, climb up the, granite cliffs with their binoculars. Years ago, it used to be the case that narwhals would come into this bay, but there are none today. The place looks like a cross between the Grand Canyon and Antarctica, a true polar desert. Back on the boats, we then scout the whole length of the southern stretch of the Inglefield Bay, moving slowly like a police boat on duty. Everywhere you look, glaciers have retreated right up to the Ice Cap, lacerating paths that hunters have used for centuries to travel by dog-sledge to the more southern settlements. It is gone midnight, the sun is still quite high in the sky and I can feel my face burning.

At Kangeq, there is one tiny hut built into the cliff. Last time I was here, I had made the journey alone on skis to what seemed like this distant outpost. We stop the boats at the entrance of the Olrik Fjord. The hunters have a short coffee break and then we are off again. Nothing is said, but the plan seems to be uncontested and somehow defined. Moving from Kangeq towards Steensby Land, we come to a sudden halt and turn off the engines. With his perfect vision, Iggiannguaq has spotted a narwhal in the distance. The hunters climb up onto the front of the boats and scour the horizon with binoculars. Narwhal pods number between four and 20. The narwhal grows up to sixteen feet long and weighs 1.6 tonnes. They come up for air every twenty minutes or so, and it is a question of just waiting in silence, hoping that we have not disturbed them. We are listening for their breathing and trying to pick up the scent of their sour breath. I hear a whale coming up to breathe to my right, but do not manage to see anything beyond perhaps a tantalising glimpse of mottled skin. There is a faint smell of blubber. A pod must be close to us. Spending most of their time in deep water, these animals are very difficult to see. Iggiannguaq thinks that we have scared it off with the sounds of the engines. They have very good hearing and will dive to the botttom of the fjord if they hear a motor engine. The narwhal dives so deep the radio transmitters that biologists put on them to track them crack under the water pressure. We wait and wait, but there is not a ripple to be seen. My hopes of seeing a pod of males 'tusking' are well and truly dashed. The hunters wish to set up camp and it is time to move on. At 3am, we snack on *mattak* and dried mackerel (*angmassak*) which are very tasty and high in Vitamin A, and then fall asleep on the rocks under the fulgent sunlight from which there is no respite. After a few days of waiting on rocky precipices, examining every inch of the horizon through scuffed binoculars, we decide to give up on the elusive unicorn of the sea. We are tired, sunburnt and the prospect of sleeping on a mattress is increasingly appealing.

Back in the town, the flags are at half-mast. Another suicide. This is the season. Nuka Henningsen, the brother of Naaja, has taken his life and hung himself. He was a 24-year-old mechanic. Nobody knows why he did it, but Mikkili thinks it is because his relationship broke down. I think Josef was right about suicide. When things go wrong, young people do not feel as if they have any other exit. They are perhaps victims of topography. People queue outside the hospital to view the corpse. Otherwise, the town is unusually quiet. Hunters are out in their kayaks, waiting for the narwhals. Many of those who do not hunt are at home nursing an *aqaguluk* ('hang-over'). Women are arched over, picking Bog Bilberries on the tundra out towards the airstrip, just as they were doing when I first arrived. At Qaaqqu's house, all the talk is of the occasional narwhal that has been spotted passing through the bay and why it is unlikely that they will meet their quota this year. We have seal meat and fermented Little Auks for supper, all washed down with Danish beer. Ana and Qaaqqu are constantly laughing, calling me *piniartoq nutaaq*. The notion of a *kadluna* hunting is so absurd to them and always makes for a lively conversation and side-splitting laughter. I am pleased that they are so easily entertained and am perfectly happy as usual to be the object of ridicule. It has taken a long time and a lot of work, but on occasions like this I feel as if I have been fully accepted by the community.

A group of young, naïve New Zealanders have flown up from Kangerlussuaq. They are working for the North American Minerals Institute and are here to do geological surveys from the air. They look about 18 years old and travel the world the whole time doing this geomagnetic work. They have no idea what they are looking for or who they work for. Mining companies are employing the most naïve people they can find and for good reason. They do not ask questions. The plane is up in the air for 8 hours a day, covering grid after grid. They know nothing about the community which they are visiting and I cannot really sum up my experience of a year in a few lines for them, as they would like.

It is soon getting to the point of saying goodbye to everybody. Marie Nielsen wanted to organise a leaving party for me, but that has come to nothing as Frederik is away hunting. I thought I would host a party at my hut, but was unsure about having a *kaffimik* as I wanted to avoid the wake-like formality that comes with it, but was not convinced that hosting a party with alcohol was a good idea either. I have invited

Susanne over for a farewell supper. She wishes to eat Western, and not Greenlandic food. She is unusually subdued, upset that I am leaving. She keeps asking me when I am going. I remind her that I am leaving on Wednesday and she asks how many days away that is, and yet every time I see her she tells me how many more days there are left before I take my leave.

The word is getting around that I am leaving, and now every conversation is centred on the subject of my departure. It is impossible to talk about anything else. Women with bruised arms and faces stop me on the dusty tracks to confirm gossip and rumours. A sense of hysteria is growing in the town. People would trickle into my hut over the next few days, looking sad and dropping off unwanted gifts. Now that I am leaving, there is some curiosity about where I am going and what England is like. Frederik Nielsen wants to know whether there are millionnaires in the UK, whether it is true that you can 'buy' women there and whether it gets dark at night. The 76-year-old woman, Ingeborg, with whom I worked intensively on language documentation, whispers furtively how difficult it was for her to come to my house every day in the month of January because people assumed that we were having an affair. She would visit me every morning knowing that all eyes were on her. I had no idea, but that would explain many of the comments and jokes that were made about me these last weeks.

Frederik Kristiansen thinks there will be lots of tears at the airport tomorrow. 'Greenlanders love to cry all the time and not just the people from here'. He asks me if I have 'mixed emotions' about leaving and I say 'no'. It is not that I have been unhappy here, but one cannot get anything done in this place. It is an inert, static community. I wanted to give it a year. I wanted to go full circle. I have done that and now I am ready to come down. The scene is just how it was when I arrived and therefore my departure seems right and appropriate. I have seen what I needed to see. There have been ups and downs, but all in all it has been a tremendous experience. The fact that that other world has not always been an easy one to live in, that there have been so many frustrations, apathy and worse is not really the point. The real point is that it is different from what I know and therefore interesting. Once again, I have found that language is the key to the cultural chest and even the hardest of the world's languages can be mastered, even if I am not quite there yet. It is

10pm. The sun is shining bright and I wish to enjoy my last evening on the balcony.

It is the beginning of August and time to come down, time to return to my old life and different, unfrozen world. I spend the morning, saying goodbye one last time to all the people I have worked with, starting with Appalersuarsuk. We exchange a joke or two, shake hands and then I am on my way. He is a kind, gentle man to whom I have always warmed. Then, I climb the littered slope to Inge's cabin. She knows that I am leaving today and begins immediately to cry. Her leathery, deformed hands wish to grip mine. She pulls me close to her; tears pour down her cheeks, etched with wrinkles. I mention that I have been out to Herbert Island again, but it only makes matters worse. She sobs and keens. She had been so happy living there, but then her husband fell ill and her life fell apart. I feel sorry for her. She is in love with me, and her life is now nothing more than a box of distant memories of happier times, which she clings onto. It is tragic and pathetic. Her face pressed against the window, tears pour down her face. She makes me a cup of tea, but I cannot stay too long as there are many people to say 'goodbye' to. It is perhaps best if I just leave.

Then, it is off to see Qaaqqu and Arnarulunguaq Kivioq. They are delighted to see me. I tell them that I am leaving later on today and Qaaqqu hugs me, holding me so tight that I fear he is going to crush the sunglasses hanging round my neck. Arnarulunguaq grips my hands and they say *nanngmanniartutin aggurruaq* ('make sure you look after yourself') time and time again. This is followed by an *inudduarit*. I joke that next time it will be me doing the drum-dancing as I am an *angakkoq mikihuq*. They find this amusing and encourage me to do so. Visiting their home is the quintessential Qaanaaq experience. I hope that my lasting memory of Qaanaaq will be Qaaqqu and Arnarulunguaq Kivioq standing at the entrance of their dishevelled, stained house, waving at me non-stop. He is smiling and squinting, as always. I have gone round the corner and up the hill, but they are still there standing, waving, standing, waving. The image of them, waving is absolutely timeless and stuck in my memory. On the way back home, I meet Josef, Bodil and Iva. Josef tells me that he will not be able to come to the airport today and that therefore we must say our 'goodbyes' now. It is quick and unemotional.

He is laughing, as always and even the farewell becomes a joke.

The afternoon feels a bit like a wake. Visitors filter in and out, saying their goodbyes: firm handshakes, grins and then a joke. Sorrow mixed with humour, as always. It ends with Susanne, Magnus and myself having a jolly game of Olsen on the remains of the balcony. The thin layer of morning mist has turned into fog and has moved towards Qaanaaq. It feels like a divine intervention, the Gods wishing to block my exit. Nothing is certain in this cold land. I keep asking whether they think the plane will come, and the answer can only be *nalorrhorruiga*.

At 5pm, my dear friend, Arqioq, comes and picks me up in the white Mercedes with dance music blaring. He drives Susanne and me to the airport. He does not hang around, but shakes my hand and tells me that we must stay in touch and that I must come back. It is just Susanne and myself left now. The feeling is slightly like that when I first arrived. The plane arrives and I give Ane her key back. There is no drama. I say goodbye to Susanne, giving her a big hug. She is brave and does not cry. It is a short farewell and she leaves me to get on the aeroplane. As I walk across the gravel, she shouts out 'Stiffi' and gives me one last wave. It will be a long walk back to Qaanaaq for her, but she is going to be fine.

The flight is on time. It is a two and a half hour flight to Upernavik where three more passengers get on and then another two hours to Illulissat. We arrive there almost exactly at the scheduled time, at 10pm. The sun will set in Illulissat for the first time this summer and the sun is setting on my trip too. Outside the tiny airport at Illulissat, passengers are greeted with flies and mosquitoes.

Epilogue

T his book was prompted by living for a year in a society quite different from my own, inhabiting and sharing a kind of existence distinct from the one I knew. Stepping out of my own familiar *Lebenswelt*, I began to wrestle with new questions concerning language, the 'experience of language', epistemology and phenomenology. Living apart is a privilege as one encounters unfamiliar ecophilosophies and new perceptual and aural experiences as one embraces the alien sounds of the language one is learning. A new social experience of language can be a sensory rich one and lead to fresh ideas regarding the question of what language actually is, and what is the role of speech as a manifestation of 'Being-in-the-world' – the Heideggerian notion that the world and reality are ontologically inseparable (Heidegger, 1990). Working in a predominantly oral culture, the perceptual experience of language became informative for establishing an ontology of language in the context of phenomenology. Using phenomenology as a framework for couching my thoughts, this meta-level discourse does not constitute an analytical, philosophical approach to language which sees language as a vehicle for exploring logic, truth and meaning. It does not represent therefore an artificial view of language where man is absent. I have instead been concerned here with the 'experience of language' as the person's subjective assessment of listening to speech and the sounds around him. Fieldwork is surely concerned with the experience of subjectivity. In this book, I have subscribed to the Heideggerian belief that if we reduce our understanding to an objective opinion, bracketing out all prior experiences and emotion, then we ultimately bracket out the meaningfulness of the experience we are trying to explore.

The approach assumed during my year was an holistic (not atomistic) approach to language that looked at 'speech situations' (Lanigan, 1972) derived from the context of certain fieldwork encounters in an attempt to answer Searle's (1969: 3) opening question of 'how do words relate to the world?' – or perhaps with Polar Eskimo it is more a case of 'how do sounds relate to the world?' In doing so, I considered words and sounds as the embodiment of the 'lived world'. That is to say, they are existentially significant, part of existence and not detached from it. In the spirit of Austin's linguistic phenomenology of the 'total speech act' that must be seen in the 'total speech situation' (Austin, 1962: 52), my views on language derived from my fieldwork pertained to real situations and contexts in which utterances occurred.

The phenomenology of language is a subject that has more or less been ignored by the majority of linguists and one that linguists and 'innatists' working in the generative framework would actively disregard. Its key ideas have been taken up by a small number of philosophers who work in the tradition of continental philosophy, but the overall impression is that it is a topic that has been on the demise following the premature death of Merleau-Ponty. At the time of his death, Merleau-Ponty was not finished with the phenomenology of language project (Merleau-Ponty, 1964) and it remains incomplete to this day. However, it is a branch of linguistic philosophy that needs to be developed further to save the study of language from the formalists and universalists who are determined to keep man out of the equation when it comes to developing linguistic theory. It is time to return to the mindset that it is acceptable to pursue the study of language in such a perceptual, non-empirical manner, taking one's inspiration from the phenomenological lifeworld and looking at language as more of an inner process rather than a cognitive code. Exploring the vitality of language need not be a literary pursuit either, but is something that should be actively undertaken by linguists, anthropologists and phenomenologists.

'Being-in-the-world' means to not simply represent the world as a pure object of knowledge from a point outside the world, but to actively participate in it as one does in long-term fieldwork. Phenomenologists want us to return to the 'immediate experience of the world' and there can be no better context for doing this than being embedded in an alien culture in a strange place, relating things as they are viewed and perceived immediately before you, and not as science describes them. A key concept of Heideggerian phenomenology is *Mitsein* 'Being-with-

(others)' and this was perhaps the most important ingredient of my fieldwork, being surrounded by those who shared a different worldview, and perhaps a different concept of what the 'experience of language' is. It is surprising that phenomenology, the work of Michael Jackson aside, has not been used more in such long-term fieldwork contexts.

The language of phenomenology, in the case of Heidegger and Merleau-Ponty at least, can be poetic and evocative and in order to develop a phenomenology of language, one needs a to have a 'feel' for the language in the same way that a poet does. The Arctic landscape gave me that 'feel' for language and put me on this path. Merleau-Ponty (2002: 217) spoke of language as 'singing in the world' by which he meant the relationship between the word and what it signifies is 'motivated' because words express the emotional essence of our encounters in the world. Different cultures express the world differently. However, Merleau-Ponty is concerned with more than the 'word', and embraces instead all the gestural 'significations' of language – phonemes, voice, intonation, gestures, movement of the body, the way the word resonates with its surroundings, etc. Thinking about language in phenomenological terms does not, however, amount to mere poetic Romanticism. Heidegger thought that the language of poetry took us back to pre-linguistic meaning, the structures of primordial human experience and the essence of phenomenology. The structure of the Polar Eskimo language permits great innovation and this is important as it shows how new lexical constructions bring out the phenomenological meaning inherent in the structures of experience.

Merleau-Ponty (2002: 84) tells us that 'we must study the subject who is actually speaking' in an attempt to unite language to the lived-experience of the body-subject. By doing so, we are able to focus on the immediacy of speech in a pre-reflective context. Merleau-Ponty believed that one could only get a sense of language by speaking and listening to it, not from reading. It is not the written word or the codified form that goes hand-in-hand with discovering a new *Lebenswelt* and that is why I have spoken about a phenomenology of speech (and not language). As Merleau-Ponty (2002: 83) put it: 'To know what language is, it is necessary first of all to speak. It no longer suffices to reflect on the language lying before us in historical documents of the past'. This is why we have to get back to the spoken word. Contemporary linguistic research with its overwhelming bias towards syntax, semantics and phonology chooses not to engage with the Merleau-Pontian perceptual experience of language. And yet, it is imperative to appreciate what people 'do with words' in a natural context in order to be able to study language. Fieldwork in maximally 'other' linguistic scenarios is a vehicle for shaping one's thoughts and ideas surrounding language because one cannot 'experience' language in the same way if one does not step outside the familiar conventions and typologies of one's mother tongue language.

Through hearing and speaking an alien language, one experiences the consciousness of the other but it is subjective because it is based on the primacy of perception which is personal, individual and coloured by one's own cultural background. The language of the Inugguit may have sounded primordial to me in the sense of perhaps reflecting the raw sound and movement of the elements, but surely not to the native speakers of the language. In such a fieldwork situation, one embraces a new level of consciousness as one's natural and cultural environment is so new and alien. The awareness of the speaking subject and his language is a perceptual one and is linked to the experience of learning the language as one tries to internalise new bundles of resonances which at this initial stage are still just the fuzzy, indistinct sounds of the language. It is not long before one tries to string these alien sounds together to see if they fit the few pre-established linguistic patterns bouncing around in one's mind. The initial perceptual consciousness of a new language is important because it introduces you to the rhythm of the language which becomes a 'determined' framework of sounds for learning the idiom. In learning a new idiom, one can soon appreciate the language at a sonic macro-level or 'immediate value as a whole' (Merleau-Ponty, 1964: 40). After all, it is when a language is not comprehensible to us that it has its biggest impact on our senses.

Once these sounds have been internalised, the language-learning process becomes much easier even if one does not yet know what the words mean or how the syntax or morphology works. Phenomenology dictates that music precedes grammar and semantics, and that was definitely the case in the experience of learning Polar Eskimo. If you are listening to an alien sounding language in which you understand almost nothing, as was my initial linguistic experience, a language where you simply cannot distinguish when one word begins and ends, a language which contains sounds that one has never heard before, one is inclined to return to this kind of primordial sense of appreciating language as first and foremost sound and music, and not words and grammar. It is a language's music, rhythm, intonation patterns and combination of phonemes that gives us its appeal and personality. It is these immediate and subjective features which contribute to the phenomenology or essence of language.

Responding to the speech and language you hear is a necessarily subjective practice. As Lanigan (1972: 102) notes, 'perception and expression in this dimension are only distinguishable by and to the other person' – the interlocutor will be making his own assessment of the other person's speech. Through speaking comes the consciousness of the person himself: 'a friend's speech over the telephone brings us the friend himself' (Merleau-Ponty, 1964: 43). Phenomenology represents a 'rediscovery of the subject in the act of speaking, as contrasted to a science of language which inevitably treats this subject as a thing' (Merleau-Ponty, 1964: 104). Words in Polar Eskimo come alive when stems and affixes combine. This means that their language has the ability to surprise, perhaps through the unusual compounding of affixes. Through metaphor, simile and unusual juxtaposition of words, poetry surprises us and makes us stop and think in new ways. Our own everyday language is, however, overwhelmingly conventional and predictable as we use for the most part a limited vocabulary time and time again.

This lived 'experience of language' that I have been referring to in the book is something one can only encounter as an adult learner of a second language. It is the experience of 'living and doing culture' that gives you bit-by-bit access to the distinct 'semantic deep structure' (Friedrich, 1979: 34) of a language – a meta-domain of semantic categories specific to the culture expressed through the language. This cultural semantic code can only be understood by being in that 'linguistic world' for an extended period of time. In the case of Polar Eskimo, this code relates principally to hunting, climate, traditional food, domestic life, what remains of animist thinking, etc.

Gaining a consciousness of language means being introduced to the 'rhythm' and phonological structure of a language which is not arbitrary as it is often assumed. The phonological patterns of its speakers are specific, peculiar and shaped by a host of complex cultural, social and environmental factors. One suspects that this is especially the case in the indigenous languages of hunter-gatherers where there has been minimal language contact and where the groups still live to some degree in 'harmony with nature' such as the Polar Eskimos. Here the sounds of the Arctic hunters' speech seem to almost merge with the noise of the wind, and the slow rhythm of their speech mirrors the moving soundscape.

There is evidence in language of a non-arbitrary relationship between the physical aspect of a speech signal and its meaning. As an example, words in English beginning with *fl-* often suggest lightness and quickness (fly, flee, flow, flimsy, flicker, and fluid) and those beginning with *gl-* often refer to light (gleam, glisten, glow, glint, glitter, and glimmer). Sound symbolism or phono-semantics as this has been called (Jespersen, 1922: 408-11) has been much discussed on and off since the time of Plato. With a few exceptions (Hinton, Nichols & Ohala, 1994), most linguists consider incidences of sound symbolism to be exceptional. Poets are of course aware of this sound symbolism and exploit it in the use of alliteration and other tools, but some speakers of indigenous languages know of this too. Polar Eskimo might look like a phono-semantic language. For instance, most words related to 'seeing' begin with *ihii-* (*ihiinnaarut* – 'television', *ihiluktoq* 'has bad eyes', *ihiggauhoq* 'is visible', *ihinnaut* 'iris', etc.) and words relating to 'flowing, pouring' tend to begin with *kui-* (*kuihiriarniq* 'drop', *kuihinniq* 'baptism'), but this is actually a different issue and what one might call lexical *ex interno* reproduction, i.e. productive stems are engineered to produce new words and phrases using indigenous stems and words already in the language. Words relating to 'seeing' begin with *ihii-* because that is the stem meaning 'to see' and *kui-* is the stem referring to 'flows, pours'. Polar Eskimo may well be phono-semantic in places, but that is not the same thing as saying that the language is shaped to some degree by the natural environment, as in phono-semantics the motivation is a sound symbolic one where groups of meanings cluster around a particular phoneme (and perhaps its reduplication). Many indigenous people speak of a subtle link between language, the senses and the landscape, reckoning that this bond takes us back to the very foundations of language. The Polar Eskimos speak of the smell of the winds in certain places and believe that their language is shaped by the natural environment. Reciting Valery, Merleau-Ponty (1968: 155) would write in *The Visible and the Invisible* of language being everything 'since it is the voice of no one, since it is the very voice of things, the waves and the forests...' – a view that would resonate certainly with some of the Inugguit. In such a context, there is a convergence of perception and expression where speaking and the *Lebenswelt* are intertwined.

Throughout the fieldwork, it was the 'speaking' that was the essence of consciousness. In such a context, surrounded and penetrated by this originality of speech, one has a chance to overcome the bias of dualism inherent in Western thinking on language. We are part of it. One cannot have this experience if working with one's mother tongue as the relationship and experience is quite different because the level of consciousness is lower. By going through this experience of 'entering into language and submitting to it' in this Heideggerian way, I found my own poetic voice.

A phenomenological approach to language allows one to grasp the dynamic of language, going beyond the ethnocentric formalist approach to language, but also enables one to capture the manifold character of lived experience. Critics will say that phenomenology lacks rigour, but the 'rigorous' framework that the generativists wish to employ impoverishes our understanding of what 'real' language is and ignores entirely the essence of language. It is the language we use (not the idealised language of Chomskyian theories of syntax) through which we construct reality and this is, perhaps, the most important lesson of all from long-term fieldwork. Language is not an objective, but an intersubjective phenomenon enabling one to experience the other as a subject and not object. Phenomenology leaves the window open to indigenous views on what language is. Those views put forward by linguists and anthropologists sympathetic to phenomenology are ultimately those of outsiders pitched in an alien environment.

It should be noted that it was immensely difficult to gauge indigenous perspectives on language. The reluctance to engage with such a discussion meant that the only way to solicit answers to such questions is through long-term ethnographic participant observation. If one really wants to know what language means to the indigenous population, one has to simply listen and observe and gradually piece the jigsaw together. Having done so, my best conjecture would be that their indigenous phenomenology of language is one that is unlikely to embrace the Saussurean arbitrariness of the sign. Instead, I think they would perceive the relationship between form and meaning to be more one of intimate symbiosis. Historically, when animist traditions, taboo beliefs and shamanic language were more prevalent, and when the bond to nature was even closer, I think the role of language would have been more evocative than it is today. More evocative still would have been the mnemonic landscape, the contours of the land, the smells of the winds and the sounds of the creaking ice. Living so close to nature, the Inugguit's extraordinary memory, olfactory sensitivity and proximity of sensory pathways might seem almost synesthetic to us.

In a society where gesture is as important as words, where speech trumps writing, where sitting in a hunters' hut on the sea ice in a gale, the sounds of the storyteller's voice merge with the sounds of nature, one begins to see language as more than just a set of arbitrary symbols and that is one of the many lessons that I took away from the fieldwork. In Polar Eskimo society, sounds relate to the world in the Searlian sense. It is clear then that the Inugguit are phenomenologists in the purest form, having always lived within a non-Cartesian framework of thinking where man and nature are largely co-extensive, where language is not an object but part of this man-nature enmeshment.

It is perhaps a cliché to say so, but I found the fieldwork process a humbling and highly self-reflexive process. It was humbling because the three communities where I worked and lived were hypersensitive and vulnerable places where tragedy lurked behind every smile and toothless grin. Daily life is a grind for many people simply because they had to live with not one, but often multiple suicides in their very close families. The narrative came back to me time and time again because it was obvious to me (and perhaps them) that in many senses, my values and priorities were diametrically opposed to those of the local people. Unlike them, I discovered that I was happiest when pushing myself to the limits physically, pulling a pulk across the sea ice in the depths of the Arctic wilderness in temperatures of -25 degrees (pre-wind chill), weaving through shimmering tower blocks of ice, on the look out for polar bears. To live so close to nature was a tremendous privilege for me. Living intensely and unrelentingly at the heart of another culture, I came to understand how environmental reality has shaped the life of the Inugguit, but also how the Arctic had deepened my sense of the infinite and unknown.

The fieldwork experience provided me with a consciousness of myself and of my world. It was often difficult to know what to make of my year in the Polar North because positive experiences juxtaposed negative experiences, day after day. A year in an Inuit community showed me certainly that to be human is to be conflicted, thwarted and thrown by circumstance and contingency. It showed me how dualistic our thinking in the West is. To damage the environment is to forget that man and nature are enmeshed.

Having now completed my research project, I am often asked what was the 'hardest thing' about my year in the Polar North. Dodging starving polar bears and stumbling over deep snow in 'white-outs' with temperatures of -40 degrees were certainly not the biggest challenges. In many respects, the hardest thing was trying to overcome the wall of mistrust that exists between the inuk and the *kadluna*. As a researcher, it was exceedingly difficult to gain people's trust and to persuade people that I was different from my predecessors, many of whom were considered exploitative. For a few, I never did cease to be an object of suspicion and that was very regrettable.

Before I left for the Arctic, friends told me that the experience would change me as a person. I do not think that is the case, but it is true that I will never be able to look at life and our world in quite the same way again. Living in the Arctic confirmed what I had suspected for a long time and opened my eyes to the lunacy of the congested, overpopulated world we live in where people have almost no concept of what 'nature' or 'wilderness' is. The society I was living in was not an ideal at all. It just happened to show me what life must have been like before industry left its mark on the world. We cannot turn the clock back now and return to pre-industrialised society, but to stay on the current path is exceedingly irresponsible and foolish. We cannot support attempts to stem climate change and explore for oil and gas in the Arctic at the same time. In doing so, we are ignoring the knowledge that we have.

In August, it was time to return to my chloroform, neutered world of tinned thought and what many people call 'civilisation', the multi-cultural zoo of modern life: a deeply unenticing prospect. I had spent much time thinking about how I would readjust to my old life and whether there would be any difficulties in doing so. The plane touched down at Kastrup Airport in Copenhagen at 9pm on a Thursday evening. It was just getting dark and after four months of 24 hour sunshine, the return to a more regular balance of day and night was very welcome. With 75kg of luggage and a pair of skis slung over my shoulder, I staggered out of the airport and was struck by the stifling humidity. After having lived in a polar desert for a year, the sweat poured off me as my Turkish taxi-driver negotiated the busy streets of the Danish capital. I dropped my bags off at the hotel, walked down one of the main boulevards and sat quietly on a bench. I had often speculated how this moment would feel. Even though I had returned to the world I knew, I felt in a sense 'displaced' and overwhelmed. The sky rumbled with the incessant noise of aeroplanes overhead, one after the other, streams of traffic poured past me in both directions. The pavements were almost empty. The only sign of life were fixed heads behind steering wheels, moving horizontally and swiftly as if on a conveyor belt in the wrong gear on an assembly-line of environmental destruction. It was the dream of Susanne Imiina who visited me every day and from whom I learnt much of their language, to leave north-west Greenland and come to Denmark or England. But, having lived in the Arctic, having lived in a pristine environment where man has barely left his mark, I would be ashamed and embarrassed to show her my world of 'progress', 'development' and 'unsustainability', a world of industry, high-rise buildings, noise, polluted skies and rivers, a place where childhoods are spent in the back of cars on clogged streets and where freedom comes at a price. And yet it does not have to be like this. We can live in sustainable ways which are simple and very gratifying.

Back at home and now acclimatised to the relative heat and humidity, I feel at times like a lone voice in a sea of madness. I am an idealist and with the Arctic environment, it seems that I finally found my cause. In those first few weeks and months back at home, I felt like I had climbed out of a cave and walked into a circus. Initially, there was the shock of acclimatising again to a temperate climate. In that first week, I would find solace in the freezer aisle at the local Sainsbury's in Cambridge. But the single biggest shock was the number of cars everywhere. I think if an alien arrived on our planet, the sheer preponderance of vehicles would be their first observation. For the first month, I would aim to avoid Cambridge at the weekends as the congestion and number of people crammed into the narrow, warm streets seemed unbearable. Inevitably, this feeling did not last for long and within about two months, I was more or less comfortable walking around London. There were times when I wondered whether the trip had been a mistake as the sense of displacement at being back at home continued to linger, and made relationships difficult. I knew that north-west Greenland would not be my chosen 'elsewhere', but I could not imagine living in overcrowded Britain either. The search for belonging continued and within two years, I had found a new home in the Scandinavian Arctic.

After having lived in the Polar North, I came to realise that living in temperate Western Europe is like being in an existential buffer zone. Life is easy and comfortable in the West. One can go about one's daily business without a care for what is really going on in the world. Climate change is the stuff of newspapers. It is in the polar regions where the reality of environmental change never leaves you. Standing at the top of the world, you can really see what is going on just as you can if you sit in the bow-seat of an Eight. At some point in the future, the buffer zone will disappear and the grim reality will slide southwards. In the meantime, living in elected ignorance is the easiest option for most.

I believe we are living through the greatest period of change the world has ever known. The vulgarity of mass air travel and excessive materialism is spreading to every corner of the world and changing irreversibly how we interact with one another and how we relate to our natural environment. In the Polar North, I was privileged to be able to escape that world for a while at least. Access to an unspoiled environment is surely an essential human right. When we exploit the environment, we usurp the rights of people across the world and of future generations. The time has come to challenge nation states, corporations and individuals whose actions cause irreversible damage to our shared environment. We have become disconnected from nature. We miss out on the beauty and secrets of the world around us when we fly across time-zones at breakneck speed and dash in four-wheeled metal boxes over the cluttered landscape.

Before living in the Arctic, I was convinced that we needed a new paradigm for looking at the world. We live in an age where the pursuit of material wealth above all else is increasingly the basis of society. We live the lie, believing that this leads to happiness when it manifestly does not. This is no longer a Western phenomenon, but increasingly a global one. Those societies who crave wealth above all else are the ugly, new get-rich quick economies of south-east Asia where the inhabitants are choking in the smog of their own 'progress'. We have surely reached the point where the pursuit of economic growth at the expense of everything else can only lead to ultimate ruin for mankind. We must now recognise the urgent need for sustainability to replace economic growth as humankind's central focus. We need a different compass: growth in knowledge, but not GDP. There is a need to develop a system which would turn this model on its head, forcing investors to allocate funds and reward companies and indeed countries not solely for their respective growth in earnings or annual percentage increase in GDP, but directly and quantitatively for their progress in having developed green, sustainable products and economies. Having spent much time talking to the Arctic hunters who bear the costs of environmental damage, I am sure of the need for a new approach to assessing what we consider to be 'economic success', but also for the introduction of urgent policies to curtail the world's population growth.

A country with 1.4 billion people and an annual economic growth rate of ten per cent should not be hailed as a success story if it is building a new coal power station every week and causing untold damage to the environment. That is effectively the view of the Arctic hunters and one which having lived with these people I endorse. Shortly after coming down from the Arctic, the population of the world reached seven billion people. The pernicious combination of this uncontrolled population growth and the finite mineral resources of the planet are undoubtedly the biggest threats to the environment. Unless we take appropriate action and implement policies on these fronts, the disappearance of a small, isolated culture in the Arctic may be a microcosm for a much more apocalyptic outcome. For many, it may seem irrelevant if we lose a culture numbering fewer than a thousand people, but if the Polar Eskimos come to be the canary in the cultural coal mine, then such a loss may have more relevance than some people feared.

The people of the Polar North believe that overcrowding in the rest of the world has meant that man has severed his ties with nature. When I told the locals how many people lived in the UK, they would screw up their faces and shake their heads. With over sixty million people crammed on one small island, it is no longer possible to live in harmony with nature, even if we still knew what that means. As more and more newcomers pour into the country, we stand to lose first and foremost the last remaining scraps of the English countryside. If you care about the green fields of England being lost to soulless, ugly housing estates and shopping centres with identical shops, then you have to care about population. Population matters here in England and in most parts of our fragile world. After having returned from the Arctic, the south-east of England appears to me as one large housing estate, an urban cancer that will eventually take over the country. Wherever man goes, things are destroyed. That is the beauty of the desert and the Ice Cap: it is surely, one of the few places where man cannot build, and therein lies its appeal.

As the world's population continues to grow exponentially, life for its billions of inhabitants will become distinctly less pleasant. The population of the world increases by approximately one quarter of a million people every single day or to put it differently, daily population growth on the planet is equivalent to five times that of the population of Greenland or more than the entire population of primates on Earth. The world's population has doubled from 3.5 billion to 7 billion in my lifetime. It may level out when it has reached 12 billion as some predict, but by that time life on this planet will be hellish. Life might become less congenial for us, but the animal kingdom is simply being 'crowded out'. The numbers are terrifying. With dwindling finite energy resources, surely anybody can see that the explosive growth in the world's population over the last 50 years is utterly unsustainable. And yet, the taboo of talking about the 'biggest issue' remains. For the sake of the future of the planet, that has to now change. Those who wish to live in blissful ignorance, those who think it will all somehow miraculously 'sort itself out', those who think that population activists are some kind of Nazi supremacists must be now tackled head-on. The argument must be won and common sense must not be sacrificed to political correctness, the scourge of modern Britain. Political correctness not only clouds judgment, but stifles debate, making it socially unacceptable to address the most pressing issues. I do not believe it is possible to persuade the majority of the people in the West to live more simply. The consumerist culture is too ingrained and there is every reason to believe that developing economies will follow our patterns of consumption. If that is the case, countries around the world need to urgently put in place population growth policies and implement linked taxation measures. Instead of doing the sensible thing, countries in Western Europe talk about the problem of falling birth rates. The idea that we need constantly more young people to look after an ageing population is the logic of an ecological Ponzi scheme, as David Attenborough so elegantly put it. At what point is the penny going to drop? We cannot grow forever, in numbers of humans or in terms of economic development. The real answer to the problem lies in education, but it is not easy to educate people about the problem when the topic is taboo and with the thinking of the Catholic Church still stuck in the Middle Ages. The longer we leave it and do nothing, the less pleasant become the solutions. That is why we must act now.

Like Inge who felt ill-at-ease in the modern town of Qaanaaq, I am a romantic and I discovered that romantics are always disillusioned because the world is no longer how they had hoped it to be. I had gone to the top of the world and had wished to find elderly folk sitting around telling stories. Instead, I found adults and children glued to television screens with a bowl of seal soup on their lap, playing exceedingly violent and expletive-crammed Hollywood video war games. Consumerism and globalisation has now made it to every corner of the world. Some Polar Eskimos may live in tiny, wind-beaten wooden cabins with no running water like Wally's, but Amazon delivers. Most eight year olds who live in Qaanaaq and the remote settlements have the latest smartphones. Media entertainment will, however, never be produced for a language of 770 speakers because it is loss-making. Technology, be it mobile phones, DVDs or video games may support the top fifty languages maximum, but never more than that. Some languages are not suited to these technologies: Greenlandic words are too long to to use in text messaging. Polar Eskimos tend to send text messages in Danish or English because it is easier.

As the world embraces the synthetic monoculture of populism and consumerism, linguistic and cultural diversity risk being erased right across the world. For consumerism to operate efficiently, it requires as few operating languages as possible. That way, the message is consistent and the producer's cost is minimised. This globalised consumerism is the product of a system which is based on an addiction to economic growth. Growth for the sake of growth is the ideology of the cancer cell, and yet it is difficult to hear American politicians or EU officials talk about anything else. Some politicians speak oxymoronically of 'sustainable growth' but the combination of a rocketing world population and finite resources is the recipe of 'unsustainability' par excellence. Growth has become an abstract imperative that is driving humanity to destroy the ecosystem upon which life depends. If we can shake off the growth habit and focus on the 'local' and sustainability for its own sake, minority languages will have a chance to prosper providing they engage with new digital media technologies. The Internet represents surely the best opportunity to help support small or endangered languages and yet 95 per cent of Internet content appears in just twelve languages. The Internet offers also a chance to move away from television which is largely responsible for the spread of a phoney, idiotic form of entertainment culture where production costs are too high to support minority languages.

I have never met anybody who is indifferent to the elimination of biodiversity or the protection of endangered animal species, but linguists and anthropologists are still being asked to defend linguistic and cultural diversity. In doing so, it should be remembered that a language is so much more than a syntactic code or a list of grammar rules. To treat language as such is to reduce it to its least interesting features. When languages die, we do not just lose words, but we lose different ways of conceptually framing things. For the Polar Eskimos, there is no one concept of 'ice', but over twenty different ways of referring to various forms of ice. Through different distinctions in meaning, languages provide insights onto how groups of speakers 'know the world'. A language is a collection of statements about the world delivered in a multitude of voices set to a background of music. When we lose a language, we lose an orchestra of voices that permeate the mind as well as knowledge and perceptions of the world which are built into local language varieties. We lose the music and poetry of words and speech which elicit so much pleasure.

The twenty-first century is the make-or-break century for cultural and linguistic diversity, and for the future of human civilisation per se. An unprecedented and unchecked growth in the world's population, combined with the insistence on exploiting finite resources, will lead to environmental and humanitarian catastrophes as mass urbanisation meets fundamental problems such as the lack of drinking water. The actions that we collectively take over the next fifty years will determine how and if we can overcome such global challenges, and what the shape of the 'ethnosphere' or 'sum of the world's cultures' is to look like in years to come.

After having spent a year in a remote Arctic community which speaks a vulnerable, minority language and whose cultural foundations are being rocked by climate change, it is clear to me that the link between environmental and cultural vulnerability is genuine and that the two are interwoven. Cultural practices of the Polar Eskimos are based on a history of survival strategies in one of the world's most hostile environments. Their language and 'way of speaking' is a representation of that. When the sea ice disappears, their stories will eventually go with it.

We, human beings, rent the world for a period of approximately eighty years. It is our duty to future tenants to leave the house as we found it. The conservation issue goes beyond everything else and should therefore be at the heart of every policy decision. To do otherwise, would be to live in the twentieth century. At present, linguists predict that over fifty per cent of the world's languages will no longer be spoken by the turn of the century. Instead of leaving the house in order, we are on the road to the fastest rate of linguistic and cultural destruction in history. Languages die for many reasons, but the current trend is driven by the juggernaut of the homogenising forces of globalisation and consumerism which seems unstoppable and whose language tends to be the new universal tongue, English.

If you live in the Arctic for a period of time, you can never quite leave it and it never quite leaves you. It does not matter how difficult the time was socially, you are always drawn back to the emptiness. Two years later, I returned briefly to the community and found that nothing stays the same for long in north-west Greenland. Nothing is constant. People die suddenly and unexpectedly. Iggiannguaq Petersen dropped dead from a brain seizure shortly after my last hunt with him. Many others had contracted cancer and had fallen seriously ill, including Magnus Qujaukitsoq and Appalersuarsuk Qaerngaq. Qaaqqu Miteq died shortly after I left the field. He was apparently suffering from cancer, but never mentioned it. Iisaaq Jeremiassen died at the age of ninety and with his and Qaaqqu's passing, the best surviving storyteller and drum-dancer were gone within a few months of each other. I had hoped to return to the community and work with Qaaqqu again as I got on with him so well and I had only begun to tap his knowledge. But, it was too late and now he is gone forever. With him went a great catalogue of stories and drum-songs about a fading life which I was only able partially to document. I was shocked to hear of his death. He had struck me as somebody who was in good health. I was reminded of the urgency of these oral documentation projects. There are now only about five or six drum-singers left in the community.

Rapid change is afoot in Greenland. Up and down the coast, international companies are looking for oil and gas and prospecting for every mineral you care to name. Iron deposits have been found on Inglefield Land, north of the region that the Inugguit occupy. China is leading the resource grab and wishes to ship them from the north of Greenland to the foreign markets across the melted Arctic Ocean to China, but they will not be employing local hunters to do the work. The election result in 2013 implies that the Greenlanders will not allow the Chinese to bring thousands of their own workers to do the mining, but the foreign mining companies will need a well-trained and educated labour force. None of these dramatic measures are in fact necessary to sustain a tiny population, and it is ironic that the Inuit who like to project the image of living in harmony with nature have pursued relentlessly this policy the moment they achieved Self-Rule from Denmark in 2009. The desire for independence from Denmark is understandable, but in the wake of an Arctic oil spill or a potential attack from a resource-grabbing country, Greenland will never be able to stand alone.

An industrialised Greenland and an Arctic free of ice would destroy and eliminate the spiritual appeal of the frozen, empty world of the polar regions that I came to know and love. It would change forever the map of our world that has been consistent for thousands of years; it would render the maps of the polar regions that used to hang in my childhood bedroom anachronistic and redundant once the white bits are gone. We would go down in history as the generation who lived in disequilibrium with the natural world and whose hunger for development was so rampant that we literally changed the colour of the map. We will have conquered the world and begun the slow destruction of humanity in the process.

Glossary

ajor – 'oh no, oh dear'

ajorpoq – 'bad' or 'not functioning' (strictly speaking, the word is West Greenlandic but is sometimes used as a synonym for *naamaangitsoq*)

ammaqa – 'perhaps'

angakkoq – 'shaman'

avataq – 'a buoy used on a kayak, made out of a seal bladder'

bosted – a Danish word which in the Greenlandic context refers to a settlement where the population has typically fallen below about 20 and where provisions are no longer delivered on a supply-ship

bygde – Danish word for 'settlement'

hermeq – 'the Greenland Ice Sheet that covers the interior of Greenland'

hiku – ' sea ice'

imaq – 'open water'

inudduarit – 'farewell'

inuk – singular of Inuit

kadluna – 'the white man, often used to refer to the European'

kaffimik – a party held on special occasions to mark birthdays and other events. Sweet and savoury food is always served and coffee is drunk

kamikker – 'seal skin boots lined with Arctic Fox or Arctic Hare fur and worn by the Inuit'

kiffaq – previously, a woman that would do chores around the house

mattak – 'the skin and blubber of a narwhal'. A delicacy in Greenland, high in Vitamin C

nalorrhorruiga – 'I don't know' in Inuktun

nannut – 'polar bear fur trousers worn by hunters'

nuna – 'the local cosmos, the land, sea, sea ice, air and all the stories, feelings and beliefs connected to the natural environment' *pujoq* – 'smoke or cloud, in particular puffs of cloud that appear over open water'

qivittoq – 'a feared, semi-mythical figure that goes out up into the mountains or onto the Ice Sheet because he has been rejected from society'

qujan – 'thank you'

tarhaq – 'a white shield that hunters hide behind when they shoot seals basking in the sunshine on the sea ice'

tarneq – 'the soul of a human being or animal'

tuurngaq – 'the spirits that would follow and help a shaman in time of need'

uuttoq – 'seal or walrus that has crept up on the ice to bask in the sun'

uuniit – 'never mind', 'don't worry'

Bibliography

Alia, Valerie. 2008. *Names & Nunavut: Culture and Identity in the Inuit Homeland*. New York: Berghahn.

Appadurai, Arjun. 1997. *Modernity at Large: Cultural Dimensions of Globalisation*. Minneapolis: University of Minnesota Press.

Austin, John Langshaw. 1962. *How to do things with words: The William James lectures delivered at Harvard University in 1955*. Edited by J. O. Urmson. Oxford: Clarendon.

–1961. *Philosophical Papers*. Edited by J. O. Urmson & G. J. Warnock. Oxford: Oxford University Press.

Basso, Keith. 1996. *Wisdom sits in Places: Landscape and Language among the Western Apache*. Albuquerque: University of New Mexico Press.

Bauman, Richard, & Briggs, Charles, L. 1990. 'Poetics and Performance as critical perspective on Language and Life'. *Annual Review of Anthropology*, 19: 59-88.

Baumeister, Roy, F. & Leary, Mark R. 1995. 'The Need to Belong: Desire for Interpersonal Attachments as a Fundamental Human Motivation'. *Psychological Bulletin* Vol. 117, No. 3: 497-529.

Bender, Barabra. 2001. 'Introduction'. In Bender, Barbara & Winer, Margot. (editors), *Contested Landscapes: Movement, Exile and Place*. Oxford: Berg.

Blake, William. 1977. *The Complete Poems by William Blake*, edited by Alicia Ostriker. Harmondsworth, New York: Penguin.

Bodenhorn, Barbara. 2009. 'Calling into Being: Naming and Speaking Names on Alaska's North Slope'. In vom Bruck, Jespere & Bodenhorn, Barbara (editors). *The Anthropology of Names and Naming*. Cambridge: Cambridge University Press: 139-57.

Clifford, James. 1997. *Routes: Travel and Translation in the late twentieth Century*. Cambridge: Harvard University Press.

De Certeau, Michel. 1984. *The Practice of Everyday Life*. Translated by Rendall, Steven. Berkeley: University of California Press.

Drengson, Alan & Yuichi Inoue (editors). 1995. *The Deep Ecology Movement: An Introductory Anthology*. Berkeley, CA: North Atlantic Books.

Fortescue, Michael. 1991. *Inuktun: An Introduction to the Language of Qaanaaq*, Thule. Institut for Eskimologi 15, Københavns Universitet.

Freuchen, Peter. 1961. *Book of the Eskimos*. New York: Fawcett World.

Friedrich, Paul. 1979. *Language, Context, and the Imagination*. Stanford: Stanford University Press.

Fromm, Erich. 2004. *The Fear of Freedom*. London and New York: Routledge.

Gilberg, Aage. 1948. *Eskimo Doctor*. London: George Allen & Unwin.

Heidegger, Martin. 1990. *Being and Time*. Translated by Joan Stambaugh. Wiley, John & Sons: New York.

– 1978. 'Letter on Humanism', in D. F. Krell (ed.), *Basic Writings*. London: Routledge: 213-65.

Hinton, Leanne, Nichols, Johanna & Ohala, John, J. (Eds.). 1994. *Sound Symbolism*. Cambridge: Cambridge University Press.

Hymes, Dell. 1974. 'Ways of Speaking'. In Explorations in *The Ethnography of Speaking* edited by Richard Bauman & Joel Sherzer. New York: Cambridge University Press: 433-51.

Jackson, Michael. 2007. *Excursions*. Raleigh-Durham: Duke University Press.

– 2005. *Existential Anthropology*. New York; Oxford: Berghahn.

– 1995. *At Home in the World*. Durham, North Carolina: Duke University Press.

Jenkins, McKay. 2005. *Bloody Falls of the Coppermine: Madness, Murder, and the Collision of Cultures in the Arctic, 1913*. New York: Random House.

Jespersen, Otto. 1922. *Language: Its Nature, Development and Origin*. London: Allen & Unwin.

Kulchyski, Peter. 2006. 'Six Gestures'. In Pamela Stern & Lisa Stevenson, eds., *Critical Inuit Studies: An Anthology of Contemporary Arctic Ethnography*. Lincoln: University of Nebraska Press: 155-67.

Lanigan, Richard, L. 1972. *Speaking and Semiology: Maurice Merleau-Ponty's Phenomenological Theory of Existential Communication*. The Hague: Mouton.

Liberman, Kenneth. 1985. *Understanding Interaction in central Australia: An ethnomedological study of Australian Aboriginal People*. Boston: Routledge & Kegan Paul

Lovell, Nancy (editor). 1998. 'Introduction'. In *Locality and Belonging*. New York: Routledge: 1-12.

MacMillan, Miriam. 1951. *I Married an Explorer*. Lonon: Hurst & Blackett.

Massey, Doreen. 1994. *Space, Race and Gender*. Cambridge: Polity Press.

Merleau-Ponty, Maurice. 2002. *Phenomenology of Perception*. Translated by Colin Smith. London: Routledge.

– 1968. *The Visible and the Invisible*. Edited by Claude Lefort and translated by Alphonso Lingis. Evanston: Northwestern University Press.

– 1964. *Signs*. Translated, with an Introduction by Richard C. McCleary. Evanston: Northwestern University Press.

Nuttall, Mark. 1992. *Arctic Homeland: Kinship, Community and Development in Northwest Greenland*. Toronto: University of Toronto Press.

Ong, Walter. 1982. *Orality and Literacy: The Technologizing of the Word*. New York: Methuen.

Rasmussen, Knud. 1908. *The People of the Polar North: A Record*. London: K. Paul, Trench, Trübner & Co.

Riches, Arqioq. 1986. *The Anthropology of Violence*. Oxford: Basil Blackwell.

– 1982. *Northern Nomadic Hunter-Gatherers*. London: Academic Press.

Rose, Gillian. 1995. 'Place and Identity: A Sense of Place'. In: Massey, Doreen & Jess, Pat (editors). *A Place in the World? Places, Culture and Globalisation*. Oxford: Oxford University Press: 87-132.

Saussure, Ferdinand, de. 1916. *Cours de linguistique générale*. (English translation by Wade Baskin. 1959, *Course in general linguistics*). New York: Philosophical library.

Searle, John, R. 1969. *Speech acts: An Essay in the Philosophy of Language*. Cambridge: Cambridge University Press.

Silverstein, Michael. 2003. 'The Whens and Wheres – As well As Hows – of Ethnolinguistic Recognition'. *Public Culture* 15(3): 531–557.

Thalbitzer, William. 1904. *A Phonetical Study of the Eskimo language*. *Meddelelser om Grønland*, bind 31. Commissionen for Ledelsen af de geologiske og geographiske Undersøgelser i Grønland. Copenhagen.

Tuan, Yi-Fu. 1991. 'Language and the Making of Place: A Narrative-Descriptive Approach'. *Annals of the Association of American Geographers* 81(4): 684-96.

Verhaar, John. 1963. *Some Relations between Perception, Speech and Thought: a Contribution towards the Phenomenology of Speech*. Assen: Van Gorcum.

Wautischer, Helmut. 1998. 'Pathways to Knowledge'. In H. Wautischer (Ed.), *Tribal epistemologies: Essays in the philosophy of anthropology*. Brookfield, VA: Ashgate: 3-14.

Willerslev, Rane. 2007. *Soul Hunters: Hunting, Animism and Personhood among the Siberian Yukaghirs*. Berkeley: University of California Press.